DEFIANCE OF THE PATRIOTS

DEFIANCE OF THE
PATRIOTS

THE BOSTON TEA PARTY
& THE MAKING OF AMERICA

★ BENJAMIN L. CARP ★

YALE UNIVERSITY PRESS
NEW HAVEN AND LONDON

Published with assistance from the Annie Burr Lewis Fund

For information about this and other Yale University Press publications, please contact:
U.S. Office: sales.press@yale.edu   www.yalebooks.com
Europe Office: sales@yaleup.co.uk   www.yaleup.co.uk

Set in Adobe Caslon by IDSUK (Data Connection) Ltd
Printed in Great Britain by TJ International Ltd, Padstow Cornwall

Library of Congress Cataloging-in-Publication Data

Carp, Benjamin L.
   Defiance of the patriots: the Boston Tea Party and the making of America /
Benjamin L. Carp.
     p. cm.
   ISBN 978–0–300–11705–9 (cl:alk. paper)
   1. Boston Tea Party, 1773. 2. Boston (Mass.)–History–Colonial period, ca.
1600–1775. 3. Sons of Liberty. 4. East India Company–History—18th
century. 5. United States–History–Revolution, 1775–1783–Causes.
6. Great Britain–Colonies–America–History–18th century. I. Title.
   E215.7.C37 2010
   973.3'115—dc22
                                                                    2010019703
A catalogue record for this book is available from the British Library.

10 9 8 7 6 5 4 3 2 1

For Jessica

Contents

Illustrations and Maps

Illustrations *page*

Maps

Acknowledgments

Thanks to Heather McCallum for asking a great question, and thanks to Frank Cogliano for recommending me as a person who could answer it. I am also grateful to Rhodri Jeffreys-Jones and Alvin Jackson for their early advice. Thanks to Sydelle Kramer, literary agent, for helping me to craft a convincing proposal. Wayne E. Lee, David Waldstreicher, and numerous unnamed scholars provided valuable feedback at the proposal stage.

This book is dedicated to my wife Jessica, who made this book possible in countless ways, and life wonderful in countless others. She read an early draft of the entire manuscript and offered wise critiques. I am also indebted to J. L. Bell, my late father Robert Carp, Frank Cogliano, Peter S. Onuf, Ray Raphael, and Alfred F. Young, who each read a subsequent draft of the manuscript in full. Their responses, coupled with recommendations from Heather McCallum and Rachael Lonsdale of Yale University Press, led me to make extensive revisions, all of which improved the manuscript enormously. Thanks also to Tami Halliday, Stephen Kent, Liz Pelton, and Jessica Lee.

I am grateful for my Tufts University colleagues, including former colleagues, particularly in the Department of History. I have been fortunate to land in such a congenial, supportive environment, and I also deeply appreciate the profound ways in which my colleagues' approaches to history and scholarship helped to shape this book. Tufts University provided me with a year of junior faculty research leave, as well as two Faculty Research Fund Awards, which were vital in enabling me to complete the manuscript. Thanks to Patrick Florance of the GIS Center at Tufts for his work on the maps, as well as Tufts students Rian Amiton, Jonathan Gale, Simcha Levental, and Natalie Susmann.

Martha R. Simms, who graduated Tufts in 2009, worked with me as part of the Tufts Summer Scholars Program, helping to compile information on the Tea Party participants. Molly Palmer, who received her M.A. from Tufts in 2009, assisted me further to compile data on the Tea Party participants, as well as other sources. She and Alexandra Mulrow, a current M.A. student at Tufts, also helped me to locate the book's images and put finishing touches on the manuscript. Without research assistance from these three promising students, I could not have finished. I am grateful to each of them. I taught a seminar course, "Massachusetts and the American Revolution" in the spring of 2007 and then again in spring 2008. In the process of writing papers for the course, these students revealed some remarkable insights and sources. Although I was not able to include all of their contributions, I have cited many of the students' names at points in the text where their research aided my own.

I enjoyed exchanging inquiries with J. L. Bell and Alfred F. Young about Revolutionary Boston and its inhabitants; I can't overstate their kindness toward me or their influence on me as scholars. I would also like to offer my warmest thanks to George A. Quintal Jr., an impressive researcher who generously shared with me some of the information from his extensive database of Boston Tea Party participants. Sarah Neale Fayen, Ethan Lasser, and Jonathan Prown of the Chipstone Foundation graciously hosted me on a trip to Milwaukee in December 2008. Thanks also to Elizabeth Ammons, Ina Baghdiantz-McCabe, Mary C. Beaudry, Russ Castronovo, John Catanzariti, Sarah Clock, Radiclani Clytus, Felipe Fernández-Armesto, Evan Haefeli, David Jaffee, Samuel Kinser, Tsong-han Lee, Michelle Craig McDonald, Maurie McInnis, Meghan McMahon, Jane T. Merritt, Francesca Morgan, Kate Ohno, Nathan Perl-Rosenthal, Linda Smith Rhoads, Jessica Sewell, John Stauffer, Beverly Tomek, John W. Tyler, Jennifer Van Horn, and Karin Wulf, who shared their work, pointed the way to useful resources, or helped me to locate sources at a distance. Special thanks to Woody Holton for motivating me to think about protests past and present.

I am grateful to Paul Grant-Costa, Daniel Mandell, and Kris Manjapra, each of whom read manuscript chapters, for their valuable insights. Thanks also to C. James Taylor and the other participants in the MHS-sponsored Boston Area Early American History Seminar, hosted by Alan Rogers at Boston College in May 2008; and to Karen Kupperman's Atlantic World Workshop at New York University in December 2008. I presented some of my research at "Cities in Revolt: The Dutch-American Atlantic, ca. 1650–1830," a conference at Columbia University in November 2009. Thanks to Ned Landsman and Peter Silver in particular for their remarks. I was also grateful for responses from audiences at the thirteenth annual meeting of the Omohundro Institute for Early American History and Culture in June 2007; the Exploring Transnational Studies Inaugural Conference at Tufts University in April 2009; the Summer Seminar Series of the McNeil Center for Early American Studies in June 2008; the Cronin Lecture Series at the Lexington Historical Society in November 2008; and the "Middays at the Meeting House" series at the Old South Meeting House in December 2009.

One can never be too thankful for librarians and museum curators; many thanks to the staffs of the institutions who provided images or facilitated access to their archives. I neglected to take names at all the places I went, but I will offer thanks in particular to Diann Benti and Paul Erickson at the American Antiquarian Society; Adele Barbato, Nicole DeLaria, Rainey Tisdale, and Marieke Van Damme at the Bostonian Society and Old State House; John W. Hooper at the Boston Public Library; Katherine A. Ludwig and Meg McSweeney at the David Library of the American Revolution; Katherine Fox, Laura Linard, and Tim Mahoney of the Baker Library, Harvard Business School; Dana Ste. Claire of Historic Tours of America for giving George Quintal permission to share some of his data with me; Cynthia Alcorn of the Samuel Crocker Lawrence Library at the Grand Lodge of Massachusetts; Anne Bentley, Anna Cook, Caitlin Corless, Jeremy Dibbell, Peter Drummey, Elaine Grublin, and Conrad E. Wright at the Massachusetts Historical Society; Elizabeth Bouvier and Bruce Shaw of the Massachusetts Supreme Judicial Court; Thomas Lannon and Jessica M. Pigza of the New York Public Library; Emily Curran, Robin DeBlosi, and Aliza Saivetz at the Old South Meeting House; Dan Finamore and Carrie Van Horn at the Peabody Essex Museum; Joan Gearin at the National Archives in Waltham, MA, and Rodney A. Ross of the Center for Legislative Archives in Washington, DC; Peter J. Knapp of the Watkinson Library at Trinity College, Connecticut; and Connie Reik of the Tisch Library at Tufts University. Eric Foner once again facilitated a year of access to the libraries of Columbia University.

I conclude with fondest remembrance of my grandmother, Selma Carp, and with warmest thanks to friends and family for their support.

My father, Robert Carp, passed away just as I returned the copy-edited manuscript to the press. He had provided wonderful feedback on an earlier draft, and accompanied me on a research trip a few weeks after his retirement from Hewlett-Woodmere Public Schools. In his 38 years of teaching social studies, he reached hundreds of students. He was a profound inspiration to me as a reader, scholar, and teacher of history, and we will miss him.

Introduction:
Teapot in a Tempest

And now, I pray you, sir,
For still 'tis beating in my mind, your reason
For raising this sea-storm?

Miranda (to Prospero), Act I, Scene II,
Shakespeare, *The Tempest*

It seams we have troublesome times a Coming
for there is great Disturbance a Broad in the earth
& they say it is tea
that caused it.
So then if they will Quarel about such a trifling thing as that
What must we expect
But war
& I think
or at least fear
it will be so.
Jemima Condict, October 1, 1774[1]

On December 16, 1773, at a crowded meeting in the largest church in Boston, the leather-dresser Adam Collson supposedly shouted, "Boston Harbor a tea-pot this night!" Collson then marched down to the water's edge at Griffin's Wharf to make his metaphor come true. If "a tempest in a teapot" describes a big disturbance about a small matter, Boston—in the midst of a turbulent political crisis over the authority of the British Empire—was in this moment a "teapot in a tempest." Collson and his companions staged an act of rebellion that would have worldwide significance.[2]

About a hundred men boarded the three trading ships that were riding at Griffin's Wharf in Boston harbor. They hoisted 340 chests onto the decks. These chests contained more than 46 tons of tea. The men smashed open the chests, releasing the leaves' bittersweet aroma into the air. It was the intoxicating smell of exotic luxury, and a couple of men were so unable to resist it that they stuffed some of the leaves in their pockets. The rest of the men remembered that there were principles at stake. They dumped the tea into the saltwater below. The ships, which had arrived in the previous weeks from London, were named the *Dartmouth*, for an aspiring port town, the *Eleanor*, for a woman, and the *Beaver*, in homage to New England's industrious work ethic.

The tea destroyers hailed from all walks of life. Men with strong backs and hard Yankee accents, they were a mix of young merchants, craftsmen, apprentices, and workers. They believed in a wrathful God, and they feared that the temptations of tea would turn them into tools of a corrupt, tyrannical empire. The grown men among them believed they were embarked on a noble deed of patriotic virtue. The younger boys thrilled to the idea of an evening spent wreaking chaos and destruction. The men and boys had names like Thomas Melvill, Joshua Wyeth, and—improbably—George Robert Twelves Hewes. On the evening of December 16, they spoke for all the dissidents in Boston who had squared off against the policies of the British government. The Boston Tea Party wasn't a rebellion, or even a protest against the king—but it set in motion a series of events that led to open revolt against the British Crown. The destruction of the tea, which became known as "The Boston Tea Party" fifty years later, was a bold, defiant act of political mobilization.

These destroyers had carefully calculated their reasons for dumping the tea on that particular evening. They needed to destroy the tea before the stroke of midnight. If they failed, then the hated customs officers would seize the tea and make it available for sale. They destroyers were trying to stop the tea from being sold at all. They would have preferred to force the captains of the three ships to weigh anchor, pilot their way back out of Boston harbor, and carry the tea back to London. But when the ships' owners proved reluctant to send their ships back, the men decided they had no other choice but to destroy the tea.

Why did the destroyers want to prevent the tea from landing in Boston? The easiest answer is that Parliament had imposed a tax on tea. Many people thought this tax was reasonable, but a dissident faction of Bostonians (the majority of the townspeople, in fact) believed that Parliament had no right to raise revenue from American colonists without the colonists' consent.

The Bostonians worried that more taxes were on the way. They knew that the revenue from the taxes paid the salaries of the civil officials that the British government had appointed to enforce the imposition of taxes. To the Bostonians—and other dissidents throughout the colonies—this was a blatant example of tyranny.

Even worse, this tea was to be sold by the preferred agents of a monopoly company, the British East India Company. Parliament had imposed this new arrangement under the Tea Act, which now threatened American merchants by cutting them out of the tea trade. If Parliament could sell tea to America this way and earn revenue from the sales, then the British government could start creating new monopolies on the sale of other products. Exorbitant prices, mammoth monopolies, and crushing taxes might leave Americans with nothing.

Dissidents were frightened, not just because of what they saw happening in Boston, but because of what they had seen happening throughout the world. Tyranny and liberty were locked in a constant struggle, and the dissident Bostonians knew which side they supported. The story of the Boston Tea Party was not just a local story, but a global story: the British East India Company, which was gaining territorial control over more and more South Asians, made much of its profit selling tea, a product grown by East Asians. When Europeans and Americans drank tea, they mixed it with sugar, farmed by enslaved Africans in the Caribbean. When the Bostonians dumped this tea in the harbor, to protest the actions of the East India Company and the British Parliament, they dressed as Native Americans. These were just some of the historical currents swirling around the Boston Tea Party.

The Boston Tea Party had revolutionary significance—it set the stage for an American rebellion and the war that followed. The Tea Party was an expression of political ideology about taxes, rights, and authority. Just as important, it was a window onto American culture and society of the time. Americans' consumer habits, including the colonists' love of tea, played a role in the way the resistance unfolded. Prevailing views of American Indians in colonial society help us to understand the disguises that the destroyers wore. Boston's colonial legacy of riotous parades, angry protest, and political organization provided the ingredients that made the Tea Party possible. These elements offer a fuller picture of why the Tea Party happened.

The destruction of the tea was a quintessential rejection of authority that became a cherished American tradition. The Tea Party involved a relatively broad segment of the population, even though this was an era when only the elite were thought fit to rule and make decisions. Because of this, the destruction set a world standard for future democratic protest. From the British perspective, the Boston Tea Party was the culmination of a decade's worth of flawed imperial policy, and the event certainly played a

Die Einwohner von Boston werfen den englisch-oftindischen Thee ins Meer am 18. December 1773.

1 Stylized figures, including Anglo-Americans, an African-American, and a Native American, observe the Boston Tea Party in this German print.

part in its imperial legacy. To Americans, the Tea Party became an emblem of their faith that a determined and organized group can accomplish momentous political change, culminating in independence. The participants were men who showed their willingness to defy the law in defense of their rights. To this day, journalists, pundits, and politicians frequently cite the Tea Party as the first and most famous example of Americans' heritage of civil disobedience, their penchant for secret conspiracies, and their aversion to foreign trade restrictions, excessive taxation, or government overreach. By reading the tea leaves at the bottom of Boston harbor, we can see the American character itself taking shape.

The day after the Tea Party, the attorney and future president John Adams called it "the most magnificent Movement of all." He went on, "There is a Dignity, a Majesty, a Sublimity, in this last Effort of the Patriots, that I greatly admire." Not everyone agreed. Some found the story of the Tea Party to be inspiring and democratic, but others called it riotous, disorderly, and disturbing. They saw a pack of rebels who had disobeyed the law, destroyed private property, and threatened anyone who stood in their way.[3]

Eighteenth-century Boston was a town where crowd action was not uncommon: from time to time, townspeople pulled down opponents' houses, brawled with soldiers, threw bricks at officials, tarred and feathered civilians, and otherwise asserted their power. In this climate, the tea consignees and senior customs officials had feared for their lives to such a degree that they

2 Father Time projects an image of an exploding teapot and the War of American Independence, as allegorical figures representing America, Africa, Europe, and Asia view the scene. In the image, the American army advances upon the British army, while a rattlesnake leaps from the teapot. A French rooster fans the flames and stands atop a defeated British lion.

fled to Castle Island offshore. By December 16, 1773, Bostonians had topped it all off with the invasion and destruction of private property as part of their political protest. The kind of political movement that birthed the Tea Party protest—and the Revolution—seems both exciting and extreme.

Throughout history, and today, the Boston Tea Party has given off mixed signals. In part because it involved so little bloodshed (no one died at the Boston Tea Party), it became a formative expression of liberty, independence, and civil disobedience, representing the finest human tradition of non-violent resistance to tyranny. The Tea Party was sublime, in John Adams's words, because it was a rejection of arbitrary rule. The Tea Party is also stirring in its radical potential for mobilizing people from all walks of life. Most people can't imagine themselves in knee breeches signing the Declaration of Independence, but they can easily imagine destroying the East India Company's tea.

At the same time, the Boston Tea Party is also downright frightening, in that it seems to justify the bullying nullification of any law that an outspoken group dislikes—whether it is slavery, damage to the environment, racial discrimination, legal abortion, court-ordered busing, taxation of any sort, or illegal immigration. The Tea Party opens up Pandora's box— out comes chaos, but also hope. In this way it exemplifies an ongoing struggle in America between law and order and democratic protest.

Perhaps we should not be too quick to embrace the Boston Tea Party— which many authorities would today classify as an act of terrorism—as a gauzy, harmless tale of American origins.[4] Americans enshrine their traditions of democratic protest, but they also profess to respect law and order, and our regard for the Boston Tea Party stands at the frontier of these two values. The Boston Tea Party remains an important historical event, not just because it brought about dramatic change in its time, but because it still resonates today.

CHAPTER 1

The Empire's Corporation

Great Britain should not only assert, but also support that Supremacy which she claims over the Members of the Empire, or she will soon only be supreme in Words.

Thomas Gage, April 13, 1772[1]

In May 1750, the Boston Town Meeting expressed concern that a provincial tax on tea and coffee would "bring on the displeasure of those two great and powerful Corporations the East India & Turkey Companys in our mother Country." Twenty-three years later, as ships bearing tea made their way to Boston, the same town meeting fumed that the "East India company" had launched "a violent attack upon the liberties of America." Although Bostonians had previously admired the East India Company from a distance and enjoyed its tea, in 1773 they cast the Company as a monster—as a danger to the colonists' freedoms. The people of Boston were caught up in the storm and stress of Great Britain's struggle to manage its expanding empire.[2]

At the dawn of the seventeenth century, the Crown of England had created the East India Company, the earliest American colonies, and other global ventures in much the same way. England was then too weak to send its military forces to the far corners of the world. So the Crown had sent chartered companies to do the work of conquest, trade, and settlement. Queen Elizabeth I granted the East India Company (EIC) its charter in 1600 as one of these private ventures, just as King Charles I gave the Massachusetts Bay Company its charter in 1629. In effect, the English government had subcontracted the business of imperialism to adventurers willing to undertake the risks and reap the potential rewards of an overseas voyage.[3]

Since its founding, the EIC had been trading, fortifying, making allies, and fighting rivals (literally, with guns) in the East Indies and beyond. Queen Elizabeth's charter granted the Company a licensed monopoly on all English trade west of the Cape of Good Hope. The EIC carried spices, silk, cotton, opium, gold, silver, and tea across enormous distances, paying out generous dividends to its shareholders. In the seventeenth and eighteenth centuries, most people assumed that such monopoly grants were beneficial: they would help the Company, as an extension of the English national interest, stand up to the country's Continental European rivals. The trade bolstered the economy, and helped to support the government through payment of customs duties. The Company became, along with the Bank of England, part of the backbone of national finance. Of course, there was a downside to monopoly companies: they stifled competition, and a corporation with such enormous power also wielded inordinate leverage over indigenous Indian Ocean traders. Nevertheless, the shareholders enjoyed the Company's relative freedom, and the Company did its best to take advantage of its trade networks, its financial power, and its government connections.[4]

During the eighteenth century, Robert Clive became the most famous of the Company's adventurers in South Asia. Clive was tough, daring, and manic-depressive, and he had amassed a great fortune during his years of energetic service for the Company. He earned his fame in Great Britain (and wheedled an Irish barony for himself), in part because he had defeated the Nawab of Bengal at the battle of Plassey in 1757. In 1765, Lord Clive was serving as the Company's governor and commander-in-chief at Bengal. He arranged for the Company to assume the *diwani*, or civil administration, over Bengal's 20 million people, convinced that its revenues could yield an annual profit of £1.6 million and more. Over the next few years, the EIC aggressively assumed the authority of an imperial government in Bengal— collecting taxes, building up its military presence, striking new (and often obnoxious) arrangements with local merchants and artisans, encouraging the development of cash crops, stripping local elites of their power, and increasing its control over the territory.[5]

Starry-eyed British optimists were enthusiastic about these developments. The Company's "new acquisitions," the *Gentleman's Magazine* speculated, "may open to this nation such a mine of wealth, as . . . in a few years to enable administration to pay off the national debt, to take off the land tax, and ease the poor of burthensome taxes." The Company already paid customs duties that amounted to around a third of the customs revenue for the entire nation. In 1767, the ministry decided to sink its teeth into the Bengal revenues as well. The EIC, hoping to keep these profits for its shareholders, did its best to beat back the ministry's efforts. As a compromise, the Company granted what was in effect an annual bribe to Parliament of £400,000 (4 percent of the Treasury's total revenue), in exchange for

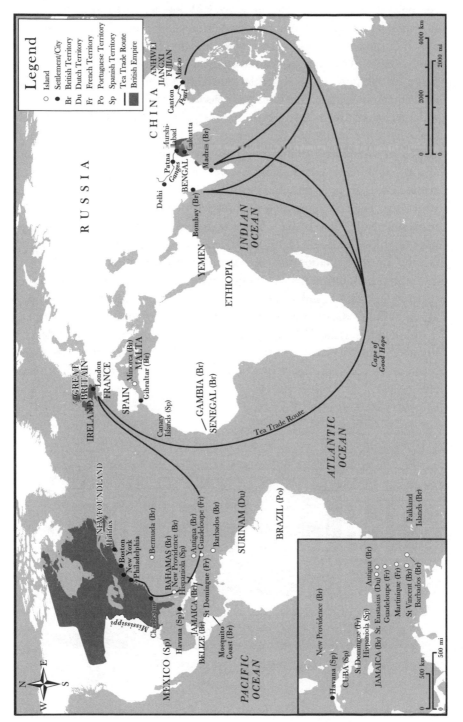

1 The World, with the British Empire and its Tea Trade Route.

keeping government oversight off its back. As the writer for the *Gentleman's Magazine* had hoped, these new Indian revenues helped Great Britain reduce the land tax on its own subjects at home. The interests of Company shareholders and the British state were now closely tied.[6]

The British public also began to comprehend the darker side of British involvement in India. The Company accumulated a long record of irresponsible greed and corruption in the 1760s. East India Company employees like Robert Clive, Thomas Rumbold, John Caillaud, George Pigot, and others returned from their service in India as "nabobs," and flaunted their newfound riches. They acquired seats in Parliament, baronetcies, Irish peerages, and knighthoods. A newspaper correspondent warned that Parliament needed to consider "new regulations in conducting the affairs of the East-India Company, and of limiting the power of their servants abroad, who . . . have all shewed an eagerness to return home early in life with Nabobs' fortunes, which can only be acquired by . . . embroiling the Company in perpetual war." In Bengal, meanwhile, money was growing scarcer and the population had become more vulnerable to natural cycles of drought and flood. Lest anyone try to fault the Company for these difficulties, EIC employees blamed the indigenous rulers of Bengal as untrustworthy, vice-ridden, and despotic. Back in its plush offices on Leadenhall Street in London (fig. 3), the East India Company

VIEW *of the* EAST INDIA HOUSE.

3 The East India House on Leadenhall Street in London, as it would have appeared in 1773.

could do little about their employees' independent trading and often rampant corruption, just two ingredients in a riot of mismanagement that almost tore apart the Company in the years 1769–73.[7]

"Suddenly the gods turned angry" in Bengal in the fall of 1769. "Not a drop of rain fell. The paddy withered in the fields and became like straw." This was how the nineteenth-century novelist Bankimcandra Chatterji described the suffering in northeast India in *Ānandamath*, the book of historical fiction that he published in 1882. For most of the eighteenth century, Bengal was a rich corner of the once-powerful Mughal Empire. Farmers coaxed crops from fertile fields. Muslin weavers and silk winders unfurled magnificent fabrics that were prized throughout the world. Traders shuttled goods up and down the Ganges river valley. Now, as the ground hardened, the drought choked the life out of half the land's crop. Scarcity soon drove the price of rice to more than twenty (in some places fifty) times its normal rate. "Once again people went hungry. First, they skipped a meal, then even the one meal they had was reduced by half, and finally they fasted throughout the day."[8]

"People started to beg. Soon there was no one to give alms, so they started to go hungry. Then they began to succumb to disease. Then they sold their cattle, their ploughs and cattle yokes, finished off their seed-paddy, and sold all their possessions. Then they sold their land. After this, they started selling their girl children, then the boys, and then their wives. Finally, who was there to buy the children and the wives? There were no buyers, since everyone wanted to sell. For lack of food, they began to eat the leaves of trees, and grass, and weeds. The low-caste and those who lived in the forests started to eat dogs, mice and cats." As corpses piled up in the streets and bazaars of Murshidabad and Calcutta, the scholar Karam Ali wrote, "people could not find the time or inclination even to bury their dead." Jackals, vultures, pigs and dogs made prey of human carcasses—there were even whispered accounts of far worse.[9]

In early reports of this disaster, observers guessed that Bengal lost a third of its population—later estimated to be about ten million people. Although the death toll was probably closer to 1.2 million, the famine's reaping of human life was undeniable: had it struck the Thirteen Colonies of North America, it would have wiped out half of the entire population. Some regions of Bengal, indeed, lost about half their people to starvation. Tigers and elephants roamed through deserted settlements as the jungle reclaimed the landscape.[10]

Bengal was starting to look like a country sucked dry—not just by the fateful shifts of Nature, but by the profit-seeking of traders and tax collectors.

"This affliction comes from the hand of your countrymen," said the sufferers who confronted one English witness. The Company provided only a few scraps of charitable relief, and it did little to ease its taxation of the region during the famine, as the earlier Muslim Mughal regime had done in times of scarcity. Instead the Company stockpiled grain to feed its own garrisons, and kept dunning its new subjects for revenue even as the carnage mounted.[11] As Chatterji wrote, "People could die of starvation, but the collection of revenue didn't stop." Warren Hastings, the new governor of Bengal in 1772, reported to London in chilling terms that revenue collection had been "violently kept up to its former standard."[12]

The pocketing of bribes by Company employees continued as well, while Parliament and the British press were a six-month journey away. But news of the calamity and the corruption eventually broke. Horace Walpole, a member of Parliament and the son of a former prime minister, wrote, "The oppressions of India, and even of the English settled there, under the rapine and cruelties of the servants of the Company, had now reached England, and created general clamour here." The public blamed the Bengal famine on the monopolistic practices of East India Company agents; "A tithe [tenth] of these crimes was sufficient to inspire horror." In the coffee-houses of London, people began to look upon the riches accumulated by Company servants like Lord Clive (the former Bengal governor) and his fellow *arriviste* nabobs with disgust. William Bolts, himself a former Company merchant in Calcutta, pointed to the Company servants who, "after exhibiting such scenes of barbarity as can scarcely be paralleled in the history of any country, have returned to England loaded with wealth." William Pitt the Elder, now Lord Chatham, despised these nabobs who had no "natural interest in the soil" and called them mere "importers of foreign gold" engaged in "private corruption." Alexander Dow, a former EIC army officer, spoke of the gloom of Bengal and warned, "The ruin, which we have brought on an unfortunate country, will recoil upon ourselves."[13]

A few whispers about the "melancholy news" of the Bengal famine eventually found their way to the western reaches of the British Empire, to Boston and New York and Philadelphia. American colonists initially said little about the news, although reports reached them just as they were contemplating their own place in the empire. Still, they must have been shocked by what they read in reprints from London newspapers. One account described an Englishman who had returned from Bengal, having "amassed above one hundred thousand pounds by a monopoly of rice; and to which monopoly, it is said, was chiefly owing the late terrible and affecting famine in that country, by which nearly 100,000 unhappy people lost their lives. Who would wish the enjoyment of riches at such a price?" Another item read, "The cruelties exercised upon the innocent natives of Bengal, for some years past, and the scene of rapine that has been carried on there, by the servants of the company, call aloud to heaven itself for vengeance." By 1773, Americans' mute bemusement would turn to fear that they might be next.[14]

Meanwhile, the fate of the Company in Great Britain was worsening. Once the British public had awoken to the possibilities for profit in Bengal in the 1760s, increasing investments had turned to frenzied speculation in Company stock. Then, when investors heard news in 1769 about a military setback in Madras (now Chennai), the bubble burst. Waves of financial panic and distress reverberated worldwide. A few years later, in the summer of 1772, Alexander Fordyce, a suave, handsome Scottish investor who was later satirized as a "macaroni gambler," bet more money than his bank had on East India Company stock. He guessed wrong, and his mistake threw an entire network of heavily leveraged banks into ruin: in Amsterdam the newspapers called it a "British Twister" and blamed the EIC. Fordyce himself fled to France, but the damage was done. As if "connected by an electrical wire," the Scottish writer James Boswell observed, "the people in every corner of the country have almost instantaneously received the same shock." The twister of bankruptcies blew throughout England and Scotland. Indeed, as it became harder to secure new loans, the shock of the banking crisis was eventually felt in the West Indies, and North America, and across Europe as far as Russia. The inability to borrow money only added to disgruntlement in the North American colonies.[15]

The East India Company's stock was sinking, and it threatened to take the British imperial economy down with it. Thomas Pownall, a member of Parliament and former Massachusetts governor, wrote that the Bengal revenues had been "wrought into the very frame and composition of our finances." There seemed to be no way of going back.[16] To make matters worse, the East India Company was bleeding its dividends out to shareholders (many of whom were members of Parliament) at rates that had ballooned from 6 percent in the early 1760s to 12.5 percent, rather than reinvesting its profits into the Company's infrastructure, or reducing its prices, or easing up on revenue collection in Bengal.[17]

The Chinese tea trade presented the Company's directors with another headache. The EIC depended on monopolizing the trade of this valuable commodity, and the British Treasury stood to gain a great deal from customs revenue. Without competition (or at least without legal competition), the Company could charge high prices, which more than covered its shipping expenses and tax obligations. And so the EIC had been steadily ordering more and more tea from China. It was a colossal mistake. British and foreign smugglers were bringing in thousands of pounds of illegally imported tea, and offering it to British customers at cut rates. Perhaps the majority of the tea consumed in the British Isles was smuggled from the European mainland, where the Dutch, French, Swedes, and other nations had their own Chinese import companies. With all of this tea business going to illegal competitors, tea began piling up in Company warehouses, unsold. The amount now stood at over 17.5 million pounds of the leaf—more than everyone in England drank in a year—potentially worth over £2 million but sinking in value.[18]

Sir George Colebrooke, a banker educated at the University of Leiden, was chairman of the East India Company in 1772, and his company now faced a desperate situation. The EIC was losing more money than it had on hand. Its expenses on military fortifications in India were eating up more and more of the budget. The Company had still not worked out the kinks of its revenue-collecting in Bengal. Meanwhile, its own agents, nabobs like Clive, were making private fortunes that cut into the Company's profits. Its stock was tanking. The banking crisis led to delays in some payments that were due to the Company. And those pungent piles of tea filled thousands of crates' worth of unrealized profit.[19]

Every year the East India Company turned to the Bank of England for a loan to cover temporary shortfalls until the Company could collect its earnings from sales. By summer, the Company's debts were mounting, and it was begging the Bank for further loans. This time, the Bank refused. The EIC also owed the British government over £1 million—£400,000 for the annual payment and the rest for customs duties. By autumn, the Company's total debts were staggering—over £1.3 million. Its only solution was to suspend payment of the annual dividend to shareholders for that year. Now Parliament and the shareholders were paying attention. John Burgoyne, a member of Parliament who would later lead an army against American troops at Saratoga, headed a parliamentary select committee to address the problem. In May 1773, his committee began inquiring into the offenses that Lord Clive and other Company employees had committed in South Asia.[20]

The British cabinet under prime minister Lord North seized on the climate of negative publicity surrounding the Company and vowed to take greater control over its corrupt practices and financial troubles. The EIC would remain an independent company, but now it would answer

to the British state. First Parliament passed the Restraining Act, which
temporarily prevented the Company from sending out any new supervi-
sors to India. A few months later, the Regulating Act gave greater power
to the Company's larger shareholders, with the idea that this would ensure
stability. The Regulating Act also prohibited private trade by Company
servants, provided for regular government supervision of Company affairs,
and put executive and judicial power in India more firmly in Parliament's
grip. The British government was attempting to resume and redefine the
authority that it had formerly delegated to its chartered Eastern venture.[21]

Imperial expansion and consolidation, the credit crisis, and changes in the
tea trade were bedeviling Parliament and the EIC, but they affected
the American colonies, too. The Seven Years War, known to Americans as
the French and Indian War, had ended in 1763, realigning the balance of
power in North America, India, and Europe. The Treaty of Paris signed
that year had granted French territories in North America and eastern
India to Great Britain, removing the French threat from these regions.
Great Britain's star seemed to be ascending. At the same time, the war had
also saddled the British government with crippling debts and massive
naval and military commitments in the Indian Ocean and the trans-
Appalachian West. The British government wanted a return on its invest-
ment in these overseas wars, naval squadrons, and troop commitments.
From the American colonies, Parliament asked for new taxes and tighter
customs enforcement. From the East India Company, Parliament asked for
the yearly £400,000 tribute in 1767, and it passed the Regulating Act of
1773. The British government also hardened its enforcement of customs
laws in America, giving new powers to judges, naval officers, and customs
officials to make sure customs duties flowed back to the British Treasury
on schedule. The colonists and Company directors, though they had little
interaction with one another, now had something in common: they had
seen Parliament's vision of an overseas empire for Great Britain, and they
felt the reins tightening on India and America.[22]

In response, the chartered companies and colonies began fighting as hard
as they could to hold onto their rights. American colonial legislatures tried
to be savvy about lobbying the government in England. The mainland
colonies, including Massachusetts, had long retained agents to look after
their interests. The attorney William Bollan (son-in-law of former
governor William Shirley) had operated on behalf of Massachusetts since
the 1740s, and was serving as agent for the colony's Council in the 1770s.
When the aged Flemish merchant Dennys DeBerdt passed away in 1770,

the Massachusetts House of Representatives appointed the Boston-born scientist Benjamin Franklin as its agent. In addition, the colonies had a few scattered allies in and around Parliament such as the scar-faced war veteran Colonel Isaac Barré, the fluent orator Edmund Burke, and the controversial John Wilkes, a former MP who became an alderman and sheriff (and later mayor) of London. These pro-American allies were useful, but the coalition was loose, because Americans had such a diverse array of economic interests. Compared to the lobbyists, agents, and members of Parliament working for West Indian sugar planters and East India Company shareholders, the Americans' influence seemed distant and uncertain.[23]

Furthermore, as a Boston merchant in London pointed out, the British aristocracy held American interests in contempt. "Manufacturers and commercial people so far as their Interest is Affected are on our side," he wrote, "but all the Landed Interest are against us." He continued, "The House of peers are not friendly; one of that house said sometime ago that in a few years he expected all his old family pictures and furniture would adorn a hall in America." The old-money British aristocracy expressed distaste for new-money nabobs from America as well as the East and West Indies.[24]

In the mid-1760s, many Americans started to resist the taxes that Parliament tried to levy. Throughout the colonies, respectable protesters and unruly crowds gathered to assert American rights. They objected to the idea of extracting revenue from the colonies without the colonists' consent. In the process, the American dissidents began to forge their objections into a distinct set of ideas about government. Politicians like Samuel Adams of Boston or Patrick Henry of Virginia believed that the local legislatures, dating back to the early seventeenth century, were the colonists' rightful representatives—not the distant members of Parliament, whom they had no power to choose. The colonists also wanted their assemblies (and not Parliament) to have power to choose and fund the colonies' executive branch.

In 1767, Parliament passed two laws affecting the East India Company's tea shipments. The first, designed to help the Company, was the Indemnity Act, which lowered the duty on all black tea and cheap green tea (Singlo tea) sold in England. The act also granted a drawback (or refund) on all import duties on tea being reshipped to America—in other words, if the Company imported a chest of tea from China and paid taxes on it, then reshipped that tea to America, it could have its taxes on that tea chest refunded. Parliament hoped that the act, by allowing the Company to sell tea to consumers at a lower price, would discourage smugglers. At the same time, Parliament hated the thought of losing government revenue from tea sales, so they insisted that the East India Company make up the difference.[25]

The Company had hoped for commercial gains from the provisions of the Indemnity Act, but the second act, which became known as the Townshend Act, threatened to wipe out these gains. Young Charles Townshend, Chancellor of the Exchequer, proposed taxes on all tea, glass, paper, lead, and paint imported into the American colonies. This measure would raise funds to offset the tax breaks of the Indemnity Act, and it would pay the salaries of civil officials in America. Most of the taxed items were relatively insignificant to transatlantic trade, except for tea, which now bore a duty of threepence per pound. Because the taxes on tea in the British Isles were particularly high, Americans still paid less for tea than British customers did. Regardless, Americans objected to the new tax on principle.[26]

The specter of taxation without representation haunted the American colonists. The lawyer John Dickinson, posing as a "Farmer in Pennsylvania," wrote that Parliament was now dictating taxes to the king's American subjects, not to regulate trade or encourage commerce, "*but for the single purpose of levying money upon us.*" This was a "most dangerous innovation." Dickinson's protest was echoed by thundering sermons and newspaper articles throughout the colonies, as well as citywide boycotts of British imports and even outright violence. The East India Company and a group of London merchants, eager for American customers and fearful of American boycotts, joined the chorus of protesters asking for the Townshend duties to be repealed, to little avail. Parliament stuck a finger in the dam with a political solution. To pacify the colonists, in 1770 they repealed most of the Townshend duties. To make sure Americans knew that Parliament retained the right to tax the colonies, and to ensure that the colonies would remain a source of revenue, they kept the tax on tea in place.[27]

In the colony of Massachusetts, many people saw these issues of taxes and legislation through the prism of protecting their rights under the Massachusetts Charter. Under the colony's original royal charter of 1629, the male colonists had the power to direct their own affairs in town meetings, and they elected their own members of the Massachusetts House of Representatives. They saw the Massachusetts Bay Colony charter as a sacred covenant between themselves and the king, akin to the covenants that God had made with Noah and Abraham in the Old Testament. After upheaval in England and New England during the Glorious Revolution, Massachusetts received a new charter from Parliament in 1691: the Crown would appoint the colony's governors, and those governors served at the king's pleasure. Members of the Council (the legislature's upper house) were chosen by a joint conference of the House and the outgoing Council, but Massachusetts governors had the power to veto the appointment of councilors or any law passed by both houses. This new blueprint for Massachusetts government did nothing to settle its politics. The Massachusetts House of Representatives, claiming the mantle of representing "the people," insisted on keeping a tight leash on the governor's salary and expenditures, as well as his powers over the legislature. When the British ministry decided to start paying the Massachusetts governor as well as the province's chief judges and attorneys directly out of the duties collected on tea, dissidents like Samuel Adams worried that this new policy would render these officials independent of the Massachusetts legislature. The ministry's decision to take these salaries wholly out of the hands of the legislature looked like another infringement on the people's liberty.[28]

Parliament had begun trying to strengthen its control over governors and councils in the American colonies as well as the East India Company. One way to do this was by making sure it had the power to appoint and supervise officials, and another was by making sure that the British government had firmer control over the officials' salaries. For Massachusetts, Parliament took the salaries of civil officials away from the local legislature and began paying them directly from the British Treasury. For the East India Company, Parliament granted greater salaries to key Company employees so as to discourage corruption, since a well-compensated official, in theory, would be less likely to seek bribes, gifts, favors, and other private profits in India. Yet a certain circle of Opposition politicians in England worried that these fat salaries would just shift the corruption to England. The politicians in the British ministry could reward their friends with plum positions, and they could lavish these British, colonial, and Company employees with grossly high salaries. This arrangement—known as patronage—led to dangerous corruption at home. In America, critics often used the derogatory term "placemen" to describe exploitative Crown officials in their midst. Nabobs who went to distant lands and made money for themselves may have offended the British upper classes—but to Opposition politicians and dissident colonists, an imperial government sending its salaried officials to distant lands to make money for the state *and* themselves was an even more fearsome prospect. As the writer "ATTICUS" wrote to Lord North, "With the Company's Wealth and Influence at your Feet, with those extensive Powers of Corruption in your Hands, America too must now submit to the wretched System of the Favourite." Tea was becoming the means by which the British Empire would degenerate into corruption and tyranny.[29]

Americans resented paying taxes on East India Company tea, but they blamed Parliament for this, not the Company itself. Some of them hoped that they could join forces with the Company as fellow defenders of "chartered rights." The Duke of Richmond (an Opposition leader in Parliament) urged the East India Company's stockholders in May 1773 not "to lie at the mercy of administration," but "to resist, like Englishmen, every illegal attack upon their chartered rights and privileges." American protests against recent acts of Parliament echoed this warning, as in the town of Beverly, Massachusetts, which described the use of tax revenue to pay the salaries of civil officers "an infringment on our Charter Rights," which "has a direct Tendancy to the Destruction of our Happy Constitution." The Regulating Act of 1773 also manipulated salaries to control (Indian) officials, and it was similarly resented.[30] In September 1773, the Boston Committee of Correspondence forwarded a letter to all the other towns of Massachusetts, detailing how under the Regulating Act, the East India Company's "sacred Charter Rights were arbitrarily taken from them," which alarmed other chartered institutions, including the City of London itself. These American radicals initially tried to cast the Company as a sibling in the struggle for liberty, a fellow victim of the British ministry's attempts to foist placemen upon them.[31]

In the event, the idea that the colonies and the Company were siblings was superficial at best. As Americans learned more about the provisions of the new East India Company laws, they realized that Parliament would sooner lend a hand to the Company than the colonies, and that the ministry had decided to play the interests of the Company and the American colonies off one another. Parliament had unmistakably tightened the reins on the EIC, but it had also preserved the Company as its partner in the pursuit of profits and in the government of its holdings in India. In 1773, Parliament bailed out the Company to the tune of a £1.4 million loan. Then the accompanying Tea Act paved the way for the EIC to pay off its debts by making it easier for the Company to unload its surplus tea at America's expense.

Where would the EIC find a market for its tea? Europe and England were out of the question—these markets were already glutted, and the Company could hardly compete with the European East India companies (and their partners, British smugglers), given its high prices and hands-off practice of using middlemen to sell tea to retailers. America, on the other hand, was the emerging market for consumer goods of all kinds. Once again, the Company's proprietors asked permission to ship tea directly to the American colonies, duty-free, but the ministry's priorities were clear. Lord North, the prime minister, was in no mood to repeal the last Townshend duty—if he did, it would look as if Parliament had conceded an important point about its right to tax the Americans. Colebrooke, the Company's chairman, suggested that North could save face by claiming that he repealed the tea tax at the Company's request. North refused, although he admitted "he had rather do it at the desire of the India company than that of America." Lord North's stubbornness led to a compromise that propped up the East India Company, but still extracted revenue from the colonists: under the Tea Act, Parliament would give a tax rebate to the Company on tea shipped to America. This measure would allow the Company to offer a lower price to American customers (the Tea Act would make tea cheaper, not more expensive), while Parliament could continue to collect the three-penny duty on every pound of imported tea.[32]

Aside from the tax, Parliament's plan for shipping the tea also offended the colonists. In the past, English and American merchants had been able to compete for the right to buy cargoes of tea in London and ship them to America for a healthy profit. Now the East India Company would be able to hand-pick its own consignees (or agents) and sell tea directly to the American colonies. To Lord North this appeared to be the perfect solution: the new arrangement would reduce the surplus of tea in the Company's warehouses, Americans would buy more tea at lower prices, the Company's profit margins would increase, and the British Treasury would take its own sanctioned cut.

In response, just a month after the Boston Committee's circular letter, the Massachusetts House of Representatives issued another missive with a new, more fearful interpretation of the Tea Act. "It is easy to see how aptly this Scheme," while helping the East India Company, "will serve both to destroy the Trade of the Colonies & increase the revenue." A committee representing Boston and its neighboring towns announced, "We know that great dependance is placed upon this master-piece of policy for accomplishing the purpose of enslaving us." The Tea Act conjured up nightmare visions of enslavement and ruin.[33]

First, it reaffirmed Parliament's right to tax the colonists without their consent, a point that more and more Americans were refusing to concede. If Parliament could continue to raise taxes on Americans without any consequences, eventually Americans would be little better than feudal vassals.

Second, Parliament had already determined that those taxes would fund the salary of the royal governor of Massachusetts and other provincial officers. The tea tax—pulled from the colonists' own pockets—robbed the New England colonists of this leverage over executive and judicial officials. This seemed the first step to tyranny—an imperial government sending hired tyrants to rob the colonies blind.[34]

Third, the Tea Act appeared to grant special privileges to a monopolistic company—the East India Company—at the expense of American merchants. The Massachusetts colonists might have felt some sympathy and solidarity with the Company in the name of "chartered rights," but not if the Company was going to make money at Americans' expense. Using its unfair competitive advantage, the East India Company could now starve the American people of their livelihood, while imperial courtiers and their cronies were scheming to take the rest of it. Americans worried that, poorly connected as they were in London, they would suffer a fate worse than Bengal's.[35]

In a series of five pamphlets, a New York Son of Liberty named "HAMPDEN" painted a picture of the East India Company as an evil monopoly built on bribes. "Wonder not then," wrote the author, "that Power thus obtained, at the Expence of the national Commerce, should be used to the most tyrannical and cruel Purposes." Referring to the famine in Bengal, the author called the East India Company "lost to all the Feelings of Humanity" as they "monopolized the absolute Necessaries of Life in India, at a Time of apprehended Scarcity." Now, "the Purchase of the *Company's* Iniquities, *Tea*, must be sent to the Colonies, the Profit of which is to support the Tyranny of the Last in the East, enslave the West, and prepare us fit Victims for the Exercise of that horrid Inhumanity they have . . . practised, in the Face of the Sun, on the helpless Asiaticks." A Newport paper chimed in, disgusted that the Company had probably shed more "innocent blood" over the previous twenty years—slaying perhaps as many as three million people—than all the world's other wars combined.[36]

John Dickinson, the lawyer who had become famous for his "Letters from a Farmer in Pennsylvania" against the Townshend duties, took up the pen name "RUSTICUS" and launched a similar attack on the East India Company. "Their Conduct in *Asia*, for some Years past, has given ample Proof, how little they regard the Laws of Nations, the Rights, Liberties, or Lives of Men." Dickinson continued, "they have, by the most unparalleled Barbarities, Extortions, and Monopolies, stripped the miserable Inhabitants of their Property, and reduced whole Provinces to Indigence and Ruin. Fifteen hundred Thousand, it is said, perished by Famine in one Year, not because the Earth denied its Fruits, but this Company and their Servants engrossed all the Necessaries of Life, and set them at so high a Rate, that the Poor could not purchase them." Having drained Bengal of its wealth and corrupted it, "they now, it seems, cast their Eyes on *America*, as a new Theatre, whereon to exercise their Talents of Rapine, Oppression and Cruelty. The Monopoly of Tea, is, I dare say, but a small Part of the Plan they have formed to strip us of our Property. But thank GOD, we are not Sea Poys, nor Marattas, but *British Subjects*, who are born to Liberty, who know its Worth, and who prize it high."[37]

In highly politicized American cities like Philadelphia and Boston, most people apparently agreed with Dickinson that the Tea Act would have dire consequences if it were allowed to stand. As the EIC began shipping tea to America under this unacceptable new law, the question became: what would Americans do about the tea?

During the 1760s and 1770s, Great Britain began to come to terms with its massive empire. It was in 1773, in fact, that Sir George Macartney referred to "this vast empire, on which the sun never sets, and whose bounds nature has not yet ascertained." Bengali weavers, Iroquois hunters, Irish peasants, Afro-Caribbean slaves, Boston shipwrights, Virginian planters, and Québécois *habitants* all fell within the British sphere of dominion. Representatives of the imperial government—governors, military officers, and other officials—depended on local cooperation, and they usually had the wisdom to be flexible with the king's overseas subjects. Ultimately, however, the British ministry became impatient with these flexible arrangements. Parliament tried to tighten its grip over trade, revenue, and governance, especially in South Asia and the "mutinous colonies" of North America. From this point of view, chartered organizations like the East India Company and the New England colonies, formed as military ventures in the seventeenth century, were no longer useful. The Company and the American colonies would either submit to the laws of the eighteenth-century commercial empire or be brought to heel.[38]

The Bengal famine was a deadly symptom of the East India Company's struggle to administer India—and the British government's struggle to administer the empire as a whole. These struggles caused a shudder that was felt, not just in Boston during the tea conflict, but all around the world.

Lord Clive, hero of the battle of Plassey, felt the shudder—he spent the year 1773 defending himself in Parliament against the Burgoyne committee's charges of corruption. He was reduced to begging, "Leave me my honour, take away my fortune." Although Parliament exonerated him and he kept both, Clive was driven into one of his habitual bouts of depression and illness, and he never recovered. Clive either committed suicide or overdosed on opium and died of a seizure in his grand London home on November 22, 1774. In another example of the connections between America and India, the trappings of Clive's wealth and fame included a painting by the American Benjamin West, a favorite of George III. It was supposed to be a series commemorating events in the life of an adventurer in Asia, but only the first was ever finished (fig. 4).[39]

4 Shah 'Alam, the Mughal emperor, conveys the grant of the *diwani*, or tax collecting privileges, to Lord Clive and the East India Company in August 1765.

China felt the shudder, even though its imperial government had done its best to keep European traders on a short leash. China made handsome profits selling tea to Europe, but Western nations became impatient with all the silver they were dumping into Chinese coffers. The British East India Company, searching for a way to make famine-scorched Bengal profitable, needed another product to trade to China. Opium turned out to be the solution to both problems. Once the EIC decided to ignore the Chinese ban on opium and seek out the profits of the drug trade, its directors declared a monopoly on the Indian opium trade in 1773. Over the next few years, the Company stepped up its shipments of this Indian-grown plant, both painkiller and poison, by smuggling it into Chinese harbors. By 1810, Emperor Daoguang vowed to snuff out "the wicked traders [who] pursue high profits on sales and purchase of opium." The following year, observing how addicts would buy opium instead of food and clothing, he wrote, "Opium will destroy our people's morality."[40]

In Edinburgh, the economist Adam Smith felt the shudder. Bengal's apparent decline struck him as proof that the East India Company's monopoly—and the "strange absurdity" of a joint stock company ruling as sovereign—was a disaster. The starving Indians were certainly suffering—and Britons suffered, too, from monopolistic price-gouging, from the rot of corruption, waste, "fraud and abuse" which were "inseparable from the management of the affairs of so great a company." Smith's writings on free trade in 1776 would have lasting influence on economic thought in both hemispheres.[41]

Urdu poets in Delhi and Patna felt the shudder as well. With haunted eyes, they saw the changes wrought by grasping British Company men and invoked the word *inquilab*, or "revolution." The social order was being disrupted. Rapacious traders and officials were pursuing profits without honor. The heavens' wrath was raining down upon India. The world was turning upside down.[42]

In the years following the passage of the Tea Act, Americans would come to know this feeling, too.

CHAPTER 2

"The Ringleader of All Violence"

[A] storm in this Town is raised in the twinkling of an Eye, without your having the least Warning. Such an absolute Sway have our leaders over the Minds of the Common people, that in an instant they will raise you a Tempest, that would threaten Destruction to the Globe.

Nathaniel Coffin, May 22, 1770[1]

In 1770, Thomas Hutchinson was in many ways the first man of Boston. He had come from a wealthy family, and had ranked third in social prominence among his classmates at Harvard College. He was proud, honorable to a fault, and extremely protective of his personal reputation. He had risen through the ranks of local and provincial office to serve as magistrate, representative, Speaker of the House, councilor, chief justice of the highest court, lieutenant governor, and governor. His attention to detail had made him successful as a merchant, a stickler for legal rectitude, and a thorough scholar—he had written two volumes of the colony's history, and was still accumulating notes for a third. If the king of Great Britain were ever to consider establishing a hereditary aristocracy in America, Hutchinson's name would be among the first on his list. In colonial America, men like Hutchinson inspired (and expected) obedience and respect.

The Hutchinson family had not had an auspicious beginning in America. William and Anne Hutchinson were farmers who had arrived in Boston in 1634 with fourteen children. Within a few years they had broken with the religious establishment of the zealous new colony, and they were exiled to what became Rhode Island. When William died in 1642, Anne moved to Pelham Bay on the outskirts of the New Netherlands. Her family's presence was an unwelcome sight to the local Indians, and Anne and five of her children perished in an attack on European settlements in the area. Her son Edward became a leader in the political and military affairs of Massachusetts until he, too, died in an Indian attack during King Philip's War in 1675.

Luck and hard work redeemed the fate of Thomas Hutchinson's forebears. As traders, the Hutchinsons made steady (if not spectacular) profits. Edward's son Elisha became a judge and a member of the Provincial Council; his son, Colonel Thomas Hutchinson (the governor's father), was a member of the Provincial Council for twenty-six years. The younger Thomas was born in 1711. While attending Harvard, the future governor began putting capital in overseas ventures. Eventually Governor Thomas Hutchinson would have a substantial fortune, including several commercial and residential properties in Boston and suburban Milton.

Thomas Hutchinson was tall, slender, and fair-skinned, and people acknowledged his judiciousness, intelligence, and competence. But they found him difficult to love. He was humorless and rational, scrupulously law-abiding, and often disdainfully judgmental. The love of his life was his wife, Margaret "Peggy" Sanford. When she died from childbirth complications in 1754, he was devastated. He later wrote that he had lost more than half his soul; for years he declined all social engagements, and although he was a wealthy widower, he never remarried.[2]

Family was important to Hutchinson, and his family became a tightly knit political clan. Peggy Sanford's sister, Mary, was married to Andrew Oliver, who became lieutenant governor under Hutchinson. Hutchinson's eldest son, Thomas, married one of Oliver's daughters, and his daughter, Sarah, married Andrew's nephew, the son of Peter Oliver, who later succeeded Hutchinson as chief justice of the superior court. Another son, Elisha, married Peter Oliver's granddaughter. These two connected families dominated some of the most important political offices in Massachusetts during the middle of the eighteenth century. Families like these were at the apex of Boston's social world.

By 1773, Hutchinson was probably the most hated man in town.

In 1773, Thomas Hutchinson's Boston was a town of about 16,000 people—small compared to London or Paris or Mexico City at the time but larger than most communities in British America. Compared to diverse American towns like Newport and Philadelphia (to say nothing of Lucknow or Istanbul), Boston might strike the visitor as a homogenous place, full of nosy Puritans and nasal accents. Yet it was still a cosmopolitan eighteenth-century city: a mix of community ties, social conflicts, and contentious political disputes. The people lived elbow to elbow on a hilly peninsula, about two miles from tip to neck. At high tide, the sea sometimes covered Boston Neck, a narrow isthmus, and washed away the pavement of the only road into town. In cold winters, the harbor froze so that a person could walk or ride a sleigh to Fort William on Castle Island (now Fort Independence, connected to the mainland by landfill). Eighteenth-century Boston was a forest of steeples and masts—it was John Winthrop's "city upon a hill" as well as a bustling seaport of taverns and brawls. The city smelled of salt air, horse manure, and trash. A simple meal at home might be a slow-cooked stew of meat and vegetables, or it might have the taste of an oyster or codfish plucked from the ocean. It was a town of traders, and on market days the air was filled with sounds of haggling shoppers and clattering carts. It was a town of observant Congregationalists, so on Saturday nights and Sundays it was plunged into pious silence, except for learned sermons and murmured prayers.[3]

As Protestants with Calvinist roots, the people of Boston believed that working hard at their calling might be a sign of saving grace. New Englanders' reputation for thrift, Yankee industriousness, and sharp-elbowed bargaining was known throughout the Atlantic world. The rocky soil of Massachusetts yielded few cash crops for market, so Bostonians exported little in the way of farm products. Instead, fishermen like Adam Beals Sr. plied the Grand Banks for glistening hauls of cod. Shipbuilders like Samuel Nowell or Gilbert Colesworthy pulled together skeletal keels and white pine masts from New Hampshire, caulked the planks together around them, and fitted the vessels out with sails and rigging. Distillers like Thomas Chase turned West Indian molasses into rum. The profits from trading these goods had created a powerful class of overseas merchants. Some imported finished goods from England along with exotic items like Chinese tea or Indian calicoes from beyond the Cape of Good Hope. Others exported or transshipped American products to other ports. A few merchants, like Thomas Hutchinson, attained the rank of "gentleman" and commanded huge amounts of capital. Commercial business put these merchants in contact with other traders, from Charleston, South Carolina, to Bristol, England.

Further down in the social hierarchy were petty shopkeepers like the bookseller James Foster Condy. In 1771, Boston had well over 500 retail shops selling merchandise—and there were many more stores and traveling peddlers who made kitchenware, trinkets, and tea available in smaller towns and in the countryside. Advertisements enticed shoppers into stores, and easy credit (when it was available) helped fuel the purchase of thousands of items. Americans were often cash-poor, and so American merchants (and their customers) sometimes struggled to pay for British imports.[4]

Boston craftsmen built and repaired a variety of goods with their hands. The silversmith Paul Revere used a hammer and sharp little burins and needles to produce fine goods for wealthy clients (fig. 5). The shoemaker

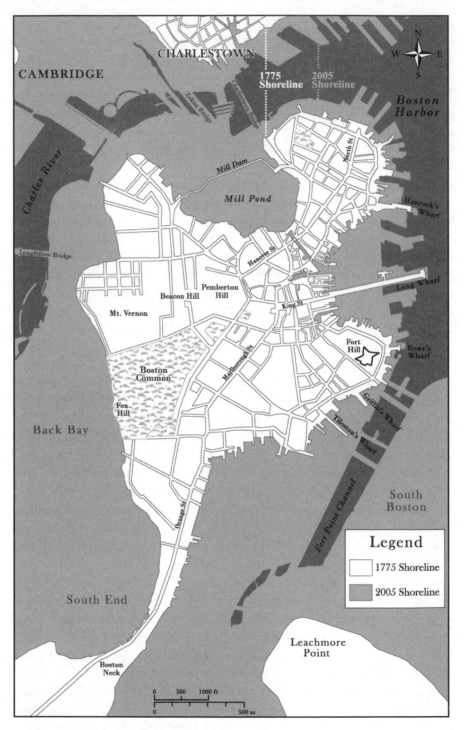

2 Boston in 1775 with 2005 shoreline depicted.

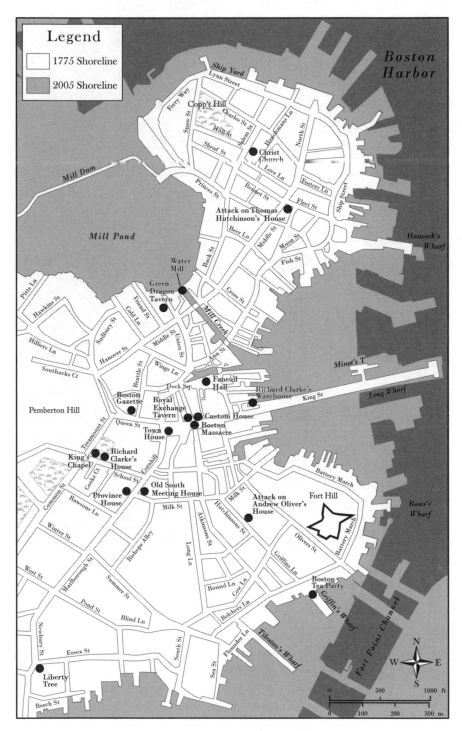

3 Boston (detail) in 1775 with 2005 shoreline depicted.

5 In this portrait by John Singleton Copley, Paul Revere holds a gleaming silver teapot, one of the products of his Boston workshop.

George R. T. Hewes used an awl, knife, and pliers to make and repair shoes for what was probably a more ordinary clientele. Other artisans made barrels, candles, oars, or hats. Carpenters and masons like John Crane, Joseph Eayres, and William Etheridge raised up houses of brick and wood, which leaned into one another amidst crooked streets and alleyways. Mariners and seamen served aboard the ships, either for short coasting trips or long overseas voyages. Dockworkers and laborers scrambled for unskilled work where they could find it. Apprentices, servants, and black slaves held in bondage toiled in the houses and workshops. These Bostonians sometimes struggled to make ends meet, especially when the economy took a turn for the worse. At the bottom of the social scale, some relied on seasonal or intermittent work, some had no property at all, and many relied on charitable relief from the town to get through the winter. Oystermen and prostitutes beckoned from the streets. Pastors and magistrates kept a stern eye on the people they saw as their charges.

While Boston had its social hierarchy, most Bostonians were also closely intertwined by kinship and marriage and by the close proximity of their houses. Many of the men, particularly wealthy and middling Bostonians, drank together in fire companies, Masonic lodges, and other clubs. John Rowe and Paul Revere were especially adept at navigating Boston's club life. Rowe, a wealthy importer, belonged to Boston's more elite Masonic lodge, and he became a Grand Master of Masons for North America in 1768. The Freemasons were a fraternal order that encouraged sociability among its members—they held public processions but also cherished their secret rituals. Rowe also held important offices in the town and his church vestry, and he belonged to a number of other social clubs, a fire club, and a charitable association. Paul Revere came from a lower social rank than Rowe— he was the son of Apollos Rivoire, who had emigrated from France at age thirteen and married into a local family of artisans and mariners. Revere, the oldest son in a family of nine, learned his father's trade and became a master silversmith, goldsmith, and engraver. Dependent on the wealthy merchants who purchased his teapots and porringers, he was nonetheless able to provide a comfortable living for his family, and he was thirty-five years old when he bought a house for them in North Square in 1770. That same year he was elected master of St. Andrew's Lodge of Freemasons, a less elite Masonic lodge, which he had joined in 1761. At St. Andrew's, Revere was able to develop business contacts, attain greater status within the community, learn leadership skills, and enjoy an evening of fellowship.[5]

Poorer Bostonians were ineligible for the elite drinking clubs and Masonic lodges, but they had their own traditions. On November 5, the English celebrated Guy Fawkes Day, in commemoration of deliverance from the Pope's alleged 1605 plot to detonate Parliament and the king. Bostonians adopted this holiday and named it "Pope's Day." Boys knocked on doors asking for money, rang bells, and threatened to break windows. At night, Boston's craftsmen and older boys formed a North End company and a South End company, who rolled out horse-drawn wagons with effigies of the devil and the Pope. People wore costumes, blew horns, and banged on drums. When the two wagons met, the North End and South End companies battled with fists, and the winners held the losers' effigies aloft and burned them atop one of Boston's hills. In the mid-1760s, the leader of the South Enders was a slender, jumpy shoemaker and firefighter named Ebenezer Mackintosh.

Crowds in Boston didn't just form once a year on Pope's Day. Early in the century, the crowd roughed up a few merchants who hoarded food or raised prices in times of scarcity. In 1747, the locals held British naval officers hostage to protest the Navy's habit of picking men off the docks and forcing them into seagoing service, a practice called "impressment." Sometimes the Boston crowds targeted whorehouses, the ostentatiously wealthy, or unfair traders.[6]

Crowd actions took place at different moments for different reasons, and they were particularly acute in hard times. Although New York and Philadelphia grew rapidly during the middle of the eighteenth century, Boston's population and economy were stagnant. Boston fell from its position as the largest city in British North America in 1700 to third place sometime around 1760. Competition from other ports threatened Boston's import trade as well as its exports of rum, fish, and ships. Without trade, mariners could not sail, shipbuilders had no demand for their services, and laborers could not work. The Molasses Act of 1733 hurt Boston shipping further by restricting the supply of cheap molasses from the French West Indies. A series of wars with the French and Indians led to the disruption of trade routes, supply shortages, and to higher prices and taxes. As military and naval casualties claimed scores of Boston's young men, the number of destitute widows and orphans increased. While some transatlantic merchants and war contractors made great fortunes, disparities of wealth were widening, and more and more Bostonians were feeling left behind.

Economic cycles that could fill the town with happy prosperity would then plunge it into debt and despair. Like any large town of the time, Boston suffered from a host of urban problems—but in Boston they all seemed to happen at once. On March 20, 1760, a fire broke out in a tanning yard in the center of town and claimed dozens of buildings (perhaps 10 percent of the town) as it swept toward Fort Hill. Then in the early 1760s a smallpox epidemic raged through Boston, causing death by a thousand lesions. In January 1765, the merchant Nathaniel Wheelwright declared bankruptcy, ruining many other businesses in town. A severe storm in March 1765 damaged a number of wharves and ships. Unemployment, desperate poverty, crime, and unrest were rampant. Boston sank into a deep economic depression in the early 1760s. The climate was ripe for airing grievances and resentments.[7]

With the Hutchinson and Oliver families having arrogated some of the choicest offices in Massachusetts, a few Boston politicians began raising the charge of nepotism. The stern politician Samuel Adams, for instance, was born into the town's popular faction, which opposed Hutchinson and his more conservative allies. Adams's father, the elder Samuel Adams, had been one of the directors of the private Land Bank, a popular institution that issued paper currency, which enabled more money to circulate in Boston. (Thomas Hutchinson was an outspoken opponent of the Land Bank.) When Adams Sr. died in 1747, the sheriff tried to seize his property for debt, even though the bank records had been destroyed by fire. The younger Samuel Adams rose to prominence as a defender of his father's legacy against local creditors and as a passionate advocate of civil liberty, particularly in the newspapers, in Boston's local government, and eventually in the Massachusetts House of Representatives (fig. 6).[8]

The printing presses of Boston were an extremely effective way for dissidents such as Adams to transmit their message to the public. Benjamin Edes and John Gill printed the *Boston Gazette* from their workshop in Dassett Alley, and Isaiah Thomas would later begin printing the *Massachusetts Spy* as a weekly paper from his Union Street shop in 1771. Since New England Congregationalists believed that everyone ought to read and understand the Bible, New England had one of the highest literacy rates in the world. Newspapers and pamphlets, which were read in taverns and homes throughout Massachusetts and other colonies, could generally expect to command a wide audience—they were "The general source throughout the nation, / Of every modern conversation."[9]

The fiery lawyer James Otis Jr. turned against Hutchinson in 1760. Otis had seen his father, a prominent Barnstable lawyer and legislator, denied a prestigious judicial appointment that had been promised to him. Francis Bernard, the governor who overturned his predecessor's promise by slighting the elder Otis, granted the post of chief justice of the Massachusetts Superior Court to Hutchinson instead. Hutchinson was no lawyer, and he had not even sought the position, but Bernard found Hutchinson's political views more to his liking than those of Otis Sr. Now the younger Otis decided to take revenge and "set the whole province in a flame," even if he "perished in the attempt." He painted Hutchinson as a grasper of "lucrative posts," holding multiple, constitutionally incompatible

6 On the day after the so-called "Boston Massacre" of 1770, Samuel Adams points to the Massachusetts charter and demands that the troops leave town.

offices at the same time. In 1761, Otis represented sixty-three Boston merchants in the Superior Court and argued, as John Adams later recalled, with a "prophetic glare of his eyes," and a "rapid Torrent of impetuous Eloquence" against "writs of assistance"—general search warrants that allowed officials to search a merchant's property for smuggled goods.

Hutchinson, as the presiding chief justice, ruled in favor of the writs, earning himself the enmity of Boston's smugglers and radical merchants.[10]

To many established merchants in Massachusetts, including the Masonic leader John Rowe, smuggling was just another way of doing business, and prominent traders such as the Hancock family relied upon the evasion of customs duties as a path to profit and wealth. Their ships imported goods illegally from Amsterdam or Lisbon, or loaded and unloaded illicit goods at the Dutch Caribbean island of St. Eustatius; New Providence in the Bahamas; or Monte Cristi, Hispaniola (now the Dominican Republic). Many prominent men in town scarcely thought twice about smuggling, and they hired plenty of local laborers to help them carry out their illegal trade.[11]

Yet the new customs restrictions of 1764 suddenly politicized overseas trade in new ways. The Boston merchants, with the help of Adams, Otis, and other politicians, were outraged when Parliament began imposing new restrictions in 1764. Parliament commanded customs officers in America to keep a stricter watch and demand more paperwork, it applied new duties and regulations to several commodities, and it made a major adjustment to the tax on foreign molasses. Naval officers now had the power to seize vessels involved in smuggling, vice-admiralty judges could now authorize seizures without the help of juries, and customs officials were immune from being sued for damages. As Bostonians' local grievances became intertwined with resistance to imperial legislation, the town soon earned a reputation as the vanguard of American resistance to Great Britain's most oppressive policies.

The Stamp Act of 1765 did the most to fuse local rivalries with imperial protest, and Boston was the first city in America whose inhabitants reacted to the act with violence. The patrons of Boston taverns had passed around pamphlets that argued against the constitutionality of this new tax on official documents, newspapers, playing cards, and other items. Hutchinson thought the new legislation was a mistake, and his private arguments against the Stamp Act were similar to those used by American agents in Parliament. But he believed Americans were duty-bound to obey the law, and he moved to blunt the colony's public outcry against the act. He thought that violent protests would foolishly provoke Parliament, and that negotiations for repeal would be more effective. This might have been sensible, but it was poor politics: to the public, Hutchinson appeared to be on the wrong side of the issue, and it did not help that his brother-in-law, Andrew Oliver, was appointed the distributor of stamps for Massachusetts.[12]

On the morning of August 14, Boston awoke to find that the Boston crowds, invoking their Pope's Day traditions, had dangled effigies of Oliver and a British minister from an elm tree in the South End. When

Hutchinson threatened to have the sheriff remove the effigies, the crowd organized guards to make sure the images stayed in place. The protesters stood under the elm, now called the Liberty Tree, and gave a mock stamp to all goods entering town. At dusk, a crowd took the effigies down and marched to the town house. From there the shoemaker Ebenezer Mackintosh, the South End captain of the annual Pope's Day parade, led the crowd to King Street, where they destroyed a new building of Oliver's, widely rumored to be a stamp distribution office. The crowd had been disciplined at first, but as the night went on, things got out of hand. The Bostonians began by throwing rocks at Oliver's home, pulling down his outhouse, and stomping on his gardens, and they finished by drinking his liquor and throwing his furniture around. Hutchinson tried to persuade the crowd to disperse, and they answered him with bricks and stones. Oliver publicly resigned the office of stamp distributor the next day.

Then at dusk on August 26, crowds attacked the homes of three more local officials. One group went to the home of William Story, a vice-admiralty court judge, gathered his court records, and destroyed them in a bonfire on Fort Hill. Another group ravaged the residence of Robert Hallowell, Boston's comptroller of customs. Mackintosh then led the crowd to Thomas Hutchinson's house at Garden Court (fig. 7), which soon became the proxy for resentment against Hutchinson himself. Using axes and clubs, the crowd ripped fixtures from the interior and shingles from the roof. They raided the wine cellar, carried off money, dishware, furniture, and clothing, and scattered Hutchinson's papers in the streets. Dawn broke over the shell of a house, with Hutchinson devastated by his losses.

A number of the Bostonians involved in these Stamp Act protests were later associated with the Tea Party. Mackintosh was the first to be arrested after the actions of August 26, though when the sheriff heard rumors that there might be further rioters clamoring for Mackintosh's freedom, he released Mackintosh soon afterward. George Pillsbury also claimed to have been "at the destruction of the Stamp office" on August 14. Years later, Pillsbury claimed, "When Governor Hutchinson was treated by the Patriots, as all traitors to their Country ought to be, I was rank'd among the number." Only a few people were thrown in jail for the destruction of Hutchinson's house on the 26th, including a young man named Will More, who later helped destroy the tea in 1773.[13]

Mackintosh and the Boston crowd were acting in concert with a group of high-end artisans and merchants called the Loyal Nine, who held their meetings at a South End distillery near the Liberty Tree. Almost half of them also became linked to the Boston Tea Party, including the merchant

7 Thomas Hutchinson's mansion in the North End was damaged by crowds during the 1765 Stamp Act riots.

Henry Bass (later the son-in-law of prominent leader Samuel Phillips Savage); Benjamin Edes, printer of the fiery *Boston Gazette*; the distiller Thomas Chase; and the decorative painter Thomas Crafts Jr. Bass was "not a little pleas'd to hear that McIntosh has the Credit of [i.e., took the blame for] the whole affair," but in fact the crowds and small businessmen had worked together. The secret coordination of these groups foreshadowed the cooperation between merchants, artisans, and the Boston crowds who later destroyed the tea on December 16, 1773. In the years between the resistance to the Stamp Act and the outbreak of the Revolutionary War, many Americans began calling themselves "Sons of Liberty." The term sometimes referred generically to anyone who opposed the new policies of the British Parliament, and sometimes referred to an active group of newspaper writers, intercolonial correspondents, and tavern organizers. In Boston the leading Sons of Liberty included Samuel Adams, the radical physicians Thomas Young and Joseph Warren, the merchant John Hancock and his associate William Palfrey, and other men who were politically active in town and provincial government, and local clubs.[14]

Parliament repealed the Stamp Act in 1766. But the Boston crowd and the nascent Sons of Liberty had shown what they could do when provoked. Merchants, printers, and crowds could all defend the waterfront community from obnoxious impositions such as stronger customs enforcement or the Stamp Act. Most merchants believed that the local economy could not survive without the ability to smuggle foreign goods for lower prices. Boston's artisans and laborers, hurting from the terrible economy, also acted out their grievances against the new British laws. These protests opened up new opportunities for popular participation—even popular initiative. Reformers in Parliament may have wanted to tighten customs enforcement, but Bostonians were afraid that this would spell the end for them. On September 24, 1766, customs officials accused the merchant Daniel Malcom of concealing smuggled wine and liquor in his basement. When Malcom barricaded his house to keep out the officials, his neighbors and a group of boys from the nearby grammar school gathered to help. Among the defenders were future Tea Party participants such as Paul Revere and insurer Nathaniel Barber. Customs officials frequently looked on, aghast, as townspeople boarded a ship and took off all its goods in plain sight before the ship's captain obtained a customs clearance. Royal governors and their superiors in London faced constant frustration at their inability to enforce unpopular customs duties in Boston.[15]

Bostonians became disgruntled again when they learned about the new Townshend duties—which included the duty on tea—in 1767. Parliament also established a new American Board of Commissioners of the Customs, and stationed it in Boston. The board was composed of hated local customs officers like John Robinson and Charles Paxton, as well as suspicious newcomers from England. Arrayed against these officials was a group of merchants who had cut their teeth working with James Otis in the 1761 fights against the writs of assistance and other instances of customs officials' aggression. Ann Hulton, the sister of one of the new customs commissioners, called Boston a "Town where every cross wind or what thwarts thier [sic] inclinations raises a Storm." In coordination with smugglers, crowds sometimes attacked overly scrupulous customs officers or informers who ratted out illicit traders. Although a writer in the Boston Gazette called for "No Mobbs—No Confusions—No Tumults," the crowd did not always blindly follow local leaders.[16]

John Hancock was rising in popularity and political prominence during these years. Hancock had the good luck to be adopted and named heir to his uncle, the merchant—and smuggler—Thomas Hancock. John Hancock inherited a fortune: extensive wharf property, vast stocks of merchandise, a sprawling network of trade, and a large house on Beacon Hill. In April 1768, Hancock's brig *Lydia* was detained on suspicion of smuggling. When two tidewaiters (low-level customs officers) boarded the *Lydia*, Hancock intimidated them until they retreated. In retaliation, on June 10, customs officers decided to seize another of Hancock's ships, the sloop *Liberty*. As the workday ended, a crowd gathered on the docks, and more than 300 Bostonians attacked customs officers with bricks and stones. When they had finished abusing Joseph Harrison, the local customs collector, and his son Richard, they marched to his house and shattered every window.[17] Upon hearing news of the *Liberty* riot, the British ministry concluded that they could not even protect their officers from bodily harm without sending armed forces to patrol the streets. These redcoats landed at the end of September 1768, and Paul Revere etched a politically charged picture of the landing (fig. 8).

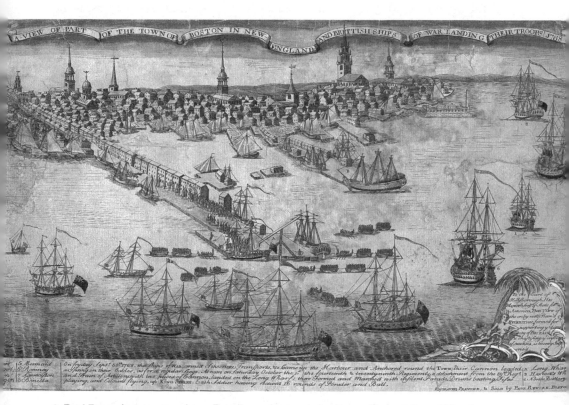

8 Paul Revere's engraving shows British regular troops landing at Boston's Long Wharf on September 30, 1768.

John Mein, a Scottish printer and bookseller who had moved to Boston, called Hancock "Johnny Dupe, Esq.," and the radicals' "*Milch-Cow*." He painted a picture of a blind man "richly dressed and surrounded with a croud of people, some of whom are stroaking his ears, others tickling his nose with straws, while the rest are employed in riffling his pockets." The implication was that Hancock was blindly funding the protests against Great Britain, although in fact Hancock had voiced his resentment of British infringements since the Stamp Act of 1765. (Mein satirized so many of Boston's popular leaders in this way that the Boston crowd treated him to a hard jab in the ribs, a barrage of brickbats, and a whack from a shovel.) In 1768, Hancock and other established merchants favored agreements to stop the importation of British goods until Parliament repealed the Townshend Acts. Their motives were not entirely patriotic—because many of these merchants already had large inventories of goods, the nonimportation agreements allowed them to sell off their overstock and regain a competitive advantage against British trading houses. Younger merchants like Hutchinson's sons, on the other hand, suffered from these locally enforced trade restrictions, as did representatives of English and Scottish firms. Discontent and disagreement plagued the nonimportation movement from the beginning.[18]

Some of the active Boston protesters did their best to enforce the agreements. They wrote newspaper polemics and held meetings to try and inspire the community against British taxes. When these methods failed, the crowd physically intimidated the more stubborn importers and their allies. At a merchants' meeting on January 18, 1770, the hardware merchant William Molineux, "first Leader of Dirty Matters," wanted to lead a crowd to the houses of the importers, including the Hutchinsons' house. Molineux may have been the grandson of the Lord Lieutenant of Ireland, the nephew of an Irish radical, and the fifth son born to a Dublin physician. He had moved to Boston in the 1740s, had done well as a trader and smuggler, and had risen to the forefront of radical politics in the Boston streets.[19]

Josiah "Wilkes" Quincy, a cross-eyed lawyer from Braintree who at the time was more moderate (though still an ardent enemy of Hutchinson), warned that Molineux's plan to lead a crowd to the Hutchinson house constituted treason. Quincy even suggested that Hutchinson himself was counting on such a disruption, which would help discredit the protest movement. Although most of the meeting's speakers (including Hancock and Otis) refused to lead a crowd, Quincy's argument failed. Molineux jumped up on a table, cried out that Boston had deserted him, and threatened to kill himself, before his companions calmed him down. Molineux and Samuel Adams then led a crowd to confront the younger Hutchinsons, only to come upon the governor, speaking in his sons' defense. The crowd dispersed peacefully that day, but it was clear to everyone that violent popular action was possible even with troops stationed in town.[20]

About a month after the dispute between Quincy and Molineux, on February 22, a large crowd of men and boys was surrounding an importer's shop, preventing any customers from entering. Ebenezer Richardson, the importer's neighbor, stepped in to see what he could do. The Boston Sons of Liberty despised Richardson as a customs informer, and the feeling was mutual. Richardson tried to knock down an offensive sign posted in front of his neighbor's shop. He got into a verbal argument with a few of the protesters, including the lemon importer Edward Proctor. Proctor and the other protesters followed Richardson to his house, and the boys followed, throwing fruit rinds and eggs, sticks and stones. Eventually the hecklers goaded Richardson so far that he aimed his musket out the window and fired a charge of swanshot, or pea-sized pellets, into the crowd. Eleven-year-old Christopher Seider, stooping to pick up a rock, was hit with eleven pellets. Two more hit nineteen-year-old Samuel Gore: one injured two of the fingers on his right hand, and another lodged itself in his thigh. Dr. Joseph Warren, a Harvard graduate and member of the local Masonic lodge, treated the wounded young men. Gore healed sufficiently for him to help hoist tea chests with the destroyers three years later, but little Seider's wounds turned out to be fatal. As the crowd roared with grief and rage, Molineux was barely able to stop them from stringing Richardson up.[21]

By this time, British troops had been stationed in Boston for over a year. The civilians and soldiers had made a regular practice of harassing, threatening, and scuffling with one another. On March 2, 1770, there was a huge brawl at Gray's ropewalk between soldiers and Boston's civilians. The apprentice Peter Slater, then only nine years old, remembered furnishing way-sticks (hickory clubs used for ropemaking) to the Bostonians. The next day, twenty-year-old Archibald McNeil Jr. was spinning rope with two apprentices when three stout British grenadiers, armed with bludgeons, asked them, "You damned dogs, don't you deserve to be killed? Are you fit to die?" If the soldiers were looking for a fight, they found it, because bats found their way into a couple more hands, and the civilians battled the soldiers to a draw. Slater and McNeil were later said to be tea destroyers.[22]

Eventually, the tension between the inhabitants of Boston and the British soldiers led to a fatal conflict. Once again, Bostonians demonstrated their singular ability to provoke the empire's minions into an explosive incident. Three days after the ropewalk brawl, on March 5, 1770, a few boys surrounded a group of eight British soldiers in front of the customhouse in King Street and began harassing them. A wigmaker's apprentice taunted Captain-Lieutenant John Goldfinch of the 14th Regiment for failing to pay his bills, and Goldfinch struck the boy on the head with his musket. The crowd of boys grew, hurling insults, followed by snowballs, followed by bricks. Someone had cried, "Fire!" which set the church bells ringing, and this brought even more people into King Street. Some carried buckets, ready to form a water brigade, but others had clubs and sticks, ready for a fight. Hundreds of people were now pressing in upon the soldiers, many of them shouting, and some even daring the soldiers to fire their weapons. Someone threw a club that hit one of the soldiers on the head. Shaking with anger, the soldier regained his feet and fired. Amid the noise and confusion and shouts of "Fire!" and "Don't fire!" a few more of the soldiers discharged their weapons.

The bullets just missed five men who would later participate in the Boston Tea Party.

The blockmaker James Brewer had been one of the first adults on the scene. He later claimed he had urged the soldiers not to shoot, but now he saw the sixteen-year-old shipwright's apprentice, Christopher "Kit" Monk, falter. He asked Monk if he was wounded, thinking that the soldiers had been firing blank charges, not real bullets.

Henry Prentiss also couldn't believe the guns were loaded; he was laughing at the crowd's fright until he saw the fallen men to his left and right, each not more than a yard away. The laugh died in his throat, and he told his father that it was "a scene the most Tragical, of any that ever the Eyes of Americans beheld . . . to see the blood of our fellow Citizens flowing down the gutters like water."

George Pillsbury, another bystander, said that he was near "Christopher Mattocks," or the mixed-race mariner Crispus Attucks, when the British "Hell Hounds" fired. Two bullets hit Attucks in the chest and killed him.

The shoemaker George R. T. Hewes was standing amid the crowd in King Street. Hewes had always been the kind of man that people hardly noticed. He was the fourth son in a family of five boys who had survived to adulthood. Although he had already reached his thirties, he had never amounted to much, economically or physically—he was only 5'1". George was muddling along as a poor shoemaker, a trade with few bright prospects, and had fared worse than most. Although he had a wife and children, he could not afford his own home for them, and he would even spend some time in debtors' prison later that year. When James Caldwell, a ship's mate, took two bullets in the chest, Hewes caught the dying man in his arms and helped carry him to a physician, but to no avail.

The mariner and horse renter Charles Conner was standing next to Patrick Carr, an Irish leatherworker, when a bullet went through Carr's hip and out his side. Conner helped carry the victim away, but the wound turned out to be mortal.

All told, there were five fatalities and a few others wounded. Eighteen-year-old Henry Mellus (another future Tea Party participant) saw the whole thing. Brewer and a few other Bostonians urged everyone to go home peacefully. The tailor David Bradlee, who helped a town watchman carry away a corpse, may have been another Tea Party participant. Seventeen-year-old Samuel Maverick, who was also slain, was related to Ebenezer Mackintosh by marriage. The incident, which enraged the town, came to be known as the Boston Massacre.[23]

The merchant William Molineux now stepped in as a go-between for the British officers and the town of Boston. He personally escorted the British troops off the peninsula, helping the crowd maintain its organization and discipline. Molineux's record as a popular leader was not perfect—he managed some Boston storehouses for a government supporter in New York, which he rented to British soldiers, and his enemies accused him of using town funds to defraud his fellow townsmen in a scheme to build a workhouse for the poor. Yet his role as an upper-class crowd leader was distinctive: he was a member of the Boston Caucus, a group of political organizers, and he was also well known and respected in the streets.[24]

After the bloody incident in King Street, British troops were stationed at Fort William on Castle Island in Boston harbor. Technically, they were ready for the governor to deploy, but it was now politically impossible for the governor to call them back to mainland Boston, and so the troops remained on the island until 1774. In the ensuing murder trials, the soldiers would claim that they had feared for their lives on March 5, and had acted in self-defense. Paul Revere produced another engraving that commemorated the radicals' version of the incident as a "massacre" instead, casting blame on the soldiers for killing unarmed civilians. Each year following the incident, Bostonians gathered to hear an anniversary speech commemorating the Massacre; Peter Edes, the son of a Tea Party partici-pant, printed these orations in a volume in 1785.[25]

Following the Boston Massacre and the trials, the next three years were a period of relative calm, compared to the destructive riots and vicious assaults that had characterized the 1760s. But when Hutchinson officially assumed the governorship in 1770, Parliament had still not given up on the idea of taxing the colonies for revenue and tightening control over them. Neither had the Massachusetts legislature, the Boston Sons of Liberty, or the Boston crowd given up on the idea of resisting Parliament at every opportunity. Under such conditions, no governor could both uphold the law and maintain authority over Massachusetts.[26]

The Boston dissidents who organized against the imperial government and its allied officials during these years drew their personnel from a loose coalition of overlapping groups. Though they came from different social ranks, each person could feel that they were making a contribution to the wider movement. Some exercised their power in official bodies like the House of Representatives or the Council, or became famous for their arguments in court. Other upper-class protesters voiced their arguments in open town meetings. In Boston (as in other Massachusetts towns), men who met a loose property qualification chose selectmen and other town officials every year, held open debates, and ruled by majority. Such town meetings were unknown in England or in the British colonies outside New England. Most New Englanders were Congregationalists who organized their towns as independent, covenanted communities, free of the church hierarchy that existed in the Roman Catholic Church or the Church of England. They believed that the public good superseded individualism, and they sought to contribute to the welfare of the whole in these meetings. The Bostonians who gathered in Faneuil Hall for town meetings expected a certain amount of self-government, and were suspicious of outside interference. Imperial governors found the independent spirit of these meetings intolerable. Governor William Shirley wrote in 1747 that "the principal cause of the Mobbish turn in this Town, is it's Constitution; by which the Management of it is devolv'd upon the populace assembled in their Town Meetings . . . [where] the meanest Inhabitants . . . outvote the Gentlemen, Merchants, Substantial Traders and all the better part of the Inhabitants." In 1766, Hutchinson wrote that at these meetings, "Otis with his mobbish eloquence prevails in every motion."[27]

Some of the dissidents operated through unofficial groups like the Boston Society for Encouraging Trade and Commerce (a group of merchants), the Loyal Nine, the Sons of Liberty, or the Boston Caucus. "I could fill my sheet," Hutchinson wrote, "with Acts of Government come into by the Town of Boston by the Cadet Company [the governor's honor guard] and by several Fire Clubs for we have no sort of Company but what look upon it they have a right to do something or other in Publick affairs."

Boston's taverns were filled with politically connected men like John Rowe or Paul Revere convincing their friends how to vote, pointing out inflammatory newspaper items, and practicing the rituals of organized club life. Some of them, like Samuel Adams or Josiah Quincy, wrote pamphlets or newspaper pieces in which they articulated their arguments. Revere expressed himself in his printed engravings.[28]

Other dissidents, like Ebenezer Mackintosh, were artisans and laborers who did their arguing in the streets. Hutchinson claimed that "they are some what controuled by a superior set consisting of the master masons carpenters &c of the town," and indeed the crowd was often willing to coordinate with the middle-class artisans and merchants who worked within the local political clubs. At the same time, the Boston crowd had demonstrated on several occasions that the "rabble" could act of its own accord, and that the members of these crowds were just as willing as the politicians to protect Boston from obnoxious soldiers, importers, and civil officials.[29]

Any coalition with so many moving parts was bound to have some trouble holding together. The rifts in Boston's popular party were particularly apparent during the nonimportation movement of 1768–70. Nonimportation created scarcities, drove up prices, and hurt commerce, and so it was difficult for Boston's popular politicians to maintain support for it. Colonial merchants in all the cities eventually became impatient with the agreements, and after New York merchants agreed to resume importing goods in July 1770, it became more difficult for the Boston leaders to keep up the pressure on the merchants. By September, it seemed to the tea merchant Richard Clarke that Boston's popular leaders had "lost much of their power." The nonimportation agreements limped along for a few more months and then died an uneasy death. When Adams, Molineux, and others demanded the continuation of these agreements, the merchants ignored them.[30]

During the "Pause in Politics" that lasted from the end of the nonimportation agreements in 1770 to 1773, supporters of the Crown rejoiced that the popular leaders of Boston seemed to be in retreat. After 1769, Otis was an intermittent presence in politics, as his sanity came and went. The lawyer John Adams briefly took Otis's vacated seat in the legislature in 1770 until he too left Boston, suffering from exhaustion. Josiah Quincy, the dissident lawyer, had become more intense in his attacks on Hutchinson, but in the early 1770s he contracted tuberculosis, and traveled to the southern colonies for his health. Dr. Joseph Warren, a vibrant young orator, stirred audiences with his speeches in commemoration of the Boston Massacre in 1772, but his debts and his management of another man's estate were distracting. Molineux was facing allegations of fraud. Dr. Thomas Young, a sharp and radical thinker, had to defend himself from charges of atheism.[31]

Samuel Adams continued to insist that England was plotting to send corrupt officials with arbitrary powers to take away American rights, liberties, and property. But most Bostonians were too distracted or divided to mount a serious challenge to imperial authority. Hancock was often too ill to attend to politics, and a group of men told Hutchinson that Hancock "wished to be separated from Mr. Adams." In January 1772, Hutchinson wrote, "Mr. Hancock I have reason to think is upon such terms with his Colleagues the Town Representatives that they will not easily be reconciled." In 1772, the Company of Cadets elevated Hancock to colonel—a position of prestige that led some to worry that Hancock might become too friendly with Hutchinson. If the friends of government could separate more moderate merchants (like Hancock) from radicals like Adams, Hutchinson wrote, "we may hope they will be less capable of mischief." Hutchinson reported that Dr. Benjamin Church, a member of the North End Caucus (and the Boston Massacre anniversary speaker in 1773), was now writing newspaper pieces in support of government. Meanwhile, provincial politics were at a stalemate, because Hutchinson moved the General Court from rowdy Boston to Cambridge in 1770. Over the next two years, the House of Representatives refused to do any business until Hutchinson brought the legislature back to Boston.[32]

Boston may have been calmer, and its popular leaders may have lost some of their focus, but most Bostonians still thought of their town as a stalwart in the radical protest against Parliament. Furthermore, as they looked around, they saw they were not alone in this fight. Since 1765, Americans had established (or attempted to establish) a series of intercolonial networks: nine colonies had sent delegates to a Stamp Act congress in 1765. Around the same time, groups of protesters in taverns throughout North America were corresponding with one another as the Sons of Liberty. As Thomas Young wrote to a sympathetic organizer in New York City in 1769, "The Society of the Sons of Liberty after lying sometime inactive have again resumed their former vigor and begin to mediate a renovation of their correspondence thro the Continent." When Bostonians stopped importing British goods in response to the Townshend duties, they knew they could not succeed without comparable agreements in the other major ports— Newport, New York City, Philadelphia, and Charleston. The Massachusetts legislature had also sent a "circular letter" to other colonial legislatures in 1768, protesting the Townshend Acts and calling for another conference.

THE RINGLEADER OF ALL VIOLENCE

Americans from different colonies were opening lines of communication for coordination and cooperation. These relations were sometimes frayed, especially in the doldrums of 1770 to 1773, when radicals sullenly accused one another of slipping.[33]

Yet Bostonians' anger was quick to revive. When the British ministry announced that it would pay civil officials out of the duties collected on tea in 1772, Samuel Adams saw it as a dangerous threat to the Massachusetts Charter. With a number of like-minded organizers in Boston, he created a Committee of Correspondence that would coordinate action with the colony's country towns, in the hopes of uniting them politically.[34] Then in 1773, the famous scientist Benjamin Franklin, who was acting as an agent for Massachusetts in London, leaked some old letters that Hutchinson had written to a correspondent in London in 1768 and 1769. In these letters, which Hutchinson had written while British troops were billeted in town to neutralize the Boston crowds, he appeared to be urging the British government to manage Boston with a firm hand, even if it required "an abridgment of what are called English liberties." Hutchinson's enemies, men like John Adams and Samuel Adams, seized on this phrase, printed the letters, and accused Hutchinson of serving a conspiracy that "threatned total Destruction to the Liberties of all *America*." Hutchinson, who had already hinted that he wanted to resign, asked his superiors in June 1773 for leave of absence to go to England. When Franklin heard a report that Hutchinson was "gloomy and low spirited," he responded, "It must be an uncomfortable thing to live among people who he is conscious universally detest him."[35]

If things had been calm during the so-called "Pause in Politics," this was in part because there had been international friction, first between Great Britain and Spain, then Great Britain and France. "When it appears a calm we never look upon it as settled," wrote Ann Hulton. "When dark clouds & Storms threaten us across the Atlantic, then the tempest subsides here, & a profound Calm succeeds for a while, but then those impending Clouds being blown away, this Calm is followd by commotions & hurricans."[36]

The Customs Commissioners knew better than anyone how nasty such commotions could be. On Boston's annual election day in May 1773, the governor was hosting the commissioners as guests at his annual dinner. The Company of Cadets was standing in a file and presenting arms. Two of the cadets, bookseller James Foster Condy and upholsterer Moses Grant, refused to show their respect: they clubbed their firelocks (or shouldered them, muzzles down) and quit the ranks. John Hancock dismissed the men on the spot, and Condy and Grant joined the local crowd, led by William Molineux and Paul Revere, who were hissing and pelting mud at the commissioners. The *Boston Gazette* voiced support for "their just resentment and contempt manifested to the Commissioners of the Customs." Lendall Pitts and Joseph Pearse Palmer, fellow cadets, dissented from the cadets' vote to expel Condy and Grant from their ranks. Molineux, Revere, Condy, Grant, Pitts, and Palmer all participated in the Tea Party later that year.[37]

Even though pre-Revolutionary Boston was linked in important ways to Great Britain, the town had its own distinctive history, culture, and daily rhythms. Amid economic woes, it was peppered with brawls, parades, and turbulent politics. Men like Samuel Adams, John Hancock, and Ebenezer Mackintosh were stepping to the forefront of Boston's politics of protest. But even more obscure men, like George R. T. Hewes, James Foster Condy, or George Pillsbury, also began demonstrating their active political stance against Parliament by appearing at protests involving troops, importers, and customs officers. The ingredients were in place for a renewed clash over the duty on tea, and the Tea Act of 1773 provided the catalyst for this confrontation.

CHAPTER 3

Tea and Scandal

Tea produces nothing; all is sunk, buried, and annihilated. We only see its effects in idleness, and . . . various distempers.

Jonas Hanway, "An Essay on Tea," 1756[1]

Standing just over four feet tall and bent under a curved spine, the Quaker gadfly Benjamin Lay stepped onto a box amid the Philadelphia market stalls in 1742. His wife had died just over six years before, and Lay rather curiously brought out her large collection of valuable china. Once a sufficient crowd of shoppers had gathered, Lay hefted a hammer and began smashing the porcelain to pieces, as "a publick Testimony against the Vanity of Tea-Drinking." The onlookers reacted in a panic. Some offered to buy the china instead, but Lay wouldn't sell for any price. Then the crowd rushed to stop him, and scurried away with as much of the intact china as they could gather. Despite Lay's preaching, they were unwilling to part with their tea.[2]

Well before the Boston Tea Party, tea inspired destruction among those who feared its effects, and frenzy among those who couldn't get enough. The tea that reached America from China inspired new addictions, new trade connections, new forms of luxury, new social critiques, and a simmering provincial inferiority. As it inspired moral and political debates in Britain and America, and as it launched smuggling ventures and boycotts, tea gave off more than a whiff of controversy.

Beginning in the 1580s, Europeans adopted a trio of warm, caffeinated drinks for the first time: chocolate, coffee, and tea. Chocolate, its dark, earthy depths roasted from ground cacao beans, made its way across the Atlantic Ocean from Mexico. Coffee beans, roasted and brewed to blackness, reached Europeans by way of Ethiopia and Yemen. Tea, its leaves filling the nostrils with bittersweet scent, came by ship or caravan from China. Compared to ancient favorites like beer and cider, tea was relatively new to the English-speaking world.

Despite their far-flung origins, these three beverages had a great deal in common. In Mexico, Yemen, and China, people revered the hot drinks as part of cultural and religious rituals. All three were packed with caffeine that loosened the blood vessels, dampened the appetite, and sharpened the senses. And all three were so bitter to taste that Europeans were slow to begin drinking them until they combined them with sugar—another new substance. Once a spoonful of sugar was added to a steaming cup, the mixture of sensations delighted the palate. Soon Europeans and Euro-Americans began revering these drinks as part of their rituals, too. New mind-altering plants like tobacco, tea, and sugarcane became the basis for world trade. As governments caught on to the idea of taxing these products, world trade became the basis for worldwide empires. The British Empire, fueled by the demand for tea and sugar, turned its attention to imperial expansion and enslavement—to amassing more land and laborers for growing these products.[3]

All pure tea comes from one species of plant, *camellia sinensis* (fig. 9).[4] Farmers pluck the small, firm leaves from this flowering evergreen shrub, which can grow twelve feet high and live for a hundred years. These leaves release caffeine, antibacterial chemicals, and perhaps other properties yet unknown. Indeed, for hundreds of years, the Taoists and Buddhists of Eastern Asia have ascribed spiritual properties to tea. Today, scientists are still investigating the medical benefits of tea, from flavonoids to fluoride.[5]

Human beings first picked tea from the skyward mountains that separate China from the Indian subcontinent, and the Southeast Asian jungles beneath them. Over a thousand years before the Boston Tea Party, the Chinese popularized and marketed the drink in Asia and beyond. Chinese emperors had their own varieties specially prepared for them, while teahouses invigorated Asian city life. In the Celestial Empire, tea became a central part of Chinese learning, high culture, and hospitality. East Asians developed a rich variety of teas, some coarse, and some delicate. It was a simple pleasure with a complex flavor: warm and soothing, yet able to spark a buzz in the brain. Chinese merchants enjoyed a thriving exchange with Japanese ships and Mongol horsemen for years before Western Europeans first tasted tea in the sixteenth century. Persian caravans also began dealing in tea: in the Muslim world, tea joined coffee as another pleasant substitute for forbidden alcohol.[6]

Until the nineteenth century, all the tea that Europeans and Americans drank grew in Chinese soil, and the Chinese closely guarded the secrets of its cultivation. Most of today's well-known varieties of tea from India, such as Darjeeling, Assam, or Earl Grey (named for a British general who fought the Americans during the Revolutionary War), were not developed until later.

9 Eighteenth-century European readers were fascinated to learn more about tea and its properties.

Throughout the 1700s, European trading companies advertised both green and black teas. Oxidation (which turns apples brown and iron to rust) and fermentation differentiated these two types of tea. Green tea comes from leaves that are steamed or heated after plucking to prevent oxidation. The result is generally a flavor as sweet and fresh as a garden, gentler and mellower than black tea. The varieties of green tea that sank to the bottom of Boston harbor included hi-tshun (Hyson, the finest) and Singlo (gathered later in the season from larger leaves). The green tea that the Chinese farmed for the European market grew primarily in the southeast part of Anhui (Anhwei) province.[7]

To produce longer-lasting black tea, the leaves are allowed to fully ferment, yielding a darker, earthier tea with a stronger taste and aroma. The black tea that Chinese hongs (merchants) sold to European traders largely came out of the Wu-i shan (Bohea) hills on the border of Fujian (Fukien) and Jiangxi (Kiangsi) provinces. Ordinary black tea, popular and cheap among Europeans, was called "Bohea," and this was the bulk of the tea dumped in Boston harbor. The discarded black tea also included finer Souchong and kung fu (Congou) teas, which varied depending on where the leaf was picked from the stem. The martial arts style "kung fu" comes from the same Chinese word, meaning "labor requiring skill and effort."[8]

The cultivation and processing of tea did require extensive effort. Though both men and women performed this arduous labor, women often made up the bulk of the workforce. In some areas of China, laborers picked tea three or four times a year, with the principal season lasting from mid-spring to early summer. Tea-harvesting was intense. Timing was crucial, since a delay of even one day might degrade the quality of the leaves. A tea picker might have to search for plants along dangerous cliffs or in mountain crevices. Once she reached the plant, the picker sat for long, tedious hours plucking each leaf by hand. Tea pickers might break the monotony by singing songs— especially love songs—and Chinese poets were enthralled by the sensuality of young female tea pickers putting their nimble fingers to work. After hauling the heavy baskets away, pickers had to sort the leaves from the stalks. The tea was then cured through a process of heating, roasting, and rolling, usually at the end of the day when the tea was picked. Tea peddlers collected the processed tea, and wholesalers sorted and packed it. Merchants then sent the tea on a tortuous and difficult route, hundreds of miles long, towards Guangzhou (Canton), via river rafts and porters on mountain paths, and sometimes by sea.[9]

The British East India Company bought tea at the port of Canton, in accordance with Chinese regulations and long-standing European practice. There the port's superintendents (known as "hoppos") and Chinese imperial administrators managed the trade by keeping prices competitive, giving discounts to large shippers, arranging loans, and making sure that duties were sent properly to Beijing. Traders from Northern Europe often conducted negotiations in Portuguese, since the Portuguese at Macao had been the earliest European overseas traders in China. The hoppos supplied all the necessary provisions, pilots, and linguists to outsiders, and controlled contact between all Chinese people and the foreign traders (fig. 10).[10]

In late November or December the tea arrived at Canton quays in light-weight tin containers from farms upriver. Once the hongs and European traders finished haggling over price, quality, and method of payment, porters loaded the cargo onto European ships docked at the Whampoa

10 Chinese laborers in a Canton (Guangzhou) warehouse carry tea for inspection.

islands. Wooden tea chests were lined with lead to prevent contamination, and the chests were packed together with strong, flexible rattan (or bamboo) matting. The East India Company ships were then ready to embark upon their six-month journey to London, where the Company held tea auctions twice a year. The auctioneer lit a one-inch candle and accepted bids on tea chests until the candle snuffed out.[11]

Before 1680, tea was a rarity in the West. At first only the wealthiest Westerners could afford Eastern silks, porcelain, and tea. Sugar and tea were principally of interest as herbal medicines rather than as everyday pick-me-ups. Furthermore, tea was expensive: it had to be shipped across great distances, the East India Company's monopoly allowed it to charge a high price, and British duties added a further surcharge. As a result, tea was a luxury item during the seventeenth century, and it was unclear whether tea would disappear as a passing fad, or become entrenched as a daily English and Anglo-American custom.[12]

By the eighteenth century, the answer was clear: tea had become a commodity of major importance in British commerce with China. Between 1719 and 1833, tea represented 70 to 90 percent of Canton's exports, and (after 1765) over 70 percent of the value of the East India Company's imports from China. Most strikingly, by 1768, tea represented 48.3 percent of the EIC's total income, and the annual haul of Company tea reached a pre-Revolutionary peak of 13 million pounds imported in 1772. Only textiles rivaled tea in importance to the Company, and the duties the British government collected from tea accounted for over 6 percent of the national budget.[13]

As the tea trade grew, tea became more affordable. Between the 1720s and 1770s, the EIC and its foreign competitors improved their trade connections with China and India and increased their shipments of tea. Retailers marketed tea to the British and colonial public, and the price of legally imported tea in England fell by half, despite higher duties. With taxes generally amounting to twice the original cost of tea, some of these retailers obtained their tea from smugglers who took the risk of slipping across the English Channel or the North Sea into a warren of cellars and caves. From there, parcels of tea made their way across the countryside, lubricated by counterfeiting and bribery, so that illegal tea from Continental European companies was provided at cheaper prices. Contemporaries estimated that around 7 million pounds of tea were smuggled into Britain annually in the 1770s, and in some years half the tea drunk in Britain was smuggled. With so much inexpensive tea available by the middle of the eighteenth century, observers were reporting that even chambermaids and common laborers took tea regularly. Some critics argued that this was not necessarily the best way to spend money—tea with sugar provides an energy boost but little in the way of substantive calories or protein—but then again, tea was more than just a new item to stock in the pantry and brew for a daily fix. Tea carried immense significance as an exotic stimulant, a status symbol, and the focus of a feminine domestic ritual.[14]

Tea imports to Massachusetts also came via legal and illegal trade routes. Most legally imported tea—90 percent—came in British or American merchant ships to Boston, New York City, or Philadelphia. For most of the eighteenth century, Boston's native wholesalers had close ties to British merchants in London and other ports, and these merchants received healthy commissions for their sales. Since the 1760s, Boston had been dealing with an influx of British agents who threatened to crowd out

American merchants, but this was not unique to the tea trade. From the warehouse, chests of tea went into the hands of shopkeepers and peddlers, who sold tea to those families who could afford it. People craved tea, and bought it whenever they could.[15] Meanwhile, smugglers slipped tea from continental ports like Lisbon or Amsterdam into isolated spots along the coast. From there, they ran tea by boat or overland to peddlers and shopkeepers: the extra profits that resulted were worth the risk. Customers often had no idea whether the tea they drank was legal or illegal—everyone just looked for the best price they could get. "We have been so long habituated to illicit Trade that people in general see no evil in it," Thomas Hutchinson wrote. In another letter, he guessed that more than three-quarters of the "prodigious consumption in America" was smuggled.[16]

In the years leading up to the Boston Tea Party, East India Company tea represented almost 3 percent of the total value of all goods exported to the American colonies from England, over £70,000 worth a year on average. If smuggled tea were factored in, the value of imported tea might be three times as high, or more.[17] One merchant guessed that each American drank more than two pounds of tea per year, or a cup of tea a day—though the correct figure was probably closer to half as much.[18]

As the British and American economies grew, and as transatlantic trade became more efficient, the British began to export a wider selection of consumer goods to America than earlier generations could possibly have imagined. American colonists did not just clothe themselves with new fabrics, but bedecked themselves in buttons, ribbons, and jewels and admired themselves in mirrors. Books, toys, and musical instruments gave Americans a broader imagination, and candlesticks helped them illuminate work and play throughout the evening. Carpets and draperies made rooms luxurious, not just comfortable. Especially after 1740 (around the time when Benjamin Lay was smashing crockery), the average American family was able to devote almost a third of its income to imported goods like these. Tea was an important part of this new American consumer phenomenon.[19]

During the eighteenth century, tea became the drink of respectable British and colonial households everywhere. The wealthiest families adopted tea ceremonies first, giving tea immense cultural cachet. In these households, tea was a regular family event. Guests might be invited, but this was not meant to be a large, showy display of hospitality like an evening banquet; tea was a quiet, pleasant household occasion. The steam from a teacup was meant to banish all thought of conflict or arguments. The woman of the house oversaw the making of tea and assigned a series of tasks and errands to other family members, bringing the family together under her direction. Proper manners were essential: brewing tea was a matter of delicacy, serving tea had its own etiquette, and even receiving a cup of tea from the hostess demanded appropriate behavior. Young men and women of the elite were trained to emulate these rules on their way to entering polite society. Tea became a ritual of family solidarity, sustenance, and politeness.[20]

To master the tea ceremony was to announce your own virtue, as you displayed your breeding and comportment. The striving "middle class" of tradesmen, professionals, and landowners couldn't resist the chance to partake in this elite pastime. You didn't have to have a hereditary title, or even be particularly wealthy, to sip respectably at the tea table. As families learned the rules of this fancy ritual, more and more of them began to drink tea in their homes.[21] Alongside tobacco and—more vitally—sugar, tea had become a new necessity. Addictive, stimulating, lightweight, and easy to prepare, these new products increased a middling family's need for cash and encouraged men and women to work more and work harder.[22] Tea could conquer sleep and thereby make a person more productive: in this way tea was contributing to the empire's growing economy.[23]

Consumers in Great Britain and the American colonies sipped their tea amid lacquered ("japanned") furniture that revealed a fascination with the Orient that came from trading with it, "discovering" it, and colonizing it. These pieces depicted Chinese figures that were often sipping tea, just like the British consumers on both sides of the Atlantic that shared a fascination with exotic beverages. Americans assured themselves that a good consumer was a good colonist, since trade and commerce helped support the mother country. Tea also allowed Americans to feel more sophisticated—tea and fancy tea things led colonists to believe that they had something in common with the English aristocracy, or even the royal family. In this way, tea and other consumer goods allowed Americans to feel a stronger connection with the British Empire, although it also unearthed deep insecurities about provincial inferiority. As they strived to become more and more like their British cousins, Americans struggled to keep up with trendsetters in London.[24]

Americans spent their money on fancy new accessories that went along with drinking tea with sugar (fig. 11). In a well-appointed household, a glittering array of glass, silver, and ceramic objects could be found on a mahogany or walnut tea table. After boiling the water in a teakettle, the hostess took tea from the house's tea canister or caddy and brewed the mixture in a teapot, perhaps of silver or ceramic. Teapots were the centerpieces of the tea set, and

11 From the 1770s, a blue and white porcelain tea service along with a copper hot water urn and silver equipage (including a milk jug, tea canister, sugar box, tongs, and spoons).

they were ornamented and styled in a variety of ways. At this point, a servant may have arranged a row of teacups on their saucers alongside the edge of the table. The hostess poured the steaming brew into the ceramic cups, and the drinker had to hold the cup carefully by its edges (handles were not common until the end of the century) so as not to scald the fingers. In England, tea drinkers avoided this problem by drinking cooler tea from the saucer, but Americans preferred their tea hot. To sweeten the beverage, the hostess picked up silver tongs or a spoon and lifted a lump of sugar from a shallow bowl. A jug or urn, sometimes called a "creamer," was used to lighten the tea with milk or cream. When a tea drinker finished her cup, she dumped the dregs into a slop bowl. In the households of less wealthy people, tea accoutrements were made of cheaper metals and glazed earthenware.[25]

Early in the eighteenth century, American and British tea drinkers bought porcelain tea things through the East India Company from the Chinese. Later in the century the British began making and marketing their own ceramics. The American colonies were the largest export market for the growing British ceramics industry, and teaware accounted for a sizable fraction of this market. Pottery manufacturers could make teapots shaped like cauliflower, fruit, or a squirrel, or imprint the sides with Chinese scenes, floral patterns, English cartoons, or a buyer's name. A

1771 advertisement in Boston even listed "several compleat Tea-table Sets of Childrens cream-coloured Toys." Local craftsmen also served the tea-drinking market: Paul Revere, for instance, made, engraved, and repaired silver teapots and teaspoons, cream pots and sugar tongs for a variety of Boston customers. English entrepreneurs like Josiah Wedgwood specifically catered to an American market at times—they shrewdly put the face of William Pitt or a phrase like "No Stamp Act" on a teapot as a direct appeal to American consumers.[26]

Bostonians were proud of their caffeine drinking, "the easiest, readiest, and cheapest refreshment, the Inhabitants of Boston, can take in a Morning."[27] New Englanders turned out to be discerning tea drinkers. As the Boston tea merchant Richard Clarke wrote to his wholesaler, "send us . . . the best quality as to strength Flavor & color"; customers turned up their noses at a poor-quality batch. Even the militiamen at isolated frontier garrisons, as well as a variety of Native American groups, were drinking tea. By the 1770s, tea equipment could be found in around half of all probated estates for the deceased in Massachusetts. Tea was not some rare treat, but an everyday satisfaction for many.[28]

Tea was foreign, strange, and new, leading to debates over whether it was a healthy beverage or an evil brew. Tea arrived in Europe just as people were reading the first popular books and pamphlets about health and diet. A Dutch physician argued that tea would make you "exempt from all maladies" and prolong your life. Authors wrote that tea could cure headaches, stomach problems, lung and kidney obstructions, and malaria. Tea could banish nightmares, clear up acne, sharpen the memory, and one Dutch pamphlet noted that it "strengthens the work of Venus serviceably for newlyweds." A couple of scientists performed experiments demonstrating that meat soaked in tea spoiled more slowly. Many experts were quick to notice tea's properties as a diuretic and a stimulant.[29]

Other writers argued that tea was harmful to the human body. One British essayist called it "utterly improper for Food" and classified it among "Poysonous Vegetables." Critics cautioned that pregnant and nursing women should avoid it—they blamed tea for infant deaths and weakened adults.[30] John Wesley, the founder of Methodism, observed in 1748 that tea made his hands shake, which he described as "Symptoms of a Paralytick Disorder." According to his further observations, tea sapped the strength, wreaked havoc on digestion, and made daily labor sluggish.[31] Jonas Hanway, a British merchant, anti-Semite, and philanthropist who later argued against American independence, compared tea to an "epidemical disease," and blamed it for bad teeth, scurvy, and weak nerves. "Can any reasonable person doubt," he asked, "that this flatulent liquor shortens the lives of great numbers of people?"[32]

Neither tea's supporters nor its detractors had the standards of scientific objectivity that we might expect today. Many pro-tea pamphleteers stood to gain from the expansion of the tea trade. Critics who attacked the physical effects of the drink, meanwhile, were mostly troubled by its effects on people's morals. These critics, skeptical whether tea was beneficial or necessary, lumped it in with other suspicious luxuries. A broad literature in the eighteenth century attempted to discourage British people from the habits of conspicuous consumption, status-seeking, and enslavement to the fickle whims of taste and fashion.[33]

Luxury was worrisome because it disrupted traditional visions of the social order. In the past, Britons judged the status of others on the basis of their parentage and honor. But luxury goods like tea changed the equation—suddenly all it took was a little cash to attain the trappings of the upper class. Luxury threatened the elite in another way: by diverting them from the more serious business of governing society at the very moment when new consumer goods were making common people more impertinent. Among strict Puritans in England and New England, luxury was also potentially sinful, if it distracted people from their duty toward God and the community.[34]

Hanway, the philanthropist, warned that luxury would lead to vanity and pride, and he worried that items like tea would "intoxicate with desires, which have no better support than fancy and opinion." Luxury would corrupt not just the human body, but the entire country—and as poorer people slavishly imitated the wealthy, the problem would only get worse. "It is the curse of this nation, that the laborer and mechanic will ape the lord." In the hands of poor men and women, tea would drain England of its wealth, military strength, and labor force. Englishmen needed to be tough enough to fight the French, Hanway wrote, while Englishwomen needed to tough enough to raise such hardy fighters. Instead, both men and women were sipping tea, insipidly.[35] The writer Samuel Johnson, a self-confessed "hardened and shameless tea-drinker," criticized much of Hanway's essay. Still, he agreed with Hanway that "tea is a liquor not proper for the lower classes of the people . . . Its proper use is to amuse the idle, and relax the studious, and dilute the full meals of those who cannot use exercise, and will not use abstinence."[36] Luxury, in other words, was supposed to be reserved for the idle rich. If the tea habit was not monitored closely, it might turn society upside down.

12 In this English painting, one of a series on "Modern Love," a young wife adds sugar to her husband's tea.

13 The caption of this image begins, "How see we Scandal (for our Sex too base)/Seat its dread Empire in the Female Race." The verse's author laments that destructive slander circulates among women at the tea table.

While both men and women drank a great deal of tea, women were at the heart of these debates, because in British and American homes, it was women who served tea. Chinese poets had sung of the beauty of female tea pickers—and for Western men, the female tea pourer held just as much sexual allure. Since tea was a foreign product, and since exotic lands have always conjured up assumptions about places with less inhibited sexuality, the very idea of Oriental tea was an aphrodisiac. A British woman's pure, white hands—unsullied by dirt or sweat and busy pouring tea—were particularly arousing to British men. In Britain and America, male suitors would show up at women's tea tables to compete for a woman's hand and offer up displays of gallantry (fig. 12).[37]

In the biblical tradition, a person's inner erotic desires were the fallout of humanity's original sin in the Garden of Eden. Ever since the story of Eve, the Western world had associated women with sinful appetites, and women's appetite for tea and other consumer goods (including fancy china for serving tea) threatened to destroy the nation. Bernard Mandeville, the Dutch-born physician and philosopher, wrote in 1714 that women would use "Deceit and vile Stratagems," such as teasing, scolding, wheedling, and the exchange of sexual favors, to drain money from their husbands and spend it on finery and hot tea. Mandeville believed this was a good thing, since spending would sustain Great Britain's burgeoning capitalist economy, but not everyone agreed. Since men could not resist women, and women were particularly seductive when they were pouring tea, this vicious tide threatened to drown the whole empire in effeminacy.[38]

In addition, teatime encouraged women to gather in groups, which led to further tongue-clucking. Men met one another in public places: in taverns (which were also sinful and corrupting, but impossible to banish) and coffeehouses, which were soberer places for conversation, news, and business. It was unseemly for respectable women to gather in taverns, and women were thought to be too uneducated and unserious for the coffeehouse. So women, perhaps reacting to their husbands' absconding to coffeehouses, took their social beverages in the home. The idea of upper-class ladies drinking tea in private boudoirs might strike us as pretty harmless, but some men, not content with having excluded women from many public places, were still disturbed by the idea of women (especially working-class women) getting together in a female setting. In the eyes of critics, the tea table was becoming a venue for women to ridicule outsiders (including men), compete cattily with one another, and spread gossip throughout the drawing rooms of London and Boston (fig. 13). Eliza Haywood wrote, "Scandal, and Ridicule seem here to reign with uncontested Sway" at the tea table, where women were quick to seize on other people's deficiencies in dress or behavior. Edward Young agreed: "Scandal's the sweet'ner of a female feast."[39]

If tea-drinking was unsupervised, women were liable to become uncontrollable. If women spent too much time at tea and too much money on tea, they might neglect their children and their chores, destroy their own health, and empty the family's coffers. With gossip they might besmirch their betters as well as their peers. Such upheaval would also "prevent that quiet Harmony which ought to subsist between Man and Wife," worried the apothecary Simon Mason. These were just some of the many ways in which critics worried that tea would destroy the British Empire. The desire for consumer goods stimulated a productive British economy (and although critics rarely noted it, women's work was a vital component of this productivity), but perhaps luxury was not worth the high price. A weakened nation, bankrupting its treasury on developing and protecting the tea trade, would be unable to face its enemies. Tea and its accoutrements also provided sparkling evidence of the inequalities that separated the lavish rich from the landless poor. The pleasure of a cup of tea, therefore, was just one side of a bargain that the industrializing British Empire made with itself.[40]

Tea-drinking endured, nonetheless, and eventually the habit became respectable all over the British Empire. From Bristol to Boston, tea had become "*a necessary of life.*" Though some worried that families were squandering their disposable income on frivolities like tea and saucers, many economists believed that such expenditures enlivened international trade and enhanced the national income. Though some questioned whether tea was healthy, others praised the way that its bitterness balanced the seductive sweetness of sugar. Though chauvinists criticized women who mixed their tea with gossip, many commentators praised the way in which women civilized men and brought the family together at afternoon tea. For women themselves, tea things could be empowering: they rewarded the woman's labor and offered her a chance to show off her shrewdness as a shopper and her sense of style. Tea things were gifts to bequeath to female relatives in one's will. Furthermore, tea was a healthy and moral alternative to gin and rum punch—which is one reason why John Wesley later changed his mind about tea. Britons and Americans came around to the idea that anyone could potentially elevate himself or herself (and, by extension, the whole country!) by partaking in tea. Yet the criticisms of tea continued to lurk beneath the surface: it might weaken the body and cripple society in the process. Thick with snobbery, suspicion, and misogyny, these criticisms could be revived at any moment, with enough provocation.[41]

All of these controversies had made their way, through printed writings and by word of mouth, to late colonial America. Some writers blamed the Bay Colony's economic woes on the purchase of foreign commodities like tea. To them, it looked as if wealthy merchants and government officials were indulging in luxuries at the people's expense. These fears were directly linked to a growing discomfort with the changes inherent in the new market economy—and many blamed Great Britain and its goods, specifically, as the sources of this corruption. Republican virtue required hard work and simple frugality, but also harmony and shared obligation. The Sons of Liberty—those who protested against the British government—began to demand that ordinary citizens consider the public good before their own private gain. Simple dress and simple tastes became badges of public virtue, and public virtue left no room for tea.[42]

One New Englander called the craving for *"needless Imported Commodities"* like tea an epidemic disease—a *"Boston distemper"*—which rural families were catching all too quickly. After 1763, many Americans, from John Dickinson to Benjamin Franklin, scolded their fellow colonists for bringing British taxation upon themselves: the colonists had indulged so much in finery and imported luxury that the British government had greedily pursued them as a fat source of tax revenue. Colonial writers defensively argued that the British were overestimating their true wealth, but they acknowledged that American consumers had perhaps spent their money too extravagantly. By buying so much tea and crockery, Americans had demonstrated that they did not quite resemble the stereotypical ideal of the hardy, self-sufficient pioneer; instead, they were shopping addicts just like the English.[43]

New Englanders quickly recognized women's special connection to tea. As early as the 1720s, preachers and social critics in Massachusetts began sniping about "the Ladies favourite Liquor" and the way tea seemed to invite gossip and idle talk. Tea became a Sunday ritual that followed church services, or a special occasion for newlyweds, or a regular afternoon pastime. These social gatherings invited women to dress up in the latest fashions: a tea table with a central pillar was perfect for showing off dress and posture. A visiting lawyer scoffed, "the ladies here visit, drink tea and indulge every little piece of gentility, to the height of the mode: and neglect the affairs of their families with as good a grace as the finest ladies in London." Another writer lamented that his wife and daughters, imitating fashions that had migrated from London to Boston to the Connecticut countryside, "spend more than half their Time in Cards, Visits, Dances, Talk and Tea." Men kept complaining, perhaps because tea was a way for women to find freedom and empowerment through companionship and new consumer choices. Again, like British critics, New England critics tended to ignore the time and effort women put into their work, which after all helped the family afford luxuries like tea.[44]

When the American colonies began to sink into a depression in 1764, many New Englanders must have wondered whether their consumer choices would remain available to them. It began to dawn on American colonists that they would never be as rich as the wealthiest Englishmen, and their obsession with keeping up with the British only made them sink lower in the eyes of many people in the mother country. "As we have grown more Luxurious every Year," wrote a man from Cambridge, Massachusetts, "so we run deeper and deeper in Debt to our Mother Country." He called for men and women alike to embrace "the Principles of Virtue and Oeconomy," and teach them to their children. As Americans protested the Stamp Act, merchants began suspending orders for manufactured goods— partly to reduce American debt, and partly in the hope that a slowdown in trade would motivate British subjects to come to Americans' aid. Although colonial consumers considered cooperation, no one had yet suggested giving up tea entirely—too many people would have found the idea unimaginable. Indeed, as the former New York merchant (and government informer) George Spencer wrote, tea "is used there by People of all Denominations, from the Gentleman even to the Slave; and is so much in Vogue, that the most menial Servant will not be Satisfied without It." In 1766, Spencer suggested a tax on tea, an idea that Parliament would take up a year later.[45]

When Charles Townshend's 1767 duty on tea sent to the American colonies came into effect, Americans responded with renewed insistence that Parliament could not tax them without their consent. This tax was hitting Americans where it hurt: in their love for tea's refreshment. In return, Americans aimed to hit the British where it hurt: in the pocket-books of British merchants and manufacturers who were getting rich from the colonial trade. If Americans stopped ordering imported goods, then these British tradesmen would complain. And if British tradesmen complained, then perhaps Parliament would listen. So once again, the Sons of Liberty began urging their allies among the merchants to stop ordering goods from Great Britain.

Here the fault lines appeared: the solution seemed to be giving up tea itself. On October 28, 1767, Bostonians gathered at Faneuil Hall and drew up a list of "Superfluities" that they hoped locals would refrain from importing—but tea was not on the list. And so the following week, the

Boston Gazette reported, "many of the Ladies of this Town have said, that in the List of Articles not to be purchased, TEA ought by no Means to have been omitted; and that they are resolved to omit the Use of it for the future." One writer cried out against "unwholsome Exotics" and criticized the "madness" and "invincible prejudice" that would lead to "a preference of rank poison if far fetched and dear bought." At the urging of Boston women, tea became another item that Bostonians were supposed to stop importing.[46]

Today we would call this movement a "boycott," though the term didn't exist until the 1890s, when Irish tenants refused to pay rent to Charles Cunningham Boycott. Americans instead called for "nonimportation" in the years after Townshend's Revenue Act of 1767. The program combined traditionalists' abstention from worldly pleasures with new ideas about American economic self-sufficiency. During the nonimportation movement, groups of New Englanders publicly declared their refusal to import British goods, circulated subscription lists of participating merchants, ostracized disobedient importers, and flaunted their self-abnegation by wearing homespun clothes and seeking alternatives to tea.[47]

By October 1768, the people of Massachusetts were convinced that the boycott was working. The students of Harvard College had resolved to drink no more tea. At least one merchant was forced to return a tea shipment. "Most of the Inhabitants of Charlestown, Dedham, Weymouth, Hingham, and many other Towns, with fifteen Hundred Families in the Town of Boston, have totally reliquished TEA."[48]

Since women were in charge of the tea ceremony and much of household spending, the boycotts needed their help. (This was particularly true in Boston, where women outnumbered men by at least 700.) Men had turned to women for help in political movements before. In response to a proposed excise tax on alcohol in 1754, the schoolteacher John Lovell had called upon "the Tea-Tables and other *Female Associations*" to give the bill "serious Consideration, and use their Influence, as the *Roman* Matrons did formerly, to save the State." The Boston minister Jonathan Mayhew similarly praised American women for their help in calling for the repeal of the Stamp Act: "such was the danger, and . . . so great and glorious the cause, that the spirit of the Roman matrons in the time of the commonwealth, seemed to be now equalled by the fairer daughters of America."[49]

While some women chose to abstain from tea and some did not, the point was that these women were able to make a choice that had an impact on imperial politics. And in choosing, they developed a political consciousness of their own. Many women directed their efforts to the boycotts in the hopes that Parliament would repeal the duty on tea.[50] "We must," wrote one of the Sons of Liberty, "depend greatly upon the Female Sex for the Introduction of Oeconomy among us."[51] The friends of government, meanwhile, were evidently worried about women's participation in the boycotts. They attacked the very idea of women making political decisions, and they argued that women were unfit to question the decisions of their male rulers. A satirist named "Squibo" wrote that a group of boycotting women "drink nothing at their meetings but *New-England Rum*" as a substitute for tea.[52]

Women resolutely defended themselves against these attacks. Under the bylines "Aspatia, Belinda, Corinna," they asked Squibo to stop throwing "his unmanly Squibs on the Ladies of Boston." After beating back attacks from a couple of other writers, they concluded that the respectable women of Boston were "willing to sacrifice every lesser Inclination at the Shrine of Public Vertue." They didn't care if this meant that they would be "ridicul'd by the little Wits and Foplings of the present Day." They were unwilling, however, to be thought "Inferior in Veracity, Honesty, Sincerity, Industry, Love of Virtue, of Liberty, and of our Country." Other women turned the drunkenness criticism back on men: "you charge us with drinking at the Tea-Table," retorted one female writer, "and cannot we charge you with drinking more unaturally at the Tavern?" Besides, she added, "When we are at the Tea-Table, you were as merry in the Chat as any of us." This sort of banter had become familiar over the years—in England and America, when men criticized women for tea-drinking, women would retort by attacking men for their alcohol consumption.[53]

Even as female writers gave as good as they got, women's participation in the boycotts became more and more crucial. In 1768, "one of the Daughters of Liberty" entered a Boston shop, selected a few items, and then asked the proprietor whether he sold tea. When the shopkeeper said yes, she walked out of the store and left her merchandise behind.[54] In 1769 a Pennsylvania poetess wrote, "That rather than Freedom we part with our *Tea*."[55] Early in 1770, hundreds of Massachusetts women joined a subscription drive where they agreed to refuse all tea both at home (except in cases of sickness) and on social occasions, until Parliament repealed the Townshend Acts.[56]

Not everyone abstained from tea during these calls for boycotts. Boycotting tea sounds easy in principle, but the ensuing self-denial forced American men and women to rely on much less tempting substitutes. Just before printing the suggestion to boycott Chinese tea, the *Boston Gazette* encouraged New Englanders to drink Labrador (or Hyperion) tea, made from a plant that grew naturally in the Northeast. Two months later, "G. J." reported on some promising (but ultimately unsuccessful) schemes to grow tea in America. In 1769, a ship's captain arrived from North Carolina with yaupon tea (also known as cassina or black drink), which some Native Americans used to induce vomiting. These alternative "teas" must have been a hard sell (one opponent of the boycotts wrote that Labrador tea caused "Disorders in Health," including vertigo). Tea—real Chinese tea—had become an ingrained American habit, one that was difficult to give up.[57]

Some men, already condescending toward women, were becoming concerned that women were undermining the boycott. "A Young American" warned that "Scandal and Detraction" reflected poorly on women. He encouraged them to be more "worthy of your charming selves."[58] And the insults got worse. In a 1768 satire, one man called his own daughters "two hearty trollups as any in town," for drinking tea in the morning and afternoon.[59]

Perhaps the boycotts weren't working as well as the Sons of Liberty had hoped? By January 1770, a writer from Worcester, Massachusetts, saw that Parliament was no closer to repealing the Townshend duties and he knew whom to blame: "the people of this country will not deny themselves a dish of Tea for the sake of their Liberty!" The writer was even more specific: "Consider what you are doing ye fair daughters of the land, and be wise for yourselves and your posterity."[60] The writer "Philagrius" warned local women that if they did not abstain from tea, they would be displaced "by the upstart kept mistress of some commissioner, inspector, informer, tide-waiter, or exciseman." If any of them were to be assaulted in the street, "Philagrius" argued, wouldn't a manly citizenry be better able to protect them than a "band of slaves"? Men assumed that women's weakness for fashionable consumption and idle teatime gossip would unravel the boycott. Such weakness would reinforce Americans' dependence rather than stiffen their resolve.[61]

Supporters of government, meanwhile, continued to attack Boston women. Peter Oliver, an associate justice of the Massachusetts Superior Court and a member of the Governor's Council, was particularly caustic. He wrote that women "were cautious enough to lay in large Stocks [of tea] before they promised [not to drink it]; & they could be sick just as suited their Convenience or Inclination." He commented on "the Ladies' new invented chymical Process, of transmuting Chocolate & Coffee into Tea"; in other words, women continued to drink tea, but pretended they were drinking something else.[62]

Abigail Dwight, the forty-eight-year-old former headmistress of a boarding school for Mohawk girls in Stockbridge, Massachusetts, witnessed the social pressure of the boycott first hand, and found it real enough. While visiting Boston in June 1769, she wrote to tell her daughter that she was feeling ill from "drinking strong Coffea in the Afternoon" at the home of Dr. Belcher Noyes—"a High liberty House." Then again, she wrote, *all* houses in Boston were "high liberty" houses: except for British government officials in Boston, she wrote, "not a Drop of Tea will one soul of them drink." All of a sudden, this new political influence on Abigail Dwight's social life was making her ill. She couldn't give up tea completely, she wrote: "at home I may drink it." Women felt compelled to furtively sip their favorite drink in private.[63]

The passage of the Tea Act in 1773 instantly infused the idea of boycotting tea with new life. Once again the Sons of Liberty called on men and women to stop drinking tea, so as to push British commercial interests into action. If Parliament would not listen to American colonists and their refusal to be unfairly taxed, then perhaps they would listen to the East India Company when their tea failed to sell in America.

Bostonians took offense when it became clear that the British were not yet willing to treat Americans with respect, despite their embrace of a genteel drink like tea. As a result, they invented a new form of respectability: a willingness to push tea aside. Tea boycotts were a way for rich and poor alike to combat the sin of worldly overindulgence. Some men hoped that tea boycotts would make women restrain themselves; some women found that tea boycotts gave them a chance to assert their own patriotism. The boycotts became a way for American men and women to organize themselves to fight for liberty. To decline tea was to voice one's protest against an unjust law, and thereby stand beside like-minded men and women in other American towns. Tea and tea boycotts had given Americans a sense of self-respect, and any threats to their self-respect might be met with violence.[64]

CHAPTER 4

"Enemies to Their Country"

A Merchant, trading to America, hath offered a bet of ten guineas to five, that not a pound of the tea, now sending out by the India Company to Boston, New York, and Pennsylvania, will ever reach those markets, that some accident will happen to it.

Anonymous Newspaper Item, 1773[1]

The storm, a real storm, hit Boston in advance of the news. Coasting ships had to clear the decks, and after the storm had blown away, people spotted shingles and clapboards floating in Massachusetts Bay. On October 18, 1773, the *Boston Gazette* printed "the current Talk of the Town that Richard Clarke, Benjamin Faneuil, Esqrs; and the two young Mess-rs Hutchinsons, are appointed to receive the Teas." The newspaper warned readers that "This new Scheme of Administration" threatened Boston's commerce and was "well calculated to establish & encrease the detested Tribute," meaning a tax to support the province's civil officials. The paper encouraged readers "to meddle with this pernicious Drug" by either returning the tea to England or by destroying it.[2]

When the Boston Sons of Liberty began battling the British government over customs duties in the 1760s, the "friends of government" sided with the royal governor—Francis Bernard in the 1760s, and his successor, Thomas Hutchinson, in the 1770s. The friends of government wanted to maintain good relations with the mother country, which they saw as the protector of Massachusetts and the fount of its commercial livelihood. Hutchinson and his supporters believed that the British government was the source of their liberty, not a threat to it. They found the Sons of Liberty and their methods obnoxious—even dangerously anarchic. They worried that reckless popular leaders like James Otis and Samuel Adams were going to throw the baby out with the bathwater: you couldn't just topple the British government without tearing down the traditions, culture, and social structure that kept colonial life going. Many of these friends of government were colonial officials like Hutchinson, parishioners of the Church of England like Bernard, or Scottish immigrants like the printer John Mein—but many others were locally born Congregationalists who held no imperial office.[3]

Richard Clarke was one of these. He was born in 1711, the son of a successful Boston merchant who died when Richard was ten years old. Although Richard's mother was still alive during his childhood, he lived with two prestigious guardians: his great-aunt (the widow of a Connecticut governor), followed by his stepfather, the secretary of the province. Richard graduated Harvard College in 1729, married soon afterward, and started a career in overseas trade. As he built a growing business, he never showed much interest in politics, apart from holding some minor town offices and even serving alongside William Molineux (who later became his adversary) to protest high provincial taxes on the town of Boston. Richard Clarke had twelve children: his two eldest sons died too young, one at 28 years old, the other at 32. At least four of his daughters married well: his eldest married the merchant and militia colonel Henry Bromfield, and another married John Singleton Copley, the talented painter (fig. 14). Richard Clarke appears to have placed most of his hopes for the future in two of his surviving sons: Jonathan Clarke, who turned 29 in 1773, and Isaac Winslow Clarke, who turned 27, became particularly active in the family's import/export business.[4]

The firm of Richard Clarke & Sons became one of the largest tea importers in Boston. Tea business was good business, they boasted, since "Bohea [common black] Teas are in . . . almost universal use, amongst us." When it first seemed, in 1767, that Parliament was moving to lower the taxes on tea, the Clarkes looked forward to "a proffit ariseing on this Article imported here." They eagerly anticipated working with English merchants who were "conversant in this Article of commerce & know how to get at it on the best Terms."[5]

But when Richard Clarke first read the text of Townshend's Revenue Act in late 1767, he was surprised: he thought it was strange to make American tea drinkers pay a new threepenny-per-pound tax. Under the new law, he wrote to his British wholesaler, the retail price of imported Company tea was sure to rise—and that helped no one, except for smugglers seeking to undercut EIC prices. These illicit traders now sprang into action, striking deals with tea dealers in Northern Europe or the Dutch West Indies so as to avoid the new taxes.[6]

Thomas Hutchinson, who had himself invested in the tea trade, confirmed that New England smugglers were doing a brisk business under

14 John Singleton Copley painted himself at the top of his family portrait, with his father-in-law, Richard Clarke, below. Clarke, one of the appointed tea consignees for Boston, was by this time an exile in London.

the Townshend Act: "As much has been imported this Fall as I have known at any time." Yet customs officials hadn't successfully seized a single chest. Hutchinson complained about the "iniquity" of it all: "The Smugglers not only buy cheaper in Holland but save the 3d duty." They were effectively nullifying Parliament's attempts to ·impose new revenue measures. Privately, even Hutchinson argued that Parliament should repeal the Townshend Act and replace it with a more subtle tax, payable in England. In his own conciliatory way, Hutchinson hoped that Parliament would stop levying inflammatory taxes upon the colonies.[7]

The radicals were not so placatory. The American Sons of Liberty made political hay from the Townshend Act, and attempted to rally protests throughout the colonies. They argued that Parliament had no right to tax a high-demand good like tea (or any other commodity) just to raise revenue from the colonists. Boston merchants began passing around a nonimportation subscription—proscribing the importation of all goods, including tea—in March 1768. Over the following year, they tried to convince their counterparts in New York and Philadelphia to join them in cutting off imports from Great Britain and obtain their tea elsewhere.

Illicit trading was not equally prevalent in every colony. Customers in the southern colonies preferred the quality of British tea, and so their traders ran fewer illegal shipments. But in the northern colonies after 1768, most merchants imported their tea from the Continent instead of the East India Company. One observer estimated that this illegal trade was worth about £160,000 a year.[8] As a result, American imports of legal tea during the boycott dropped by a third. During 1769 and 1770, legal tea imports to New England fell from a pre-boycott peak of almost 300,000 pounds to around 86,000 pounds a year. New Yorkers and Philadelphians had even better smuggling connections, and so they were better able to satisfy their craving with illegal tea. New York and Pennsylvania merchants imported 500,000 pounds of legal tea in 1768, before the boycott dramatically slashed imports to a total of 269 pounds for New York in 1770, and zero legal tea for Pennsylvania. Tea-drinking continued throughout the Thirteen Colonies—American addicts couldn't bear to drop the habit entirely—but only in New England and the South did tea drinkers continue to rely on substantial imports of Company tea.[9]

The Boston Sons of Liberty, having encouraged rival merchants in New York City and Philadelphia to join the nonimportation agreement, now had to enforce compliance to keep the alliance alive—colonial unity in the face of Parliament's new laws depended on trust and concerted political action. The merchants of the middle colonies watched, enraged, as the committed friends of government among the Boston merchants continued to place orders for a variety of items, including tea. Thirteen of the 143 import businesses in Boston initially refused to sign the nonimportation agreements, including the governor's sons, Thomas and Elisha Hutchinson, Richard Clarke & Sons, and the Scottish printer John Mein.

The reason Clarke abstained, as he explained privately, was because "we fear it wont have the Effect that is proposed & think it may be attended with many Inconveniences." The Clarkes might not have liked the British taxes, but they had good reasons to distrust the Sons of Liberty. For one thing, many of the so-called "patriot" merchants were smugglers who were detrimentally affecting the Clarkes' business. They could also see that the enforced scarcity of British imports would raise prices, and play right into the hands of merchants with existing inventories of British goods. They believed that dissident merchants like John Hancock and William Molineux—bullies and opportunists—would profit handsomely. The Sons of Liberty were bound to use ugly, heavy-handed tactics to coerce people into signing the nonimportation agreements. The Clarkes wanted no part of it, but "notwithstanding our own Opinion," they admitted, "it may be inconvenient to act against the general Sentiment." They saw how Governor Hutchinson's sons, Elisha and Thomas Jr., had become the "Butt" of local resentment, and they knew that such political animosity might be bad for business. They were torn.[10]

Despite their observations about the town's "general Sentiment," the Clarkes had trouble believing that there was widespread support for the agreements; they thought (perhaps wishfully) the so-called Sons of Liberty were a weak faction that would melt away if the friends of government showed proper firmness. The Clarkes were eager to see the British troops arrive in town in 1768, when "we shall be able to judge, whether this Scheme has been generally engaged in from ye principle of fear; or patriotism, & consequently how far it will be abided by."[11]

John Mein, the type of man who mixed ink by the barrel, decided to put these principles to the test. His rivalry with the *Boston Gazette*, which was published by Benjamin Edes and John Gill, erupted in violence—Mein was prosecuted for assault after beating Gill with a cane in January 1768—and Mein's attitude toward the Sons of Liberty hardened. Mein received a tidy government contract as stationer for the American Board of Customs Commissioners, which drove him even further away from Boston's dissident faction. Then he lashed out vigorously at the professed boycotters. In August 1769, he printed the cargo manifests of all the vessels that had imported goods into Boston over the previous months. Mein wanted to show just how little the Bostonians were honoring the nonimportation agreements: the offenders included nonsubscribers like Richard Clarke & Sons and out-of-towners like the Nantucket whalers Joseph Rotch & Son, but also staunch protesters such as James Pitts and even John Hancock.[12]

Mein intended that these revelations should embarrass the Boston Sons of Liberty, especially among their allies in other colonies. The Boston committees charged with monitoring the nonimportation agreements were usually inclined to let small packages or necessities (like medicine) slip through their net of enforcement. But Mein took the Sons of Liberty literally: no imports meant no imports. The Sons of Liberty, caught in the act of allowing violations of the intercolonial agreements, tried to defend themselves. They claimed that the imported goods were actually bound for neighboring colonies, or that the London exporters had ignored instructions from their American correspondents. The radical Dr. Thomas Young argued that

Mein's propaganda had exaggerated the extent of the importations, and he lamented that the Boston Sons of Liberty had not yet had a chance to mount a proper defense. Gleefully Mein continued his attacks: he depicted Hancock as wearing a "fool's cap," and gave other popular leaders names like "William the Knave" (William Molineux) or "Counsellor Muddlehead" (James Otis). In any case, events had proven the Clarkes' suspicions correct: "patriotism" appeared to be in short supply, and fewer people were boycotting tea. In April 1769, they wrote, "we are informed that the consumption increases."[13]

In a climate of wary suspicion among the colonial merchants in different seaports, Boston's dissident leaders did their best to encourage people to sign the agreements and ostracize those who refused. In the spring and summer of 1769, handbills and newspapers named the Hutchinson brothers, their cousin Nathaniel Rogers, Richard Clarke & Sons, and John Mein as importers who "must be considered as Enemies to the Constitution of their Country."[14] Eventually the pressure forced the Clarkes to give up: "the opposition against the importation of goods from Great Britain," they wrote, "is so firmly fixed & extensively prevalent, that altho' we were determined to maintain the struggle as long as prudence would admit, we were obliged at length to give way to the torrent" or lose all their customers.[15]

Thomas and Elisha Hutchinson tried to hold out even longer. When a nonimportation committee visited them, they stood firm, but their friends became anxious that the Boston crowd would mark the brothers out for violence. The Hutchinsons were persuaded to submit on October 2, 1769: "besides the danger to their persons they had good reason to fear there was a design to destroy the Tea." Governor Hutchinson blamed smugglers in particular for the clamor against legal importers like his sons. The legal sales "enraged the Smuglers who expected a great harvest from the agreement not to import goods from England." The brothers stored the offending goods in a warehouse, and gave the key to the committee for safekeeping, to make sure the goods remained unsold. Eventually, bad publicity and threats drove the young Hutchinsons to sign the nonimportation agreement. Governor Hutchinson later lamented that Boston's Sons of Liberty "have persecuted my Sons with peculiar pleasure."[16]

Outside of Boston, American protesters were watching these struggles. In Philadelphia and New York City, the Sons of Liberty (some of them tea smugglers) fought like cornered animals to help the nonimportation agreements succeed against powerful groups of conservative politicians and merchants. Boston's casual lapses were infuriating. A writer with the pen name "Philadelphus" grumbled that Boston had made "large Importations, both contrary to the Spirit and Letter of their Agreement." By doing so, they had "lessened the Weight of the Non-importation Scheme, and were instrumental in preventing the Repeal" of the tea duty in 1770. In addition, once Boston had imported goods, there was little to prevent those goods from reaching other parts of America, which depressed prices and profits. Technically, the merchants of New York City were the first of the three largest ports to break the agreement in July 1770 and begin placing orders for imported goods (except tea, which they smuggled from Holland anyway). Technically, Philadelphia merchants had been the slowest to sign on to the agreements in the first place. Regardless, in both cities, leading Sons of Liberty blamed Boston for its breaches of faith. The humiliated Bostonians sullenly ended their own nonimportation agreement in October 1770, and everyone went back to business, many with great relief; the restrictions had cost Boston's merchant community a lot of money.[17] "The Article of Tea is so generally & openly sold in this Town," one Boston merchant reported to his brother, "that was it in my way as it is in some other People, I should sell it my self. I see no advantage in your being the only person that Excludes themselves from the sale of it."[18]

Radical patriots still disdained the drinking of dutied tea, but most people went on buying tea and didn't worry much about whether it came from London or from smugglers. The years 1767 to 1773 were banner years for tea smugglers, who were newly aware that they were engaging not only in illicit activity but in a political act. They secreted their tea in wine casks or under containers of coal, and unloaded their cargo at night onto small boats or shallops before arriving at port. They bribed His Majesty's customs men, or posted lookouts to warn the longshoremen that a customs officer was approaching. Once the ships arrived in port, smugglers made sure the crews scattered, so that no one could testify against them in court—and the merchants themselves were careful never to get too close to the goods. When it came time for a ship's captain to declare goods at the customhouse, he had no qualms about swearing a false oath. The town watch looked the other way, local magistrates hesitated to prosecute smugglers, and local juries would never find in favor of a customs officer. By enforcing customs regulations and levying new taxes, Parliament had turned the smugglers' profitable avoidance into political defiance.[19]

Up and down the American coast, this defiance was liable to turn violent. On November 23, 1771, in the Delaware River, Thomas Mushett's customs schooner stopped a pilot boat that was headed upriver from Chester to Philadelphia. He found the boat loaded with fifteen chests and twenty quarter-chests of tea, as well as some wine. The customs officers aboard the schooner seized the pilot boat and began escorting their prize up to Red Bank, until the wind died down and they were forced to drop anchor.

At ten o'clock that night, another pilot boat and three other small ships came alongside the schooner and the seized prize boat. The customs officers were nervous, but they saw only two men on the pilot boat.

Suddenly, more than thirty armed men burst from the pilot boat's cabin and hold, "rushed out & boarded the prize." Their faces were covered in black, and witnesses later guessed that they were "some of the principle Merch" in this City in disguise," because although they had on sailors' jackets, their white stockings flashed in the moonlight. These men brandished clubs, cutlasses, and guns, and swung at the customs officers "with such violence that they . . . laid most of them flat upon the Deck." The armed men forced the officers below deck and fastened the hatches. Captain Mushett almost died alone in his ship's hold. Luckily for him, one of his men heard his groans and begged the boarders to send down a bucket of water. While Mushett suffered, the boarders cut the schooner's rigging, sails, and cables. They took the anchor, carried away the schooner's small boat, and then left the schooner stranded in the mud. Mushett and his wounded men didn't make it back to Philadelphia until 3 a.m., having endured a five-hour ordeal, and by then the pilot boat, the rescued prize, and its tea were long gone.[20]

In August 1771, Hutchinson guessed that around 83 percent of the tea Bostonians drank was smuggled, and estimated that the percentage in New York and Philadelphia was even higher, at 90 percent. Still, legal tea was finding a market, at least in the Boston area. Although a merchant named Jolley Allen reported being harassed by a committee for buying EIC tea from the Hutchinsons, for the most part legal tea transactions continued without incident. Even advocates of colonial rights partook. In February 1771, John Adams had tea at John Hancock's house with Dr. Warren, Dr. Church, and other prominent Sons of Liberty present: "Drank Green Tea," he wrote in his diary, "from Holland I hope, but dont know." Only a year before, selling tea could cost a merchant his reputation, but now even anti-government leaders only hesitated for a second before drinking it.[21]

From the perspective of Samuel Adams, Thomas Young, and the other active leaders of the Sons of Liberty, these legal imports threatened Boston's credibility. They knew that the radicals from New York City and Philadelphia were looking on in disgust as Bostonians sheepishly swallowed Company tea. William Palfrey, an associate of John Hancock, gave his perspective on the trade during a visit to London in early 1771. "The N Yorkers and Philadelphians adhere very strictly to their resolution of not importing any of that baneful and pernicious article. Not an ounce has been suffer'd to go on board any of their Vessels, while those in the Boston trade take large quantities." He continued, "I am sorry for the honor of my dear native Country that any opportunity should be given our enemies to triumph over us. Tea is an article we can most assuredly do without, and if we were honestly firm in a determination not to import it the Act must infallibly be repeald."[22]

The East India Company was making its own plans. After a successful lobbying effort by its Directors, the Tea Act became law in the summer of 1773. Parliament had granted the Company a tax rebate on tea shipped to America, as well as the right to select their own agents to sell it there directly. Prospective traders came flocking, and competed for the contract to sell the tea on the EIC's behalf. The winners had impressive insider connections. From New York, Frederick Pigou was a former employee of the East India Company—he had traveled to Canton and made careful recommendations about the Company's diplomatic and trade relations with China. Pigou's firm got one share of the New York consignment. The other New York consignees were the treasurer of the province and a member of the Governor's Council. The Pigous in turn recommended the Quaker merchants Abel James and Henry Drinker of Philadelphia, who put off retirement for the chance of a low-risk 6 percent commission. Three of the other Philadelphia firms had representatives in London who had been offering the East India Company advice on tea-selling schemes. The Charleston contract went to two firms with a long record of connections to England. These traders now enjoyed preferred treatment from a monopoly company.[23]

From Boston, Richard Clarke's son Jonathan won the EIC's tea contract for his family firm. Brook Watson, a London merchant who lost his leg to a shark in Havana harbor in 1749 (later depicted in a famous painting by John Singleton Copley), recommended another of the tea consignments for Jonathan's cousin, thirty-seven-year-old Joshua Winslow, and his partner Benjamin Faneuil Jr., who was about 44. The final tea contract went to the Clarkes' family friends and relatives by marriage: the brothers Thomas Hutchinson Jr., 33, and Elisha Hutchinson, 27, who also had a London connection. Richard Clarke, now 62, was the only Boston tea consignee who belonged to the older generation. His son Jonathan was pleased to receive the commission, but he made sure to ask that his firm "be free from the risk of fire or any other accident that may occur before the delivery of the tea."[24]

These consignees hoped to honor their contracts with the Company and sell the tea. They would earn a healthy commission, and perhaps open up a solid connection for future dealings with the Company. They found that most of their neighbors had other ideas.

On October 18, the *Boston Gazette* reported that the tea was on its way, and urged readers to copy "the resolutions of Philadelphia and New-York to destroy it." Though no such resolutions had been reached—yet—the reference to resistance in Philadelphia and New York was significant. For all that Boston's protest against tea echoed through history, it was actually the two cities further south that first sounded the alarm about the Tea Act. The earliest letters from London about the East India Company's plan arrived in Philadelphia and New York. Boston heard second hand that a few American ship captains had refused to transport the tea; these mariners had guessed— correctly—that the controversial cargo wasn't going to be worth the trouble. It was the *Pennsylvania Journal,* a Philadelphia newspaper, which first boasted that Americans "are not ready to have the yoke of slavery riveted about their necks" and would "send back the tea from whence it came."[25]

New Yorkers and Philadelphians gave two principal reasons for their opposition. First, the Tea Act reaffirmed the tax that Townshend had imposed in 1767: for every pound of tea that entered an American port, the merchants would still have to pay threepence. Thomas Mifflin of Philadelphia had been to Boston that summer and sat for the portraitist John Singleton Copley (Richard Clarke's son-in-law); in October, he addressed a letter to the tea agents (which was reprinted in Boston newspapers) arguing that the tea law was "designed to raise a revenue, and to establish *parliamentary despotism,* in America." A retired trader, "RECLUSUS," echoed this concern, writing that the revenue from the tea tax would line the pockets of the "harpy Commissioners" of the customs, "a Curse to Society."[26]

Second, the Tea Act gave the East India Company an unfair competitive advantage in selling tea in America. Throughout the month of October, a New York author "HAMPDEN" (possibly the ex-privateer Alexander McDougall) published a series of essays called *The Alarm.* He allowed that, in theory, a merchant or company might be granted exclusive trading rights as a reward for the risk and uncertainty involved in a new invention or in initiating "Commerce with a Nation unknown." But the East India Company had obtained "a Monopoly beyond this" which was "manifestly injurious to the Community." Through bribes, the Company had stretched its monopoly for decades, well beyond what was fair to other traders.[27]

Now, "HAMPDEN" wrote, the American colonies would be forced to overpay for Asian goods. Although the Tea Act actually lowered the price of tea, this was merely a seductive trick designed to get Americans to accept an offensive law. The East India Company, which could set any price it wanted with its new privileges, would begin its fleecing of America in due course. These writers from the middle colonies had good reasons to emphasize the EIC's threat to economic competition. The tea trade there was dominated by smugglers who, along with many law-abiding merchants, objected to any law that showed such favoritism to the agents of a monopoly company. Even with the duty paid on EIC tea, its new low price would threaten all American tea traders with stiff, probably insurmountable, competition.[28]

"We heard of an opposition forming in New York and Philadelphia," wrote the Reverend Dr. Samuel Cooper of Boston's Brattle Street Church. "Our patriots determined to second their brethren in the other Colonies."[29] Most Bostonians also resented parliamentary taxation. When they weren't furtively sipping tea, they objected to dutied tea on principle. Bostonians also feared the East India Company monopoly—they worried not just that their merchants would be cut out of the tea trade, but that the Tea Act would set a precedent for further government-supported monopolies. Beyond these principal reasons, they had further grounds for resisting the arrival of the tea. In Massachusetts, the revenue from the tea tax paid not just customs commissioners, but it also stuffed the pockets of Governor Hutchinson and other local officials. Even before Boston had learned about the Tea Act, the Boston Committee of Correspondence was warning everyone about "our Enemies," and their "fixd Design to make our Executive dependent . . . & subservient to their own purposes."[30] The fact that Hutchinson's sons were the carriers of the tea made the whole situation all the more insidious. "HAMPDEN" had articulated the problem: "the 'Civil Government' to be maintained by the produce of that act, is a Government totally independent of the people, and dependent on the Crown . . . which must inevitably effect [Americans'] slavery, and all the terrible consequences of it."[31]

As a result, Bostonians' anger at the tea importers seems to have been more personal, or even tribal. Their hatred of Governor Hutchinson was transferable to his sons, to his extended family, and to their close friends and business associates. Another writer, "PRÆDICUS," accused Governor Hutchinson of "establishing an American revenue for the support of . . . [his] *children* incapable of any considerable employment in church or state." As Hutchinson had observed in the past, whenever his sons' business dealings were at issue, "Everything done by me" was "construed to proceed from private and sinister views."[32] Unlike in New York or Philadelphia, the

Boston consignees more or less belonged to a single social circle, a small group of prominent families connected through ties of business and political allegiance. Leading Sons of Liberty like Joseph Warren and Samuel Adams—who were also Harvard men from old Massachusetts families— sought to stigmatize Hutchinson and his circle. They worried that the British government and the East India Company were injecting themselves into local politics, creating unfair advantages for a hand-picked group: political appointments, plum contracts, and the higher status that went along with exclusive power and wealth. Besides, there were political advantages to focusing people's energies on the tea agents. Charles Thomson, a Philadelphia radical, rather cynically suggested that Adams and Hancock should "raise a storm of indignation" against the consignees themselves rather than the Tea Act, thus allowing them to keep "the spirit of Liberty" alive without widening the breach with Great Britain.[33]

Ironically, the constant pressure and tormenting of Hutchinson had already succeeded. In the summer of 1773, the beaten governor had asked for a leave of absence so he could travel to England. Lord Dartmouth, the Secretary of State for American Affairs, granted this request in the middle of August, but the ship bearing his letter was slow to reach Massachusetts: Hutchinson did not receive it until the evening of November 14, after the news of the Tea Act had already arrived. By then it was too late in the season for him to arrange a passage to England. Hutchinson—a magnet for the dissidents' resentment—decided to stay in Massachusetts and take "proper measures" to ensure the orderly landing of the tea. "As there had been no exception [i.e., objection] to the duty for sevral years past," Governor Hutchinson wrote in December 1773, he was convinced "that there would be none now."[34]

The Boston Sons of Liberty were also feeling significant pressure from their counterparts in New York and Philadelphia to stand fast and prevent the tea from landing. A writer in New York reminded his audience, "that the Non-Importation Agreement, respecting Tea . . . still exists; and the honour of the parties to it, is bound to maintain it inviolable." But the Bostonians had not given a good account of themselves thus far. They had never completely abstained from importing tea, and continued to purchase legal (as well as illegal) tea even as the middle colonies sustained themselves exclusively on smuggled stuff. If importers of tea were enemies to commerce and liberty, then what did that make the people of Boston? A Philadelphia correspondent warned Bostonians that if they continued to accept dutied tea, it would "confirm many prejudices against them, and injure the common cause essentially, in future." Bostonians were, at the same time, reassuring Philadelphians,

"You may depend no Tea, if it should arrive, will be landed here. The spirit of opposition to that measure is daily gaining strength." Boston's smugglers, it was rumored, particularly encouraged resistance to the Tea Act.[35]

The Boston Town Meeting and a writer for the *Boston Gazette* were forced to acknowledge the truth: while the middle colonies had "punctually observed" the nonimportation agreements and bought tea only from Holland, Boston's record was not nearly so unblemished. Bostonians tried to make excuses: Boston's commerce had "peculiar circumstances," such as friends of government ("*pirates*") who were willing to import legal tea. Besides, Boston was only importing a "small" amount of tea, or at least less than before 1768. Regretfully, Bostonians also had to admit that "such small Importations" had encouraged the British government to pass the Tea Act and encourage the East India Company to send its tea to America. This was, in fact, true. As a result of Boston's continued imports, the British ministry hoped that the East India Company's 1773 tea shipment would be a wedge for a new scheme. "Should the English Tea be cheaper than the Dutch," wrote the New York consignee Frederick Pigou Jr. to two of the Philadelphia consignees, "Philad[elphi]a New York & other ports on the Continent will smuggle it from Boston instead of Amsterdam." Observers in England as well as America knew that if the tea could be landed at one American port, it would flood the entire American market at a cheaper price than smuggled tea.[36]

A year after the Boston Tea Party, when John Adams was spending an evening with members of the Continental Congress and other radicals at Philadelphia, they asked him pointedly "about the Conduct of the Bostonian Merchants since the Year 1770, in importing Tea and paying the Duty." They criticized John Hancock, Adams's fellow congressional delegate, in particular. Adams defended himself lamely, saying the merchants were "not wholly justifiable," but that "Their fault and guilt has been magnified." He blamed Hancock's English merchant partner for the tea shipments, not Hancock himself, but he wasn't sure what to think. Still, the point was clear—even after the Tea Party, Philadelphians still resented the Boston merchants for their legally imported tea. The friends of government scoffed at the Bostonians' hypocrisy: as one wrote, "Boston the loudest in the Cry for supporting the Asociation, did actually import great Quantities of English Tea & slyly with great profit supplyed their Neighbours, as appeared by the Custom House Books."[37]

The people of Boston, with the exception of the increasingly isolated friends of government, seemed ready to meet the tea crisis with new resolve.

If they were going to stand with the other colonies against unjust British laws—and prevent the lapses they had permitted over the years—they would have to get organized. The writer "RECLUSUS" called on not just merchants, but also artisans "and even the Labourers" to "resolutely oppose this Plan and quash it in Embrio." Two groups were particularly well suited to organize the townspeople behind the resistance to the Tea Act. The first was the North End Caucus, a group of sixty political operators, including Samuel Adams, Joseph Warren, and William Molineux, who met at the Salutation or Green Dragon taverns to coordinate and influence elections for town and provincial office. Now they met, as an early historian wrote, "to awake the *north wind*, and stir the *waters* of the *troubled sea*." The other organization was Samuel Adams's Boston Committee of Correspondence (BCC), which was in charge of coordinating resistance with other towns in Massachusetts and with the other American colonies. On October 23, the North End Caucus met and voted to oppose the sale of any imported East India Company tea "with our lives and fortunes." They appointed three of their members, Paul Revere and the merchants Abiel Ruddock and John Lowell, as a subcommittee "to correspond with any Committee chosen in any part of the town" that might be involved in protesting the Tea Act.[38]

These were shrewd choices. John Lowell, a thirty-four-year-old merchant on Hancock's Wharf, was the son-in-law of John Scollay, one of the town's selectmen or elected leaders. Lowell's sister was married to John Hancock's brother, and Lowell had been a member in 1770 of a town committee monitoring tea importers.[39] Revere, aged thirty-seven, was an important Freemason at St. Andrew's Lodge (where Lowell was also a member), and an engraver of propaganda for the Sons of Liberty. His connections, to fellow artisans as well as prestigious politicians, linked him to most of the Sons of Liberty in Boston.[40] Abiel Ruddock, a thirty-one-year-old storekeeper and the son of a late town selectman, was also known as "formerly head of the mob on the 5th of November."[41] In other words (according to this unfriendly source), he had been a leader of the crowds in the annual Pope's Day parades. This subcommittee of Lowell, Revere, and Ruddock would be able to coordinate the resistance with other townspeople, whether they were wealthy, middle class, or poor.

Paranoia was permeating the town. The Caucus, the BCC, the newspapers, the Boston Town Meeting, and the crowds formed a flexible, overlapping coalition to protest the Tea Act. These groups, sometimes generically called the Sons of Liberty, were newly energized with resentment against Parliament, the East India Company, and the designated consignees. Their first tactic was to concentrate pressure on the consignees, who were closest to hand. If the Company's hand-picked agents resigned their commissions, there would be no one to receive the cargo. If the colonists could show Parliament that the Americans would not stand for a duty on tea—even if it was tacked onto lower prices—then maybe Parliament would reconsider its decision to try and raise revenue from the colonies.[42]

The consignees, however, had no desire to turn down the lucrative Company contract. Richard Clarke took to the newspapers, as "Z.," to argue that the Tea Act wasn't such a bad thing. By eliminating the middleman, the new law would make tea cheaper. He was confused about why the Tea Act suddenly caused Bostonians to yelp about the Townshend duty, since the people of Massachusetts had been importing plenty of dutied tea over the last few years. For that matter, Americans silently paid much more to Parliament in duties on wine, sugar, and molasses—why complain about tea? (The answer, as Clarke probably well knew, was that the long-standing duties on wine, sugar, and molasses were designed to regulate the trading of foreign goods, whereas the tea duty was designed to raise revenue.) Finally, Clarke argued, the East India Company could prove to be an ally in the fight for charter rights, and might help Americans get the tea duty removed—so long as the colonists didn't try to ruin the Company's sales with "unsuitable Behaviour."[43]

But these arguments failed to sway public opinion in Boston, where the people were forming ranks alongside the Sons of Liberty.

Instead, the consignees began to hear warnings about what would happen to them if they defied their neighbors. On November 1, the *Boston Gazette* reprinted a letter from "PHILELEUTHEROS" (Greek for "freedom-lover"). "Secure yourselves," this New York writer warned, "from the gathering storm, before it . . . overwhelms you with a sudden, dreadful, and sure destruction." If the consignees persisted in injuring their country by importing tea, they would not be safe no matter how many troops and fortified walls might surround them. "You cannot readily become your own cooks, butchers, butlers, nor bakers: You will therefore be liable, to be suddenly, and unexpectedly taken off, in the midst of your confidence and supposed security, by those whom you may chance to confide in, and employ." The author called upon a local Brutus or Cassius "to sheath their daggers in the hearts of such base, such abandoned and infamous Parricides." If the consignees hoped to profit from their treason, the author warned, the triumph would be short-lived. Guilt, hatred, and infamy would be their lot for generations to come. The choice was now the consignees' to make. Threats to their safety lurked around every corner. The consignees would have to watch their backs.[44]

As early as October 16, the merchant Henry Bromfield wrote, "People here are much enraged at the India Company's Intentions of Sending their Tea here." He continued, "the Consequence is uncertain but I believe Messrs Clarke will have a good Deal of Trouble wth it." A week later his predictions were more specific: "unless the Gent.ⁿ to whom it [the tea] is Consign'd should agree to Send it back it will be destroyed by Fire or Water as Sure as it comes."[45]

The reckoning came at one o'clock in the morning, on Tuesday, November 2. Richard Clarke was awakened by a "violent knocking." As he looked out the window of his School Street manor, the waning gibbous moon, just past full, showed two men in the courtyard. One called up, claiming he was carrying a letter from the country. This was the exact ruse a crowd had used at a customs commissioner's country house in June 1770, just before smashing the windows and terrorizing the family.[46] This time there really was a letter, but it was from the town, not the country:

Boston, 1st Nov., 1773

Richard Clarke & Son:
   The Freemen of this Province understand, from good authority, that there is a quantity of tea consigned to your house by the East India Company, which is destructive to the happiness of every well-wisher to his country. It is therefore expected that you personally appear at Liberty Tree, on Wednesday next, at twelve o'clock at noon day, to make a public resignation of your commission . . .
   Fail not upon your peril.

O.C.

The initials almost certainly stood for "Oliver Cromwell," the Puritan, republican military leader of seventeenth-century England. Cromwell was regarded by many New Englanders as a folk hero, a deposer of oppressive monarchs. His image adorned a tavern in town. "O.C." asked the Clarkes to meet at Liberty Tree in Hanover Square, a huge elm that was over a hundred years old. Andrew Oliver, brother to Clarke's sister's husband, had been forced to resign his appointment as executor of the Stamp Act at Liberty Tree in 1765 (fig. 15).
   "O.C." had made similar early-morning calls at the other consignees' houses, and had posted broadsides all over town inviting "the Freemen of this and the other Towns in the Province" to the meeting on November 3.

15 John Husk, a former Boston merchant who supposedly supported the Stamp Act, hangs from the Liberty Tree in Paul Revere's cartoon. "Mounted aloft perfidious H[us]k you see,/Scorn'd by his Country, fits the Rope & Tree," reads the verse below.

The postscript threatened, "Show me the man that dares take this down." Some joker had even posted a notice on the gate of the Province House, but one of Hutchinson's servants took it down so it could be sent to England as evidence.[47]

The letters from "O.C." tried to convey the impression that the entire town of Boston was against the consignees. But one handbill, the *Tradesmen's Protest against the Proceedings of the Merchants*, did appear in support of them. The author, claiming to represent "The True SONS OF LIBERTY," warned Boston's artisans to *"AVOID THE TRAP"* that anti-government merchants had set for them; after all, under the Tea Act, tea would cost "less than half the Price" that local merchants could afford to charge. The handbill urged the tradesmen "to walk *uprightly*, and to eat, drink, and wear" whatever they pleased. Bostonians should ignore the "thundering Bulls" of whatever *"Bellowing* PATRIOT" would be mouthing off at the "illegal and underhanded" meeting beneath Liberty Tree on November 3.[48]

Still, Bostonians were apparently interested in what the bellowers had to say.

The day before the Liberty Tree meeting, the North End Caucus had met at the Green Dragon Tavern and invited the merchant John Hancock to join them. Although Hancock had been drifting away from the Boston radicals since 1770, the tea crisis helped spur him back into the center of the action. The Caucus also invited the Boston Committee of Correspondence to meet with them. The Caucus voted that they were "determined that the Tea shipped or to be shipped by the East India Company shall not be landed." Finally their three brilliant physicians, Church, Warren, and Young (members of the Caucus and the BCC), drew up a resolution to be read to the consignees at Liberty Tree. The trio of doctors called the consignees "enemies to their Country," and warned that patriotic Bostonians "will not fail to make them feel the weight of their just resentment."[49]

Summoned by the town's church bells, a sundry crowd around 500 strong gathered at Liberty Tree at noon on Wednesday, November 3. Richard Clarke described them as being "chiefly . . . of the lowest rank," while Governor Hutchinson said they were "generally of the very lowest class mixed with boys and negroes." Friends of government often described the Boston crowds in these terms, as a way to express their scorn and undermine their enemies' significance. Yet the group surrounding Liberty Tree also included artisans and traders, as well as leading Sons of Liberty like Samuel Adams, John Hancock, and Joseph Warren. The North End Caucus was on hand, and they had hung a flag from the tree. Yet one group was conspicuously absent: none of the tea agents appeared. As Clarke later wrote, "none of us ever entertained the least thoughts of obeying the summons." Instead, the consignees convened at Clarke's warehouse at the foot of King Street and agreed to "oppose the designs of the mob."[50]

Those milling about beneath Liberty Tree were insulted that the consignees had failed to show. With the disgruntled crowd at their backs, William Molineux and eight other designated leaders walked up Newbury Street, halfway across town, past the Old South Meeting House, and down King Street to Clarke's warehouse. The nine delegates confronted the consignees in Clarke's counting room.

Clarke asked some pointed questions. Who, exactly, did this committee represent?

They were "from the whole people," Molineux replied. No doubt the noise of 500 onlookers made it seem that way.

Clarke asked the delegates to identify themselves. Molineux was flanked by Joseph Warren, Benjamin Church, Nathaniel Barber, Edward Proctor, Ezekiel Cheever, and others, and Clarke made sure to take down their names.

Clarke then asked the delegates what the people wanted.

Molineux informed the agents that they "had committed an high insult on the people," by ignoring the summons. And how dare they? Molineux slid a paper across the table for Clarke to sign. The delegates had helpfully drawn up a written promise that the consignees would not land the tea or pay the duty, but would send the tea back to England.

Clarke pushed the paper away and replied, "he had nothing to do with them and should give no answer." In other words, the consignees "firmly refused" to meet the committee's "extravagant demand," and treated it "with a proper contempt."

In that case, Molineux replied, the consignees "must expect to feel . . . the utmost weight of the people's resentment" as "enemies to their country."

The committee then left the warehouse and informed the crowd of the consignees' refusal. The crowd was gathered in front of Vernon's Head Tavern, on the northeast corner of King Street and Merchant's Row. After some hesitation, people began rushing purposefully toward the warehouse. One of Clarke's servants frantically tried to shut the door. Nathaniel Hatch, a justice of the peace, moved to help. He warned the crowd to disperse, in His Majesty's name, and in response the crowd taunted Hatch and struck him. They forced the door from his hands and ripped it off its hinges. The Clarkes' friends, a group of about twenty men, retreated to the counting room on the second floor. Because the building had a narrow stairway, a few men were able to prevent the swarm from advancing any further. The crowd made a few more feints, and kept the Clarkes and their friends confined to the second floor for about an hour and a half. As the rush of rage melted away, people split from the group and drifted home.[51]

The Sons of Liberty still needed to sustain the resistance, however, and they did their best to keep the people's anger alive. On Thursday, November 4, a radical newspaper, the *Massachusetts Spy*, printed a couple of letters that threatened the consignees with violence. A member of Molineux's committee wrote of the "danger of lives being lost, which is not to be ventured upon till the last extremity." It was the same "no mobs, no tumults" warning that the crowd had heard in 1768. But if the consignees persisted in their stubbornness, the writer continued, "all the world will applaud the spirit that, for the common preservation, will exterminate such malignant and dangerous persons." The tea protesters were willing, it seemed, to resort to violence after all.[52]

That evening, "O. C." left another message under Benjamin Faneuil's door, addressed to all the tea agents. Remarking on the consignees' anxiety about their reputation, the writer affected sympathy: "We do not wonder in the least that your apprehensions are terrible, when the most enlightened humane & conscientious community on the earth view you in the light of tigers or mad dogs, whom the public safety obliges them to destroy." Theft was still punishable by death in Massachusetts—the province had just hanged twenty-one-year-old Levi Ames for burglary two weeks before. And while the letter-writer professed to abhor the idea of "spilling human blood," he reminded the consignees that they were playing "a principal part in the robbery of every inhabitant of this country, in the present and future ages," and perhaps they deserved to share Ames's punishment. The letter encouraged them to do as the Philadelphia consignees had done and promise not to land the tea when it arrived. Further delays, "O. C." warned, would result in the consignees receiving "the just rewards of your avarice & insolence . . . from the insulted, abused, and most indignant vindicators of violated liberty in the Town of Boston."[53]

Friday, November 5, was Pope's Day in Boston, which was, as Governor Hutchinson wrote, "a day of disorder every year." Bostonians gathered at Faneuil Hall for their first town meeting since May ("tho' by Law," Hutchinson wrote, "Towns have no more Authority in such cases than to declare war against France"). With John Hancock as moderator, the free-holders of Boston took their cues from Philadelphia, their sister city to the south. First they heard a petition expressing alarm about the East India Company tea: "they esteem it a political plan of the British Administration" that threatened to destroy the local trade along with their liberty. The meeting asked the 400 tradesmen who were present to gather on the south side of the hall, where they unanimously disavowed the support for the consignees outlined in the *Tradesmen's Protest* that had been printed two days before. From this point onward, few people, except the most ardent friends of government, were willing to speak in favor of the Tea Act.[54]

Instead, the assembled meeting agreed to the eight resolutions that the Philadelphia Sons of Liberty had previously adopted: these resolves affirmed the doctrine of no taxation without consent, and argued that duties such as the Tea Act would replace representative assemblies with "arbitrary government and slavery." Americans had a duty to oppose the tea plan and the Company that was enforcing it, while anyone who sold the Company tea was an "enemy to America." Finally, a committee would wait on the consignees and demand their resignation "from a regard to their own characters, and the peace and good order of this town and province." The Town Meeting was speaking as much to New York and Philadelphia as it was to locals: they were determined to stand fast with the other colonies and refuse to import dutied tea, no matter how poorly they had kept to such agreements in previous years. The Tea Act had given them new energy.

But the consignees stayed stubborn. They developed a strategy of throwing up every technicality and stalling tactic they could. Hancock and the rest of the Town Meeting's delegation approached the consignees on November 5 with a formal request that they resign their appointments as agents of the EIC. In response, Clarke and Faneuil asked for "an authenticated copy of the Town's vote." When this was provided, they concluded that "It is impossible for us to comply with the request of the Town," because they did not yet know the terms of the consignment. The Hutchinsons had fled to their father's Milton estate to avoid the annual Pope's Day ruckus, but when Adams, Hancock, Warren, and a few others tracked them down anyway on the 11th, their answer was essentially the same. This did nothing to satisfy the Town Meeting held that day, which proclaimed the consignees' answers "DARINGLY AFFRONTIVE." Had the consignees offered to store the tea under the town's watchful eye, a town selectman later claimed, the town would have accepted this as a compromise.[55]

The Clarkes could take some comfort from supportive letters like this one from Worcester: "I hope you will persevere in so good a Cause, and by so doing convince these lawless Raskalls, that you even dare to withstand those Devils, that call themselves *Sons of Liberty*. But from such Liberty! good God! deliver us."[56]

By the following week, as Boston had its first ice of the winter, the excitement had shrunk to an angry simmer. The editors of the *Boston Gazette* were uneasy that Governor Hutchinson had asked Hancock, in his capacity as colonel of the Company of Cadets, to keep themselves armed and ready in case of a disturbance. Why was this necessary, they asked, if the townspeople had not given the tea consignees "the smallest affront"? (Never mind the assault on the Clarke warehouse.)[57]

Hutchinson had good reason to drum up armed patrols. He was worried that it would be impossible to secure the tea even if the consignees could land it. Hutchinson wanted to protect the liberty and property of the king's faithful subjects, he wrote, but he felt incapable: "I wish we had it more in our power." The *Gazette*, meanwhile, warned that Hutchinson's "design is to set up a military tyranny," as people waited anxiously for the tea to arrive. Lieutenant Governor Andrew Oliver heard a rumor on the 12th that Boston's "sons of violence" were about to break into the consignees' houses, "secure their persons," and compel them to resign their commissions. Before evening fell, the consignees quietly slipped away from their houses for a restless night in the homes of friends.[58]

Jonathan Clarke finally arrived in Boston on November 17 aboard the *Hayley*, one of John Hancock's merchant ships. His trip to England had been a triumph: he had wheedled a consignment of tea from the East India Company for his family's firm, with a 6 percent commission. The tea was still on its way: the *Hayley's* captain, James Scott, had refused to carry the Company's tea, though he had carried dutied tea before, but he had safely returned Jonathan to the Clarke household. Scott reported that four Boston-bound vessels, and several headed for the other American seaports, had come down the English Channel at the same time as him, and couldn't be far behind. That evening a concerned crowd of one or two hundred people surrounded Governor Hutchinson's house, where one of his sons was living. Finding that the sons were not at home, the group proceeded to the Clarke residence.[59]

In retrospect, young Clarke should have realized that firing a gun out the window was bound to anger the mob.

Then again, who was thinking clearly? Perhaps the Clarkes had passed around a bottle of wine to celebrate Jonathan's safe passage across the Atlantic—no sure thing in those days. Then the neighbors had to ruin the party. A growing crowd approached the house on School Street. The Clarkes had just enough warning to secure the doors before the townsfolk showed up in the front yard at around 8 p.m. The noise had been deafening—whistling, catcalls, and horns—as the crowd pounded at the door in an attempt to force it open. The women, frightened, had fled to the upper chambers for safety, where Richard Clarke, the family patriarch, tended to them. History does not record which of the Clarke brothers shouted, "You Rascals, be gone or I'll blow you[r] brains out!" When the crowd responded with hisses and shouts, this Clarke apparently lost his temper and fired a pistol.

No one was hit, luckily for all (the gun might have only been loaded with powder, not shot), though there was a rumor that a wounded man was dragged away. But it could have been worse—many people probably recalled the incident in February 1770 when Ebenezer Richardson, his house surrounded by Bostonians who were angry about breaches of the nonimportation agreements, had fired into the crowd and killed young Christopher Seider.

That night in 1773, after the gun's report had echoed in School Street and the smoke had wafted upward, the crowd renewed their assault. The angry Bostonians unleashed their fury on the Clarke house. They shattered the windowpanes, smashed the window frames, and threw as many stones, brickbats, and pieces of wood as they could through the openings.

After about an hour, some steady hands intervened. A few of the Clarkes' friends showed up to encourage them to persevere. Some "worthy Gentleman of the Town" tried to broker a compromise with the crowd: would the assembled people disperse if the Clarkes promised to appear at the town meeting scheduled for the following day? But the Clarkes refused to negotiate with a mob. Things had reached an impasse, but the tension had leaked out of the scene, perhaps out of respect for the "distressed" women in the house. Everyone went home after another hour, leaving the Clarkes to clear the broken glass and furniture and tend to a couple of small injuries. With no defense against the chill, the Clarkes spent the night at the homes of relatives and friends. It was now not just unpopular to support the East India Company's tea shipments, but unsafe.[60]

The townspeople of Boston were ready to confront the Clarkes again the next day, having decided that the consignees' excuses were up. The Boston Town Meeting sent a committee to visit Richard Clarke & Sons. Surely the East India Company's orders had arrived on the *Hayley* with Jonathan Clarke. Instead, once again the consignees turned the committee away. This time the consignees said that all they knew was that their friends in London had entered into a commercial engagement on their behalf, "which puts it out of our power to comply with the request of the Town." The Town Meeting replied that this was still unsatisfactory, and adjourned. Selectman John Scollay later wrote that the townsfolk had hoped that the consignees would agree to reship the tea, "as they knew this measure would prevent the destruction of the Company's property, which they judged would be the case if it was not sent back."[61]

"People's minds were daily more and more agitated," wrote Scollay. The crowds over the past few weeks had unnerved the consignees, as the shot fired from the Clarkes' window on November 17 made clear. The Company's agents did not trust the Town Meeting, but they were, after all, close with the governor. So the consignees now turned to Hutchinson and his Council on November 19, asking whether they might give the tea (when it arrived) to the Council, "the guardians and protectors of the people," for safekeeping.[62]

Now Governor Hutchinson learned once again how few allies he had in his Council. Writing to his boss back in England (the Earl of Dartmouth, the Secretary of State for American Affairs), he complained, "If I had the aid which I think the council might give, my endeavors would be more effectual." Instead, the councilors were "infected" with the "distemper of the people." Rather than help Hutchinson "discourage an opposition to the landing of the teas," they believed, too, that the consignees should resign. The Council's lack of responsiveness made sense—its twenty-eight members were elected by the House of Representatives and represented all political views. While the governor had the power to veto the House's choices, he had less power than governors did in almost all other colonies, where the king and his officials usually appointed councilors directly. The Massachusetts Council met on November 19 but did nothing about the consignees' petition until November 23, postponed action again until the 27th, and then again did nothing. This was important, because Hutchinson would be extremely reluctant to order the king's troops to protect the tea without his Council's consent.[63]

With the governor powerless to help them, the consignees turned desperately to the Town of Boston. Jonathan and Isaac Clarke met the town's selectmen at 4 p.m. on November 24. Jonathan was probably still shaking with fear and rage from his homecoming ordeal the week before. With as much false sincerity as he could muster, he tried to persuade the selectmen not only that he had not sought the tea commission for his family's firm (this was a lie, as a few of the selectmen suspected), but that "it was very disagreeable to him." He offered to do whatever he could, within reason. When the selectmen replied that the people would be satisfied with nothing less than the return of the tea to London, Clarke answered that if he did so, customs officials would seize his ship and cargo for sure—it was illegal to bring tea back to England. All Clarke could promise was that he wouldn't secretly try to unload any of the tea onto American shores: "nothing underhanded." The irony must have stung like the spit of the sea in high winds. The East India Company had been trying to quash tea smugglers for years, and now Boston's Sons of Liberty were trying to make sure that the Company's own consignees didn't imitate the smugglers' tactics.[64]

By November 28, the time for dancing around the issues had passed. Early that morning, a pilot guided the *Dartmouth* to anchor at King's Road in the harbor. The ship had arrived from London with 114 chests of tea aboard. If the Clarkes and Hutchinsons remained stubborn, one Boston merchant wrote, "I tremble for y^e. consequences." Another merchant, in town for business, predicted that if the consignees attempted to land the tea, "there will be blood shed on the Occasion."[65]

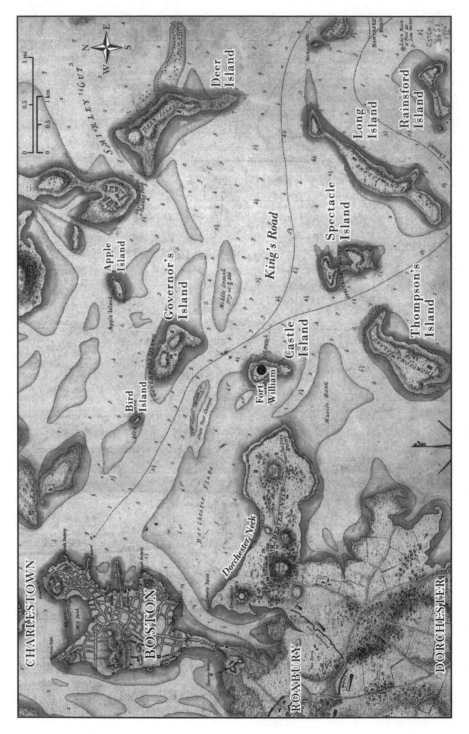

4 Boston Harbor, from "Boston, its environs and harbour . . . ."

CHAPTER 5

The Detestable Tea Arrives

A fatality seems to attend the Tea concern.
Thomas Hutchinson, December 9, 1773[1]

Francis Rotch was standing in a church filled with five or six thousand Bostonians. A resolution was read, on behalf of this huge meeting, which threatened him and his ship's captain with "Peril" if he allowed his cargo of tea to land in Boston. One could forgive Rotch if his mind flashed, at that moment, to the Boston martyrs. Back in the years 1659–61, these four convicts had swung from the gallows on Boston Common, only a couple of blocks from where Rotch was standing. Their crime was preaching Quakerism back in the days when Massachusetts Puritans brooked no dissent. Rotch himself, twenty-three years old, was a member of the Society of Friends—a Quaker. We don't know whether he was thinking about the Boston martyrs on November 29, 1773, but we can guess that he was starting to think of Boston as a rather uncomfortable place.[2]

Rotch (the name rhymes with "coach") and the thousands of people who made up this massive gathering were packed into the Old South Meeting House—the only building in town big enough to contain a crowd of that size. They had gathered to discuss the tea that had just arrived in Boston harbor aboard the *Dartmouth*, a share of which was owned by Rotch's family. This wasn't even an official town meeting (which would have been smaller and more proper), but a gathering of the "Body of the People." By holding a meeting without official notification by the selectmen and the town clerk, these officials would be able to deny responsibility for anything illegal that might occur. This "Body of the People" was telling Rotch, as owner of the ship, and James Hall, as its captain, "that if they suffered the Tea to be landed it would be at their Peril."[3]

Before he received this warning, Francis Rotch had stood, perhaps uneasily, to explain his gloomy predicament. The *Dartmouth* could not leave the harbor without a pass from the governor, and the governor would not give him a pass without clearance from the customhouse. If Rotch tried to break the law and his shipping contract, he would not only lose the freight charges he had earned for shipping the tea (this was a business, after all), but he was liable to have his ship seized by customs officials in London, if he even made it that far. Rotch would lodge a formal protest with the customhouse, he said, and then he sat down.[4]

Rotch was trying to act in the best interests of his family's merchant firm. Francis, his elderly father Joseph, and his oldest brother William were part of two linked firms at the heart of a prominent Nantucket whaling family. Spermaceti oil was a big business in the eighteenth century, since the oil was rendered into radiant, clean-burning candles; and the Rotches were big players in the industry. Joseph Rotch Sr. had recently relocated to the town of Dartmouth (near what is now New Bedford), and named the firm's ship for this new venture.

Francis was only twenty-two years old when his older brother Joseph Jr. died in England. The younger Joseph had left in 1772 for his health (and for the family business), and the black poetess Phillis Wheatley had written a poem in his honor. "Leave these bleak regions and inclement skies," she suggested, and although she hoped Joseph would return to Massachusetts "Replete with vigour not his own before," he died in England at age thirty. In Joseph's will, he bequeathed the brick warehouse and other property in bleak Boston to his younger brother.[5]

By 1773, the Rotches had managed to anger quite a few people in Boston. In the 1760s, the Rotches had engaged in a vicious trade war with John Hancock's family firm over the price of whale oil. In 1769, local newspapers listed the Rotches among the handful of families (like the Clarkes and the younger Hutchinsons) that continued to import British goods in defiance of the boycott. Around the same time, a Boston family sued William Rotch for the wages of a black slave, "Boston," who served aboard one of Rotch's ships. A jury of Nantucketers declared "Boston" a free man, a decision that almost went to the province's Superior Court. The Rotches, like most Nantucket Quakers, were cool to the campaign against Parliament, and the Boston Sons of Liberty knew it.[6]

Knowing Rotch as they did, the "Body" of Bostonians was a bit testy when it ordered him not to enter his ship at the customhouse "at his Peril," and similarly threatened Captain Hall not to unload the tea. The towns-people were asking Rotch to break the law, or else. All Rotch wanted to do was unload his cargo, load the *Dartmouth* with his family's whale oil, and send the ship back to London. Every day's delay potentially cost the family hundreds of pounds' worth of business. Rotch was in a terrible position.[7]

The Boston Sons of Liberty were in a tricky situation, too. The day before the assemblage at the Old South Meeting House, the *Dartmouth* (185 tons), laden with tea, had anchored beneath the stern of Admiral John Montagu's flagship, H.M.S. *Captain*, about 400 yards off the Long Wharf. It was 11 a.m. on November 28, and the weather was pleasant. British warships had been stationed in Boston harbor ever since Parliament had decided to tighten its enforcement of customs regulations. In addition to the *Captain*, a 64-gun ship of the line, two other British warships rode in the harbor: the frigates *Active* and *Kingfisher*. These ships remained an armed, menacing presence in the harbor throughout the tea conflict of 1773. At first, it looked as if the tea ship would be safe under the guns of the British Navy. That evening, two customhouse officers came from Castle Island and boarded the *Dartmouth*, which was unusual, but this was no usual cargo. As the ship's mate wrote, they had "the East India Company's *accursed dutiable Tea* on board."[8]

The *Dartmouth* was now under the jurisdiction of the port's authorities, and so a customs regulation kicked in that would have a profound effect on the timing of the Boston Tea Party. When a ship entered Boston harbor, the owners of any taxable goods aboard it had twenty days to make payment to the customs office in King Street. If they failed, customs officers would seize the ship and have the vessel and everything aboard it sold at auction. The customs office, the governor, and the informer would split the proceeds. In cases where the Navy was involved, half went to the crew, and half to the customs office.

The people of Boston now had an intractable problem to resolve. On one side were the Bostonians who were working to actively resist the Tea Act—led by the North End Caucus and the Boston Committee of Correspondence, but the catch-all term "Sons of Liberty" will suffice. By now the Sons of Liberty had managed to sway most of the town to its side, and quieted almost everyone else. Their only remaining opponents were the increasingly friendless shipowners and consignees who wanted to obey the laws and execute the consignment. The Boston Sons of Liberty had 20 days to resolve the issue of the tea, or there would be no opportunity to stand on principle. Any protest against the tax, the revenue, or the monopoly would be a waste of time, because Parliament and the East India Company would succeed in executing their scheme under the Tea Act. Using tea as their lure, they would hook Americans into paying—without their consent—taxes, monopoly prices, and the salaries of hated officials. The Sons of Liberty in New York and Philadelphia would turn away in disgust.[9]

So the Boston Sons of Liberty had twenty days. The looming deadline for the cargo aboard the *Dartmouth* was December 17.

Several groups swung into action on November 28, even though it was a Sunday. The Town Board of Selectmen (Boston's executive branch) met at noon to see what they could do, in their official capacity, to prevent Boston from erupting into further violence. They hoped to convince the consignees to send the tea back to London. Now that the tea ship had arrived, the consignees had no more excuses to delay a firm answer about their intentions, so the selectmen called on the Clarkes to see what they would do. When they arrived at the School Street manor, they were told that Richard Clarke and his sons were out of town. The selectmen adjourned to attend afternoon church services, and met again at 5 p.m., hoping they could get a straight answer in time to call a regular town meeting the next day. After waiting until late in the evening, the Clarkes crushed their hopes: a brother-in-law (probably John Singleton Copley) finally told them they would have to wait until the following day for an answer. From this point onward, the selectmen stepped back from their attempts resolve the tea crisis. Instead, the coordination of Boston's response shifted to two groups: the North End Caucus and the Boston Committee of Correspondence (BCC).[10]

On the same day as the selectmen's meeting, and in the same room, the radicals of the BCC were hatching their own plans for the Company's tea. For the last year, this group had coordinated communication with other Massachusetts towns, spreading the word through circulars and letters, to make sure that town and country were united in guarding their constitutional rights. On November 19, the BCC had invited committees from Boston's neighboring towns of Roxbury, Dorchester, Brookline, and Cambridge to discuss matters relating to "our common Liberties" at Faneuil Hall on the 22nd. The five towns agreed to "use their Joint influence to prevent the Landing and Sale of the Teas." They agreed to inform the rest of Massachusetts about the "evil tendency" of the Tea Act and the "absolute necessity of making an immediate & effectual opposition to this detestable measure." As Thomas Hutchinson put it, Bostonians were drawing in these other towns "expecting them to share in the Criminality and so lessen their own share."[11]

Now that the Boston Town Meeting had failed to persuade the consignees to send back the tea, the Boston Committee of Correspondence turned to Francis Rotch. They sent William Molineux and two others to visit Rotch and urge him not to enter the *Dartmouth* at the custom house until Tuesday. The Townshend Act required shipmasters to report their vessels "directly" upon arrival (the fine for failing to do this was £100), but forty-eight hours of leeway was generally allowed. Rotch agreed to Molineux's request but warned him that he couldn't risk delaying any longer than Tuesday. The committee was hoping that if they could get the *Dartmouth* to leave the harbor without registering at the customhouse (though this was technically illegal), they would avoid a crisis entirely.[12]

While they waited for Rotch, the BCC invited the committees from the neighboring towns to meet with them at Faneuil Hall at 9 a.m. on Monday, the 29th, and "send as many Friends to our assistance at this important crisis as you can possibly spare." Only with widespread support from the people in Boston and its surrounding towns could the Boston Committee be certain that no one would land the tea.[13]

The Clarkes were preparing their answer to the Boston selectmen on Monday, the 29th, but according to Scollay, this was a day too late. "Very early next morning hand bills were dispersed, by unknown persons, inviting the people to meet at Faneuil Hall."[14] Bostonians awoke that Monday to find notices pasted up throughout the town. "Friends! Brethren! Countrymen!" they began. "The Hour of Destruction or manly Opposition to the Machinations of Tyranny stares you in the Face." The notice called upon "every Friend to his Country, to himself and Posterity" to meet at Faneuil Hall at 9 a.m. A real town meeting was now pointless.[15]

The selectmen, as formal leaders of the Town of Boston, had failed to persuade the consignees to act. Instead, Bostonians convened in a larger mass meeting as "the Body," which accomplished several goals. First, a "Body" meeting broadened the base of interested, mobilized participants to include poorer Bostonians and residents of the outlying towns (only qualified property-owners were eligible to vote at a regular town meeting). Second, a "Body" meeting granted a broad, popular legitimacy to the political movement against the Company's tea—and perhaps this would further intimidate the consignees. Finally, as the selectmen learned from a "Lawyer and high son of Liberty"—possibly Josiah Quincy or John Adams—the Town of Boston could not be held liable for the tea if anything untoward happened to it. In theory, the authorities could not hold a spontaneous gathering of a "Body" of people accountable for anything. Despite the somewhat illegal nature of the meeting, the most important men of the town (apart from the governor's faction) were present: the three radical physicians, Dr. Thomas Young, Dr. Joseph Warren, and Benjamin Church were all there. So were Boston's four representatives to the Massachusetts House: Samuel Adams, John Hancock, William Phillips, and Speaker Thomas Cushing. The merchant William Molineux and the lawyer Josiah Quincy also stood at the front of the meeting, along with the town selectmen and other members of the Caucus and the BCC.[16]

As church bells rang throughout the town, Bostonians began crowding their way into Faneuil Hall with the goal of making "a united and successful Resistance to this last, worst and most destructive Measure of Administration." The moderate merchant Jonathan Williams (who was married to Benjamin Franklin's niece) presided over the meeting. William Cooper, the clerk of Boston's town meetings and the BCC, served this secretarial function here, too. As the meeting began, Faneuil Hall overflowed with people, and the lines outside were growing. So the meeting voted to move to the Old South Meeting House, the largest building in town (fig. 16).[17]

The Old South Meeting House had no fireplace, so unless people had brought foot warmers or portable stoves (which was considered dangerous, especially in a packed house), they had no choice but to stamp their feet and huddle closer together to ward off the late November chill. Since bathing was not a regular practice, the church must have reeked of human sweat, leather shoes, and musty wool. Hundreds of excited murmurs probably bounced from the walls, the galleries, and the pews. Given the size of the crowd, the meeting was impossible to ignore, and very difficult to defy. Governor Hutchinson thought the whole idea outrageous. "This meeting or assembly consisted principally of the lower ranks of people," he sniffed, "and even journeymen tradesmen were brought to increase the number and the rabble were not excluded." Hutchinson particularly remarked upon the young artisans and the "rabble," but even he conceded that a few "gentlemen of good fortune" were present—and he hoped they would exert a moderating influence. Scollay, the town selectman, tried to put a more positive spin on the meeting. He noted that "men of the best character and of the first fortunes" were present, and that people of all political stripes were impressed "that the utmost decorum was observed."[18]

Samuel Adams, Boston's foremost dissident politician, proposed a number of resolutions, which grew in insistence as the day went on: first, that the tea should return to London; second, that neither the consignees nor anyone else should pay the duty to the British Treasury; and finally,

OLD SOUTH CHURCH.

16 Although some details had changed, this image largely depicts the Old South Meeting House as it would have appeared in 1773.

that the tea should go back in the same vessel, to make sure it didn't fall prey to a legal technicality, a trick, or a mishap. The meeting approved all of these resolutions unanimously. Although some later reported that Dr. Thomas Young proposed to destroy the tea, Scollay later insisted that the meeting's attendees wanted "to preserve the tea from destruction." The meeting adjourned until 3 p.m. to give the consignees a chance to respond. Once again they delayed. The assembled Bostonians agreed to give them until the next day, "out of great Tenderness to these Persons," even though they had wasted so much of everyone's time.[19]

In the meantime, the reassembled inhabitants were determined to accomplish something useful that afternoon. They confronted Rotch and

Hall, insisting that they delay entering the ship at the customhouse, and heard Rotch's protests. Samuel Adams tried to reassure Rotch: shipowners regularly entered protests because of storm damage to protect themselves from liability; therefore, since Rotch "was now compelled by a *Political Storm* to return the Tea" and since "it was necessary for the Safety of his Person and Property" to send the tea back to London, this should excuse Rotch from his legal obligations toward the Company (to deliver the tea), the consignees (to hand over the tea), and the customhouse (to land the tea properly so that the duties could be paid).[20]

The gathered Bostonians also worried that either the ship's owner or the consignees would unload the tea no matter what they said. To prevent a clandestine unloading, they appointed a guard of twenty-five men "as Assistants to the Captain and Ship's Crew to take Care that the Tea was not smuggled out of the Ship or the Ship removed out of their Power." The men were led by lemon importer Edward Proctor, a member of the North End Caucus and one of the town's wardens. The meeting claimed that these men were there "for the Security of Captain Hall's Ship and Cargo," which was deliberately ambiguous: although the men could claim that they were protecting the East India Company tea from Boston's crowds, they were in fact (as they later told the customs officers stationed aboard the other tea ships) protecting the tea from the Company's own appointed merchants. In any case, Proctor's crew agreed to spend all night aboard the *Dartmouth* where it lay at anchor. By 9 p.m. on November 29, the guards had boarded boats at the wharves and rowed out to the ship.[21]

Just before adjourning, John Hancock told those present that Governor Hutchinson had ordered the town's magistrates "to suppress any Riot that might ensue on Account of the Tea." According to Hancock, Hutchinson was expecting that the magistrates would do nothing, which would give him a "Reason for again introducing Troops and thereby Bloodshed in the Town." The meeting cried out against this as an insult to Boston, and approved Hancock's statement that those gathered "were perfectly peaceable and quiet." They had no desire to feed the bad impression of Boston that Hutchinson had *already* given the king, and they were shocked (shocked!) that Hutchinson would whisper such aspersions.[22]

Over at the Province House, Governor Hutchinson finally got an answer out of his Council. The councilors protested against taxation without representation, and particularly against the Townshend Act's provision for using tax revenue to pay the salaries of the civil government (including Hutchinson's own salary)—this was a threat to the charter rights of the

Massachusetts Bay Colony. The Tea Act, they argued, was just an excuse to confirm Parliament's right to tax, and it was "introductive of monopolies" besides. (One thing they didn't add was that the East India Company monopoly appeared to be favoring Hutchinson's own sons.) Seeing that Parliament had no desire to save them from the ruin of their liberty and property, they expressed "a distress that borders on dispair." The Council would take no responsibility for protecting the consignees or the tea—they left the consignees' safety to the town's magistrates (most of whom sided with the Sons of Liberty), and vaguely recommended that colonial authorities prosecute anyone who had engaged (or would engage) in violence against the consignees. This sounded like tough talk, but of course none of the perpetrators of previous acts had been identified, and there was no assurance that anyone in Boston would be willing to give evidence against a townsperson for disrupting the peace. Most importantly, the Council said nothing about giving its blessing for the governor to call the 64th Regiment from Castle Island to protect the tea or the consignees.[23]

In other words, the consignees and the governor were on their own. If a crowd gathered to harass or assault the tea agents, or even strip them bare and smear them with hot tar and feathers (the "American torture"), there was little that could stop them. Although the town magistrates were supposed to intervene on a victim's behalf, past experience had shown that these town appointees often looked the other way when a crowd with popular support committed an act of violence. Hutchinson called his Council's response "An indirect countenancing and encouraging the disorders." In response, four of the consignees—the Clarke brothers, Thomas Hutchinson Jr., and Faneuil—immediately packed a few possessions, jumped aboard boats, and took shelter at Fort William, on Castle Island in the harbor (fig. 17).[24]

There, surrounded by the king's soldiers in their barracks, thick stone walls, a porcupine's array of cannon, and the depths of Boston harbor, was the only place they could feel certain of their safety from the anger of the Boston crowds. Castle Island, which was sometimes used as a breezy summer retreat for the colony's governors, was thought to be uninhabitable for genteel folk in colder weather. One of the customs commissioners, Henry Hulton, was already visiting Lieutenant Colonel Alexander Leslie at the fort, and thought it prudent to stay. Later that week, a handbill from "The PEOPLE" warned any customs officers that allowed the *Dartmouth* to unload its tea that they would be "considered and treated as Wretches unworthy to live, and be made the first Victims of our just Resentment." So Hulton's family and fellow commissioners joined the others at "the old

17 A view of Boston harbor from the edge of Long Wharf. Fort William, on Castle Island, is toward the right of the image, with the flag waving above it. During the tea crisis, many of the consignees and customs commissioners fled to Castle Island for safety and shelter. The fort housed a British garrison.

place of refuge." As for the other consignees, Joshua Winslow was in declining health and convalescing at Marshfield. Elisha Hutchinson stayed with his in-laws in Middleborough. Richard Clarke, "whose constitution being hurt by the repeated attacks made upon him," had left town on November 23, giving his sons full power to deal with the matter of the tea, until he arrived at Castle Island, too. The governor, meanwhile, so afraid that he almost went to the fort himself, spent most of his time at his country estate in Milton. The East India Company's supporters were doing their best to stay out of the crowd's reach.[25]

Just before leaving town, the consignees sent a letter to John Scollay, one of the town's selectmen. They claimed that it was "utterly out of our Power" to return the tea, but they agreed to store it until they could receive further instructions from the East India Company. Privately, they were betting that the tea would be landed successfully at New York before the twenty days expired at Boston, and this would cool the enthusiasm of the Sons of Liberty. Scollay read the consignees' letter to the meeting of the "Body" that gathered on Tuesday morning, November 30. Those present were still "irritated" with the consignees' obvious stalling.[26]

Just as they began to prepare a further response, the town sheriff, Stephen Greenleaf, interrupted with a letter from Governor Hutchinson. Hutchinson called the meeting an unlawful assembly, and ordered them "to disperse and to surcease all further unlawful Proceedings at your

utmost Peril." While everyone knew what sort of "Peril" the Boston crowds could offer, it was less clear that Hutchinson had the teeth to back up his threats. Greenleaf was chased away as "a loud and very general Hiss" filled the Old South Meeting House. In case this wasn't clear enough, the meeting voted to ignore the proclamation. Hutchinson later explained that there was little he could do to disrupt the meeting. He could not convince any magistrate to raise a posse to break it up, because "no other posse except the meeting itself would have appeared." In other words, who would form a posse if almost all the men in town were already at the meeting?[27]

Hutchinson's proclamation made Samuel Adams furious. This was a man who had helped ruin Adams's father—the enmity was long, bitter, and mutual. Adams harangued the crowd for fifteen to twenty minutes about Hutchinson's insulting decree: he mocked Hutchinson's claim to be "His Majesty's Representative . . . He? He? is he that Shadow of a Man, scarce able to support his withered Carcase or his hoary Head! is he a *Representation of Majesty*?" Adams also defended their right to assemble: "a free and sensible People when they felt themselves injured" had a right to meet "to consult for their own Safety." After the applause died down, Dr. Thomas Young stood, arguing that since the province was "in a State of Nature," the people assembled had the right to redress their grievances.[28]

As the meeting became more agitated, the painter John Singleton Copley stepped forward to try and arrange a truce. Copley, who was Richard Clarke's son-in-law, asked if the meeting could guarantee safety and "Civility" to the consignees if they appeared before it. Still eager to show

how orderly and peaceable they were, the attendees agreed. They allowed Copley two hours to fetch the consignees from the fort.[29] While they waited, the meeting summoned Rotch and Hall again, and demanded that they pledge to return the tea to London on board the *Dartmouth*. Hall and Rotch agreed, but Rotch again announced his intention to protest. The meeting also summoned the owners of the other tea ships that were expected to arrive: the merchant John Rowe was part owner of the *Eleanor*, and one John Timmins acted as agent for the owner of the *Beaver*. Timmins gave his assurances that the tea would not land, but Rowe really played to the crowd.

Rowe "expressed his Sorrow that any Vessel of his should be concerned in bringing any of that detestable and obnoxious Commodity, (Tea)." When the audience roared with approval, he asked "whether Salt Water would not make as good Tea as fresh." As shouting and clapping filled the hall, a few turned to their neighbors and bragged "that now they had brought a good Tory over to their Side." Rowe, for his part, later confessed to his diary that the tea "hath given me great Uneasiness." Still, when he was chosen to be on a committee to transmit the meeting's resolutions to New York and Philadelphia, he wrote that it was "much against my will but I dare not say a word."[30]

Rowe was probably telling the Bostonians what they wanted to hear. He was, in the end, a businessman trying to protect his profit margins. He had been known to evade customs duties, but also to supply the British soldiers. He supposedly helped inspire the destruction of Hutchinson's house in 1765, but he was breaking bread with Hutchinson in 1770. While Timmins, the Rotches, the Clarkes, and ship captains James Bruce, James Hall, and Hezekiah Coffin—that is, all those concerned in owning and captaining the ships—sympathized with the British government, Rowe never threw in his lot entirely with these future Loyalists. As Governor Hutchinson wrote, "He has kept clear [of the Sons of Liberty] of late but by a strange infatuation comes in again just at the end." Hutchinson admitted, "It was some surprize to me to see Master Rowe again engaged in so dangerous a business." Although Rowe fired up the crowd on the 30th, a week later he was offering to lend the Hutchinsons money to pay the tea duty, "Rather then the Affair should be any Longer kept up in Anger in the minds of the People."[31] Rowe was a trimmer, and he was probably apolitical at heart—he wanted to go back to making money. But his public pronouncement about destroying the tea demonstrates that the neutral faction was receding. Most Bostonians were now fired up and preparing to resist the East India Company's tea.

Meanwhile, the "Body" still needed to ensure that the tea stayed on board the ships. Six horsemen were appointed to rouse the countryside, if anyone raised an alarm. Another twenty-five men were appointed to the watch, under the distiller and rum-seller Ezekiel Cheever. Cheever, like Proctor, was a North End Caucus member and a town warden. The watchmen "were directed in Case of Molestation to give Warning to the Inhabitants by tolling the Bells in the Night and Ringing the Bells in the Daytime." The idea was to sound a warning like the signal given in case of a fire, and not the signals—like lighting a beacon or beating drums—that smacked of a military emergency or mob action. Samuel Adams added, however, that "he had for some time kept and should keep his Arms in Order and by his Bedside as every good Citizen ought," and that everyone should be prepared to support the watch in case they should be assaulted. Adams felt sure that "no one . . . would go out without being prepared and determined what Part to act." The next day a Boston merchant would report, " 'twould puzzle any person to purchase a pair of p[isto]ls in town, as they are all bought up, with a full determination to repell force by force."[32]

Copley the painter rowed (or had himself rowed) across the harbor to Castle Island, where he met with the Clarkes—his wife's father and brothers—and the other consignees. He returned to the Old South Meeting House alone. He apologized for his lateness and blamed "the Difficulty of a Passage by Water at this Season." Copley was nervous. His goal was to "draw the people from their unfavourable oppinion" of his in-laws. He had to convince the crowded meeting that the consignees were acting out of neither "obstinacy or unfriendliness to the community." He begged the audience to understand that if the consignees failed to discharge the tea contract, it would "ruin" their "reputation as Merchants." And when you regularly dealt with people on the other side of an ocean, reputation was everything.

The meeting may have been suspicious that the consignees had failed to appear because they felt unsafe. If this was acknowledged openly, it would make the Bostonians look like a crowd of thugs rather than a body of wise citizens—and the people of Boston held themselves in higher regard than that. Copley hastened to deny that the consignees were afraid—he had assured them, he said, that they would be safe in Boston. Now Copley drew breath and continued. "The Consignees were very desirous of seeing Peace restored in the Town," he said, "and thro' a tender Regard for their Families etc. would do their Utmost to give their Fellow-Citizens Satisfaction." But, they said, it "would serve no valuable Purpose to appear at the Meeting and might create some new Disgust." Through Copley, the consignees reiterated their offer from the evening before: they could not be "Active instruments" in returning the tea "without ruining themselves," but they would agree to store it—or if the Bostonians wanted to send the tea back themselves, there was nothing the consignees could do to stop them. Since they had played no part in "introducing the Tea" to Boston (though in the case of the Clarkes this was disingenuous at best), they would "do nothing to obstruct the People" if they decided to force the tea to be returned to England.[33]

Samuel Adams took great satisfaction in this. The meeting had "humbled the Consignees." Having learned "what it was to displease their Fellow-Citizens," the Consignees "were now willing to yield to any Terms." Copley, meanwhile, felt certain that he had "cooled the Resentment" of the people against the consignees. Doing his best to sound chipper, he later wrote to his brothers-in-law, "I have no doubt in my own mind you must stay where you are" at Castle Island until the *Dartmouth* left Boston, "but I beleive not Longer." Copley would continue his discussions with Warren and Hancock, but he warned his in-laws in no uncertain terms to "avoid seeing the Govournor." Someone at the meeting had said "some very warm things" about the consignees "acting under the Imediate influance of the Governor," and Copley had tried his best to refute this. If the Sons of Liberty noticed too much chatter between the governor and the consignees, that would only deepen their sense that a conspiracy was afoot. The people at the meeting were still annoyed and unsatisfied. The consignees were pretending to wash their hands of the whole affair, but it was too little, too late.[34]

The meeting then voted to send their anti-tea resolution to London and all Massachusetts seaports, and to send a report of their entire proceedings to New York and Philadelphia. Those in attendance agreed to prevent the tea from landing "at the Risque of their Lives and Property." They asked for volunteer watchmen to submit their names at the office of the *Boston Gazette*. "My Fellow Countrymen," said John Hancock by way of valediction, "we have now put our Hands to the Plough and Wo be to him that shrinks or looks back."[35]

Captain Hall entered the *Dartmouth* at the customhouse on Tuesday, the 30th, and turned the ship up to Rowe's Wharf. The ship was now out of the Royal Navy's power, and in the hands of Boston's patrols. On Wednesday, December 1, Hall warped around to Griffin's Wharf, where his crew put the sails and cables ashore, and over the coming days, stevedores unloaded all the ship's cargo except for the tea. The tea was now in limbo—not officially landed (but due to clear customs by December 17), and under no one's clear control—certainly not the consignees', nor the control of the ship's owner or captain, all of whom had been given dire warnings about trying to unload the tea. The British warships in the harbor couldn't fire on the ships without hitting the town. Governor Hutchinson's only option would be to order British troops to seize the *Dartmouth*, but he was reluctant to do this without the Council's blessing (which it wouldn't grant). Everyone would have to wait until the 17th, when His Majesty's Customs Service— probably with the help of the Navy—would have the power to seize the ship.[36]

In the meantime, the only group that could plausibly claim some control over the tea was the "Body of the People." During the day, the Sons of Liberty evidently relied on the watchful eyes of the townsfolk to make sure the tea stayed aboard the *Dartmouth*. Once night fell, the vigil belonged to a rotating crew of volunteers. "They have kept a constant military watch of 25 men every night," Hutchinson reported, "generally with their fire arms to prevent the Tea being privately landed." Every half hour they called to one another the watchword "All is well!" like garrison sentinels. When Hutchinson confronted the colonel of one of the militia regiments (perhaps John Hancock) about allowing his men to patrol Griffin's Wharf under arms, the colonel consulted with his fellow officers and replied simply, "it was not in their power to restrain the men from appearing on this Occasion." Several sources later confirmed that the Cadet Company supplied the men of the watch one night. Captain Hall, along with a cadet, both said that John Hancock himself went aboard, though perhaps "only out of curiosity."[37]

On December 3, the Committee of Correspondence ordered Captain James Bruce to bring the *Eleanor* (250 tons) up to Griffin's Wharf to join the *Dartmouth*. The third tea vessel, the brig *Beaver* (about 100 tons), arrived near Boston on the 7th, "not only with the Plague (TEA) on board, but also with the Small-Pox," joked the *Boston Gazette*. The paper supposed, rather unscientifically, that the tea itself had absorbed some of the disease. Some of the men aboard had indeed come down with smallpox, so the ship lay at Rainsford's Island in the harbor to be smoked and purified—the selectmen allowed the *Beaver* to join the other ships at Griffin's Wharf on December 13. There was also a fourth vessel with Company tea aboard, the brigantine *William*. Owned by the Clarkes, the *William* had foul luck: during a violent storm on the 10th, it struck a sandbar off Cape Cod, taking on four feet of water in the hold until the crew were forced to cut her cables, which drove the ship ashore. It would never sail again; eight days later another storm would rip up the ship's decks, and the crew decided to set the wreck on fire to save the iron.[38]

Now the three remaining vessels were all at Griffin's Wharf, and December 17 was drawing closer. What if Captain Hall ended the crisis by leaving the harbor, as the Sons of Liberty wanted him to do? Hutchinson heard a rumor of this. "Hall is preparing for the Sea and it is given out that the Tea shall be carried back in the Ship," he wrote, "but that cannot be." He was determined: "at all events she must be stopped at the Castle."[39] Stubborn and unbending, Hutchinson steeled himself to uphold the proper legal procedures for ships entering Boston harbor, and he refused to bend the rules just because an illegal gathering of townsfolk had made a few insolent demands. When Hall hinted that his ship might leave Boston harbor by another route, Hutchinson reported the intelligence to Admiral Montagu, so Montagu could stop the *Dartmouth* no matter what route it tried to take. The admiral woke the *Active* and *Kingfisher* from their winter slumber so they might be ready to pursue the *Dartmouth*. Hutchinson also made sure to notify Lieutenant Colonel Leslie "to suffer no Vessel . . . to pass that fortress from the Town without a permit signed by the Governor, and a sufficient number of Guns were loaded upon this special Occasion."[40]

Bostonians learned about all these military moves from the newspapers: they read that the soldiers at Fort William "have cleaned and loaded their muskets, have charged their cannon, even the 42 pounders," that a battery of artillery had sprouted on Governor's Island, and that the warships were moving to prevent the *Dartmouth* from leaving the harbor. There was nowhere the *Dartmouth* could go that wasn't in the line of cannon fire. Once the twenty days elapsed, the people of Boston fully expected that the customs officers would "call in the naval and military force to their aid."[41]

Well, if the British military and navy were ready for a fight, then so were the people of Massachusetts. Although friends of government and apolitical trimmers like Rowe could be found throughout the province, public opinion had swayed decisively against landing the East India Company tea. Of the Massachusetts towns that spoke up, almost all did so in opposition to the Tea Act, while the minority was usually too cowed to speak up. A Salem newspaper reported that the Boston-area locals were "determined upon hazarding a Brush," and the paper advised sympathetic readers "to get suitably prepared."[42]

Furthermore, the opposition was spreading deeper into Massachusetts. In the towns closest to Boston, town meetings voiced resolutions that were brimming with anger at Parliament and the tea consignees, and they offered full-throated support for the actions of the Boston-area committees of correspondence. Cambridge adopted the Philadelphia resolves on

November 26, and Charlestown declared its support the following day. Dorchester vowed to stand with their "patriotic brethren" should a "day of trial" come. The following week, Roxbury declared the consignees to have forfeited the town's protection. Soon Marblehead, another large port town, was also resolving that no tea would be landed there. From Brookline and Medford and Plymouth, from Lexington and Portsmouth, New Hampshire, word came back that Boston could count on an extended network of support.[43]

Even as early as December 1, one Bostonian could boast, "Its not only y^c. town, but the country are unanimous against the landing it." Abigail Adams, wife of the lawyer John Adams, was similarly enthusiastic. "The flame is kindled and like Lightning it catches from Soul to Soul," she wrote. "Great will be the devastation if not timely quenched or allayed by some more Lenient Measures."[44]

The closer the deadline drew, the tighter the tension thrummed. "There certainly is danger of some violent explosion," Hutchinson predicted. "A few nights ago they were under great apprehensions that one of the Ships with the Tea on board would have been burnt by the Mob." Apparently someone tried to burn one of the ships, but a "grave man," one of the volunteer watchmen, had restrained the would-be arsonist.[45]

Meanwhile, the newspapers mocked Hutchinson relentlessly. "ARGUS" accused Hutchinson of having "hoped, prayed and incessantly labored to effect" the landing of his "darling baby Bohea tea."[46] Another writer added, "your enemies (*that is the whole community!*) say you are busied in the affairs of your *Cubbs*." This author accused Hutchinson of taking orders from the East India Company because he and his children had a direct commercial interest in the tea. The letter called him "*incorrigible*," a "pestilence," a "culprit," and "beneath . . . resentment." Hutchinson was a disgrace to his office, and "the sooner you take your departure, the *better!*"[47]

Weeks earlier, Hutchinson had hoped that the tea ship bound for New York would arrive before the Boston tea ships did. He had estimated that New Yorkers were "less disposed to any violent proceedings" and would set a peaceful example. Once the situation at New York was defused, the Boston radicals might give up on their insistence that the tea be returned. But the news from New York must have disappointed him and gladdened Boston's Sons of Liberty. On Pope's Day, some New York City boys burned an effigy of the Irish merchant William Kelly (a former resident of the city) for recommending one of the local tea consignees and bragging that the colony's governor would have no trouble forcing the tea upon New

Yorkers. "LEGION" gave detailed instructions to local pilots not to bring the tea ship into harbor, lest they meet "the vengeance of a free people." The following week, "The MOHAWKS" promised to pay "an unwelcome visit" to anyone who helped to land the tea. The consignees agreed to resign their commissions in late November, and on December 1, they asked New York's governor to take responsibility for the tea when it landed. Whereas this proposal had failed in the Massachusetts Council, New York's more conservative Council agreed to it.[48]

Mass meetings in the State House Yard, as well as a number of printed pieces, helped mobilize Philadelphians against the Tea Act. A "Committee for Tarring and Feathering" threatened pilots with the mark of treason if they helped to bring in the tea ship. In Philadelphia as in Boston, the consignees tried their best to stall and delay, but eventually the firm of James & Drinker stood alone against the anger of local Sons of Liberty. On December 1, they, too, resigned their commissions. "Indeed," they later wrote, "no consideration would have induced us to have stood the Storm that has been raised." Far away in Charleston, South Carolina, the consignees in that town did the same. Only in Boston had the consignees, with the support of the governor, been able to hold firm against popular outrage at the Tea Act.[49]

Bostonians sensed the pressure from the other colonies. During the meeting of November 30, Samuel Adams had originally suggested a resolve that castigated Massachusetts merchants for having imported dutied tea and "justly incurred the Displeasure of the other Colonies," especially those at New York and Philadelphia. Adams saw this as "basely preferring their own private Interest to the general Good," but William Cooper moderated the language and the meeting only resolved that the merchants had "inadvertently" imported the dutied tea.[50]

The New Yorkers and Philadelphians still didn't quite trust the New Englanders—once bitten, twice shy. On December 13, the *Boston Gazette* printed a letter from Philadelphia, dated the 4th: "Our Tea Consignees have all resign'd, and you need not fear; the Tea will not be landed here or at New-York. All that we fear is, that you will shrink at Boston." The writer reminded Bostonians that they "have fail'd us in the Importation of Tea from London since the Non-importation Agreement, and we fear you will suffer this to be landed."[51]

William Palfrey, a close associate of John Hancock's, had left for New York and Philadelphia on December 1, to report the "regularity" of the proceedings of the "Body" meetings, as well as their "spirited and firm conduct." As Palfrey later told a correspondent, "Our Committee of Correspondence tho't proper to employ me to negociate certain business of an important Nature."[52] Palfrey reported that New Yorkers and Philadelphians were "highly pleas'd" with the Bostonians, who stood to "retrieve their almost expiring Credit" with the skeptical Sons of Liberty in these cities. He urged the Boston Sons to "strongly recommend a steady uniform conduct," and urged them not to make any promises that they couldn't keep. "For beleive me Sir, . . . If by any Means you should relax, or fall back in any degree from your late resolutions you will be a scorn & reproach among your Neighbours & never, never more be able to retreive the public Confidence." He concluded, "Now is the Time to convince the World that the People of Boston *can* Act with Virtue & resolution."[53]

Although the Bostonians had learned that New Yorkers and Philadelphians were preparing to reject the tea, the tea ships had not yet arrived in either port. As far as the people of Boston knew, they were the first port to face the test of what to do with the East India Company's tea.[54]

Francis Rotch was still worried that the tea crisis would ruin him. Accompanied by Captain Hall and a notary public, he went to Fort William and told the tea consignees he was ready to deliver their cargo. The exiles replied that they had no power to receive it, since the armed guard on board the *Dartmouth* and the "Body's" resolves against landing the tea made unloading impossible. Rotch asked for the bill of lading, which would release him from responsibility for the tea, and asked the consignees to pay his freight bill of over £91. The agents refused. When Captain Bruce made a similar trip four days later, he got the same answers. Both entered formal protests, so the record would show they tried their best to deliver the tea.[55]

On December 9th, the Committee of Correspondence summoned Rotch to remind him of his promise (though it was under duress) to send the *Dartmouth* back to England along with its cargo of tea. Rotch answered that although he had not asked for a permit from the customs officers, he had been led to believe that such a request would be denied. The committee suggested that he make the request anyway, but Rotch still delayed. On the 11th, the committee warned, "the People are greatly alarmed with the Report, that he [Rotch] is making no preparation for carrying his engage-ments . . . into execution." A delegation also visited John Rowe to make sure he was still with the Sons of Liberty.[56]

Four days before the deadline for the *Dartmouth* expired, the Boston Committee of Correspondence met to prepare for another meeting of the "Body." At 9 a.m. on December 13, they sequestered themselves with repre-sentatives from the five neighboring towns for a full day of meetings. They called forth Rotch. Rotch had sought legal advice from John Adams and another attorney, Sampson Salter Blowers, who probably told him that his vessel would be liable to seizure if it tried to leave the harbor without a clearance. Rotch complained that he had been under duress when he had made his earlier promise to return the tea, and "so terrified" that he would have promised them anything. No promise, he argued, could be valid under those circumstances. The committee decided, in response, that more duress was in order. They called another meeting of "the Body" for the next morning.[57]

The assemblage of people at the Old South Meeting House on Tuesday, the 14th, was the largest gathering yet, with people arriving from twenty miles' distance. This time the meeting appointed a suburbanite as moderator, Samuel P. Savage of Weston. Henry Bass, a member of the Loyal Nine who had married Savage's eldest daughter, had been one of the first to volunteer to guard the tea ships on November 29. The two corresponded regularly. Although Savage had previously been a selectman of Boston, his appointment may also have served to demonstrate that the countryside stood with the town. (Oddly, Savage's estranged brother was a customs officer for the port.) The meeting's leaders repeated the previous day's conversations with Rotch and Bruce for the crowd.[58]

Once again Rotch complained that he had only made his earlier promises "thro' Fear . . . he wold go as far as any reasonable Man should say that he ought for the Good of his Country, but he could not see the Justice or Patriotism of his being put in the Front of the Battle." He even proposed to bear a share of losing the vessel, if the local merchants were willing to appraise the doomed ship and pay for their share of the loss, too. As he had done in 1770, the lawyer Josiah Quincy once again played the moderate. He stood up and defended Rotch: "since this was a Business of public Concern," he said, "the People ought to be Sharers with him in the Loss of the Vessel." Quincy even pledged fifty guineas himself. Perhaps many in the crowd thought Quincy was being reasonable, but one person shouted out with the suggestion that Rotch had bribed Quincy to speak so finely. Quincy shot back, calling the man a "Scoundrel." Rotch said he was surprised no one else was willing to support his venture to return the tea.[59]

Finally Rotch agreed to request a clearance for the *Dartmouth*. A committee of ten would accompany him to make sure he kept his word. Samuel Adams was there, along with the trio of activist doctors, a handful of lawyers and merchants, the decorative painter Thomas Crafts Jr., and the distiller Thomas Chase (the last two were members of the Loyal Nine, coordinators of the Stamp Act protests of 1765). The committee escorted Rotch to the home of Richard Harrison, the port's collector.[60]

Harrison was no fan of the Boston Sons of Liberty. On June 10, 1768, Richard had accompanied his father (who was then Boston's collector) in the attempt to seize John Hancock's sloop *Liberty*. First the angry crowd threw dirt at them. Then came "Volleys of Stones, Brickbatts, Sticks or anything that came to hand." For 200 yards, Richard tried to shelter his father. The crowd knocked Richard down, grabbed him by his legs, arms, and hair, and dragged him through the filth of the gutter. The crowd went on to burn a pleasure boat belonging to the family. Richard Harrison had been about eighteen years old at the time.[61]

Rotch already knew what his answer would be, but he went through the motions. "I am obliged and compelled by a Body of people assembled at the old South Meeting House," the shipowner said, "at the utmost hazard and Peril of my life to demand of you a Clearance for the Ship *Dartmouth* to go to Sea in her present Situation with the Tea on Board." Harrison promised to make a decision by the following morning, so the "Body" adjourned to December 16, the last day before the *Dartmouth*'s deadline expired. That evening, Harrison sought out his colleague from the customs office, the Boston comptroller Robert Hallowell, whose house had been a target during the Stamp Act riots of 1765. Together, the two customs officers determined that Harrison had no authority to give Rotch clearance for an illegal voyage, since he had failed to unload his tea. Harrison told Rotch and his escorts as much the following day, and denied the request for a clearance. Without a customs clearance, Rotch could not legally leave the harbor.[62]

Thursday, December 16, was the last day that Boston's leaders could call people together to speak out against the East India Company's tea. It was possible that just a minute after midnight that night, as December 17 began, officers from the customhouse, backed by armed forces, would swoop down on the three ships at Griffin's Wharf and land the tea. If they did that, the duty on the tea would be paid, the revenue would pay the salaries of Governor Hutchinson and other civil officials, local merchants would be undersold by the Company, and any chance at colonial unity would be lost. Although the payment of customs duties on one tea shipment might seem to be a small matter, the radicalized Americans in Boston and the other seaports saw the successful execution of the Tea Act as an affront to their liberty.

A cold rain was falling over Boston. Once again, thousands of people packed the Old South Meeting House. It was 10 a.m. Many had come through muck and mud and miserable weather from the countryside. Samuel P. Savage of Weston once again stood at the head of the meeting. Speakers informed the people that the customhouse had denied Rotch his clearance and his pass. The Bostonians had rejected the idea of storing the tea on land—either because this solution was illegal or because they didn't trust the consignees and the governor not to secretly remove the tea from storage. There was only one more person in Massachusetts whose authority could override Harrison's decision and allow the tea ships to return to London: the governor, Thomas Hutchinson. If he refused, then one of three things would happen: the consignees would unload the tea and store it in Boston, customs officers would seize the tea and sell it at auction, or the tea would have to be destroyed. If either of the first two things happened, the tea would likely be sold and the customs duty would likely be paid. So the "Body" instructed Rotch to ask the governor to allow the *Dartmouth* to leave Boston harbor.[63]

Rotch began his seven-mile journey to Milton, the town south of Boston where Hutchinson had his country home. The meeting adjourned until 3 p.m., which was thought to be enough time for Rotch to get to Milton and back. The muddy roads must have been a nightmare. As he wiped the cold and damp from his face, Rotch must have felt frustration, dread, and perhaps only a faint flicker of hope that the governor would bend the rules for him in his miserable situation. He did not return until just before the gloomy day gave way to night.

CHAPTER 6

The Destroyers at Griffin's Wharf

I see the clouds which now rise thick and fast on the horizon; the thunders roll, and the lightnings play, and to that God who rides on the whirlwind and directs the storm I commit my country.

Josiah Quincy, December 16, 1773[1]

We can imagine the men's excitement and anxiety filling the room as their arteries pulsed with anticipation. According to later tales, they were gathered at various locations across town: above the offices of the *Boston Gazette*, under the boughs of Liberty Tree, in a carpenter's living room, in a cabinet-maker's shop, atop Fort Hill overlooking the harbor, and in a dozen other places across the city. Painted and cloaked, they waited for a signal, hefted their tools and weapons, and looked at one another. Perhaps some were nervous. Perhaps others were grimly resolute. Perhaps the nervous ones took courage from the men who hid their anxieties better. Perhaps all of them took comfort from being part of something larger.[2]

The Boston-area Sons of Liberty—plotters whose identities we'll never know—must have anticipated what Hutchinson would say. So they hatched what Hutchinson later called a "concerted plan" to go down to Griffin's Wharf, board the three ships that were anchored in the harbor, and destroy the tea. They determined that it would take a few dozen men with knowledge of how to unload a ship, and so the men who signed on for the task included a mix of traders and craftsmen. Each man would disguise himself as an Indian and swear an oath of secrecy, to be sure their identities would remain secure. Everyone agreed on the ground rules: no one would steal or vandalize any property except the tea itself, and no one would commit any violence or mayhem. If the destroyers worked quickly and efficiently, the job would only take two or three hours.[3]

This small band of rebels was preparing for a defiant act against a distant government and its pet corporation. As night crept up on

December 16, these men smudged their faces with soot, charcoal, paint, lampblack, or grease. They wrapped blankets and shawls around their clothing. They rehearsed their coded signals and chose their leaders.

Women later told their grandchildren about the way they helped men prepare for the Tea Party. James Brewer, a pump and blockmaker in Summer Street, gathered friends at his house so his wife and daughter could spread burnt cork over their faces.[4] But not every rebel confided in his family: the twenty-three-year-old merchant Joseph Pearse Palmer kept the plot so secret from his wife Elizabeth that she thought he was out with his club that night.[5]

Some masters encouraged their apprentices to attend, while others prevented them from leaving the house. The blacksmith's apprentice Joshua Wyeth, age fifteen at the time, remembered fifty years later that "a paper was handed around in a very confidential manner," ordering the men to be ready to destroy the tea. Wyeth said "that he came to the knowledge of it from his master who ever placed particular confidence in him." Six years after giving this account, Wyeth said "that most of the persons selected for occasion were apprentices and journeymen; not a few of them . . . living with tory [pro-government] masters." Thirteen-year-old Peter Slater, for instance, was apprenticed to a ropemaker who locked Slater in his room to prevent him from joining up. Slater had to slip out the window to join the rebels. Before Samuel Peck went off to the tea ships, he ordered his journeymen and apprentices to stay home all evening. But the apprentices were too curious to obey. Some masters granted permission: the laborer Robert Sessions, age twenty-one, "went immediately to the spot"—that is, Griffin's Wharf—after hearing that the tea was being destroyed. Master carpenter Thomas Crafts Sr. helped his twenty-year-old apprentice, Amos Lincoln, find an Indian disguise, and then he sank to his knees and prayed for his safety.[6]

Over at the Long Room above the *Boston Gazette* printing press, the printer Benjamin Edes's son Peter kept the punch bowl filled for the so-called "Mohawks" there. In those days, alcohol was thought to give a man strength, and the men would need it that night.[7]

It was time to solve the tea problem once and for all. As Thomas Jefferson would say, months afterward, "An exasperated people, who feel that they possess power, are not easily restrained within limits strictly regular."[8]

Francis Rotch arrived at Hutchinson's house on Unquity Hill in rural Milton, Massachusetts, as evening fell on December 16, only to get the answer he expected. No ship could pass Castle Island without a permit from the governor, and technically the governor could not grant a permit for any ship that hadn't been properly cleared at the customhouse. Would

Hutchinson be willing to grant a permit anyway? Hutchinson replied, "he could not think it his Duty in this Case and therefore should not." (A newspaper scribbler later called this a "fallacy," claiming that Hutchinson had granted such permits in the past.)[9]

Hutchinson then asked, what did Rotch think the people would do with the tea? Rotch "supposed they had no other Intention than forcing it back to England." Rotch thought that extreme measures were unlikely, and so he hatched a hypothetical plan: perhaps he could send the *Dartmouth* away from the wharf without a permit. At that point, Alexander Leslie, the commander at Fort William, could fire a warning shot to stop the ship. The *Dartmouth* would then fall under the protection of the Navy or return to the wharf (Rotch wasn't clear what he thought would happen next). Then the assembled protesters at the Old South Meeting House could "say they had done all in their power," and the crisis would be over. In other words, Hutchinson and Rotch just needed to stage this bit of theater, and then Rotch could land the tea. But there were problems with this plan. First, Rotch would never be able to hire any seamen willing to man the *Dartmouth* unless the ship was really returning to London. Second, neither Hutchinson nor Rotch could be sure that the Boston Sons of Liberty would go along with a fake attempt to depart that resulted in the ship being seized. Hutchinson tried to offer Rotch the protection of the Royal Navy, but Rotch refused: if he had accepted the offer, he later explained, "his life would have been in Danger." Rotch paid his respects to the governor and made his way back down Unquity Hill. He set off for Boston to see what the Fates had spun for him.[10]

In Boston, the "Body of the People" had reconvened at 3 p.m. at the Old South Meeting House. Rotch was still in transit, so the locals found ways to keep busy. First, they discussed the measures that certain neighboring towns had passed to prevent the drinking of tea. That day's *Massachusetts Spy* had reported on the town of Lexington, which had "unanimously resolved against the use of Bohea tea of all sorts, Dutch or English importation." To show their sincerity, they brought together every ounce of tea in the town and made a bonfire of it. The *Spy* went on to report that Charlestown was likely to follow the Lexington example, and the editor had suggested that Massachusetts town selectmen ought to deny liquor licenses to any tavern or inn that served tea. The examples of Lexington and Charlestown held a clear lesson: true patriots would rather destroy tea, despite its temptations, rather than buy it at a time when drinking tea might support a monopoly or parliamentary despotism.[11]

The "Body of the People" had no power over the selectmen of any town, but they still passed a resolution "that the use of Tea is improper and pernicious," and they hoped the official town meetings would follow suit. The "Body" also urged other Massachusetts towns to form committees of inspection to prevent the importation of "detested Tea." All this was well and good, but what about the thousands of pounds of tea in the holds of the ships down by Griffin's Wharf? By 4 p.m., some of the meeting's attendees were getting restless. Someone moved that the meeting should be dissolved so people could go about their business. Here a group of the out-of-towners stood up, saying "that their several Towns were so very anxious to have full information as to this matter." Boston's visitors would be happy to stick around for two more hours, they said. As the light dimmed, candles were lit. The flames guttered and licked the air, and thousands shuffled and waited in the Old South Meeting House. Meanwhile, a few "gentlemen" suggested to Captain Hall of the *Dartmouth* that he'd better haul his ship away from the wharf. People knew something was about to happen.[12]

Rotch finally returned from Milton sometime before 6 p.m., and reported the bad news to those assembled. The "prodigious shouts" that greeted Rotch were so loud that the merchant John Andrews heard them from two blocks away. The meeting asked Rotch, would he order the *Dartmouth* to return to London with the tea on board? Rotch answered (again) that he couldn't possibly do so without ruining himself. Would he land the tea, then? No, Rotch said, since the consignees wouldn't accept their cargo. That was the nub of the problem: Rotch could take the tea neither backwards nor forwards—all he could do was wait in misery for the morrow, when customs officers were scheduled to seize his ship. Dr. Thomas Young, one of the radical leaders, pronounced Rotch "a good man who had done all in his power to gratify the people." Rotch was hardly to blame for the stubbornness of Hutchinson and the consignees; the people should "do no hurt to his person or property." Rotch should be left unharmed, but the same could not necessarily be said for the tea aboard his ship.[13]

Either at this meeting or a previous one, the people in the Old South Meeting House's gallery had called out a number of suggestions about what to do with the tea. One person said they should haul the ships up to the Boston Common and "burn Tea and all together," or at least just the tea. "There were enough of 'em to do it and it would take but little Time." Another person shouted out, "Let us take our Axes and Chissels and split the Boxes and throw their Contents into the Harbor!" He then added, "then we shall have Tea enough without paying any Duty." The crowd cheered at this, but the meeting's leaders were smart enough not to introduce any motions to this effect, nor did they record these suggestions in the newspaper accounts of the meeting.[14]

Since the meeting had already agreed that the tea should not be landed, and since the governor was refusing to let the tea leave the harbor, everyone now understood that the destruction of the tea was the last alternative. Josiah Quincy, his body slowly being ravaged by tuberculosis, warned the assembled people, "Whoever supposes that shouts and hossannas will terminate the trials of the day, entertains a childish fancy." Quincy encouraged standing tall against the East India Company and the British Empire. But he also warned that a tough stance would invite "the sharpest conflicts." No one ever struggled for liberty without stirring up a hornet's nest. Their enemies, near and far, were too powerful, and too malicious to lie down without a fight. "Let us consider the issue," he urged. "Let us weigh & consider before we advance," lest the Bostonians and their allies "bring on the most trying & terrible struggle this country ever saw."[15]

At this the colony's treasurer, Harrison Gray, stood up to warn Quincy about some of his intemperate language. The British government would tolerate it no longer, Gray said, and would deal out punishment to the offenders. Quincy, suspecting that Gray aimed to "terrify and intimidate," brushed off any such warning. "Personally, perhaps, I have less concern than any one present in the crisis which is approaching. The seeds of dissolution are thickly planted in my constitution. They must soon ripen." Even as the audience sympathized with the ailing Quincy, no one would have missed his reference to the British constitution, which was just as much in crisis. Tea would be the source of the colonies' dissolution, unless the people of greater Boston did something to stop it.[16]

Samuel Adams now said "that he could think of nothing further to be done—that they had now done all they could for the Salvation of their Country." Rotch, he said, should "go Home, set down and make himself as easy as he could." The meeting even voted Rotch's conduct "satisfactory to them."[17] In the end, the "Body of the People" decided that they had displayed "exemplary patience and caution," and done everything possible to try and prevent their own enslavement, without damaging the tea. It was the fault of the greedy consignees and their allies, the meeting said, if the community degenerated into "violent commotions."[18]

At that moment, the "Body of the People" was formally abandoning any role in handling the tea crisis. Back in November, when the tea had arrived, the Boston selectmen and the town meeting had similarly shrugged off responsibility for the fate of the tea. Now, it seemed, the "Body of the People" and their leaders were preparing to step back as well.

When Rotch had first announced the failure of his errand, those standing in the western end of the church began to notice that "many People" had begun melting away to the exits. It's possible that a few of them were runners dispatched to the groups of men who were putting on disguises throughout the town. Those runners would have gasped out the news: Rotch would not send his ship back to London.[19]

Fifteen minutes later, the war-whoops began. A new party of men now arriving on the scene had resolved to execute the plan of last resort. They were not part of an assembly, official or unofficial. They were not debaters or deliberators. They were destroyers.

Those inside the Old South Meeting House first heard a "War Whoop" from "a number of persons, supposed to be the Aboriginal Natives from their complection," who had approached the church door (fig. 18). This was "a band of eighteen or twenty young men, who had been prepared for the event," though to one observer it sounded like the noise of a hundred people (another person guessed it was two or three hundred people). The band of newcomers made Indian noises and whistled like boatswains— signals that the Boston crowd had used in the past. A few people in the galleries echoed the whoop. Some exclaimed, "The Mohawks are come!" while others cried out, "A mob! A mob!" Two or three hundred more people from the assembly streamed out of the exits before the moderator could restore order.[20]

The "Body of the People" may have done "all they could," but now a new, separate group of "Mohawks" was stepping up to confront the tea crisis. These "Mohawks" may have coordinated with leading Sons of Liberty like Samuel Adams or Thomas Young beforehand. Almost fifty years later, a newspaper reported, "Mr. Samuel Adams is thought to have been in the counseling of this exploit and many other men who were leaders in the political affairs of the times." Two of the destroyers, Thompson Maxwell and Joshua Wyeth, later asserted that John Hancock had summoned them to the Tea Party earlier that day, but there is no proof of this. Regardless, observers at the time were meant to think that the "Mohawks" were a new group of outsiders, separate from the assembly at the Old South Meeting House. This distinction gave Adams, Young, Warren, and the other speakers a way to disavow responsibility for what was about to happen. The "Mohawks" were not part of the "Body," which was in turn an unoffi-cial gathering rather than an official town meeting. As long as these "Mohawks" wore their disguises while they set about destroying the tea, there would be no one the authorities could blame. Although the meeting

18 In this twentieth-century mural, men disguised as Indians enter the Old South Meeting House as the meeting of the "Body of the People" on December 16, 1773, began to dissolve.

had not yet officially dissolved, pandemonium was eating away at its edges. The last thing the shoemaker George Robert Twelves Hewes remembered hearing was John Hancock crying out, "*let every man do what is right in his own eyes!*" Others said, "Let every man do his duty, and be true to his country." The leather dresser Adam Colson supposedly shouted, "Boston Harbor a tea-pot this night!" and "Hurra for Griffin's Wharf!" Benjamin Simpson heard someone shout, "Every man to his tent!" from the gallery.[21]

Samuel Adams, John Hancock, Thomas Young, and a few other leaders tried to call for "order and regularity." As one observer later wrote, "silence was commanded, and a prudent and peaceable deportment again enjoined." To stall for time, Adams asked Dr. Young to make a speech—and Young was able to use up fifteen or twenty minutes. He attacked "the ill Effects of Tea on the Constitution," and called on his countrymen to stop using it. He also made sure to remind the attendees that they should be virtuous, "standing by each other in Case any should be called to an Account for their Proceedings."[22]

With the carnival of commotion outside the church, the giddy crowd wouldn't have been able to stay still much longer. When Savage finally dissolved the meeting, a "general shout" resounded inside and outside the church, followed by three cheers. The shouting, plus the noise of over 5,000 excited people rumbling out of the building, led John Andrews to remark, "you'd [have] thought that the inhabitants of the infernal regions had broke loose." Andrews "contentedly" stepped out to finish a cup of tea he'd left steaming at home. Between fifty and a hundred people stayed at the meetinghouse for a while, including the meeting's principal leaders: Adams, Hancock, Cooper, Scollay, John Pitts, Young, and Warren. They stayed visibly away from the doings down on Griffin's Wharf, so that no one could later accuse them of having participated in any illegal acts. The meeting's leaders were anxious to dissociate the proceedings at the Old South Meeting House from the activities down by the water.[23]

The cheers buoyed the crowd. Hutchinson later wrote that the disguised men "were surrounded by a vast body of people" who had come en masse from the meeting. Despite the winter chill, a multitude of people now crushed and jostled each other on the way to Griffin's Wharf to see what would happen. The new moon, little more than a sliver, was setting over Boston harbor. Yet "Everything was as light as day," Robert Sessions remembered, "by the means of lamps and torches; a pin might be seen lying on the wharf." For such a large crowd of spectators—at least a thousand or two—people were surprisingly silent. One participant recalled that the onlookers "crowded about so as to be much in our way," but few words were exchanged. John Adams wrote that the town was as still and calm as if it were a Sabbath's eve. Of course, it was in the Bostonians' interests to say that everything was churchly and quiet.[24]

The fearsome warships of the British Royal Navy were anchored in the harbor, and a garrison of British troops was only a short distance away, at Fort William on Castle Island. Would the troops and ships act to protect the pungent cargo that was stored in three smaller ships beside the wharf? As one newspaper reported, everyone "expected that the men of war would have interfered." The captains and officers had all been ordered aboard the warships the night before; the admiral had ordered lanterns brought aboard his flagship; and several armed schooners were rigged and fitted for action.[25]

Lieutenant Colonel Alexander Leslie of the 64th Regiment, who commanded the forces at Castle William, later reported, "I had the Regiment ready to take their Arms, had they been called upon," but "the Council would not agree to the Troops going to Town." As for Admiral John Montagu, he wrote "that during the whole of this transaction neither the Govr Magistrates, Owners or the Revenue Officers of this place ever called for my Assistance." He added, "If they had, I could easily have prevented the execution of this plan but must have endangered the Lives of many innocent People by firing upon the Town."[26] Instead, lacking orders from the governor and his Council, the troops and the warships did nothing. Most of the men boarding the tea ships probably knew that Hutchinson, far away in Milton, had neither the time nor the political clout to order the armed forces to intervene. But they could not be certain.

In the end, the warships and the troops remained still, even though, as one of the exiled customs commissioners wrote, the Tea Party's "threats and noise were heard very plain at Castle William." The commissioners later reported that "the Body of the People who had been at the Meeting" acted "as a Guard" for the perpetrators on board the ships. In other words, the crowd was a "covering party" that protected the tea destroyers, making military interdiction impossible. The British were smart enough not to provoke more bloodshed. The Bostonians would be safe—for the time being.[27]

Danger or no danger, the men aboard the ships had determined to carry out their plan of action, which they saw as a last resort. Their timing was important. A supportive observer wrote that "The Savages . . . began their ravage previous to the dissolution of the meeting." This supporter was trying to show that the meeting and the "Mohawks" were separate groups. Thomas Hutchinson, when he published the third volume of his history of Massachusetts, wrote that the tea destroyers had appeared on Griffin's Wharf even before Rotch returned from Milton—an accusation that was probably false. Hutchinson was hoping to demonstrate that the Sons of Liberty had never intended to negotiate in the first place.[28]

In the dim light, the crowd saw that dozens of men had already threaded their way to the dock. Two hundred of them had mustered on Fort Hill and then marched two by two to Griffin's Wharf. According to one legend, two of these men came upon a British officer, who unsheathed his sword. "One of the *Indians* drew a pistol, and said to the officer: 'The path is wide enough for us all; we have nothing to do with you and intend you no harm—if you will keep your own way peaceably, we shall keep ours.' "[29]

Some of the party apparently had elaborate disguises, some wore slight disguises, and some wore none at all. Many were armed—some with "Clubs, Sticks or Cutlasses," and at least some with firearms. With silent precision, the men spread out into three groups and began crawling all over the ships.[30]

The people of Boston and the surrounding towns had struggled and debated for weeks over the issue of the tea. Now a band of so-called "Mohawks" had formed and made the decision to destroy the East India Company's cargo. They would drown the tea rather than pay an unjust tax. As the crowd watched apprehensively, the destroyers began their work. In Boston's chilly darkness, with the tide beginning to flow, the tea destroyers showed the crowd how a group of vigilant Americans could band together to challenge tyranny.[31]

No one there by the water could have anticipated that the American Revolution was being set in motion that night. Yet the crowd surely understood it was witness to the resurgence of a revolutionary movement. Beneath the disguises, the destroyers were mostly craftsmen, but the men boarding the ships also included merchants and political leaders, laborers and apprentices from Boston and beyond. These men, from almost all walks of life, were acting together to dispose of the tea. They called out a ringing challenge to authority, rather than meekly submitting to the whim of royal officials and stubborn consignees.

Ebenezer Stevens, a twenty-one-year-old carpenter who was destined to be a general in the Revolutionary War, was preparing to board the *Dartmouth*. Suddenly he realized his future brother-in-law, Alexander Hodgdon, was the ship's mate. To keep his identity hidden from Hodgdon and the rest of the ship's crew, Stevens switched to a different vessel.[32] Once he had safely left, the rest of the men boarded the *Dartmouth* and warned Hodgdon "to get out of the way." Then the group confronted William Elliot and George Lilly, the tidewaiters the customs office had assigned to monitor the *Dartmouth* when it arrived in Boston. These "Mohawks" asked Elliot and Lilly who they were. When they answered that they were customs officers on duty, "some Persons then came forward and ordered them to depart, (or they would certainly lose their Lives)." The same scene was repeated on each ship. Aboard the *Eleanor*, the tea group's leader "in a very stern and resolute manner" ordered the captain and crew to open the hatchways and hand over the hoisting tackle and ropes. Captain Bruce asked what the men intended to do. The commander replied that they were there to unload the tea, and they ordered the captain and crew below decks, assuring them that no harm would befall them. "They instantly obeyed without murmurs and threats." The tide-waiters, meanwhile, slinked away to watch the entire event from the wharves "by mixing with the Crowd as indifferent Persons."[33]

When the Tea Party men boarded the *Beaver*, Captain Hezekiah Coffin protested. Because of the smallpox scare, his vessel had only just arrived at the wharf the day before, and they had not yet had time to unload all their cargo. He "begged they would not begin with his vessel, as the tea was covered with goods, belonging to different merchants in town." Coffin asked the boarders not to damage anything other than the tea. Lendall Pitts, the destroyers' commander aboard the *Beaver*, may have replied it was "the tea they wanted, and the tea they would have." If Coffin "would go into his cabin quietly," he said, "not one article of his goods should be hurt." Pitts then sent a man to the brig's cabin to politely ask the ship's mate for some candles along with the keys to the hatches, "so that as little damage as possible might be done to the vessel." The mate handed over the keys without a word, and sent his cabin boy for candles to help the boarders light their way.[34]

As working men in a port town, the boarders knew their way around a ship's deck. In 1788, a Roxbury historian wrote that the disguised Indians were "chiefly masters of vessels and ship-builders from the north end of town." Indeed, James Brewer was a pump and blockmaker, Gilbert Colesworthy a caulker, and Samuel Nowell a boat builder and ship carpenter. But even aside from these maritime craftsmen, many of the destroyers, as sons of coastal New England, had spent their lives around wharves and aboard ships as seafarers and fishermen. They knew how to sift through cargo, lift it above decks, and offload it. Just like the old hands they were, they whistled signals to one another. According to one source, "a considerable number of sailors, and some others, joined them from time to time, and aided in hoisting the chests from the hold."[35]

Each man had a duty; as Hutchinson observed, this was "a concerted plan." Some broke open (or borrowed the keys and opened) the hatchways and jumped into the hold. Others had fixed tackle, and once the men in the hold affixed the chests to the hoists, the men on deck began to haul the chests of tea upward. "No noise was heard except the occasional clink of the hatchet in opening the boxes," Samuel Cooper (not the minister) later told his son. In reality the crash of axes on splintering wood probably made a bit more noise than that. The men on deck hefted their tools, knocked the tops and bindings off the chests, and smashed the chests to pieces (a difficult task, according to one account, because the crates were covered in canvas). "Others raised them to the railing, and discharged their contents overboard," remembered Wyeth, the blacksmith's apprentice. "I never labored harder in my life."[36]

According to an unfriendly observer, a number of men were "watching for Spies." Another source, who supported the destroyers, clarified that the watch "was stationed to prevent embezzlement, and not a single ounce of Tea was suffered to be purloined or carried off." Indeed, one man armed with a musket "swore he would shoot any Person that offered to touch the Tea." Wyeth said that there were at least five sentries, and they were unarmed: one at the head of the wharf, one in the middle, and one in the bow of each ship. "Our object in stationing the sentries, was to communicate information, in case we were likely to be detected by the civil or military power. They were charged, to give us notice, in case any known tory came down to the wharf. But our main dependence was on the general good will of the people."[37]

The sentries actually did catch one or two offenders aboard the *Beaver*—men who couldn't resist the rich smell of all that pricey tea. A long-legged Charlestown horse renter of Irish descent by the name of Charles Conner originally "pretended . . . to be particularly zealous in the good work." But Hewes noticed him subtly slipping his hands into his clothes, stuffing his pockets with tea. Hewes reported this to Pitts, his commander, and Conner tried to slip away, but the men raised the cry of "*East Indian!*" and Hewes went after him. A group of the destroyers tore off some (or possibly all) of Conner's clothes, coated him with mud, and gave him "a severe bruising." As Conner retreated up the wharf, the throng of onlookers "cuffed and kicked him as he passed." Indeed, Andrews wrote, "nothing but their utter aversion to make *any* disturbance prevented his being tar'd and feather'd." The Reverend Samuel Cooper called it "A remarkable instance of order and justice among savages." The next day someone nailed the skirt of Conner's coat to a whipping post in Charlestown, and attached a note explaining the "popular indignation" that had occasioned his disgrace. The tea men had made their point: this was supposed to be a mission of destruction, not a free-for-all for looters.[38]

John Hooton, then a nineteen-year-old oarmaker's apprentice, remembered a man in a small boat rowing near one of the tea ships to try to steal some of the tea. He and three or four other North Enders "jumped over and beat up the poor man's canoe from under him in the twinkling of an eye."[39]

The Mohawks went first to the *Dartmouth*, where they "hoisted out the Chests of Tea, and when upon Deck stove the Chests and emptied their Tea overboard." Once finished, they proceeded to the *Eleanor*, then the *Beaver* (though other accounts later said that the work aboard these ships had already begun). Over the next two or three hours, the tea destroyers undertook the hard work of an eighteenth-century stevedore. Each of the full-sized tea chests weighed about 400 pounds, and there were 340 chests (including smaller chests of more expensive tea) in the holds of the three ships. Block and tackle made the hauling easier, but it was still hard work. The ropes groaned and stretched with the weight of the heavy tea crates filled with Bohea, Congou, Singlo, Souchong, and Hyson. Decks creaked with the sounds of the men's boots. It took muscle and know-how to swing an axe into a chest of tea with that much efficiency, and the hatchets crunched and smashed the tea crates, an irrevocable act of chaos and destruction that must have given the men a frisson of excitement and foreboding. The destroyers then shoveled the tea over the sides of the ship, and threw the broken chests after it (fig. 19). There must have been a satisfying plunk, slap, hiss as the clumps of tea made contact with the water, loose leaves spiraling downward like apple blossoms in the spring or a tree's fading foliage in the fall.[40]

Though observers expected a noisy, riotous affair, the Mohawks worked quietly, without clamor or chatter. "We were merry in an under tone," Joshua

Americans throwing the Cargoes of the Tea Ships into the River, at Boston

19 Disguised men wield axes and empty the tea chests into the water, as spectators observe from the Boston wharves. This print has some inaccuracies: there is no evidence that the destroyers were bare-chested, nor that anyone carried away tea chests in small boats.

Wyeth remembered, "at the idea of making so large a cup of tea for the fishes." They were as still as could be. They were so careful not to damage anything other than the tea that they swept the ship's decks and even replaced a broken padlock. The boarders even called up the ships' mates "to report whether every thing (except the tea, of course) was left as they found it." Even Hutchinson had to admit that the whole affair was "conducted with very little tumult."[41]

Since the tide was extremely low—perhaps fourteen feet below high water—the ships were riding in only a couple feet of water. As the Mohawks dumped the tea over the side, the leaves piled so high off the sea bottom that they spilled over the gunwales. Some unscrupulous folks tried to row by in small boats to pocket tea for themselves, but the watch ordered them away. To solve this problem, the commanders ordered apprentices like Henry Purkitt and Edmund Dolbeare to wade into the tidal flats, break up the piles of crate fragments and loose tea, and stir them into the shallow water or stamp them into the mud. Other apprentices stood aboard the ships and used poles to break up the clumps. The harbor had become a teapot indeed.[42]

The work went smoothly until suddenly a hoist collapsed under the strain of so many heavy crates being hauled up in rapid succession. When rigging snapped on a ship, the results were often fatal—a taut rope or a spike of wood could maim or kill someone if it lashed out in the wrong direction. In this case a chest struck carpenter John Crane while he was working in the hold and knocked him senseless. His friends, thinking he'd been killed, carried him to a woodshop nearby and hid his body under a pile of shavings. They hurried back to finish dumping the tea, and went to recover the body hours later when everyone had gone home. They found Crane still breathing, dazed but alive.[43]

The destroyers were heaving more than 90,000 pounds of tea over the side of the ship—physically demanding work. "I was then young, enterprising and courageous," Samuel Nowell later stated in a petition to Congress. "And I presume my broad axe was never more dexterously used than while I was staving the Chests and throwing them overboard."[44]

How many people participated in the Boston Tea Party? There is no way to know for sure, and the reports vary. One participant later recalled that there were between 100 and 150 "more or less actively engaged": either aboard the ships or keeping watch on the wharf. The master, mate, and boatswain of the *Beaver* said that about forty people boarded the brigantine (the smallest of the three vessels). Some accounts indicate that bystanders wandered on and off the tea ships freely, which would make the numbers hard to pin down. Other accounts portray a tightly controlled, almost military operation, where such milling about would have been intolerable. Still, it seems there were opportunities for some of the bystanders to participate in the action as it unfolded.[45]

Who led the way? Who was taking orders? Who joined the Tea Party on the spot? And why were all these men motivated to join? Even today, the answers to these questions are elusive. The apprentice Joshua Wyeth remembered that the men had "pledged our honor, that we would not reveal our secret." Over two hundred years later, this sworn secrecy largely still holds. Beginning in the 1820s and 1830s, a few men told tales of taking part in the Tea Party. Most of the participants had died by then, but spouses, children, and other witnesses filled in the gaps left by the deceased. Most of these stories are impossible to verify. Nevertheless, these fragmented accounts hint at the names of over a hundred men who supposedly participated in the Boston Tea Party. Although a few of these names should be struck from the list due to contrary evidence, the names of ninety-nine likely Tea Party participants, all mentioned before 1853, remain. After 1853, there were few people alive who could prove or disprove a claim to Tea Party participation, and so we are left with a list that, though imperfect, at least eliminates the stalest or most implausible names.[46]

Most surviving accounts left little indication of why the men had joined the Tea Party. Yet the men's age, station in life, and associations offer clues about the Tea Party men's connections to one another, and answers to why they boarded the tea ships. Many of the men had strong ties to Boston's most politically active groups, and so they well understood the constitutional objections to the Tea Act. Their destruction of the tea was an informed argument against taxation without representation, government-sponsored monopolies, and interference with the Massachusetts Charter. These men probably understood the pressures from the Sons of Liberty in New York City and Philadelphia, and they knew something had to be done about the tea. If they failed to resist the temptations of the Tea Act that evening, they would be little better than slaves to a corrupt British ministry. All of the men aboard the ships probably shared these fears and principles to some degree, and all of them agreed on the need for action.

Some joined the Tea Party because of their social relationships. They may not have been the most politically active men on the block, but they were connected to—and persuaded by—relatives, neighbors, employers, and other associates who wanted to protest the Tea Act. Witnesses to the landing of British troops in 1768 and the Boston Massacre of 1770, angry at Hutchinson and his cronies, and accustomed to working together—in organized meetings and in the streets—these men were ready to translate the town's complaints into action, and they took the opportunity to make a bold statement. A sense of loyalty and camaraderie motivated them, along with a general sense of grievance that Parliament's obnoxious impositions had exacerbated the economic hardship of trying to earn a living in Boston. Finally, the visceral thrill and excitement of destroying so much valuable property must have appealed to many of the participants, particularly the younger men and boys.

The men chose a commander and boatswain for each of the three boarding parties, who helped direct the offloading of the tea. According to one memoir, the leaders were the merchant Lendall Pitts aboard the *Beaver*, the insurer Nathaniel Barber, and the lemon importer Edward Proctor. Pitts was a member of Hancock's Cadets, Barber was captain of the North Battery, and Proctor was captain of a militia company, so all three had some familiarity with organizing men in formation. Pitts had a father on the Provincial Council and a brother on the town's Board of Selectmen. Proctor was at the forefront of confrontations with importers and customs informers in 1770; a satirist called him "a retailer of lemons and Oliverian principles" (after Oliver Cromwell). He was one of the town's firewards and wardens, a member of the North End Caucus, and he had commanded the first watch aboard the *Dartmouth* on November 29. Barber was a member of the Boston Committee of Correspondence and had led several meetings of the North End Caucus. Ever since the radical events of the 1760s, he had begun naming his children after his heroes: the London radical John Wilkes, Oliver Cromwell, and the sympathetic historian Catharine Macaulay. A 1775 satire said Barber was "remarkable for bullying and rioting." These were local leaders, men of acute political awareness with experience in militia musters and in the streets.[47]

Other names among the supposed Tea Party participants stand out as leaders of radical Boston. As Henry Bromfield, a supporter of the consignees, wrote, "The who[le] Affair was conducted with the greatest dispatch, Regularity & Management, so as to evidence that there were People of Sense & of more discernment than the Vulgar among the Actors." Barber, Proctor, and William Molineux had led the crowd from Liberty Tree to the Clarkes' warehouse on November 3. There's no evidence that they lingered at the Old South Meeting House with Adams, Hancock, and the others, which lends credence to the claims that they were busy boarding the tea ships instead. Benjamin Edes, the radical printer, and the distiller Thomas Chase were both members of the Loyal Nine, the group that had helped arrange the Stamp Act protests, and they may have helped plan the tea action as well.[48]

Others, by virtue of their jobs as merchants or professionals, commanded respect from those aboard the ship: young merchants like nineteen-year-old James Swan or twenty-seven-year-old Stephen Bruce, a professional like Dr. Elisha Story, and two college graduates: the merchant Thomas Melvill had a B.A. from the College of New Jersey in Princeton and an M.A. from Harvard College, and Joseph Pearse Palmer had a B.A. from Harvard. Many of these men had been born into prestigious families and were destined to start life a step ahead; as a nineteenth-century historian wrote, the young men were "dressed, and armed, and painted like Indians; though it was said that many a ruffled shirt, and laced vest, appeared under their blankets." But not all of the leaders were so lace-ruffled: the poor shoemaker Ebenezer Mackintosh, who had led the Stamp Act crowds in 1765, later told a young boy in New Hampshire that "It was my chickens that did the job" at Griffin's Wharf in 1773. Boston offered multiple avenues toward respect: wealth and education gave some men pride of place, while Mackintosh's experience as a crowd organizer had earned him trust in certain circles.[49]

These leaders relied upon a network of dependable allies from the middling and lower ranks to help them execute a variety of political activities. On election days or at the town meetings, these men lent their votes and voices. When it came time to rough up a customs man, the crowds were ready. On the night of the Tea Party, these were the men who lent their eyes and ears, their strong backs, and their still tongues. Many of them had experience with anti-government protests over the years—the Tea Party men included veterans of the Stamp Act riots of 1765, the confrontations with Ebenezer Richardson or the soldiers in 1770, and the harassment of the customs commissioners earlier in 1773. Had leaders like Proctor and Adams, Warren and Mackintosh persuaded these men to risk joining the Tea Party—and if so, how? Why did artisans, laborers, and apprentices feel motivated to join the uprising against the Tea Act?

A number of Boston men had proven themselves reliable to the Sons of Liberty. They held positions of minor importance in the local economy, town government, the militia, voluntary associations, and political groups. These associations were important: as Hutchinson once complained, "we have no sort of Company but what look upon it they have a right to do something or other in Publick affairs." Indeed, on December 3, the members of fire engine company number one had pledged to oppose the Tea Act. Paul Revere had demonstrated his commitment time and again, by engraving political prints or celebratory punch bowls, by participating in political committees, and as a leader in St. Andrew's Lodge of Freemasons. Ship joiner Thomas Urann was a fifty-year-old fire engine company master, a senior officer in St. Andrew's Lodge, and a member of the North End Caucus with Revere. They would have known several of their fellow Tea Party participants through these organizations. These were the types of men who either had long-standing connections to the leading Sons of Liberty, or joined resistance groups after becoming radicalized.[50]

All in all, at least a third of the North End Caucus had either kept watch aboard the tea ships in late November, helped lead the "Body" meetings, or were later said to have actively participated in the Tea Party.[51] Among the purported participants, at least twelve had dined with the Sons of Liberty in Dorchester to celebrate the anniversary of the Stamp Act protests in 1769.[52] A smaller number of men aboard the ships have been identified as Freemasons (most were members of the Caucus as well). St. Andrew's Lodge had cancelled its December 16 meeting (with Thomas Urann presiding) because only five members were present. Just over two weeks earlier, on November 30 (the day of the second "Body" meeting, also St. Andrew's Day), the Lodge had similarly postponed its meeting because "Consignees of Tea took up the Brethrens Time." The men aboard the tea ships had previously met one another at several of Boston's politically active clubs.[53]

A few of the men aboard the ships had already made their voices heard. James Foster Condy, Moses Grant, Edward Proctor, Paul Revere, and James Swan joined Samuel Adams in a petition calling for a town meeting to protest the Tea Act on November 5. Nathaniel Barber, Stephen Bruce, ropemaker Edward C. Howe, Joseph P. Palmer, and Swan joined Adams in a petition again on November 17 to call for a clarification from Richard Clarke & Sons about the tea. Whether in clubs or in petitions, these men had protested the Tea Act and other acts of Parliament prior to taking action aboard the tea ships.[54]

These men may have been encouraged to join the Tea Party by the town's leaders, but it appears more likely that they destroyed the tea from their own political motives. In colonial Boston, artisans and laborers generally deferred to their betters—the men who had the most seniority, standing, influence, and wealth. At the same time, if these gentlemen wanted to lead, it helped to have a personal connection: leverage or the power to dispense favors. The North End Caucus and the Boston

Committee of Correspondence were built to grease the wheels of these mechanisms of exchange. So how, exactly, did the gentlemen from these groups reach out to the artisans and laborers who boarded the tea ships?

The surviving papers of the merchant Caleb Davis offer some clues. Deacon Davis was a member of the Boston Committee of Correspondence, like Adams and Warren, and he would later serve as Speaker of the Massachusetts House of Representatives. In the two years preceding the Boston Tea Party, Davis had paid Thomas Gerrish for a month's service aboard the brig *Kingston*, housewright Joseph Payson for work on his house and barn, and William Etheridge for masonry work on his ships and buildings. James Brewer did pump and block work, Samuel Howard received payment for the caulking work he did with his father, Thomas Urann did extensive shipjoining work on one of Davis's sloops, and ship carpenter Daniel Ingersoll repaired the schooner *Friendship* and the sloop *Sally*. The laborer Robert Sessions may also have had a connection, since he later recalled that he was living "in the family of a Mr. Davis, a lumber merchant, as a common laborer." Sessions, Gerrish, Brewer, and the others are all listed among the participants in the Tea Party. This was a face-to-face town—the artisans and mariners Davis employed were obliged to him for work, and Davis would in turn be obliged to them for political support. While the BCC coordinated the tea protest, Boston's artisans did the work aboard the tea ships.[55] As one nineteenth-century historian wrote, these were "trust-worthy persons," who "had been prepared in conformity to the secret resolves of the political leaders, to act as circumstances should require."[56]

Yet who says these artisans were merely following orders? The way the caulker Samuel Howard remembered it, a band of young men had met in a cabinet-maker's shop earlier in the day on December 16, to put their disguises on. But at that point they "hesitated to proceed, and finally resolved to consult two or three influential men of the city." None of these men of influence (and perhaps Davis was one of them?) offered their opinion. None would take any responsibility for encouraging the scheme. The furthest they were willing to go was to hint, "if you go you will find friends." The young men in the cabinet-maker's shop looked at one another. One appointed himself leader, and he went around asking for each man's vote. Each man agreed to "Go ahead," and signed their names to a "Round Robin."[57]

Unlike the college graduates and overseas merchants, most of these Tea Party men were pursuing jobs with less potential for great wealth. Some were retailers and other petty traders, and a few others worked in the service trades, as mariners or farmers, or as laborers. The majority—almost two-thirds—were artisans at various stages of their careers—ranging from skilled trades, such as shipjoining or silversmithing, to more common forms of craftwork, such as shoemaking or cooperage. Because his "whistling talent was a matter of public notoriety," the struggling shoemaker George R. T. Hewes was named a boatswain on the crew that boarded the *Beaver* (though Thompson Maxwell, age thirty-one, later remembered a "Captain Hewes"). Men in the building trades, such as bricklaying and carpentry, were particularly well represented. Since Boston's population growth had been stagnant for decades, perhaps many of the young men trying to make it in construction had fallen on unusually hard times. Their grievances were linked to the town's economic troubles, and they probably realized that if Parliament and the East India Company threatened Boston's prosperity, then this was a threat to them as well.[58]

The Tea Party participants already knew each other from the militia, church congregations, drinking clubs, or town offices. They knew each other as neighbors who lived on the same streets. "From the significant allusion of some persons in whom I had confidence," Hewes later told an interviewer, "together with the knowledge I had of the spirit of those times, I had no doubt but that a sufficient number of associates would accompany me in that enterprise." Kinship and marriage also tied a few of the Tea Party participants to one another. John Gammell married Thomas Urann's daughter Margaret two months before the Tea Party. Margaret went to her parents' house to await the return of her father and husband. "Oh! that dreadful night," she later recalled, "and they knew not if any would return alive." In 1770 Joseph Shed had married Hannah Gammell (possibly John's sister), and later kept a grocery shop next to where Urann lived. The carpenter John Crane had married the sister of his fellow carpenter, Josiah Wheeler, in 1766. Not all families were of the same political mind, but some men evidently felt comfortable reaching out to kinfolk on the night of December 16.[59]

Henry Purkitt, then an eighteen-year-old apprentice, later recalled that commanders like Proctor were merely acting as interpreters for the five or six men aboard each ship that wore the most convincing Indian disguises. These men were either the true directors of the Tea Party or figureheads designed to inspire the men. They issued orders in mock-Indian dialect, and the three commanders relayed "what the Chiefs said." Was it Molineux, Edes, Revere, and Chase under the face paint? We have no way of knowing, unless we trust the stories told decades later.[60]

Many of the men and boys on the ships probably had little knowledge of any advance planning—Joshua Wyeth said he had no more than a few hours' warning. They were, as one chronicler later wrote, "extempore volunteers, who could not resist the temptation of the moment." Some, including most of the young apprentices, had joined the Tea Party on the spot. Robert Sessions, working as a common laborer for a lumber merchant, got permission from his master to join. "The appointed and disguised party proving too small for the quick work necessary, other young men, similarly circumstanced with myself, joined them in their labors."[61]

Henry Purkitt and Edmund Dolbeare were cooper's apprentices in Essex Street. Through the open door of the barrel-maker's workshop, they heard a loud whistle, a traditional crowd signal. They followed the sound to Griffin's Wharf, where a commander put them to work. Tall, athletic Samuel Sprague, a bricklayer's apprentice of twenty, was on the way to visit the young woman he would eventually marry when a couple of boys told him what was happening. He smeared his face with soot and joined the party. Romance could wait.[62]

It was an exciting moment for the young men. More than half of those for whom ages are known were between 18 and 29 years old, and more than a third were 21 or under. As one memoirist remembered of that time, "It is perfectly natural that the spirit of insubordination, that prevailed, should spread among the younger members of the community." Local loyalty, the chance to free themselves from the restraints of their apprenticeships, and the thrill of destroying the tea gave these boys a feeling of autonomy and self-respect. Ann Hulton, a supporter of government, had once warned, "the Independancy & Liberty with w[ch] the Youths are brought up, and indulged, makes too many of 'em proficients in Vice." The young boys of Boston (over half the people in town were under sixteen in 1765) had been prominent in the annual Pope's Day brawls and Stamp Act protests, as well as in the harassment of importers, the confrontation with Ebenezer Richardson, and the Boston Massacre.[63]

Boston Selectman John Scollay later told his correspondent that the disguised men "came from the country," but of course he had every reason to deflect blame from his town. Wyeth, the apprentice, also later recalled a proposal "that young men not much known in town, and not liable to be easily recognized, should lead in the business." On the other hand, Robert Sessions reported that the disguised men, the men who knew about the Tea Party in advance, were "largely men of family and position in Boston," while men from out of town, like himself, were merely volunteers on the spot.[64]

The majority of the Tea Party participants appear to have been Boston-born, although many others had been born in the New England country-side, in places like Montville, Connecticut, or Thomaston, Maine. Some had shallow roots in the New World—Paul Revere and merchant Thomas Melvill both had immigrant fathers—while others came from families that had been in New England for generations. William Molineux was born in England or Ireland; James Swan came from Fifeshire, Scotland; Nicholas Campbell was born on the island of Malta; and John Peters hailed from Lisbon. New people washed up in Atlantic seaports every day in the eighteenth century, though Boston had not enjoyed much immigration in recent years. Nevertheless, a few of these immigrants found themselves swept up in the swirl of excitement.[65]

One group of men "not much known in town" were the teamsters and coasters who brought goods to and from the Boston markets. Thompson Maxwell of Bedford, for instance, was loading a team bound for Amherst, New Hampshire. Apparently at John Hancock's request, Maxwell joined Hewes aboard the *Beaver*.[66] Samuel Hammond was driving a team from Newton, and stayed late in Boston that night. His relatives discovered tea in his shoes the next day.[67] Samuel Larrabee was shipping a load of wood from North Yarmouth, Maine, and later said "he assisted that night in throwing the tea overboard." Benjamin Burton, similarly, was a mariner on board the schooner *Cumberland*, and heard about plans for the Tea Party on his way back from visiting his relatives in town. None of these men explained why they joined the Tea Party. Perhaps, like the young apprentices, they were caught up in the day's excitement. Perhaps the Boston Committee of Correspondence had succeeded in its efforts to reach out to rural New England towns and galvanize them politically. The political movement against the East India Company tea appealed to a broad range of participants. Many country towns, affected only indirectly by customs duties, had paid scant attention to the doings of Parliament; now, at the moment of the tea crisis, country traders were awakened to the threat of the Tea Act. The news that Hammond and Larrabee brought home to Newton and North Yarmouth would help to spread the idea of resistance.[68]

By around 8 or 9 p.m., the Boston Tea Party was over, and the disguised chiefs, the appointed assistants, and the young volunteers gathered on the wharf. Here they discovered that an "old gentleman" had pocketed some tea; the group unceremoniously stripped off his coat, but otherwise left him unharmed. Lendall Pitts had his men empty the stray tea leaves from their shoes and then ordered them to line up in military formation. A fife struck up, and the men marched back up the wharf and up Hutchinson (now Pearl) Street. After breaking up the procession, the marchers snuck home with as much anonymity as they could. "No other disorder took place," wrote a historian in the 1830s, "and it was observed, the stillest night ensued that Boston had enjoyed for several months." All over town, the destroyers cleaned their faces, knocked more tea out of their shoes, and went to bed. When they rose the next day, they pretended to know nothing about what had happened, though the town's grandchildren later heard that a few still had telltale paint behind their ears.[69]

Elizabeth Hunt Palmer, a young Boston housewife, heard her front gate swing open. Thinking her husband Joseph was back from a night at the club, she opened the parlor door. "And there stood three stout looking Indians!" she said, when she later told the story to her grandson. "I screamed and should have fainted of very fright, had I not recognised my husband's voice, saying 'Don't be frightened, Betsey, it is I.' " With James Foster Condy and Stephen Bruce standing next to him, he announced, "We have only been making a little salt-water tea."[70] It was far from a little. The men had thrown about 92,600 pounds of tea—over 46 tons—into the harbor.[71]

The tide swelled into Boston harbor overnight. There was no moonlight to mark the tea's passage as it slipped away on the churning waves. Eventually the broken chests and clumps of tea formed a floating line, like a winrow of hay, along the surface of the water. The line ran from the South End of Boston along the Dorchester shore to Castle Island, almost as a taunt to the consignees and commissioners. "Those persons who were from the country returned with a merry heart; and the next day joy appeared in almost every countenance, some on occasion of the destruction of the tea, others on account of the quietness with which it was effected."[72]

Of course, not every countenance was joyful. Admiral John Montagu had been forced to watch the destruction of the tea without being able to lift a finger in response. On the morning after the Tea Party, he took a stroll on the wharf and looked with astonishment at the scene of devastation. He asked some of the Bostonians, "who was to pay the fidler" now? Perhaps they answered with a sudden fear and foreboding, perhaps with a jeering smugness. "The Devil is in this people," Montagu concluded, "for they pay no more respect to an act of the British Parliament, which can make England tremble, than to an old newspaper." He then stalked off the wharf.[73]

For the tea destroyed in Boston harbor, the East India Company later claimed losses of over £9,659. For that amount of money, Paul Revere could have purchased his modest, two-story house in the North End, which cost him just over £213 in 1770, more than 45 times. For that amount of money, the Crown could have paid Governor Hutchinson his lavish annual salary for six years, and still bought Revere's house three times.[74]

Revere and his companions had no way of knowing their actions would lead to the outbreak of an eight-year war between Great Britain and the American colonies. Yet they did believe that they had shared in a bold act of patriotism—a revolutionary moment.

CHAPTER 7

"Resolute Men (Dressed as Mohawks)"

How many ships, that have been loaded with the choicest treasures of the earth, have been swallowed up in the ocean, many times just before they enter their desired haven?

Samson Occom, *A Sermon, Preached at the Execution of Moses Paul*, 1772[1]

The disguises worn by the tea destroyers—which gave them the appearance of Native Americans—remain an indelible part of our memory of the Boston Tea Party. Hasty and rough as these costumes were, the act of concealment was iconic and important. These Bostonians were "playing Indian," yet they had serious reasons for wearing their disguises. Indian costumes *meant* something to the Tea Party participants and their audience.

The decision to look and sound like Indians was made in advance by the core group of Tea Party organizers. Most of the disguises were crude, but they are noted in almost every contemporary account of the Boston Tea Party. Witnesses gave varying accounts of their effectiveness. In the disparaging opinion of the merchant Henry Bromfield, Richard Clarke's son-in-law, the destroyers were merely "assuming the Name of Indians." Others were more persuadable: as the Boston merchant John Andrews wrote privately, "They say the actors were *Indians* from *Narragansett*. Whether they were or not, to a transient observer they appear'd as *such*, being cloath'd in Blankets with their heads muffled, and copper color'd countenances."[2]

The destroyers also sounded like Indians. The disguised men were said to have entered the Old South Meeting House with "an hideous Yelling . . . some imitating the Powaws of Indians and others the Whistle of a Boatswain." (George R. T. Hewes was an expert at sounding a whistle to summon a crowd, and government supporters had often compared the terror of the whistle to an Indian war cry.) In the log-book of the *Dartmouth*, the mate wrote that the participants were "*dressed and whooping like Indians."* The *Boston Gazette* told readers that the Tea Party participants were "supposed to be the Aboriginal Natives from their complection." These "Savages" gave a "War Whoop" at the Old South Meeting House and received their answer from the galleries. In the *Boston Post-Boy* account, "a Number of very dark complexioned Persons (dressed like Mohawks or Indians) of grotesque Appearance" made "a most hideous Noise" and then proceeded to Griffin's Wharf. John Andrews remarked on the men's "*dialect*" and wrote, "their jargon was unintelligible to all but themselves." One of the young destroyers also remembered that "Indian jargon" was a key part of the commanders' disguise: posing as "chiefs," they used an unintelligible, mock-Indian language, which an interpreter relayed to the workers aboard the tea ships.[3]

You could tell how close a Tea Party man was to the inner circle by how seriously he took his disguise. The eighteen "chiefs" were so thoroughly disguised that they even pretended to speak exclusively in Indian tongue. The men under their command, who had been given some advance notice of the Tea Party, cobbled together the best disguises they could. Hewes ducked into a blacksmith's shop on Boylston's Wharf to smudge his face, then found a blanket to wrap around his shoulders at an acquaintance's house near Griffin's Wharf. Peter Mackintosh, who had been a black-smith's apprentice, remembered that several men had visited his master's shop to grab some soot for their own faces. At the bottom of the Tea Party hierarchy were out-of-towners, apprentices, or other hangers-on who joined spontaneously—these had the shabbiest disguises, or none at all. The men aboard the ships were dressed in a motley of "old frocks, red woollen caps, gowns, and all manner of like devices."[4]

Whether crude or elaborate, the disguises must have added to the thrill of the encounter. The blacksmith's apprentice Joshua Wyeth later reminisced, with not a little fervor, "We surely resembled devils from the bottomless pit, rather than men." Putting on a costume allows people to step outside their everyday lives and rebel against normality. The Tea Party organizers recognized this. As the Loyalist judge Peter Oliver stated, "it was the Rule of Faction to make their Agents first look like the Devil, in Order to make them Act like the Devil." At the same time, a disguise can make you self-conscious, by calling attention to the real person beneath. Disguises are creative and meaningful, and touch upon the deepest questions of identity. At the moment of the Boston Tea Party, the participants lingered between two worlds: the normal lives that they had left behind that morning, and something wilder and more rebellious.[5]

Why the masquerade? The most obvious answer is that the Tea Party participants were trying to conceal their identities. If, as some of the stories claim, people had been summoned from out of town (as had supposedly happened during the Stamp Act riot of August 26, 1765), then a smudge of soot would probably be enough to obscure the perpetrator's identity from eyewitnesses. But at the same time, this answer is too simple—Boston was a small town of about 16,000 people, and most of the Tea Party men were well known there. Any careful observer would likely have recognized the way a disguised neighbor walked or carried himself, rendering such simple disguises useless.[6]

Perhaps the "Mohawk" disguises were a transparent attempt to scapegoat actual American Indians. As a Loyalist memoir later put it, "After the Affair was over, the town of *Boston*, finding that it was generally condemned, said it was done by a Crew of Mohawk Indians." When British authorities started asking who had committed the crime, the Bostonians could just shrug and blame the Mohawks. This seems such a guileless lie that not even a ten-year-old would try to get away with it, but for two salutary points. First, Boston protest crowds were often multiethnic in character, and locals were accustomed to dark-skinned rioters. Second, white Bostonians were fond of blaming youths and people of color after a violent crowd action got out of hand, whether they had participated or not.[7]

For instance, after the Boston Massacre of 1770, John Adams (in his defense of the soldiers) called the rioters "a motley rabble of saucy boys, negroes and molattoes, Irish teagues and out landish jack tarrs." He blamed much of the affair on Crispus Attucks, who was part black and part Indian, leading a "rabble of Negroes, &c." This was how it always was, Adams argued: a low crowd of non-whites would "sally out upon their thoughtless enterprizes," and then others would later "ascribe all their doings to the good people of the town." His argument enabled the Boston jury to acquit the soldiers without blaming respectable white Bostonians for provoking them.[8] Thomas Hutchinson referred to the crowd who attacked customs officers on John Hancock's behalf in 1768 as "chiefly sturdy boys and negroes." When tea protesters gathered at Liberty Tree on November 3, 1773, he said they were "generally of the very lowest class mixed with boys and negroes."[9]

Indeed, Bostonians blamed youths and non-whites so often that outsiders criticized them for it. In 1772, the *Massachusetts Spy* reported that Indians or "*Savages*" at Newport, Rhode Island, had beaten two custom-house officers, climbed aboard a seized vessel, and removed the smuggled goods. A Rhode Island man, after reading this account, remarked that he and his countrymen "are not used to such low Methods of Representation—They pretend not that these Actions were done by Indians, Negroes or Boys; but by Persons unknown." The Rhode Islander was reminding the Bostonians of what everyone knew: it wasn't necessary to blame young men or non-whites: it was sufficient to say that people performing illegal acts of patriotic resistance were "unknown," and therefore immune from prosecution.[10]

Despite this history of mixed-race rioting and scapegoating, no one seriously believed that genuine Mohawks had traveled over 200 miles through white settlements to dump tea into Boston harbor. Rather, it was an open secret that white men had disguised themselves—yet they did this to make a statement. Colonial Americans and Europeans had long celebrated playful carnival traditions where social rank, gender, and the usual rules of propriety were turned upside down. At times these festivals inspired people to imagine a new social and political order: not just a festive rebirth, but genuine rebellion. Poachers in England's Windsor Forest blacked their faces to intimidate their enemies, and European villagers harassed outcasts and deviants by riding them on rails or burning them in effigy, accompanied by the "rough music" of ringing bells, honking horns, and clanking pots and pans. The scene in front of the Clarke house on November 17, 1773, illustrates this idea. Topsy-turvy disguises and loud noise signaled a protest that was both playful and pointed, cathartic and chthonic.[11]

The early Puritans of Massachusetts had stamped out almost all of the festival traditions of the Old World (including Christmas and Easter) as being immoral or Roman Catholic in nature. The last remaining festival was the annual Pope's Day parade, and provincial lawmakers tried to discourage the disguises and effigies that went along with those festivities, too. A Massachusetts law passed early in 1753 sought to prevent "all riotous, tumultuous and disorderly Assemblies" and the "horrid Profaneness, Impiety and other gross Immoralities" that went with such gatherings. The law forbade gatherings of more than three persons, especially if they were armed, begging for money, or "disguised with Vizards (so called), or painted or discoloured Faces, or being in any Manner disguised . . . having any Kind of Imagery or Pageantry for a publick Shew."[12]

Still, "rough music" and festive crowds survived: they were a way for men like Ebenezer Mackintosh, the shoemaker at the head of the Stamp Act protesters, to gain notoriety. Both before and after the passage of the Massachusetts law, Bostonians continued to don disguises. In 1732, a group of men, "several of them having blacked their faces to prevent a discovery" of their identity, leveled a selectman's barn that blocked a planned street. In March 1737, when "a great Number of rude and disorderly Persons (many of them being painted or otherwise disguised)" pulled down a market building, some were dressed as clergymen. The Stamp Act rioters of August 26, 1765, also evidently disguised themselves.[13]

As Bostonians reached a consensus in the 1760s about protesting against British laws, they directed their raucous impulses—their "rough music" and menacing disguises—squarely at British officials and their supporters. When a crowd attacked the country house of Customs Commissioner Henry Hulton in June 1770, for example, witnesses saw "Parties of Men that appeard disguised, their faces blacked, with white Night caps, & white Stockens on, one of 'em with Ruffles on & all with great clubs in their hands." The observers tried to identify the rioters by social rank (the ruffled collar was a dead giveaway for a wealthy man) and ethnic origin. "They did not know any of 'em, but one Fisherman spoke to 'em, to be satisfied whether they were Negroes or no, & found by their Speech they were not, & they answered him very insolently."[14]

Mobs were menacing of their own accord, of course, but disguised mobs blatantly misdirected onlookers about their members' true ethnicity and status. They played on the community's paranoia about non-white or lower-class rioters, which in spite of the widespread support for riots against the British government, had never really gone away. The men of the Boston Tea Party wore their Indian disguises in part as a way of provoking fear in their enemies. Yet the disguises—precisely because they were so obviously mere disguises—also helped them overcome their neighbors' fears about disorder getting out of hand.

When a group of Rhode Island smugglers burned the *Gaspée* in 1772, a judge sent to inquire into the matter wrote that although hundreds probably knew who the perpetrators were, it was "kept so profoundly secret that all our enquiry has been ineffectual to fix with certainty upon any particular person concerned in the outrage, and to keep the matter secret is now become a common cause." The lieutenant of the *Gaspée*, hoping to cast the Rhode Islanders in a negative light, reported that the perpetrators "appeared to me to be merchants and masters of vessels." By contrast, the colony's deputy governor, who was answerable to the people, reported that some of the perpetrators "were either blacked or negroes; but it was so dark, we could not tell which." Like the *Gaspée* rioters, the men of the Tea Party may have worn flimsy disguises, but it was their fellow colonists who truly kept their identities secret. The disguises served partly as a warning, signifying that the boarders of the tea ships demanded anonymity on principle, whether or not they had achieved it in fact. If these disguises did not quite conceal, they still demanded concealment.[15]

This warning was crucial to the plans of the Sons of Liberty on December 16, 1773. As we know, the town leaders such as Adams, Warren, and Young had been careful to ensure that the tea destroyers were seen as separate from the formal protests of the Town Meeting and the "Body of the People." By dressing as outsiders to the Boston community, each of the Tea Party men was effectively saying, *I am not one of the "Body of the People."* So long as the men's anonymity held, it would be impossible for the authorities or the East India Company to assign liability for the wasted wealth in the harbor. The leading Sons of Liberty hoped that the disguises would protect the town of Boston from blame.

The participants probably knew that the government and its supporters would consider their actions riotous and unsavory. Rather than proudly proclaim themselves as defiant white patriots, they skulked around with unshapely blankets and sooty faces. They hid behind the masks of scapegoats. Yet their disguises were a cry of defiance and intimidation: the participants knew their disguises were shabby, but they dared the British government to unmask them anyway. So long as they had the support of their fellow Bostonians—so long as they embodied the will of the community—they were confident that their secret would be safe.

It is clearer, then, why the men of the Boston Tea Party disguised themselves as non-white outsiders: but why Indians, and why did they come to be known specifically as "Mohawks"? These Indian disguises were especially pertinent for dissident Americans—they were envisioning a new world as they seized the New World for themselves.[16]

Encounters between Europeans and Native Americans had been going on for almost three hundred years, and it was an ugly history. European diseases such as smallpox, influenza, and the measles had accompanied the European conquest. John Winthrop, the first governor of the Massachusetts Bay Colony, wrote with satisfaction that these diseases had "cleared our title to this place."[17] Meanwhile, whites, their livestock, and their crops also cleared the place itself, uprooting the plants and animals that were familiar to the local Indians. White New Englanders appropriated increasing amounts of the Indians' land in the seventeenth century, enforcing their claims to it with steel and gunpowder. In the 1630s, Bostonians sent a military expedition after the Pequot tribe of Connecticut, which spiraled into open warfare. In the 1670s, further conflicts over land and sovereignty brought white New England colonists into a cycle of escalating violence with the war chief of the Wampanoag Indians, a sachem named Metacom or Philip. The result was King Philip's War, a terrifying and devastating conflict for whites and Indians alike. The governor of New York prevailed upon the Mohawks to attack the poorly organized Indians who were arrayed against the New Englanders, and the resulting Mohawk victory was the turning point that ultimately led to Metacom's defeat. The colony imprisoned hundreds of Indians on Deer Island in Boston harbor, and a few allied groups, such as the Mashpees, were granted tiny, self-governing districts within the colony. The New England Indian population fell to about a quarter of its previous size: the remainder had died in combat or from starvation, been sold as slaves, or fled west and north as refugees.[18]

In the early 1770s, as the centennial anniversary of King Philip's War approached, reprints of captivity narratives from the conflict suddenly became hugely popular in Boston. "Oh the roaring, and singing, and dancing, and yelling of those black creatures in the night, which made the place a lively resemblance of hell," wrote Mary Rowlandson—who had been taken captive by the Wampanoags—in her 1682 narrative, reprinted in Boston in 1773. To accompany a new edition of a history of the war published in the previous year, Paul Revere had engraved a portrait of King Philip, armed, with a blanket wrapped around him and a hatchet at his feet (fig. 20). Other accounts of Indians in combat described them as "skulking." The Indians' dress, as much as a sense of their fearsomeness and cunning, would thus have been fresh in the minds of the tea destroyers.[19]

By the eighteenth century, American colonists and Indians alike were caught up in the wars waged by the English and the French for control of the continent. The French and their Indian allies raided English settlements in New York, New Hampshire, and Maine. In 1704, for example, a party of raiders—including Mohawks—swept into Deerfield, Massachusetts, and destroyed it. The narrative of John Williams, who was captured during the Deerfield raid, was reprinted in 1773. He described how the raiders broke open his doors and windows "with axes and hatchets," and "some were so cruel and barbarous as to take and carry to the door, two of my children and murder them, as also a Negro woman."[20]

British attempts to fight the French, corral its settlers, and fence off the Indians culminated in the French and Indian War that began in 1754. The Mohawks allied themselves to the British during this conflict—an alliance they came to regret. As the French pulled back toward the St. Lawrence River and the Great Lakes, opening up vast swaths of eastern Iroquois lands to eager settlers, the Mohawks complained to British officials in 1761

PHILIP. *KING* of Mount Hope.

20 The 1772 edition of a history of King Philip's War shows the Wampanoag chief Metacom holding a rifle and draped in a blanket. The image illustrates white New Englanders' understanding of Native American dress.

that they were in "danger of being made slaves." Victory over the French in 1763 deprived the Mohawks and other Native Americans of a counter-weight both to British power, and to white American settlers. Indeed, when the British government then attempted to prevent American settlers from moving onto Indian lands beyond the Appalachian Mountains, the colonists reacted with increasing animosity towards the empire.[21]

In April 1773, Great Britain's superintendent for Indian affairs wrote that the Iroquois could be "our best friends, or most dangerous enemies." The Mohawks, with their excellent military and organizational reputation, and lands close enough to white settlements to serve as a constant reminder of their presence, inspired a particular fear and respect. It is not hard to see how the Mohawks' military might—and their desire to retain their independence in the face of British interference—would have chimed with the hopes and principles of the tea destroyers. Even as groups of white and Indian Americans battled each other, they both had good reasons to distrust British interference.[22]

Indians and Anglo-Americans sometimes enjoyed amicable and fair diplomatic dealings. The communities traded with each other, and Native Americans fought alongside Massachusetts white men in all the wars of the eighteenth century. A 1764 census counted 37 Indians in Boston, out of 72 in all of Suffolk County, although the Indian presence in Boston was likely greater; after all, Natick traders, Nantucket sailors, servants, and sojourners came to town for the same reasons as blacks and whites, yet they were often invisible to census-takers. The Rotch family, owners of the *Dartmouth*, probably employed a few Indians aboard their whaling vessels. One of the most popular authors of the early 1770s was a Mohegan minister named Samson Occom, who became a celebrity for his 1772 *Sermon, Preached at the Execution of Moses Paul* (a Connecticut Wampanoag convicted of murder), two reprints of which appeared in Boston in 1773. (Occom, one of the first Native Americans to be published in English, was also a correspondent of Boston's Phillis Wheatley, the first African-American to publish a book of poetry.)[23] However, with Indian lands shrinking, the native population drifted further away from Boston. The remaining Indians in Southern New England were confined to a few scattered enclaves such as Mashpee or Narragansett (both names that would later be adopted by tea protesters). By 1763, white people in coastal New England faced a startling new reality: they had less to fear from the local Indians than their ancestors had.

This did not mean that the New Englanders ever quite shook off their hostility and distrust towards Indian peoples. Neither did it prevent land-hungry settlers from exaggerating the Indians' savage violence and "barbarity" and using these as an excuse to annex Indian lands, or just to affirm white superiority. If the idea of an Indian attack on Boston was far-fetched in 1773, the memory of fights with Indians still lingered. Indeed, as land in eastern New England filled up, young sons with dreams of owning their own farms would have to seek out new lands in northern New Hampshire, the Maine district, and northern New York: all lands closer to Indian territory. The terrifying prospect of further Indian violence thus weighed heavily on the minds of New England colonists still simmering over past conflicts. The tea destroyers' disguises struck at the heart of these fears. Old prejudices against these non-white neighbors died hard. "We are particularly charm'd with the

Conduct of the Indians," the Gorham Committee of Correspondence archly remarked in February 1774, referring to the disguised men who had destroyed the tea in Boston. This, the town committee wrote, would "incline us almost to forget the Wounds we have received from their Tribes in these parts; as we esteem the Deceit, Murder and Cruelties of those Native Savages not worthy to be mentioned in the same Day in Comparison to the Hellish conduct of the present Enemies of America." The Indians might have been fearsome in the past, but Gorham's thundering condemnation suggests how the disguised Tea Party participants had assumed and indeed surpassed the Indian legacy they had adopted, and used it to strike fear into their political enemies in Great Britain and at home.[24]

As for the New England Indians themselves, they did their best to retain their autonomy and craft communities of their own despite various hardships. Local Indians adapted, converting their wigwams into shingled houses, buying tea tables and other fancy trappings for their homes, inter-marrying with whites and blacks, and plotting out new homelands west of Mohawk country. Like their white neighbors and adversaries, Indians spent the eighteenth century striving to forge a new American identity.[25]

Elsewhere on the continent, other Indians chose more overt resistance. Communities in the Southeast had long cultivated a caffeinated evergreen holly plant that could be used to brew an infusion called cassina, yaupon tea, or black drink. It was used by Indian men (especially the Creeks, and later the Shawnees) as a ritual emetic. By the 1760s they had passed on this prac-tice to the Delaware Indians: the town of Wakatomica (a refuge for the Delaware Prophet Neolin near what is now Dresden, Ohio) became known as "Vomit Town." By purging their bodies, these Indian activists hoped to be purified of "White peoples ways & Nature." They wanted to be free of a humiliating dependence upon trade goods from whites. While it's unlikely that the Boston Sons of Liberty had this distant practice and its meaning in mind (though it was known to some white traders), the echoes are striking: a group of rebellious American men regurgitating tea in protest against the British Empire and its consumer goods. Furthermore, in Boston, the Sons of Liberty did call for yaupon tea as a substitute for Chinese tea from England. Both Indians and whites embraced this native American plant on the road to freedom from English ways.[26]

Even as Americans used the supposed savagery and barbarity of the Indian as justification for targeting real Indians for conversion or extermination, they also admired and applauded a different set of stereotypes when they thought of Indians in the abstract. The pure, primitive image of the Indian provided a basis for criticizing decadent, tyrannical Europe: according to this view, Americans of all colors were natural natives with natural rights. These were the very rights that the tea destroyers, as they boarded the ships, were defending.[27]

Bostonians had wrestled with their own conflicted image of the Indian throughout their history. The original seal of Massachusetts from 1629 (fig. 21) depicted an Indian holding his bow in one hand, and an arrow (pointing downward) in the other, saying, "Come over and help us." Atop the Province House (traditionally the governor's residence) was a copper weather vane, about four feet high: the weather vane was an Indian drawing a bow, and his arrow pointed in the direction of the wind (fig. 22). Indians were featured on an obelisk that Paul Revere designed to celebrate the repeal of the Stamp Act in 1766: each side of the obelisk told a story, with America as an Indian prostrate before the Stamp Act and the devil's minions, then on

21　In the seal of the Massachusetts Bay Colony, an Indian pleads, "Come over and help us."

22 This weather vane stood atop the Province House in Boston during the eighteenth century.

one knee, seeking help from English allies, and finally standing beside Liberty and a beneficent King George III. Revere also included Indians in two 1768 prints. He incorporated the Province House weather vane into a political cartoon of a fire-breathing hellhound and two claw-footed demons; called "A Warm Place—Hell," it was aimed at a bloc of legislators who had voted against a Massachusetts circular letter seeking the other colonies' support for protesting the Townshend Acts. Another of Revere's prints depicts the British troops landing in Boston, and a half-naked Indian princess teaming up with a rattlesnake to subdue a British soldier (fig. 23). Although the meaning of these imagined Indians had changed since 1629, the Indian remained the accepted symbol for the white colonists of Massachusetts, especially when they were anxiously defending their liberties.[28]

The people of the British Isles also played with the idea of Indian disguise, which arose from their own, more distant fascination with American Indians that dated from the time of Pocahontas. In 1710, they celebrated the Mohawk and Mahican "kings" who visited London and had

23 A detail of Revere's engraving of troops landing in Boston shows a Native American woman with her foot atop a British soldier.

an audience with Queen Anne. Shortly afterward, a gang of devilish rakes called the "Mohocks" or "Hawkubites" threw London into hysteria. Satirists and playwrights began exaggerating (or inventing) stories: these marauders roamed the streets, terrorizing constables, slitting nostrils, and stuffing people in barrels. The writer Richard Steele mistakenly thought the name "Mohock" came from India, and wrote that their leader sported a "*Turkish* Crescent" as a coat of arms. Even after the fervor died down, the name "Mohock" became shorthand for any group of genteel ruffians. The tradition of adopting Indian guise in London continued: a 1772 guide to masquerade dress showed a dark-skinned Mohawk with a pipe tomahawk and a blanket draped over one shoulder (fig. 24). That year, Bostonians also read of an "exceedingly brilliant" masked ball in Soho, where there were "Several Indians, Cherokees, and Mulattos, some of them exceedingly well dressed." The British had come to appreciate Indian disguises as a symbol of rakish, daring, and mischievous behavior.[29]

24 A Mohawk draped in a blanket, as portrayed in a European guide to disguises for masquerade balls, published in 1772. European masqueraders were attracted to the "dresses of different nations, antient and modern."

When a member of London's high society dressed as a Mohawk, he stepped outside of polite society with the expectation that he could return to it without any blemish on his reputation. But many people in Great Britain, as they came to see white Americans and American Indians in the same light, believed that Americans could never shed their savagery or their inferior status. As early as the 1670s and as late as the 1720s, writers were calling an American-born white New Englander a "tame Indian" and worrying that American-born English people were taking on "Indian" characteristics such as dishonesty, laziness, and indulging their children. As Americans, New Englanders sensed that the English thought of them as ruder and dumber, not far removed from being Indians themselves. In the 1760s and 1770s, Parliament (and many British writers) encouraged this insecurity by treating Americans as inferior and degenerate: as little better than foreigners, savages, or slaves.[30]

By the eighteenth century, London political cartoonists were also regularly using Indian figures to symbolize America. When the colonies were groaning under the burdens of the stamp tax, cartoonists showed an Indian on his knees (fig. 25), or with Lady Liberty prostrate at an Indian's feet

The Great Financier, or British Œconomy for the Years 1763.1764. 1765.

25 A London cartoon about the Stamp Act portrays America as a kneeling, supplicant Indian, reeling from British policies. Around the Indian's neck are heavy wooden billets reading, "Taxed without Representation."

(fig. 26). John Singleton Copley's own Stamp Act protest cartoon was more sympathetic, depicting America as a white woman and Liberty as an Indian lying down beneath the Liberty Tree, an object of pity—and his skin was much lighter (fig. 27). Copley was reminding his audience that Americans were British subjects, deserving of the same rights, and he made a plea for mercy from Parliament. However, English cartoonists continued to condescendingly portray America as a child, an animal, or an Indian. In these pictures, Americans learned that the mother country regarded them as inferior—but they also adapted the symbolism for their own purposes. The British Empire, Americans warned, would suffer the independence of a willful child, the attack of the wild animal, and the fearsome bravery of the American Indian. Americans were readying themselves for a tough frontier encounter. A week before the Tea Party, "A

26 A London cartoon shows a standing, dark-skinned Indian, which represents America, saying, "Secure Me, O, Goddess, by thy Wisdom, for I abhor it [the Stamp Act] as Death." Liberty lies prostrate, lamenting, "It is all over with Me," while Mercury, god of trade, departs.

27 John Singleton Copley's version of this print showed a lighter-skinned Indian, half-draped in a robe, lying beneath the Liberty Tree.

RANGER" wrote in to the *Boston Evening-Post*, saying that he was looking for a *"bush fight."* If Great Britain was going to treat the colonists like Indians, then the colonists were prepared to fight like Indians.[31]

As real Indians retreated from white conquest, the symbolism of the Boston Tea Party legitimized the colonists as "new and improved" Indians who deserved America for themselves. This symbolism also pointed to the popular idea of the New World as purer and freer than a corrupt and tyrannical Old World. Thus, an Indian disguise could be a statement about a new American identity, and perhaps a new source of American citizenship. A white man in Indian costume could envision himself as an American ideal, both civilized and free—the best of both worlds. But he might worry that instead he was too crude for Europe and too corrupt to truly identify with the Indians. The Indian disguise carried all of these mixed meanings with it.[32]

Given this background of conquest, estrangement, and the adoption of Indian imagery, the choice of Indian disguises at the Boston Tea Party becomes clearer. The disguises celebrated the uniquely American identity of the white colonists. Even before the Tea Party, American rioters and protesters borrowed an Indian identity time and again, both in words and deeds. New England newspapers sometimes published political satires that were written in a mock-Indian dialect—misspelled English and improper grammar with occasional references to Indian culture. These fictive Indians were knowledgeable about politics and handy with a tomahawk. In one case the faux-Indian writer "Jacob" repeated the Boston dissenters' criticisms about tea-drinking. Tea was "poor nasty stuff, it make it man week" as well as his "poor old squaw." He criticized those who imported tea from England to Boston: "Jacob he no let pay dutys for Te if he can help it, cause tis spress revenue [expressly for the purpose of raising revenue], gainst Constitushun and Magnum Cartum." Foreshadowing the Tea Party by almost two years, he concluded, "Jacob say he [would ad]vise try ebry spedient first, *for liberty and freedom*, if cant get it—den best way sound *Warhoop*."[33]

Such war-whoops had already echoed from Maine to Dorchester, Massachusetts. Men dressed and whooping like Indians burst into a tavern in Exeter, New Hampshire, in 1734. They headed for a group of men sent to claim mast trees for the Royal Navy, and beat them with clubs. In 1767, Bostonians read of the ordeal of Dr. Sylvester Gardner, a Maine landholder attacked by settlers. "Savages in human Shape, muffled in the Shades of Night, invested his Abode," the author wrote. "How great was his Surprize at the unexpected Yell of Indians in the Night, demanding him for their cruel Sport? How was he struck with Horror?" In late 1768, a similar dispute in Woolwich, Maine, led twenty or thirty men "disguised in an Indian Dress" to pull down another man's house.[34] Earlier that year, the wife of Customs Commissioner William Burch told a friend that the Sons of Liberty often surrounded her house "with most hideous howlings as the Indians, when they attack an Enemy."[35]

During the Stamp Act crisis of 1765, Rhode Island governor Stephen Hopkins reportedly "said publickly that the parliament of Great Britain, had no more right to make laws for them than they had for the Mohawks."[36] According to an earlier account, Hopkins had actually asked, "What have the King and Parliament to do with making a Law or Laws to govern us by, any more than the Mohawks have? And if the Mohawks should make a law or laws to govern us we were as much obliged to obey them as any Law or Laws the King and Parliament could make."[37] In both accounts, Hopkins denied parliamentary authority over the colonies—in one case, he characterized Mohawks and colonists as American cousins in defiance of a distant Parliament; in the other, he characterized the British and Mohawks as two threatening bodies that each lacked authority over the free colonists in between. In the same vein, an American wrote to London in 1768 that Americans feared the establishment of the Church of England in America even more "than ten thousand Mohawks, or the most Savage Indians in this Quarter of the Globe."[38]

We have already seen how pressure from New York and Philadelphia motivated the Bostonians to protest against the Tea Act and ultimately destroy the tea. It also appears that New York was the source for the use of the name "Mohawk," as well. Three days before the Boston Tea Party, the *Boston Post-Boy* reprinted a New York City notice signed by "The MOHAWKS." The notice announced that "our nation have lately been informed" of the Tea Act and the arrival of the East India Company ships. "We do therefore declare, that we are determined not to be enslaved, by any power on earth." It also promised that the Mohawks would pay "an unwelcome visit" to whomever helped to land the tea. In this case, the Mohawks symbolized a nation of American natives who would resort to violence in the face of any attempt to enslave them. It was the perfect disguise for the Bostonians to adopt: they showed solidarity with the New Yorkers as brave Americans defending their rights. Fifty years later, a historian wrote that someone in the Old South Meeting House shouted, "The Mohawks are come!"[39]

The Boston Tea Party became the ultimate piece of political theater, inspiring similar resistance (and other Indian disguises) throughout the continent. Like many effective pieces of theater, it involved humor. The disguises could be understood as a punning nod to Christopher Columbus's mistaken belief that he had reached India in 1492. In 1773, the Tea Party participants themselves apparently played up the historical confusion about the word "Indian," and chose their disguises accordingly. Since the East *India* Company was the monopolistic enemy, *American* Indians would have to make sure that none of their tea would land in Boston. When the innkeeper Charles Conner was caught pocketing tea on board the *Beaver*, Lendall Pitts and George R. T. Hewes raised the cry of "*East Indian!*" to distinguish him from the so-called American Indians who were virtuously destroying the tea. And in a satire from January 1774 (supposedly written by Edward Proctor, one of the Tea Party commanders), the "Chief Sachem of the Mohawks" began by affirming that "Tea is an Indian Plant, and of right belongs to the Indians of every Land & Tribe."[40]

Both the witnesses to the Boston Tea Party and those who heard or read about it later were in on the joke: the men aboard the tea ships weren't really Indians, but everyone still made a big show of pretending that Indians (we might call them "fauxhawks") had dumped the tea. As with the "Mohocks" of London, these Indian identities survived through embellishment by the press. Governor Hutchinson, usually all too quick to point to black-skinned members of a crowd, knew to blame white Bostonians this time around: "Such barbarity," he wrote, "none of the Aboriginals were ever guilty of." No doubt any genuine Indians who heard the joke failed to see the funny side. It was a minstrel show: white people appropriating native customs (badly) while committing property crimes in their name.[41]

The British also remarked on the Tea Party disguises, because these cut to the core of the identity crisis they were facing when the American Revolution erupted. Back in the old days, an English person knew where everyone stood—man and woman, insider and outsider, light-skinned person and dark-skinned person, high-born and low-born, civilized and savage. But new consumer goods and new political protests had disrupted everything: almost everyone was a tea drinker, and many people now believed they were entitled to equal rights under the law. How dare the Americans question Parliament! Weren't they proud to be loyal subjects of the empire? What did it mean to belong to the British Empire, if Americans could just decide to leave it on a whim? Or did these noisy Americans have a point?

In early 1776, the dissenting minister Richard Price and John Wesley engaged in a heated exchange of pamphlets on the subject of the American rebellion. As he discussed the tax on tea, the pro-American Price noted that at Boston, "some persons in disguise buried it in the sea." Price believed that the American cause was just, and he argued that Great Britain shouldn't treat the colonies too harshly just because a few disguised men had done a bad deed.[42]

Wesley, a critic of the American rebels, had a different view. He argued that the Bostonians had only disguised themselves to deflect blame from the man everyone knew was the ringleader of Boston's rebellion: John Hancock. By then Hancock was president of the Continental Congress, and therefore a natural target for British attacks—but Wesley had also heard the rumors that Hancock had imported tea during the time of the nonimportation agreements, and he accused Hancock of paying the Tea Party men for their work.[43]

Price, like the Americans themselves, preferred to mention the disguises in order to blame the Tea Party on "persons unknown." The genuine, righteous leaders of the colonial protest, like John Hancock or Samuel Adams, could disavow what the riffraff had done (even if that riffraff was allied to the cause).

Wesley was having none of it. In a subsequent pamphlet, he embellished his account of the Tea Party still further, talking of how the Bostonians under Hancock, "scorning to do any thing secretly, paraded the town at noon-day with colours flying, and bravely threw the *English* tea into the sea." A year or two afterwards, they "wholly threw off the mask," and avowed independence overtly, "without any disguise, or reserve." Had Americans, at the Tea Party, suddenly shown their true colors? Perhaps the Indian disguises were no disguise at all, but evidence of their true nature as savages and frauds? Or were the disguises little more than the darkly playful costumes of a few bad seeds? For pro-American writers, the latter argument was the most convenient, allowing them to gesture toward a reasoned discussion with one hand, while threatening violence with the other. But British hard-liners like Wesley had their own opinions about the Indian disguises, and what they meant—they concluded that the Bostonians were no longer faithful Britons, but now enemies of the mother country.[44]

CHAPTER 8

———◆ ◆———

Boycotting the Accursed Leaf

The storm has lowered dark upon us, but I really think the prospect rather brightens, and that there is reason to hope [our] united efforts . . . will extricate [us] from the hand of the oppressor.

Mercy Otis Warren, December 29, 1773[1]

Ladies, this wiser Caution take,
Trust not your Tea to Marcus Brutus,
Our draught he'l spoil, our China break,
And raise a Storm That will not suit us;
Then, for the sake of Freedom's name,
(Since Brittish wisdom scorns repealing,)
Come, sacrifice to Patriot fame,
And give up Tea, by way of healing,
This done, within ourselves retreat,
The Industrious arts of life to follow,
Let the Proud Nabobs Storm & fret,
They Cannot force our lips to swallow.
Tho' now the boist'rous surges roul,
Of wicked North's Tempestuous ocean,
Leave him, for Justice to Controul,
And Strive to Calm our own Commotion,
With us, each Prudent Caution Meet,
Against This Blushing son of Thunder,
And Let our firm Resolve, defeat
His Lordship's Ministerial blunder,

Hannah Griffitts, "Beware the Ides of March," February 28, 1775[2]

When the schoolteacher William Russell returned to his Temple Street home after helping to destroy the tea, he took off his shoes and carefully

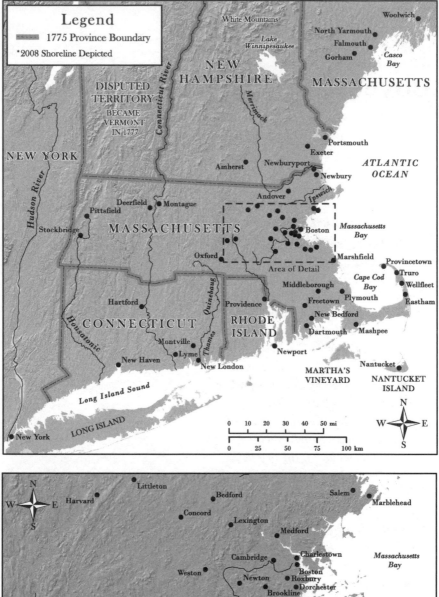

5 New England in 1775.

dusted them over the fire, "being careful that none of the tea should remain." He then went to the family's closet, took out the tea canister, and emptied it into the fire. The next morning, he printed "Coffee" on one side of the canister and "No Tea" on the other.[3]

The men who had boarded the *Dartmouth*, the *Eleanor*, and the *Beaver* were almost fuzzy with tea. Priscilla Cotton, who was then a thirteen-year-old girl boarding with a woman on Milk Street, remembered that after the family's manservant came home with tea in his boots, everyone in the house was drinking it the next day. When George R. T. Hewes came home, his wife Sarah supposedly said, "Well George, *did you bring me home a lot of it?*" Many years later, Hewes's biographer wrote, "We shouldn't wonder if Mrs. Hewes was more of a tea-drinker than a Whig." In other words, Sarah Hewes was a working-class woman trying to scrape together a little luxury—and she chose this tasty luxury over the luxury of holding fast to a political principle.[4]

Other families, however, reacted the way William Russell's family did— at least, that's what they told the grandchildren. Boston women, according to these stories, put their politics above their cravings. Housewright Josiah Wheeler pulled off his long boots and some tea leaves fell to the floor. Wheeler's wife and a female neighbor had waited up for him, and the neighbor supposedly urged her to save the tasty delicacy for later. Instead, the patriotic Mrs. Wheeler swept all the tea into the fire, saying, "Don't touch the cursed stuff."[5] Benjamin Wallcut's mother (who had helped him dress as a Mohawk) similarly swept the tea from his boots into the fire, and ordered her daughter to put the teapot away "untill this quarrel of *three pence* on a pound of *tea* is settled." Wallcut's nephew, in a manuscript memoir for his daughter that he composed sometime after the Civil War, wrote proudly, "Such were the *women* of those days, and such is the blood that flows in my veins."[6]

The destruction of the East India Company tea was big news. Throughout the American colonies, it was uncertain whether people would respond to the Boston Tea Party with a chorus of support, or with shock and disapproval. A complex blend of motivations had led the Bostonians to destroy the tea. They had feared an East India Company monopoly on American trade. They were offended by taxation without consent. They disliked the fact that the tea revenue paid for the salaries of certain civil servants. And they wanted to demonstrate their solidarity with New York City and Philadelphia. They saw the Tea Act as an accumulation of almost ten years of obnoxious legislation. The Boston Sons of Liberty hoped that their message would spread throughout the continent, and they hoped that the rest of America would approve.

In the coming months, a boycott of tea became a simple and effective way for people throughout the American colonies to show their support. The protests refocused the prevailing discontent on the original complaint from the 1760s—taxation without representation—and gave ordinary men and women a way to participate in a broad, almost national movement.

The lawyer John Adams was one enthusiastic supporter of the Tea Party. "This is the most magnificent Movement of all," he said the next day. "There is a Dignity, a Majesty, a Sublimity, in this last Effort of the Patriots, that I greatly admire." He continued, "This Destruction of the Tea is so bold, so daring, so firm, intrepid and inflexible, and it must have so important Consequences, and so lasting, that I cant but consider it as an Epocha in History." To a friend he wrote, "This is the grandest, Event, which has ever yet happened Since, the Controversy, with Britain, opened! The Sublimity of it, charms me!"[7]

The merchant John Rowe, part owner of one of the tea ships, had a very different view. Although he had stood in front of the Old South Meeting House and sounded off like a Son of Liberty, in private he had grave doubts. "Tis a Disastrous Affair," he wrote in his diary, "& some People are much Alarmed." Many people were inclined to be neutral, or apathetic, or to support the British government. They worried that the Tea Party and its attendant boycotts would only provoke further acrimony and invite the Crown's punishment.[8]

The Boston Sons of Liberty were hoping that most Americans would share Adams's reaction rather than Rowe's. After all, they had partly resisted the Tea Act in the first place because they were seeking the approval of the New York and Philadelphia Sons of Liberty. The fractious colonies had squabbled over nonimportation, tea, and many other issues. By disposing of the East India Company's tea, Boston's protesters had done their part for colonial unity. Now they needed to see if the other colonies would stand behind them. In the first of his famous rides as a messenger for the Sons of Liberty, Paul Revere rode to New York to give the radicals there a first-hand account of the events in Boston.[9]

The results were everything Samuel Adams and his allies could have hoped for. "Many people here," wrote one New Yorker, "think you have fully retrieved the honor you lost" by importing duted tea between 1767 and 1773. Had the East India Company's tea arrived in New York City before it had arrived at Boston, it's possible that New York governor William Tryon would have been in a stronger position to land the cargo by force. Instead, the tea had arrived at Boston first, and the acrimonious relationship between the weakened Governor Hutchinson and the Sons of Liberty had had an explosive outcome. Now, with Revere's news electrifying New York City on December 21, New York's governor "made a Virtue of Necessity," and promised to support the people's decision not to allow the tea to land. As it turned out, this compromise wouldn't be tested until four months later: the ship *Nancy*, carrying 698 chests of tea, had run into such a terrible storm that it had diverted to Antigua in February 1774 for repairs, and didn't arrive in New York harbor (after another storm that claimed two of its masts) until April 18, 1774. Within five days, the New York Sons of Liberty had sent the ill-fated *Nancy* back to London with its tea (at a cost to the Company of over £1,458 in wasted freight charges). Just before the departure of the *Nancy*, another ship had slipped into port with a shipment of eighteen half-chests of fine Hyson green tea. The captain of this ship, the *London*, James Chambers, had drawn the ire of the crowd because he had earlier boasted of refusing to transport East India Company tea. After confronting Chambers, a crowd of "Mohawks" threw the tea into the harbor.[10]

When the news from Boston reached Philadelphia on December 24, 1773, it was greeted with more cheers from the Sons of Liberty. Bells rang throughout the town, and a broadside with the news was headlined, "Christmas-Box for the Customers of the *Pennsylvania Journal*." The following evening, the ship *Polly* was spotted in the Delaware River, carrying another 698 chests of tea. The Sons of Liberty compelled Captain Samuel Ayres to come ashore before his ship reached Philadelphia. On December 27, almost 8,000 people gathered at the State House Yard (the square behind what is now Independence Hall) to persuade the captain to return to London. Ayres formally asked the local consignees whether they would accept the tea. They declined, and lent the captain some money to purchase provisions for his return journey. On the 28th, Ayres left the city, pulled up his anchor, and set sail for England with all his cargo aboard (costing the Company another £1,168 in wasted freight charges). British authorities later chastised John Penn, the deputy governor of Pennsylvania, for doing nothing to intervene.[11]

Meanwhile, the northern colonists learned in January that the East India Company's tea had made no headway in Charleston, South Carolina, either. In Charleston (unlike the other cities), the tea had been allowed to land. Evidently, within the close-knit South Carolina gentry, the Sons of Liberty trusted the acting governor not to do anything underhanded. Therefore the tea remained stored in damp, dark rooms beneath the city's Exchange, where it was left to rot. Local leader Henry Laurens approved of the Charlestonians' actions (which showed an admirable

"Constitutional Stubbornness"), and he shied away from arguing, as some had done, that the other towns had "proceeded too far in drowning & forcing back the Tea."[12]

As reports came in with this news from New York, Charleston, and Philadelphia, Bostonians cheered.[13] Samuel Adams exulted at the disintegration of "Old Jealousies" and the new "perfect Harmony" among the colonies. John Hancock agreed. "No one Circumstance could possibly have Taken place more effectually to Unite the Colonies than this Manœvere of the Tea." Friends of government like Peter Oliver later complained that with "the Cunning of the Serpent," the Massachusetts Sons of Liberty had contrived to involve the other colonies in their own colony's disgrace.[14]

Boston was working hard to get the New England countryside involved, too. Oliver, a critic of the Tea Party, argued that these rural towns had little choice but to side with Boston, due to the "Connection of Trade" among them. Yet these towns weren't mere dupes or dependants of Boston. They bellowed their own outrage at the constitutional wrongs that were being committed. Like the Bostonians, they feared that cheaper tea was meant to lure them into accepting an unjust tax. Like the Bostonians, they feared the establishment of a government that was independent of popular control, funded by revenue from the tea. And like the Bostonians, they feared the idea of the East India Company's monopoly crowding out American merchants. These towns were self-governing, and their leaders were responsible to the people. They were confronted with an imperial, monarchical system that didn't see things that way at all. American republicanism was born of this conflict—and the fight over the Tea Act was the latest and most dramatic example.[15]

Already by late December 1773, Samuel Adams was finding it "a great Consolation . . . that our Friends in the Country approve of the Conduct of this and the Neighboring Towns at the late Meetings." Indeed, at least eighty towns lent their voices to resist the actions of Parliament; twenty of them had never corresponded with Boston before. Towns like Montague and Gorham explicitly cheered the destruction of the tea, but these were exceptions. In York, for example, the government supporter Jonathan Sayward was able to get the town to soften its language so that it didn't go on record with a dangerous endorsement of the Tea Party. Other towns pronounced the Tea Party justifiable, but in vague terms. The town of Harvard, for instance, disapproved of "Tumultuous assemblies," but hardly expected the people to remain quiet and submissive when their rights were being "trampled in the dust." Most towns offered cautious praise for the *constitutional* actions that the Boston-area towns had taken to protest the Tea Act. That way, if the Bostonians were punished for their actions, the rural towns wouldn't be on record endorsing the destruction. Yet at the same time, these towns hinted at a belief that the tea's destruction was a proper response to tyranny.[16]

On the other hand, many Massachusetts colonists shared John Rowe's alarm, and believed that the Bostonians had crossed a line. A majority in Littleton thought things had gone so far that they voted to dissolve the town's committee of correspondence completely.[17] At Freetown, Massachusetts, the inhabitants criticized the Boston-area Body of the People for failing to prevent the destroyers "from acting their savage Nature in the Destruction of the Tea," which was "contrary to Law, and we fear will bring upon us the Vengeance of an affronted Majesty, and also plunge us in Debt and Misery, when the injured Owners of said Tea shall make their Demand for the Value of the same."[18] (Angry though they were, the Freetowners were nevertheless making a distinction between the destroyers and the Boston populace, so in that respect, the disguises had worked.) The townspeople of Pittsfield thought the destruction of the tea "unnecessary and highly unwarrantable," subversive of "all good order and of the Constitution." They advocated the punishment of any "persons connected in the destruction." Yet the residents upheld the principle of fighting taxation without representation, and they rejected the idea that Massachusetts should have to pay restitution for the destroyed tea.[19]

Some communities were bitterly divided. A group of Marshfield residents met on January 31, 1774, and resolved to call the Boston Tea Party "illegal and unjust and of a dangerous Tendency." Yet this resolution passed by only a single vote, and soon spurred a reaction. Another group announced that they were "determined to contribute to our last mite" in the defense of liberty "against the machinations of assuming, arbitrary men."[20]

The Clarke family, meanwhile, was scrambling to snatch a small victory from an otherwise disastrous turn of events. The last of the tea vessels bound for Boston was the brigantine *William*, which the Clarkes themselves owned. The *William* was carrying 300 street lamps for the town of Boston as well as 58 chests of tea. On December 10 and 11, before the Tea Party took place, stormy weather had forced the brig to run aground on the back of Cape Cod. The Clarkes were afraid that their vessel and all its cargo would sink into the sea—and if the sea didn't claim the tea, the people would destroy it just as they had destroyed the other 340 chests. "The People there have catch'd the Flame that at present prevails in this Country," wrote Henry Bromfield, an in-law of the Clarkes.[21]

John Adams was worried, too. "Are there no Vineyard, Marshpee, Metapoiset Indians, do you think, who will take the Care of it [the tea], and protect it from Violence"? Adams wasn't referring to real Indians from the vicinity of Cape Cod, but to patriotic white citizens from the region. And he didn't mind if those "Indians" destroyed the tea as the so-called Mohawks had done in Boston; instead he was trying to protect the tea "from the Hands of Tyrants and oppressors, who want to do Violence with it, to the Laws and Constitution, to the present Age and to Posterity" by selling it under the terms of the Tea Act.[22]

Young Jonathan Clarke, the man who had first won the tea commission for his family firm, rushed to rescue the cargo. Sometime on the 16th he slipped away from his place of exile on Castle Island. He paid laborers (in tea!) to cart the cargo to Provincetown: a few chests were damaged and some more may have been stolen. Clarke had difficulty getting any ships to agree to carry the politically volatile tea, but two sloops did bring the rest of the cargo to Boston. Finally Clarke convinced Captain John Cooke of Salem, master of the fishing schooner *Eunice*, to carry about fifty-one chests and a barrel of tea to Castle Island, despite rumors that a group of Bostonians was coming down to Cape Cod to destroy the tea. The consignees once again refused to receive the tea themselves, but Governor Hutchinson had it stored at the fort's army barracks for safekeeping.[23]

The local Sons of Liberty did their best to recover and destroy this last shipment of tea, but for the most part, they were too late. A group of disguised Indians searched one of the two sloops when it arrived at Boston, but found no tea aboard. A newspaper encouraged Bostonians to keep their eyes on Castle Island and make sure no tea was sold. But there was little that they could do from the mainland. At Salem, "A Company of Natives, dressed in the Indian Manner" and armed with hatchets, tried to harass the owner and the captain of the *Eunice*, but the owner was recovering from smallpox inoculation. Later the town of Salem met, found the two men blameless (they had transported the tea out of ignorance), and agreed to leave them alone.[24]

Samuel Adams was almost nauseous with disgust. Jonathan Clarke had traveled a hundred miles through Massachusetts and did "not meet with a single Instance of Contempt." If the tea could be safe in Provincetown, then Adams's enemies would start to "whisper among themselves that probably it might have been safe in every part of the Province" except for Boston itself. If this rumor gained traction, Adams's plans to unite the towns of Massachusetts would fall apart. Had the "Indians" of Boston known that "the Marshpee Tribe would have been so sick at the knees,"

Adams wrote, they would have marched in snowshoes to destroy the Cape Cod tea themselves.[25]

Now everyone knew that some of the dutied East India Company tea had landed securely in Massachusetts. If the Company felt that they could safely send tea to America after all, the work of the Boston Tea Party would be undone. Bostonians had "to convince the impoverish'd *Company* that our virtue is superior to the lust of the noxious weed," so that the Company would push Parliament to have the Tea Act repealed. But there were problems. First, there was still dutied tea in New England that had been imported before the passage of the Tea Act, as well as smuggled tea from Holland and elsewhere. How could you tell the difference, and make sure that no one was drinking dutied tea? Could you rely on merchants to stop selling tea? Could you rely on ordinary people to stop drinking it? Who would enforce a boycott—town meetings, watchful consumers, or the mob?[26]

Even before December 16, people had rediscovered their interest in doing away with tea. Since the importation of tea was "connected with the ruin of government," argued one writer, "we ought to consider and treat it as we would THE PLAGUE."[27] The newspapers reminded Bostonians that they didn't need tea for their diet: it was a luxury unknown to their "frugal ancestors."Writers repeated their dire warnings about the unhealthy effects of tea. And they began recommending native substitutes like yaupon or Labradore tea, sassafras and strawberry leaves. Nathaniel W. Appleton, whose father was a member of the Boston Committee of Correspondence, looked forward to the positive "moral & political Consequences" of boycotting tea, which caused only "Vexation, Expence & Luxury."[28]

Although most people had been relatively quiet about the tea boycotts after the failure of the nonimportation agreements in 1770, the Tea Act had abruptly reawakened people to the idea that tea was dangerous to colonial rights. Thus, even before the Bostonians destroyed the tea, they had heard of tea being destroyed in Lexington, plans to do the same in Charlestown, and statements of support from half a dozen other Massachusetts towns. From Boston, a writer calling himself "MILLIONS" took up the cry: the Lexington tea-burning was "truly worthy the notice and imitation of every town in this province."This writer called on his patriotic neighbors to collect all their tea and "sacrifice it to the flames in the Common." Not only that, people ought to shun friends or merchants who used, bought, or sold tea.[29]

Yet people like Sarah Hewes, the wife of shoemaker George, still wanted to drink tea. The destruction of over 90,000 pounds of tea on December 16 had helped make tea even scarcer than it already had been. The paltry supply and persistent demand caused the price to rise on the open market. Skeptics had spread rumors throughout Massachusetts that local tea dealers had promoted the destruction of the tea for exactly this purpose: to inflate the price of the tea they had previously stockpiled. In other words, "they meant to monopolize that Article, and so mask their Avarice with the Appearance of Patriotism." In part to dispel such rumors, Boston's "principal dealers of teas" met soon after the Tea Party. Over bowls of punch at the Royal Exchange Tavern, the tea merchants agreed to unite with their patriotic neighbors "in exterminating this destructive herb from the province." For the next month, they would sell their remaining tea at a fixed price, and would suspend sales completely after January 20, 1774.[30]

Caleb Davis, the merchant from the Boston Committee of Correspondence who had employed a handful of Tea Party participants, joined forces with a committee of local tea dealers. The group went from shop to shop, encouraging compliance from all the tea merchants in Boston. They eventually generated a list of 99 tea dealers. Of these, 51—just over half—signed, including a few men who were later revealed to have helped dump the tea themselves: Thomas Melvill, Joseph Pearse Palmer, and James Swan. The rest hesitated slightly. Some wanted nothing to do with the patriots—seven made themselves scarce and four "gave no satisfactory answer." Eleven of the merchants knew better than to sign any agreement before it became unanimous. Seventeen "were for quitting all Tea," but wouldn't commit themselves to signing a political agreement. (Later these twenty-eight were counted with the signers as "against the Sale and Use of all Tea.") The remaining nine wanted to ban only the sale of dutied tea from London, but continue to sell smuggled tea—Henry Prentiss, another man who supposedly helped destroy the tea, was one of these.[31]

But when push came to shove, you just couldn't trust merchants as a group. Merchants like John Rowe were after profit and solvency—many of them were one failed business venture away from bankruptcy—and they couldn't always afford the luxury of patriotic scruples. As Samuel Adams warned, you could always find merchants "who for the sake of a paltry Gain would ruin their Country." The Sons of Liberty had already discovered during the nonimportation agreements of 1768 to 1770 that the merchant wolves would always be looking over their shoulders to make sure other merchants didn't break away from the pack. Most were too afraid to take a leap on their own, and rightly so. As long as people craved a cup of tea, merchants could make a profit from selling it. And as long as merchants could make a profit, at least some would stay in the business of selling tea.[32]

But perhaps that was fine, so long as no one drank the Company's tea from England. What would be wrong with drinking smuggled tea? Tea smuggled from Holland and other places offended no one's constitutional sensibilities. Buying it didn't put a single shilling in the coffers of either the East India Company or the British Treasury. Drinking it conceded nothing to Parliament. But plenty of writers saw through this: after all, Hutchinson's sons had done their best to "smuggle *stored Teas*" in the midst of the 1770 boycott. Dutch tea and English tea tasted exactly the same, and there was no practical way to distinguish between the two. Therefore, "I say no Tea of any Kind," concluded "SYDNEY"; "for if you suffer Dutch Tea, you will soon be over run with dutied Tea, under that Name." Another writer, "Deborah Doubtful," also saw the problem: although "female friends to liberty" were keeping "a strict watch" on tea merchants, "The only sure way to avoid being imposed upon by duted tea" was "to oppose the trade in all tea."[33]

In other words, the best way to get merchants to stop trading tea was for families to stop buying any tea at all. In late November 1773, Bostonians read an item from Newport, Rhode Island, reporting that 50 or 60 tea-drinking families in that town "have lately entirely refrained from that pernicious herb; and that numbers of others are on the point of abandoning the disgraceful practice of tea-drinking." In a month, the number swelled to 300 families. By late January, people had cut their tea-drinking by a third. The Newport item even informed readers that tea stored for too long would breed flea-like insects that would further damage health. The Company tea from England, having been stored for months, was probably particularly dangerous, "but the surest way to be safe is to drink none."[34]

Tea, tea, tea—it was tea itself that was the problem! Tea was "the idol of America": a false god of luxury that Americans had worshiped at the expense of their liberty. Americans had been "so very fond of it," wrote a newspaper contributor, "that they had rather part with any enjoyment in life." Indeed, government supporters were apparently boasting "That the people have not virtue enough to quit India Tea, or any one superfluity, to save themselves and posterity from eternal slavery." Samuel Adams had said as much himself: "he could not trust the private Virtue of his Countrymen in refraining from the Use of it."[35]

Yet Samuel Adams and his allies trusted that "public Virtue" would overcome private temptation. They claimed, as one author wrote, that Americans now "begin to detest the drug entirely which has been the medium of so much abuse." Americans could indeed "root out" the plant that threatened to choke the colonies to death. "SYDNEY" urged readers to stop weakening their bodies and morals through luxury, for this would inevitably lead Parliament to enslave the colonists. In theory, the solution was easy: tea sellers needed to stop selling tea, and families had to stop using it. Unfortunately, one couldn't always rely on the "publick Spirit" of the individual: only on "the People in general." The best solution, "SYDNEY" argued, was for each town to appoint committees of inspection to make sure that no one would buy, sell, or use tea. Failing that, other writers argued that destroying even small amounts of tea had unmistakable symbolic power. People could make a celebratory event out of destroying more tea—not just on its way to American shores, but even the tea for which they had already paid the hated duty. Destroying tea was good for the spirit—specifically, the colonists' political spirit.[36]

Many town governments duly appointed these committees of inspection. On the morning of the Boston Tea Party, the *Massachusetts Spy* had suggested that the selectmen of every Massachusetts town should start denying licenses to all inns and taverns that sold tea to guests. Otherwise it would be difficult for tavern-keepers "to avoid dishing out this poison." Some town governments took this specific step, while others broadly tried to prevent the purchase, sale, and use of tea from Great Britain. In Concord, for instance, any person to trade or use tea "shall be for the future deemed unfriendly and enemical to the happy Constitution of this Country." Shame would keep retailers in line.[37]

For instance, "CONCORDIA" told a story of a man from the country shopping at a Boston store. Before completing his purchase, he hesitated, asking the shopkeeper if he sold tea. Once the customer heard that there was no tea for sale, he was happy to pay for his items.[38] Storekeepers at fixed shops were easy to find. But peddlers moved throughout the countryside to sell their wares—and they might easily find a gray market in tea. In the early months of 1774, in Montague and Shrewsbury, Massachusetts, and in Lyme, Connecticut, local Sons of Liberty exposed peddlers (or their customers) and forced them to burn their tea (or did it themselves). An article reporting on incidents like these reminded peddlers that peddling was technically illegal, and hinted that tarring and feathering would be the punishment.[39]

Yet everyone knew this was a weak way to enforce a boycott. As Samuel Adams had warned, tea "would be bought up underhandedly." To demonstrate this cheating in action, one mischief-maker stopped at a tavern twenty miles from Boston and tried to order tea. When the landlord replied, "it is entirely against my Constitution to let one Drop of Tea be drank in my House," the writer decided to persist (he needed it for his health, he said) until he got the landlord to admit that he refused to serve tea "for Fear of the

Displeasure of his Countrymen." The writer urged readers to "examine all the pretended Water-Pots that are brought to the Table." When fear rather than patriotism motivated innkeepers, it seemed likely that the innkeepers would cheat. And once cheating became common, it would be easy for the enemies of the Sons of Liberty to mock the tea boycotts.[40]

No, in order to get Parliament to repeal the tea duty, ordinary consumers would need to participate. These shoppers wouldn't just respond to angry pamphlets and high-minded rhetoric. They needed to get their hands around something physical—like a cup of tea. By persuading ordinary men and women to push away their tea, the Sons of Liberty could build a national movement that wouldn't require the help of skittish, cautious businessmen. Even the Boston merchants themselves recognized this: on December 23 they resolved, "We will not ourselves make use of Tea, nor will we permit it in our respective Familys . . . but will do our utmost to discourage it in others." The port of Newbury passed a similar resolution: "we will absolutely forbid the use of it in our houses as a species of entertainment for visitors, whether relations or others." Townsfolk were coming together to ensure that tea canisters were empty, and that colonial liberty was safe.[41]

With the help (and pressure) of town committees, American families could make a tea protest into a political reality. Thomas Newell, nephew of a Boston selectman, crossed the Charles River to attend a tea protest in Charlestown on December 31, 1773. A few days earlier, the Charlestown Town Meeting had voted to collect tea from any interested families in town and reimburse them for the price they had originally paid. In this they were following the example of local merchants, who had already agreed not only to stop selling tea, but to destroy their existing inventories of tea. The town crier announced the collection, so that "those who had a Mind to part with their Tea, knew where to carry it, and be sure of their pay; those who had a Mind to keep it by them, were left at Liberty." Non-participating families were on their honor not to use or sell their tea. At noon, with thousands of spectators present, the people of Charlestown celebrated New Year's Eve by collecting all the tea and setting it on fire in Market Square. Newell was delighted that their hosts treated them to punch and wine, at the town's expense.[42]

Boston had its own tea bonfire later that night. A few days after the Tea Party, the laborer Ebenezer Withington, age fifty-four, had stumbled upon a half-chest of tea that had washed up in the marshes near Dorchester. "Thinking no Harm," he brought home the tea and began selling some of it to his neighbors. When the local Sons of Liberty got wind of what "Old Straddlebug" was doing, a committee of "Cape or Narragansett-Indians" visited him at his home, seized his contraband goods, and burned the tea on the Boston Common at 11 p.m. All over Massachusetts, people now believed they shared a responsibility to defend American liberty by preventing the sale of dutied tea.[43]

The trick, after December 1773, was to get the movement to spread. "The Towns of *Lexington & Charlestown* have set us laudable examples," cheered one writer. "Let us bravely sacrifice the obnoxious Drug at the Shrine of American Liberty." The Sons of Liberty hoped that flaming pyres of tea would light the countryside, radiating outward from Boston. These bonfires would ratify town resolves by showing that Americans were people of action, not just words. As everyone had learned during the nonimportation agreements of the late 1760s, colonial unity could easily collapse unless everyone cooperated. When the Charlestown merchants agreed not to sell tea on December 25, they had to make sure their neighbors in Boston and Medford would join the embargo, too.[44]

The Boston merchants' agreement to stop selling tea came into effect on January 20. The merchants observed the occasion by yielding up three barrels of tea and pulling it on a sled from Tileston's Wharf to King Street. The Sons of Liberty then gathered a cheering crowd in front of the customhouse and set the barrels on fire. A government-friendly newspaper sniffed that the tea was "supposed to be damaged," and believed it was smuggled Dutch tea in the first place.[45]

Such skeptics abounded, of course. "A TRUE WHIG" scoffed at how little tea had actually been sacrificed at Lexington and Charlestown. The writer also hinted that the Boston tea dealers had only entered into the boycott because they had large inventories of coffee and chocolate that they wanted to unload. In general, "A TRUE WHIG" had no trouble with a ban on duties tea, but he thought that "discarding all Teas without Discrimination" was not just a "stupid Plan," but possibly a plot hatched by the friends of government. Not only would this scheme ruin Boston's trade (which Boston would lose to smugglers in the middle colonies), but since tea was such a hard habit to break, the inevitable violation of a boycott on *all* tea would "expose ourselves to contempt." A week later, "A LADY" wrote in to thank the "TRUE WHIG" on behalf of "my discerning Sex."[46]

Nor did everyone think that destroying further shipments of tea would be a good idea. Some, like "A TRUE WHIG" (who may have been a smuggler himself) believed that colonists should be able to drink smuggled Dutch tea, or at least whatever tea consumers (or merchants) still had on hand. Many Americans wanted to keep on consuming their favorite beverage without worrying about costumed vigilantes knocking at their doors. Would the colonists' insatiable appetite for tea override their civic obligation? The Sons of Liberty worried that if people were too weak to resist temptation, America would drown in tea. The Boston Tea Party had been a rousing statement, but it might not be enough.[47]

Destroying tea by fire and flood continued to be popular. In early January, local Sons of Liberty stopped a barrel of tea after it crossed on the ferry from Boston to Charlestown. Some merchant was trying to market the tea in the countryside, but the Sons of Liberty put a stop to his plan by dumping the cargo in the river.[48] Two months later, John Hancock gave a rousing speech on March 5, commemorating the anniversary of the Boston Massacre at the Old South Meeting House. The next day, a rainy Sunday, Captain Benjamin Gorham arrived from London in the brig *Fortune* with $28\frac{1}{2}$ chests of Bohea (common black) tea on board. The tea was consigned to Boston merchants—it wasn't a direct East India Company shipment like the tea that arrived in late 1773, although the press was confused about this. Regardless, the *Boston Gazette* predicted that it would "Certainly not [be] suffered to be landed in Boston."[49]

Indeed, the *Gazette* emphasized that justice and honor obliged Bostonians to oppose the landing of the tea. Since the governor and customs officers would once again prevent the tea from being sent back to London, it would be pointless to try and pressure the consignee. Instead, "The SACHEMS must have a *Talk* upon this Matter."[50] The *Massachusetts Spy* took this theme and ran with it. In a fanciful account of what happened next, it described how "His Majesty Oknookortunkogog King of the Narragansett tribe of Indians" summoned a council, which advised him to destroy the tea aboard the *Fortune*. "Orders were then issued to the seizor and destroyer-general, and their deputies" to proceed to Boston. As Captain Gorham later reported, at 8 p.m. on March 7 a group of men "disguised and dressed and talking like Indians Armed with Axes and Hatchets with force and Violence" boarded the *Fortune*, searched it for tea, and dumped the tea chests into the dock. Later, when the "Hearts of Steel" took to the pages of the *Spy* to thank Oknookortunkogog, they wrote, "your late order for the destruction of the poisonous weed *Tea*, otherwise called *Kill-all*, is a fresh proof of your Majesty's love to your people, and inviolable attachments to their liberties." Meanwhile, the owners of the *Fortune* rushed to assure readers that they had not intentionally imported any tea.[51]

The tea from the *William*, however, was still at large: William Palfrey, one of the Boston Sons of Liberty, boasted that "no Person would dare to bring away a Chest of it," since "the People are so determin'd, that Tar & Feathers would be the least part of the punishment inflicted on any one who should attempt it." The Sons of Liberty did their best to single out offenders who flouted the rules blatantly. First they would hurt their pocketbooks, by destroying the tea. If that didn't work, or proved impossible, then they could threaten offenders personally—with ostracism or even bodily harm. Despite Palfrey's enthusiasm, however, small amounts of the Cape Cod tea were found close at hand (in Truro, Massachusetts) and further away (in Lyme, Connecticut, where it was burned).[52]

The conflicts that arose from the *William* cargo and other mysterious tea shipments exposed the difficulty that the Sons of Liberty would have in enforcing a tea boycott. At a Wellfleet town meeting, they demanded two chests that John Greenough, a justice of the peace, had purchased from the Clarkes. Greenough had left another chest at Provincetown, which was burned by seven "Indians." After receiving threats from Boston and scorn from his own father and brother, Greenough later quietly recovered some of the tea from Wellfleet, but he was clearly shaken by his ordeal. "Can we imagine," he asked his father, "a more absolute State of Tyranny and outrageous Cruelty than when every private gang of Plunderers & Assassins may wreek their Vengeance against any Person or their Property unpunish'd; nay what greater Curse can befall us!"[53]

When the nearby town of Eastham found out that Colonel Willard Knowles had bought some of Greenough's tea and offered it for sale, a radical faction voted to strip Knowles of his duty to procure arms for the militia. To enforce this resolution, a group of people disguised as Indians accosted a town selectman, tarred his hands and face, and forced him to swear not to reveal their identities (since the selectman called some of them by name). After a standoff between the radical crowd and the town militia, a more moderate group seized control of the Eastham Town Meeting and restored Knowles to the town's good graces.[54]

In March 1774, Isaac Jones of Weston was caught bragging that he sold tea to a number of customers between Weston and Boston, in spite of their resolutions "not to use, much less buy any Tea." The writer "RUSTICUS" was outraged: either Jones was right, and the town meetings were making worthless resolutions, or Jones was insolent, arrogant, and deserving of "the severest chastisement." As a result of these accusations, some people from Weston and neighboring towns gathered together on March 28 to teach Jones a lesson. Though Jones was away, a crowd of thirty painted men broke his windows, stole some of his liquor, dishes, and foodstuffs, "and shewed other tokens of their resentment." Jones soon made a public apology, claiming that the tea he was selling (which he'd picked up in Albany) was duty-free.[55]

Merchants like Greenough and Jones were reluctant to stop selling tea, and consumers—especially female consumers—were reluctant to stop drinking it. Would the women of New England behave more like Mrs. Hewes or Mrs. Wheeler? What was striking, of course, is that this was a time and place where women couldn't vote and weren't supposed to speak out on political questions. Yet when it came to the success of the tea boycott, men very much cared what women thought. Writers like "*A Friend to the Cause*" tried their best to enlist women. "I . . . hope my countrymen, and the *fair Sex* in particular, will convince the world of our *uprightness*, by destroying *all Tea* for which they have imprudently paid the duty."[56]

Prior to the destruction of the tea, an elderly seamstress and "Daughter of Liberty" wrote a poem urging Bostonians, "Don't suffer any Tea to land." For the radical newspapers, it was important to include women's voices, to show that men and women alike wanted to turn back the tea.[57] Remarking on the military and naval preparations in Boston harbor in the week leading up to the Tea Party, one writer suggested, "the Ladies are apprehensive that the musty Teas kindly conveyed to them from London, will be crammed down their throats with all expedition." Although this author cast women as victims of the Tea Act, the women's apprehension showed that they were awake to the political importance of resistance.[58]

Women's literary voices became particularly important for disseminating radical ideas. A week after the Boston Tea Party, John Adams asked his talented friend, Mercy Otis Warren, to write a poem about it, which was printed in the *Boston Gazette*. The poem celebrated not just the "Hero's of the Tuskarora Tribe" who had dumped the tea in the ocean, but also the women who supported them. "For Females have their Influence o'er Kings," she wrote, and:

Nor when in weighty Matters they engage:
Could they neglect the Sex's sage Advice,
And least of all in any Point so nice,
As to forbid the choice Ambrosial Sip,
And offer Bohea to the rosy Lip?

By the end of the poem, the Bostonians have dumped the tea in the ocean as an offering to the sea-gods, as one nymph triumphs over her rival (and her rival's devious, shape-shifting servant). Tea, the poetess wrote, was fit for the sea, but was a "baneful Poison" to those on land: and the so-called Indians wanted nothing to do with faction, tyranny, greed, and luxury. In her allegorical poetry, Warren portrayed Boston's legendary men and

women working together on behalf of liberty against its enemies such as
Thomas Hutchinson and other despoilers of the American coast.[59]

Later, in an issue that reprinted a London essay on the effects of luxury
as well as a local writer's determination to give up tea for the sake of his
country, the *Virginia Gazette* featured another poem, *"A Lady's Adieu to her*
TEA TABLE," which was reprinted in Boston.

> FAREWELL the Tea Board, with its gaudy Equipage,
> Of Cups and Saucers, Cream Bucket, Sugar Tongs,
> The pretty Tea Chest also, lately stor'd
> With Hyson, Congo, and best Double Fine.
> Full many a joyous Moment have I sat by ye,
> Hearing the Girls' Tattle, the Old Maids talk Scandal,
> And the spruce Coxcomb laugh at—may be—Nothing.
> No more shall I dish out the once lov'd Liquor,
> Though now detestable,
> Because I'm taught, (and I believe it true)
> Its Use will *fasten slavish Chains upon my Country*,
> And LIBERTY's the Goddess I would choose
> To reign triumphant in AMERICA.[60]

In the month following the Tea Party, Bostonians heard an increasing
chorus of reports that women were joining the boycott. The *Newport
Mercury* picked up a rumor of a Boston boycott: "The ladies in Boston, to
their immortal honour, are entering into an association against the use of
India Tea; and we hope the ladies in this town will universally do the
same."[61] In Exeter, New Hampshire, a town meeting in January 1774 led
to an outdoor gathering on Tower Hill, where the local townsfolk burned
"a considerable Quantity" of tea. "As the weather was very cold, the ladies
were not backward in feeding the fire, and perhaps took as much pleasure
in destroying said fuel, as they would in sipping so baneful a commodity."
Meanwhile, David Mason of Salem wanted to allow his ill wife permission
to use tea, but she said, "no, she would sooner endure any inconvenience,
than it should be said, she was enjoying a privilege her husband was
employed to take from her friends and neighbours."[62]

Nevertheless, both men and women had trouble giving up their tea
addiction. After John Adams had ridden north for thirty miles to get to a
tavern in Falmouth, Maine, in July 1774, he asked the landlady, "is it
lawfull for a weary Traveller to refresh himself with a Dish of Tea provided
it has been honestly smuggled, or paid no Duties?"

"No sir," said the landlady, "we have renounced all Tea in this Place." She offered him coffee instead, which Adams said he was able to tolerate. "Tea must be universally renounced," he concluded. "I must be weaned, and the sooner, the better."[63]

In November 1774, Mary Noyes of New Haven, Connecticut, proudly reported, "There has not one drop of Tea been drink'd by any of our family," although she did note that "very particular company" on two afternoons had led her to make an exception. "Our Gen^ln would none of them touch one drop. I find my self weand from it in a good measure."[64] Women were in a particular bind—they could not vote at town meetings on boycotting tea, yet tea was at the center of their social world. They were being asked to give it up, but men were making the decision for them.

The men's rebellion aboard the tea ships had been violent and dramatic—women's rebellion would have to be quieter and subtler. Some of women's fondest memories of the year 1774 were the furtive sips of tea they took when the men of the house (or the radicals of the community) weren't watching. Clara Barton, the founder of the American Red Cross, remembered hearing that her grandmother Dorothy and her great-aunt, Martha Moore Ballard, of Oxford, Massachusetts, secretly sipped tea in the cellar while her great-uncle, Dr. Stephen Barton (a supporter of the tea boycotts) was away. In another version of the story, the tea was reserved for ailing women who needed its medicinal balm. "Poor Souls!" cried Peter Oliver, sarcastically, observing that many women "were forced to take Turns to be sick, & invite their Acquaintance[s] to visit them; & so the Sickness went on by Rotation."[65] Helen Maxwell-Read of Norfolk, Virginia, remembered her father, Maximillian Calvert, coming home one evening, laughingly telling his family that they must drink no more tea, "at least, not in my sight, for if you do, I shall be obliged to break your China for you." As Helen recalled, "So we banished the teapot from the table, but as we could not give up our tea, and saw no good to come in spiting ourselves in that way, we used to sip a little, now and then, by ourselves." Helen's mother Mary, she remembered, would serve tea in front of her father, but would pour it from a coffee pot.[66]

Innocent as these small acts of family rebellion might seem, Oliver (a government supporter) was outraged by them: the boycotts were part of "a truely infernal Scheme; it was setting the nearest Relations & most intimate Friends at irreconcilable Variance." Nonimportation, he wrote, "had that most accursed Effect, of raising a most unnatural Enmity between Parents & Children & Husbands & Wives." John Adams had noticed such conflicts, too: "We have been told that our Struggle has loosened the bands of Government every where," he wrote. "That Children and Apprentices were disobedient—that schools and Colledges were grown turbulent—that Indians slighted their Guardians and Negroes grew insolent to their Masters." Even women, a "Tribe more numerous and powerfull than all the rest were grown discontented."[67]

Other friends of government tried to capitalize on women who might feel that the tea boycott was an imposition on them. A writer named "SUSANNA SPINDLE" wrote a series of mock resolutions, modeled on the resolutions of town meetings. The resolutions argued that women, exhausted from making homespun clothing for a country mad with nonimportation agreements, found tea to be their only relief. The writer offered a resolution, "That the Women in America, are entitled to all the Liberties which the Women in Great-Britain enjoy, and particularly to drink Tea."[68] Many friends of government used misogynistic arguments: for instance, they claimed that women were too far seduced by tea to give it up. A *Boston Post-Boy* contributor seemed to ridicule the "fair Daughters of Liberty" by publishing another set of phony resolutions: "as hanging, drawing and quartering, are the Punishments inflicted by Law in Cases of High-Treason, we are determined, constantly to assemble at each others Houses, to HANG the Tea-Kettle, DRAW the Tea, and QUARTER the Toast."[69]

In some cases, the Sons of Liberty were no better. They enjoined women to give up tea, but used the emptiest possible arguments. One writer, "A WOMAN," finally became annoyed with some of the more ridiculous justifications for abstaining from tea: it was packed by the "nasty feet and legs" of Chinese porters, it bred fleas, it caused smallpox. Instead of inventing "bug bears to scare children," why not act as if readers—particularly female readers—were "capable of using their reason"? It would be more effective to enumerate the political reasons for boycotting tea than to use name-calling and "scare crow stories" to try and frighten tea drinkers away from the beverage.[70]

In March 1776, when Abigail Adams instructed her husband John, then cloistered with the Continental Congress, to "Remember the Ladies," it was a pointed reminder that women had acted as patriotically as men when it came to acts like boycotting tea. Yet by the end of the American Revolution, Abigail's plea had gone unheeded. Women still gave up their property in marriage, and they were still barred from voting or serving on juries. During the Victorian era in the nineteenth century, women were consigned to the household and the parlor as mothers and housewives in the private sphere. The whistling teakettle had become a safety valve: tea allowed women to gather and gossip, but it gave them few avenues for making their voices heard in the wider realms of business and politics. In the eighteenth century, men complained about the dangers of tea because it was new and suspicious; but by the nineteenth century, they must have been satisfied that tea-drinking women posed little threat to a male-dominated society.[71]

In any case, in late 1773 and early 1774 it seemed that tea boycotts were becoming a way for radicalized men and women in towns throughout New England to express solidarity with Boston. The Boston Tea Party had inspired a movement that gave both men and women an opportunity to protest against the acts of Parliament. All that remained was to see how Parliament would respond.

CHAPTER 9

Boston Bears the Blame

The arrival of all these thundering regulations (which very quickly succeeded one another) caused the greatest alarm in America. Here was a full avowal of tyranny in its most frightful form. We did not view the storm merely at a distance; it was almost at our very doors. The measures affecting one colony only, made no difference in the general indignation they caused.

James Iredell, 1775 or 1776[1]

"After the Destruction of the Tea," wrote the Loyalist Peter Oliver, "the *Massachusetts* Faction found they had past the *Rubicon*; it was now, Neck or Nothing."[2] On the morning after the Tea Party, Admiral Montagu had asked "who was to pay the fidler," and the town of Boston would soon have an answer.

At first, people reacted to news of the Tea Party with shock. Many immediately began looking for someone to blame.

The Boston radicals were firm in their conviction: the consignees, the customs officials, Admiral Montagu, and the governor were the ones at fault—but certainly not the people of Boston. Sure, a "number of persons unknown and in disguise" had actually destroyed the tea—but they had been driven to do it by the stubbornness of the people's enemies. Had the consignees resigned their commissions, had the customs officers granted a clearance to the *Dartmouth*, or had Governor Hutchinson given the ship a pass to depart the harbor, the waste of all that tea would have been avoided. The power to save the tea had been in the hands of government officials—but instead they took "malicious Pleasure" in standing by idly as the Bostonians struggled to preserve their liberty. The consignees and their allies had goaded the tea destroyers for the purpose of making Boston look bad in the eyes of the British.[3]

If anything, the Bostonians "did their utmost to preserve the property of the East-India company," as the townspeople of Dedham wrote in support.

"Upon the whole," wrote Boston Selectman John Scollay, "I do lament the loss of the Honourable Company; I also lament the original cause of that loss, which I think is most unrighteous, and which has proved a source of unhappiness to the Americans." According to the Boston town representatives, the tea destroyers had been trying to prevent violence, since they foresaw that the consignees and customs officials would have attempted to land the teas "by force."[4] "There was no other Alternative but to destroy it or let it be landed," John Adams wrote in his diary. "To let it be landed, would be giving up the Principle of Taxation by Parliamentary Authority, against which the Continent have struggled for 10 years." To concede the principle of taxation without representation would have squandered "all our labour for 10 years . . . subjecting ourselves and our Posterity forever to Egyptian Taskmasters—to Burthens, Indignities, to Ignominy, Reproach, and Contempt, to Desolation and Oppression, to Poverty and Servitude."[5]

Governor Hutchinson, meanwhile, reported that he was taken unawares by this turn of events. From seven miles away in Milton, he had assumed that the Bostonians (especially men of property like Hancock and Rowe) would be content to allow the tea to be seized and stored, rather than allow it to be destroyed and risk being held liable. He could not have granted a pass to the *Dartmouth* without violating his oath to uphold the laws of trade, and he could not have ordered troops or marines to prevent the destruction of the tea without bringing on "a greater convulsion" than anyone had considered possible during the clashes of 1770. In many ways, Hutchinson had been a victim of circumstance. He had less power in Massachusetts and in Boston than his position would suggest—the House of Representatives, the Council, the Boston Town Meeting, and many of the local magistrates were all lined up against him. Furthermore, he could count on little support from his masters in London: they were too distant, they had been nervous about challenging the colonies, and their previous experiment (1768–70) of using troops to enforce the law had been a disaster, culminating in the Boston Massacre. Indeed, Parliament had not even provided Hutchinson or the other governors with advance notice about the tea shipments in the fall of 1773—so the governors hadn't had much of an opportunity to prepare, nor did they have time to ask London for advice about their options.[6]

Now, in the aftermath of the tea's destruction, Hutchinson recognized that the Tea Party could not go unanswered—he would be forced to respond. But once again, he failed to spur his Council to action. As everyone knew, the Council answered to the elected members of the House of Representatives, not to the governor. Due to illness and bad weather, not enough Council members showed up to make a quorum in Boston on December 17. John Adams heard a rumor that Hutchinson had concluded that "the People had been guilty of High Treason." Adams may have been misinformed about this, and many Bostonians were skeptical about whether the government could make treason charges stick. As the young Nathaniel W. Appleton wrote, "perhaps he thinks that *great Words* will put this People in Terror, but I believe he is mistaken." Hutchinson tried to summon his Council again in Milton on December 18, and again failed to make a quorum. On December 21, he tried a third time, gathering Council members at William Brattle's home in Cambridge. This time he had enough members present, but the results were once again disappointing. If Hutchinson had really considered treason charges, then by the 21st the Council had urged him to tone down the seriousness of his prosecution: he and Attorney General Jonathan Sewall now spoke of bringing perpetrators up on charges of burglary and rioting. To add to the indignity, Hutchinson could not even get his Council to approve an offer of reward for information on those who had destroyed the tea. The Council would only advise Sewall to investigate the destruction of the tea and lay his findings before the grand jury—but the grand jury, packed with Sons of Liberty and their sympathizers, was expected to do little. Regardless, Sewall never found anyone to prosecute.[7]

It was the same frustration that Francis Bernard, Hutchinson's predecessor in the governor's office, had faced whenever riots broke out in the 1760s. It was impossible to enforce customs laws or punish those who broke them. Bostonians no longer respected or accepted the British power to tax the colonies. British leaders, therefore, had two options: to aim for the neck, or do nothing.

As the objects of Bostonians' blame, the consignees didn't feel safe in town for months after the destruction of the tea. Many of them, considered "obnoxious to their countrymen," remained in their island asylum. Thomas Hutchinson Jr. slipped away from Castle Island to his father's house in Milton ("having only changed one prison for another"), where he wrote bitterly about the consignees' inability to show their faces in Boston. On the morning of January 15, Bostonians read a handbill posted by "JOYCE, jun., Chairman of the Committee for Tarring & Feathering." George Joyce had been a seventeenth-century English army officer under Oliver Cromwell who arrested King Charles I and assisted in his execution on January 30, 1649. Now "JOYCE, jun.," with ambitions to slay tyrants in 1774, called the consignees "odious Miscreants and detestable Tools to Ministry and Governor," as well as "Traitors to their Country" and "Butchers." Young "JOYCE" warned

Bostonians that the consignees were hoping to move back to Boston (actually the rumor had been about two of them: Thomas Hutchinson Jr. and Benjamin Faneuil Jr.), and he urged the town to be ready "to give them such a Reception, as such vile ingrates deserve." Two days later, Elisha Hutchinson attempted to visit his father-in-law at Plymouth. Church bells rang their solemn peal, which summoned a crowd to the house, demanding that Hutchinson depart immediately. The local committee of correspondence stepped in and everyone agreed to allow Hutchinson a night's sleep. In the morning, Elisha either overslept or decided to try the patience of the local Sons of Liberty—but once he "was fully convinced that his safety depended on his departure," he left town in the middle of a snowstorm.[8]

Jonathan Clarke sailed for England in February. His father and the other consignees entertained the idea of defending their injured reputations in the newspapers or in court, but appear to have concluded, with the Clarkes' brother-in-law John Singleton Copley, that the people of Massachusetts were "too much disposed to beleive the Worst" of them. As late as March 9, the governor was reporting that Isaac Winslow Clarke, Richard Clarke, and Benjamin Faneuil Jr. were still confined at Fort William on Castle Island. Admiral John Montagu was heard to lament, "There never was any Thing in Turkey nor in any Part of the World, so arbitrary and cruel as keeping old Mr. [Richard] Clark, at the Castle all this winter, an old Man, from his family." To the friends of government, the Boston townsfolk were the tyrants.[9]

Back in England, officials in the British government heard protests against the Tea Act first as whispers, and then as a roar. By late 1773, English correspondents were already hearing that the Tea Act had provoked unpleasant reactions in the middle colonies.[10]

Two men in England were particularly important for connecting Massachusetts to the center of power in Great Britain. One was Benjamin Franklin, the agent for the Massachusetts House of Representatives (and for three other colonies). Although Philadelphia was his adopted city, Franklin had been born in Boston and baptized at the church that preceded the Old South Meeting House. He kept Thomas Cushing, Speaker of the Massachusetts House of Representatives, and other important provincial officials informed of relevant developments in Great Britain. He also heard grievances from the Sons of Liberty and advised the leaders of Massachusetts how they might best achieve their goals in Whitehall.[11]

The other man was William Legge, the second Earl of Dartmouth and the stepbrother of Lord North, the king's prime minister. When Dartmouth joined North's Cabinet as Secretary for American Affairs in 1772, Americans felt encouraged to hope for the best. They knew that Dartmouth had played a role in the repeal of the Stamp Act in 1766. They celebrated his reputation for piety, philanthropy (the college in New Hampshire is named for him), and mildness. Benjamin Franklin, who disliked Dartmouth's predecessor, Lord Hillsborough, was also optimistic. Franklin looked forward to a more cordial relationship with the new secretary. He also believed, as he reassured Cushing, that Dartmouth would encourage more favorable policies for Massachusetts.[12]

Since the Tea Act was primarily aimed at resolving the affairs of the East India Company, Lord North had not seen fit to consult his stepbrother about it. On the surface, the Tea Act was only tangentially related to Dartmouth's department of American affairs. Dartmouth had also been absent from his office and tending to his estates from August to November of 1773, when the tea ships first sailed down the Thames. Hutchinson and the other colonial governors had received no advance word of the Tea Act or the tea shipments because Dartmouth was unable to provide any instructions.[13]

By early January 1774 (before anyone had heard about the destruction of the tea at Boston), Dartmouth was already writing to his American subordinates with instructions for how to act if the colonists resisted the tea shipments. He told General Frederick Haldimand, who was stationed at New York City, "to protect the King's Subjects from Insult & Oppression, and remove any unlawful Obstruction that may be given to the Commerce of this Kingdom," but only in the case of "a proper Requisition." To New York governor William Tryon, he wrote that no such requisition for troops should be made "upon a slight ground, but only in cases of absolute Necessity when every other effort has failed."[14]

The king also seemed relatively unconcerned, at first. Upon hearing of the troubles in the colonies, the East India Company had instructed the consignees that if they met resistance, they should send the tea to Halifax, Nova Scotia. This advice, as it turned out, arrived far too late for Boston, Philadelphia, and Charleston—but in any case King George looked forward to seeing the tea "spread southward" from the northern provinces (present-day Canada) to the recalcitrant American colonies. The radical colonists had been both wrong and right about the intentions of the British government: the ministry didn't intend to force the tea upon the American colonists at sword's point, but they did intend to impose the tea duty by sneaking tea into the stubborn colonies and undermining any attempts at striking a nonimportation agreement.[15]

Once again it was John Hancock's ship, the *Hayley*, whose swift passage brought important news across the Atlantic. The *Hayley* had left Boston on December 22 and arrived at Dover, England, on January 19, 1774. Over the next few days, English newspapers reprinted an account of the destruction of the tea from the *Boston Gazette*, which supported the anti-tea resistance.[16] At first, newspaper audiences in Great Britain saw little reason to be alarmed. King George III commented to Dartmouth, "I am much hurt that the instigation of bad men hath again drawn the people of Boston to take such unjustifiable steps; but I trust by degrees tea will find its way there." The king was optimistic that the Bostonians' resistance was just a small obstacle that could be overcome.[17]

But his optimism was misplaced. Soon Whitehall and the British public learned how widespread American resistance to the tea had been. The *Polly* had returned from Philadelphia with its rejected tea on January 25, and London received the news from Charleston on January 28 that the tea there had been seized and stored, but not sold.[18] As the people of Great Britain absorbed the shock of the news, reactions turned against the people of Boston. In the *Middlesex Journal*, "LYCURGUS" attacked the "seditious as well as turbulent and insolent behaviour of the Bostonians," who were committing "every species of licentiousness and cruelty, common to a state of anarchy." In the next issue, the paper reported, "The whole Continent is in a flame, from Boston to Charles Town, and the whole of the inhabitants, to a man, appear unanimously resolved to dispute with their lives the right of taxation in the mother country." Two days later, "An ENGLISHMAN" wrote in: "The Americans, it appears, are absolutely in open and avowed rebellion."[19]

Lord Dartmouth, meanwhile, was gathering his own intelligence. He read official reports from the colonial governors, Admiral Montagu, Lieutenant Colonel Leslie, and the East India Company. He read accounts of the resistance in American newspapers, and he personally interviewed witnesses such as Captain James Scott of the *Hayley*, Dr. Hugh Williamson of Philadelphia (who had been visiting Boston), and Gilbert Barkly, one of Philadelphia's failed consignees. With every account, the news seemed to get worse and worse.[20]

In this climate of increasing alarm, Franklin was running into trouble. Franklin had sent to Massachusetts some of the private letters that Hutchinson and Andrew Oliver had written to Thomas Whately, a member of Parliament (who had since died) in 1768 and 1769. In those letters, Hutchinson had expressed his antipathy toward the Sons of Liberty, complained about the weakness of the Council, and asserted that restraints on colonial privileges would be necessary to tie the colonies more firmly to the British Empire. The publication of these letters, the outrage they had spurred in Massachusetts, and the mystery of who had leaked a dead man's letters had already led to a duel in London on December 11, 1773, between two of the men involved in the affair. Shortly afterward, to prevent any further violence, Franklin sent a letter to the *London Chronicle* confessing that he had been the one responsible for sending the letters to Boston. Franklin claimed that he was trying to show the public that Hutchinson and his cronies had been trying to drive a wedge between the mother country and the people of Massachusetts. London gossip-mongers were scandalized at Franklin's involvement, but few believed he had acted alone in obtaining the letters. William Whately (brother of the deceased Thomas) sued Franklin in the Court of Chancery in January 1774.[21]

The old letters had also led the Massachusetts House of Representatives to petition for the removal of Governor Hutchinson and Lieutenant Governor Oliver. This petition came before a committee of the Privy Council on January 11, 1774. After a request for delay, the committee reconvened on January 29 before a huge crowd of spectators (fig. 28). The Privy Council met at the Cockpit, so called because it had been built on the site where King Henry VIII had once made sport of watching roosters hack each other to death.

The ostensible purpose of the hearing at the Cockpit was to determine whether Hutchinson and Oliver ought to be removed because of their unpopularity. The government easily dispensed with the Massachusetts petition. The Massachusetts representatives had not proven that Hutchinson and Oliver had engaged in any serious misconduct, and the Privy Council could find no other fault with Hutchinson's administration. The committee in the Cockpit dismissed the petition.

In the process of arguing for the dismissal, Solicitor General Alexander Wedderburn (who had been a friend of the late Thomas Whately) lit into Franklin with gleeful ferocity. With the audience laughing and applauding at each of his jabs, Wedderburn supposedly said that Franklin would "hence-forth esteem it a libel to be called *a man of letters*." He also held Franklin responsible for the actions of the Bostonians, who had, "with their usual moderation destroyed the cargo of three British ships." Franklin remained stone-faced throughout this verbal assault, but the public humiliation must have cut him deeply. Two days later he was sacked from his position as deputy postmaster general for North America. Since his appointment twenty years earlier, Franklin had made the royal mail more efficient, but the

28 Benjamin Franklin, an agent for the Massachusetts House of Representatives, faces the
Privy Council in London just after news of the Boston Tea Party had reached England.

mischief and mayhem he had caused by transmitting a dead man's private
letters to Massachusetts had angered his superiors. Franklin was the first to
take the blame for the rebellious actions of Massachusetts—and most
government supporters thought Franklin deserved his punishment.[22]

On January 29, after watching Wedderburn's attacks on Franklin, the
cabinet held a meeting and decided to take "effectual steps . . . to secure
the Dependance of the Colonies on the Mother Country." The issue,
according to one hard-line member of the House of Lords, was "whether
we were to be free, or slaves to our colonies."[23]

In the past, the British ministry had tempered its responses to American
resistance: it had affirmed Parliament's right to legislate for the colonies in
1766, but it had also repealed the Stamp Act. It had kept the tax on tea in
1770, but it had repealed the other Townshend duties. Now, as Lord Chief
Justice Mansfield said, Americans would learn the hard way that Parliament
intended to "temporise no longer." Parliament was now unwilling to make

concessions—and they certainly would not give up asserting their power to tax the colonies. The destruction of the tea at Boston had forced the British government to take a hard look at its American possessions.[24]

At meeting on February 4, the British Cabinet had already made a few suggestions about possible punishments. First, the Cabinet would consult Wedderburn and the attorney general, Edward Thurlow, about whether it would be proper to prosecute any individuals for treason. The Boston Sons of Liberty may have feared that such a prosecution was possible, but in any case the Cabinet's attempt went nowhere. After reviewing the facts and eyewitness testimony, Wedderburn and Thurlow concluded that although treason had been committed, the Crown did not have enough evidence to secure the conviction of any specific individuals. The ministry also toyed with the idea of bringing offenders to Britain for trial, or disqualifying them from holding office, but again, since witnesses couldn't or wouldn't name names, nothing ever came of these ideas. One of the officials involved later recalled that the Cabinet had approved a warrant of arrest for Thomas Cushing, John Hancock, Joseph Warren, and Samuel Adams, for their involvement in resistance prior to the destruction of the tea. But even after the Cabinet gathered more evidence, the Crown's law officers gave their opinion that it wasn't enough to make a treason charge stick.[25]

With the British public clamoring for a firm response to the Tea Party, the Cabinet chose to seek justice from the entire town of Boston. According to hostile observers, Boston was a treacherous, seditious Sodom that needed a strong hand to teach it compliance. Dartmouth was confident that even most Americans would agree that Boston deserved some punishment.[26]

The Cabinet's first proposal for a general punishment was to shut down customs oversight at Boston and move it elsewhere. Essentially, this meant that the port of Boston would be closed to almost all commercial shipping. If the Cabinet couldn't identify particular individuals for punishment, it could at least chastise Boston as the site where the destruction of the tea had taken place. Even though New York had initiated much of the resistance, the *Polly* had been turned back at Philadelphia, and the tea remained unsold at Charleston, Boston was singled out as the place where the most visible—and most outrageous—resistance had occurred. As Lord Chancellor Apsley said, it was desirable "to mark out Boston, & separate that town from the rest of [the] Delinquents." Dartmouth sent reassurances to Hutchinson, a commendation to the lieutenant governor of South Carolina, an acknowledgment of the difficulties Governor William Tryon could expect to face at New York, and a reprimand to Deputy Governor

John Penn of Pennsylvania (who had not even sent in a report about the *Polly*).[27]

Dartmouth could only shake his head over Boston's fate. Of the Bostonians he lamented "how fatally and effectually they have now shut the door against all possibility of present relief," from taxation and other restrictions, and he remarked "how utterly vain it must be to expect that Parliament will ever give it them, till there appears to be a change in their temper and conduct." It would be madness, he wrote, "if I was to say a word of repealing the Tea-Duty now, and yet I don't give up the hopes of seeing it done at some time or other." He continued, "If they had made no opposition to the East India Company Teas, I don't see why it might not have been done this Session: they have now put it at a greater distance, but I hope not rendered it for ever impossible."[28]

By February 19, the Cabinet had begun secretly sketching out what would become the Boston Port Bill in Parliament. This law would mandate the closing of the port of Boston until the town of Boston had indemnified the East India Company: in other words, the town would not just have to make financial restitution to the Company, but admit its collective guilt. Benjamin Franklin, still agent for Massachusetts, scolded the Bostonians for destroying private property "in a Dispute about Publick Rights." In early February, he had advised the Massachusetts Assembly to repay the East India Company before Parliament could pass legislation like the Boston Port Bill. Franklin called the destruction of the tea "an Act of violent Injustice on our part," which might well give Great Britain a pretense for waging war, if the cost of the tea was not repaid. Though he later changed his mind, at the time Franklin thought it was reasonable to charge "the Society at large" for the actions of "Persons unknown."[29]

The ministry rolled out the Boston Port Bill in the House of Commons on March 14—and by then almost two months had passed since London had first learned of the destruction of the tea. Lord North conceded that the law would punish an entire community, not just the persons responsible for the destruction of the tea. Yet, he argued, Boston "has been the ringleader of all violence and opposition to the execution of the laws of this country. New York and Philadelphia grew unruly on receiving the news of the triumph of the people of Boston. Boston has not only therefore to answer for its own violence but for having incited other places to tumults." This was something of a half-truth. If anything, it was New York and Philadelphia who had pushed Boston to resist the Tea Act; still, Boston's bold move had stiffened the resolve of Sons of Liberty in the middle colonies.[30]

Lord North also pointed to precedents where Parliament had punished communities to answer for public crimes: Glasgow for the Malt Tax riots in 1725, and Edinburgh for the Porteous riots of 1737. Boston had behaved far worse, and the destruction of the tea had been a culmination of years of violence and defiance. For all the petty disputes about taxes, Lord North said, "we are now to dispute the question whether we have or have not any authority in that country." When Lord North finished speaking and sat down, "there was a perfect silence for some minutes." Although a couple of MPs did object to the Boston Port Bill, even some of the American colonies' greatest allies in Parliament spoke in favor of singling out Boston for its "act of rebellion." As Franklin sadly concluded, "I suppose we never had . . . so few Friends in Britain. The violent Destruction of the Tea seems to have united all Parties here against our Province, so that the Bill now brought into Parliament for shutting up Boston as a Port till Satisfaction is made, meets with no Opposition."[31]

The Boston Port Bill passed without dissent in both houses, and the king gave it his royal seal on March 31 (fig. 29). This proved to be the first of what came to be called the Coercive Acts (or later, the Intolerable Acts). All trade

The able Doctor, or America Swallowing the Bitter Draught.

29 Lord North, author of the Boston Port Bill, pours tea down America's throat, while Britannia looks away, ashamed. Lord Sandwich and Lord Mansfield, two more members of the British Cabinet, hold America's feet and arms.

in and out of Boston was prohibited as of June 1, except for ships bringing food and fuel to the inhabitants, or military supplies for the British armed forces. The idea was to bring Boston's commerce to a halt, throwing almost all its inhabitants out of work, until the Crown was satisfied that the town had compensated the East India Company for its losses. The members of Parliament expected that Boston would quickly end its own misery by voting a payment for the lost tea. As it turned out, they guessed wrong.[32]

Next Parliament debated the Massachusetts Government Bill, the second of the Coercive Acts. British leaders had long ago concluded that the Massachusetts Charter, though sacred to the colonists, also made the colony ungovernable, for a number of reasons. First, the Council, which was supposed to support the royal governor, was instead in thrall to the Massachusetts House of Representatives. This had been a problem for Governor Hutchinson, both before and after the destruction of the tea, whenever he had tried to enforce the laws of Parliament. Second, the frequent town meetings, especially in Boston, had proven to be nurseries for resistance. Although the Boston town meeting had stopped discussing the tea crisis after November 18, and responsibility had shifted to the "Body of the People," the British ministry made no distinction—town meetings were dangerous. Third, the colony's tradition of electing its juries and magistrates was also a problem—how could you enforce unpopular customs regulations, or punish popular rioters, if the jury and justice were sympathetic to guilty parties? How could a British soldier or government official get a fair trial in a province where the juries were stacked against them?[33]

So Parliament set about passing two more bills that would help prevent crises like the tea resistance from forming again in Massachusetts. Under the Massachusetts Government Act, the Crown rather than the House of Representatives would nominate the Council. This was the way it was done in most colonies, like Virginia or New Hampshire, but the people of Massachusetts were used to having input into the makeup of the Council; now both the governorship and the Council were out of their reach. The governor was now authorized to act alone in times of crisis, and he now had the power to appoint or remove judges and magistrates (except the five judges of the Superior Court) himself. Court officers and judges would be serving at the governor's whim—they would be unaccountable and prone to schemes of patronage and corruption. The method of selecting jurors was also amended—they would be appointed by sheriffs (who were the governor's appointees). Townspeople now had little say in jury selection, which threatened to put debt cases, property seizures, and the power to imprison people into the hands of local elites. Finally, town meetings could be held only for annual elections of local representatives and officials, and any other agenda items or town meetings required the governor's consent. The governor, therefore, had the power to prevent towns from appointing committees of correspondence, passing resolutions against acts of Parliament, or subscribing to boycotts of tea.[34]

Parliament's third punishment for Massachusetts was the Administration of Justice Act, which was to be a temporary measure in effect for three years. If a civil or military official was put on trial in Massachusetts for a capital offense (such as murder), the governor had the power to transfer the trial to another colony, or to London. The idea was to allow soldiers and customs officials the power to exercise their duties without fear of being convicted by a colonial jury and executed; to the people of Massachusetts, who called this law the "Murder Act," it would allow soldiers to perpetrate a repeat of the "Boston Massacre" without fear of answering to a local jury.[35]

Finally, Lord Barrington, the Secretary of War, moved for a new Quartering Bill. In the past, the people of Massachusetts had argued that Fort William on Castle Island was sufficient to house any British troops in Boston. This new bill gave the governor the authority to billet soldiers in taverns and uninhabited houses, if necessary. The measure passed without much debate in Parliament, but American colonists were suspicious of any law that made it easier for troops to be housed in their midst.[36]

While these laws were being discussed, the Opposition pleaded with the ministry to consider a conciliatory measure to counterbalance the Coercive Acts. In mid-April, Opposition politicians in Parliament raised the possibility of repealing the tea duty, to soften the impact of the harsh laws the ministry had already introduced. On the floor of the House of Commons, Edmund Burke gave a famous and lengthy speech on April 19 about imperial character. "Reflect how you are to govern a people," he said, "who think they ought to be free, and think they are not. Your scheme yields no revenue; it yields nothing but discontent, disorder, disobedience." To this, Lord North replied that a repeal of the tea duty would do nothing. It would not stop the resistance in Boston—indeed, repealing the duty would "give to the town of Boston the merit of having delivered America from this burden," and a reputation for having won the battle over taxation without representation. Parliament rejected the motion 182 votes to 49.[37]

Isaac Barré, a pro-American Opposition member of Parliament, could only shake his head. "We had been the aggressors from the beginning," he said on May 2, 1774, "and like all other aggressors we shall never forgive them the injuries we have done them."[38]

In early February, the king had interviewed General Thomas Gage, commander of the British Army in America (then on leave in Great Britain). Gage reported that he would be ready to return to the colonies and enforce coercive measures; he thought four regiments (the same number that was sent to Boston in 1768) would be enough to pacify the town. By March, the Cabinet had decided that Gage would also serve as governor of Massachusetts. Gage was to be sent to Boston with two additional ships to support Admiral Montagu's naval force: these ships would now aid in enforcing the new restrictions on ships entering Boston's port. Gage's instructions also indicated that he should try to prosecute the ringleaders of the Boston Sons of Liberty, if possible.[39]

By the time Gage arrived in Boston on May 13, the colonists' political resistance to the Boston Port Act had already begun. News of the law had reached Massachusetts by early May 1774. Samuel Adams poured his outrage into letters that he sent throughout America. "The people," he wrote, "receive this cruel edict with abhorrence and indignation." On May 13, the Boston Town Meeting called upon the other colonies to "come into a joint Resolution, to stop all Importations from Great Britain & Exportations to Great Britain, & every part of the West Indies," until the Boston Port Act was repealed. Back in March, the Massachusetts House of Representatives had voted to purchase 500 barrels of gunpowder for the province. At that time, Hutchinson had written, "an opposition to His Majesty's forces is so wild and extravagant a design that I cannot bring myself to believe even the present leaders of the people so mad as in earnest to be engaged in it." Now, in May 1774, the idea of armed American resistance didn't seem nearly so far-fetched.[40]

Hutchinson departed for England on June 1, the day the Boston Port Act came into effect. Church bells tolled in the town of Boston, mourning the closing of the port. Lord North and Lord Dartmouth took great pains to praise Hutchinson, and emphasize that he had not been sacked for incompetence; instead, they claimed, Hutchinson was only leaving for Great Britain because the ministry was honoring his earlier wish for a leave of absence. Still, at least one member of Parliament publicly criticized Hutchinson for provoking the people of Massachusetts, for allowing his own sons to accept the East India Company consignment, and for failing to order Admiral Montagu to guard the tea ships.[41]

On the day after the Tea Party, John Adams had begun speculating in his diary about how the British ministry in Parliament would punish the people of Massachusetts: "By quartering Troops upon Us? By annulling our Charter? By laying on more duties? By restraining our Trade? By sacrifice of Individuals[?]" He worried that the East India Company might launch lawsuits, or that the British government might initiate prosecution. While he hoped that these were mere "Phantoms" or "Bugbears," he had believed that it was better for Massachusetts to suffer such consequences than to give up the principle of no taxation without representation. As many of his horrific predictions became brutal realities in the spring of 1774, Adams grew more and more convinced that Britain and America could never be reconciled. He was not alone.[42]

The Coercive Acts, rather than isolating Boston from the rest of the colonies, caused the rest of Massachusetts to rise up in protest. In Springfield, for instance, the townspeople spoke out in July 1774 against taxation without consent, against being judged by people other than their peers, and against the swift, arbitrary nature of the Boston Port Act. The new laws were "virtually annihilating our most Essential Charter Rights," and this gave them "Such apprehensions of the designs of administration against our Liberties, as we have never before allowed ourselves to Entertain." The opposition politician Edmund Burke had tried to warn the ministry about this: "There is combination not of Boston but of all America against it [the Tea Act]. . . . Observe that the disturbances are universal, that the people are almost unanimous." Indeed, the Coercive Acts were drawing more and more people in the Thirteen Colonies together in support of beleaguered Boston.[43]

Many American colonists, even those who had not approved of the destruction of the tea, now took up the cry against the acts of Parliament. They "look upon the chastisement of Boston to be purposely rigorous and held up by way of intimidation to all America," wrote Pennsylvania's deputy governor, John Penn. The Bostonians' "delinquency in destroying the East India Company's tea is lost in the attention given to what is here called the too severe punishment of shutting up the port, altering the constitution, and making an Act as they term it screening the officers and soldiers for shedding American blood." Boston had been punished for the sins of the "Mohawks" in spite of all the townspeople's efforts to distance themselves from the destruction of the tea. Now public opinion was beginning to paint Boston as the martyr for the "common cause of all America." Villages throughout New England and port towns in the other colonies sent material aid (particularly food) to help sustain Bostonians in their time of need (fig. 30). American clergymen helped to sponsor fast days in New York, New Jersey, Virginia, and New England, which gave parishioners the opportunity to reflect and pray for Boston. Massachusetts had its fast day on July 14, and the merchant John Rowe, still grumpy from the destruction

The BOSTONIANS in DISTRESS.

Plate II.   London Printed for R.Sayer & J.Bennett Map & Printsellers, N°53 Fleet Street, as the Act directs 19 Nov°1774.

30 Sailors feed fish to the Bostonians, who are held captive in a cage suspended from the Liberty Tree, surrounded by British troops, warships, and cannons.

of the tea (he was part owner of the *Eleanor*), wrote in his diary, "I cannot Reconcile this measure & should much Rather the People would do Justice & Recommend the Payment for the Tea instead of losing a Day by fasting." Indeed, two months before, the friends of government had almost tempted a large faction of moderate Boston merchants to sign a subscription to compensate the East India Company for its lost tea, in the hope of keeping the port of Boston open. The Boston Committee of Correspondence had been able to outmaneuver this alliance—in June, over the objections of local merchants, it circulated a "Solemn League and Covenant" that urged nonimportation and nonconsumption of British goods.[44]

With Boston divided, the farmers of rural Massachusetts, normally a less politicized group, stepped forward. The "Murder Act" and Parliament's interference with the Massachusetts Charter struck these country folk as an outrageous provocation. In Worcester County, representatives from twenty-two towns convened in early August to reaffirm their allegiance to the king, but also to "disclaim any jurisdiction in the commons of Great Britain over his majesty's subjects in America." Over the following month, the western counties of Massachusetts took action to nullify the recent acts of Parliament. Everywhere but in occupied Boston, organized groups of Massachusetts townspeople forced the councilors that Gage appointed to resign their seats—many were forced to flee their country estates under threat of violence. In Berkshire County, the locals refused to allow the judges of the Court of Common Pleas to sit. At Worcester, county delegates suggested the formation of a Provincial Congress, and called on residents to defend themselves against British troops with arms and gunpowder. At Salem (where Gage temporarily decided to move the government), town leaders decided to ignore the Massachusetts Government Act and hold an unsanctioned town meeting. Gage angrily arrested the leaders of the Salem Committee of Correspondence, and almost sparked an armed confrontation, but then backed down. Even in Boston, right under Gage's nose, grand and petit jurors refused to serve when the Superior Court of Judicature opened at the end of August. In short, Massachusetts began to overthrow British rule. During the tea crisis, the Boston Committee of Correspondence had awoken the farmers of Massachusetts to the dangers the colonies might face. But the Massachusetts Government Act, along with the other Coercive Acts, demonstrated that the Bostonians' fears had been justified. Boston, occupied by General Gage and his troops, was no longer taking a leading role. The farmers and craftsmen of the countryside, instead, had stepped in to lead Massachusetts out of the British Empire.[45]

Fearful of an uprising, General Gage had already begun dispatching troops to key New England towns to seize stores of arms and gunpowder. He sent a detachment to a provincial powder house in western Charlestown (now Somerville), which so inflamed the people of Massachusetts that 4,000 men gathered on Cambridge Common on September 2, 1774. Things started out peacefully, but the growing numbers of armed men became rowdier under a broiling sun. When customs officer Benjamin Hallowell rode through Cambridge on his way from Salem, someone called out to him, "Dam you how do you like us now, you Tory Son of a Bitch[?]"

As false rumors spread of shots having been fired, thousands more were ready to march, in arms, to the defense of the province. Tempers soon cooled, and a thunderstorm that evening sent everyone home. Yet these events turned out to be the dress rehearsal for the outbreak of war.[46]

Colonists were taking rapid steps toward cohesive action, not just in Massachusetts, but up and down the eastern seaboard of North America. Over the summer of 1774, every colony from New Hampshire to South Carolina voted for a slate of delegates to send to a Continental Congress in Philadelphia. Massachusetts sent a group of easterners: Samuel Adams, John Adams, Thomas Cushing, and the lawyer Robert Treat Paine. Just as Congress was convening, representatives from Boston and the surrounding towns met to air their grievances on September 6 and 9. The resulting Suffolk County Resolves denounced the Coercive Acts as unconstitutional and informed the public of the county's refusal to abide by them. The resolves urged the people to begin a boycott of *all* British goods, especially tea, and cautiously urged them to begin military training in case self-defense should become necessary to preserve American rights. These resolutions were not necessarily original—they echoed those of other Massachusetts counties—but they received the most publicity, once Paul Revere carried them to Philadelphia. There the Continental Congress promptly endorsed the Suffolk Resolves, causing delegate John Adams to crow, "This was one of the happiest Days of my Life. . . . This Day convinced me that America will support Massachusetts or perish with her." Congress also drew up a program called the Continental Association, which endorsed nonimportation as of December 1, included a policy of nonconsumption (which, as they had seen with tea, helped to encourage compliance), and promised nonexportation if these measures proved unsuccessful. The delegates promised that "all America" would support Massachusetts should General Gage resort to force; they also empowered local committees of correspondence to enforce the embargo. By the time it had disbanded in late October, Congress had also published a statement of American rights and grievances and agreed to reconvene in 1775 if their complaints went unheeded.[47]

Meanwhile, tea protests continued, particularly outside Massachusetts. Groups of Americans burned tea at Portsmouth, New Hampshire, Providence, Rhode Island, and Greenwich, New Jersey, and threw it overboard in the York River in Virginia. The merchant Thomas Charles Williams had sent a cargo of tea from London to his brothers Joseph and James at Annapolis, Maryland, aboard the brig *Peggy Stewart*. After the ship's owner, Anthony Stewart, paid the duty on the tea, the residents' threats against him became so violent that Stewart and the Williams brothers agreed to set fire to the ship on October 19, 1774. The *Peggy Stewart* burned to the waterline with all its tea aboard. These incidents were evidence that the tea protest had spread well beyond Boston, New York City, and Philadelphia: Americans were abjuring British goods of all kinds, but tea had become a particular symbol of the wider boycott movement and the protest against the Coercive Acts.[48]

In October, a Massachusetts Provincial Congress met and essentially operated as an independent government outside the authority of Governor Gage and the Coercive Acts. The Congress raised taxes to procure arms and established a Committee of Safety with the power to muster militia companies and appoint commanders. As Gage reported, "Nobody here or at home could have conceived that the Acts made for the Massachusetts Bay could have created such a ferment throughout the continent and united the whole in one common cause; or that the country people could have been raised to such a pitch of frenzy as to be ready for any mad attempt they are put upon." Nothing but a massive show of force would suffice if Great Britain hoped to maintain any authority over its American colonies. The Coercive Acts, which had been a direct result of the Boston Tea Party, had galvanized the Massachusetts colonists against the imperial government and set them on a path toward armed revolt.[49]

The resolutions of the Continental Congress and Americans' continued resistance to the acts of Parliament infuriated the king. "The New England Governments are in a state of rebellion," he wrote to Lord North in November 1774, and "blows must decide whether they are to be subject to this country or independent." Lord Dartmouth sent a letter of instruction to General Gage on January 27, 1775, directing him to arrest and imprison "the principal actors & abettors in the Provincial Congress" which had sprung up in Massachusetts. Although Gage was ordered to avoid bloodshed if possible, he was authorized to use force if it would head off "a riper state of Rebellion." On April 19, he dispatched troops to Concord to seize and destroy the military stores there. Groups of Massachusetts militia exchanged fire with the redcoats at Lexington Green and at Concord's North Bridge. In response, "minutemen" marched from all over the countryside and surrounded the town of Boston. The Revolutionary War had begun. The destruction of the tea had raised a new and fatal tempest.[50]

Samuel Nowell, one of the men who claimed to have dumped the tea in Boston harbor, also told some startling war stories. In his old age, he described his daring escape from occupied Boston, his service aboard two privateers, his capture at sea, his imprisonment for sixteen months in Halifax (three of those in shackles as punishment for attempting to escape), and his recovery from yellow fever. While he and his fellow prisoners were being transported from Halifax to occupied New York City, he helped lead a mutiny when a storm separated their ship from the rest of the convoy, and the American mutineers then led the boat to Marblehead and safety. Many other Tea Party participants served as officers, soldiers, and sailors during the eight-year war between America and Great Britain.[51]

Many of the principal actors on both sides of Boston's political disputes never lived to see the Treaty of Paris that brought the Revolutionary War to a close in 1783. The merchant and crowd leader William Molineux took his last breath less than a year after the Tea Party in October 1774, crying out, "O save my Country, Heaven!" Claims that he committed suicide by overdosing on laudanum, or that he was poisoned after dining with British officers, were never proven.[52]

The lawyer Josiah Quincy spent several months in England arguing for the American cause, and he was aboard a ship, in sight of Massachusetts, when tuberculosis finally consumed him on April 26, 1775—a week after the fighting had begun. Almost two months later, on June 17, Dr. Joseph Warren was killed in action while defending the hills above Charlestown from a British assault at the battle of Bunker Hill. Dr. Thomas Young continued traveling and spreading radical ideas, and he gave the state of Vermont its name while he was supporting Ethan Allen's efforts for secession from New York. He died of a fever in June 1777 while working as a surgeon in a Continental Army military hospital. Dr. Benjamin Church was exposed in the fall of 1775 as a traitor for whispering secrets to the British, and he spent over two years in prison. While on his way to exile in Martinique in January 1778, a winter storm roared across the sea, and his ship was swallowed by the waves along with all its crew and passengers. In May 1783, the lawyer James Otis Jr., after years of mental health troubles, was struck and killed by a bolt of lightning.[53]

The merchant John Rowe, owner of the *Eleanor*, did survive. Rowe was always a step ahead of allowing anyone to figure out his true political allegiances, but he did remain in Boston, both during the British occupation and after the troops were evacuated in March 1776. He was elected to the Massachusetts legislature in 1780 and died in Boston in 1787, still a wealthy man. Francis Rotch became an erratic figure as well. While he supported the Crown, much of his Quaker family attempted to remain neutral during the conflict—and as the owners of a whaling firm, they traded and negotiated with whatever country would best help them do business. After 1773, Francis spent much of the next forty years in

England and France. Ultimately he died in New Bedford, Massachusetts, in 1822, after a painful two-year struggle with poor health.[54]

Samuel Adams, John Adams, and John Hancock all represented Massachusetts in the Continental Congress and signed the Declaration of Independence. John Adams became a wartime diplomat, the first vice-president of the United States, and its second president. John Hancock served as the first governor of Massachusetts under its 1780 Constitution, and was followed by Samuel Adams. When Samuel Adams opposed the uprising in western Massachusetts called Shays' Rebellion—which involved the shutting of courts and a raid on the Springfield armory in 1786 and 1787—one of his friends accused him of betraying his old principles. Adams later came in for some rough treatment from his biographers, who represented him as a Machiavellian manipulator.[55]

Thomas Hutchinson, who never returned to America after his departure in 1774, lived out the remainder of his days in exile. He died in London of a stroke on June 3, 1780, during the anti-Catholic Gordon Riots, and Richard Clarke was one of his pallbearers. Joshua Winslow had died of an illness in Boston in March 1775, a month before the outbreak of fighting. He was in his late thirties. The other tea agents of 1773 survived to see the Americans celebrate their victory, but from a distance. Like their father, Elisha Hutchinson and Thomas Hutchinson Jr., as well as Benjamin Faneuil Jr. and the Clarkes, were proscribed and banished from their native Massachusetts. Faneuil and the Hutchinsons ultimately took up residence in England. Richard Clarke moved in with his son-in-law, John Singleton Copley, who was working as a successful painter in London. Jonathan Clarke and Isaac Winslow Clarke pursued new careers in Canada.[56]

The East India Company never recovered any of its lost money from the town of Boston or its inhabitants. The British government, which had begun to arrogate more political power over the Company in 1773, tightened the reins further in the 1780s, while corruption and scandal continued to plague the Company's endeavors. One of the governors-general who helped consolidate British power in India was Lord Cornwallis, the same man who had surrendered to George Washington at Yorktown, Virginia, in 1781. In 1813, Parliament stripped the Company of most of its monopoly powers except for its monopoly on the China trade, including the tea trade; in 1833, Parliament abolished these remaining commercial privileges, too. After that, the Company essentially stopped trading. Following the Great Rebellion of the sepoys (the Company's South Asian soldiers) in 1857, the British government dismantled the

East India Company's nominal political powers and assumed direct control through its India Office. The Company's London headquarters on Leadenhall Street were demolished in the 1860s, and the Company itself, now little more than a dried-up husk, was finally dissolved in 1874.[57]

Americans continued to enjoy tea. Although many people assume that Americans' preference for coffee over tea dates to the Tea Party, Americans switched to coffee for economic reasons rather than out of principle. Coffee became available on plantations in the Caribbean and Brazil, close at hand for American markets, while tea could only be grown in the distant hills of China and India, subject to controls by the British and Chinese governments. Since coffee was therefore cheaper and more plentiful, Americans developed more of a taste for it while Great Britain remained a nation of tea drinkers.[58]

Whether they drank coffee or tea, both Americans and Britons flavored their hot drinks with sugar. Most of this came from Caribbean plantations, where it was grown by slave labor. As the mother country and her colonies came to blows over notions of liberty and independence, few stopped to think about the connections between tea, sugar, slavery, and freedom. But the evidence was there, if you knew where to look: in the background of the Boston Tea Party, more and more Bostonians were clamoring for abolition.

CHAPTER 10

Sugar, Slaves, and the Shadow of the Tea Party

Where is the balm to heal so deep a wound?
Where shall a sov'reign remedy be found?
Look, gracious Spirit, from thine heav'nly bow'r,
And thy full joys into their bosoms pour;
The raging tempest of their grief control,
And spread the dawn of glory through the soul

Phillis Wheatley, "On the Death of a Young
Gentleman," Published 1773[1]

No country can be called free where there is one Slave.

James Swan, *A Dissuasion to Great-Britain
and the Colonies*, 1772[2]

The Boston Tea Party and the Coercive Acts helped to bring about the Revolutionary War and American independence. These events ushered in a political climate where white men from all ranks of society could make their voices heard. For this reason, Americans celebrate the Tea Party as a crucial step on the road to American liberty. Yet "liberty" was a contentious concept in the eighteenth century. To some it merely meant freedom from government abuses of power; others emphasized freedom from interference with personal property; for a small minority, "liberty" implied genuine individual freedom for all. People in Massachusetts were arguing about liberty, to be sure, in 1773—but they were also debating slavery. A few people on both sides of the tea issue, like James Swan or the Rotch family, began to wonder whether the Americans' quest for liberty was doing enough for those who were actually held in bondage.

During the 1760s and 1770s, the British government had tried to tighten its control over its subordinates throughout the empire—not just the white American colonists who eventually led the rebellion, but also the East India

Company, Native American groups, the Caribs of St. Vincent, and other parts of its empire. Although powerful white colonists sympathized with some of these actions, they were horrified by the overall tenor of increased authority and control. The American colonists had no desire to be scrutinized and ordered about. They had heard about the hundreds of thousands of Bengalis who had starved to death in 1769–70 (they thought) at the hands of the East India Company, and they had no desire to end up like the victims of the famine. The Tea Act seemed like just another conspiratorial effort to crush Americans beneath an imperial heel. After all, most white Americans rated themselves more highly than the benighted non-white peoples of the world who lived in tyranny and ignorance—the Chinese, South Asians, Africans, and Middle Easterners. Nor did they feel equal to the Native Americans or African-Americans in their midst—the subjects of conquest, enslavement, and discrimination. The Revolution enabled Americans to forge a new identity, separate from Great Britain, but it was also increasingly a white identity, separate from the darker-skinned people who also walked upon American soil. Whatever their rhetoric, theirs had been a revolution for local power, not universal liberty.[3]

The Revolutionary War, for instance, did nothing to free the vast majority of the slaves in the British colonies. The Boston Tea Party could have been a moment to protest slavery. Since many of the empire's slaves were employed in sugar production, and since the people of the British Empire drank their tea with sugar, the tea protests could have been linked to a remonstration against slavery. But they were not. This is not because eighteenth-century Americans were unaware of the connections between tea, sugar, and slavery. While tea conjured up images of refinement and afternoon repast in Europe and America, far removed from the agricultural labor that produced it, sugar told a different story. Many Americans knew from first-hand experience or second-hand tales that the sweet, white lumps that they stirred into tea were the product of a brutal regime of enslaving black people. Even as Americans in the 1760s and 1770s began pushing away tea in the name of liberty, it did not occur to them to push away sugar in the name of doing away with slavery.

New England's economic growth after 1750 was based largely on trade with slave-based economies in the Caribbean. Exports to the British West Indies quadrupled after 1750, although Boston shared much of this trade with its competitors: Salem, Rhode Island, and Connecticut. The New England slave trade doubled after 1750; one scholar estimates that New Englanders owed as much as 10 percent of their income to the West Indies trade. New England farmers couldn't grow enough food to nourish a big city like Boston, and in order to pay for its food, Boston relied on the reshipment of Caribbean sugar, rum, and molasses to New York and Pennsylvania in exchange for livestock and grain. Much of the eighteenth-century economy of the British Empire relied on sugar and slavery, and New England was very much a part of these exchanges.[4]

The sugar business helped fuel the tea business in turn. West Indian lobbyists in London encouraged the East India Company to keep importing tea because it stimulated sugar consumption; by the mid-eighteenth century, for almost all Europeans, the two went together. Taking tea with sugar became the habit of the poor as well as the rich in Great Britain. Chinese tea pickers and enslaved African laborers, working thousands of miles apart, grew products that swirled together in the teacups of British consumers. Tea, sugar, and other such goods provided such fantastic potential for profits that they helped encourage the expansion of the British Empire, the conquest of native peoples, and the enslavement of Africans.[5]

Most historians trace New Englanders' first stirrings of resistance to Parliament to the Sugar Act of 1764. This law, by maintaining a duty on imported foreign molasses, threatened many Bostonians' ability to make money from their Caribbean imports. The Sugar Act was the first parliamentary law that really got Boston's elite merchant class upset about taxation without representation. The resistance movement led by James Otis and the Boston merchants in those days, therefore, had deep ties to the profits made from sugar and slavery. When Americans' attention switched to tea in 1767 or 1773, almost no one explicitly made the connection between tea-drinking and sugar consumption (much less the connection between sugar consumption and slavery), but in hindsight we can easily observe the global connections that drew these issues together.[6]

James Otis and Samuel Adams were fierce and dedicated in the cause of liberty—but only occasionally did they or their allies take notice of the people arguing for freedom of another kind. There were over 800 persons of color in Boston in 1765, far more than in any other Massachusetts town. Bostonians hosted slave auctions, they enforced restrictive slave codes with the whip, they pursued runaways through newspaper advertisements, and they shook with fear at the occasional rumor of insurrection. Peter Faneuil's donation of Faneuil Hall was made possible in part by the slave trade. John Hancock, John Rowe, and Thomas Hutchinson ran some of the largest slave households in the colony. Slaves in Boston crewed ships, plied crafts, and worked their backs and knuckles as household servants. They did the crucial tasks that allowed slave-owners to grow their businesses, pursue their professional careers, or strive for leisured status.[7]

In the 1770s, as Americans became increasingly exercised about the oppressions of the Lord North ministry in Parliament, a few Bostonians were questioning black slavery in the New World. Criticisms of slavery were not new—indeed, they seemed almost as old as the practice of slaveholding. In 1700, the Boston judge and merchant Samuel Sewall had argued that it was wrong to deprive African-Americans of their liberty. In 1764, while arguing against the Sugar Act, the lawyer James Otis wrote, "The Colonists are by the law of nature free born, as indeed all men are, white or black." Otis wrote that slavery "threatens one day to reduce both Europe and America to the ignorance and barbarity of the darkest ages," and he called the slave trade "the most shocking violation of the law of nature." Finally, he wrote, "those who every day barter away other mens liberty, will soon care little for their own." Nevertheless, there was a big difference between talking about slavery's ills and actively working to cure them.[8]

Few people advocated a boycott of the slave trade, or of the products of slave labor. However, a significant exception could be found among the Quakers. Such exhorters as Benjamin Lay (the teacup-smasher of 1742), John Woolman, and Anthony Benezet pricked the conscience of many Quakers (and non-Quakers), forcing them to reassess whether people ought to be held as property. In the fall of 1769, Woolman (who had formerly traded in rum and sugar) wrote that he had for a few years stopped sweetening his palate with sugar. The following spring, he had a dream in which "Tea Drinking, with which there is Sugar" symbolized to him "the Slavery of the Negroes, with which Many are oppressed." The American Quakers' detachment from slavery had particularly influenced the Rotch family, which owned the first of the tea ships that sailed to Boston in 1773, the *Dartmouth*. William Rotch, Francis's brother, had been involved in anti-slavery efforts. A few years before the Tea Party, Rotch paid wages to a slave named Prince Boston, a crewman aboard one of his whaling ships, instead of paying the heirs of Prince's late owner. A Nantucket jury and magistrate found Boston to be a free man, and an appeal attempt was dropped. According to nineteenth-century sources, slaveholding in Nantucket (which had a large Quaker population) was effectively over after this case.[9]

From the 1760s onward, the impulse to do something about slavery in Massachusetts accelerated. By 1766, quite a few persons of color, like Prince Boston, had sued for their freedom. Several local town meetings and the provincial legislature also took up the issue of slavery. In 1766 and 1767 the Boston Town Meeting, for instance, called upon its representatives to abolish the importation and purchase of slaves. Nathaniel Appleton, later a member of the Boston Committee of Correspondence, asked the Sons of

Liberty, "Is your conduct consistent? can you review our late struggles for liberty, and think of the slave-trade at the same time, and not blush?" Appleton hated the fact that luxury goods were corrupting the African continent, in much the same way that imported luxuries bothered white critics of tea and Native Americans at "Vomit Town." In 1767, the Massachusetts House of Representatives considered bills to abolish slavery and the slave trade, but these failed. Four years later, the legislature passed a bill to end the importation of slaves, but Governor Hutchinson would not give his assent, and this bill also ran aground.[10]

Then, in 1772, a year before the Tea Party, a court case in distant England injected new energy into the anti-slavery movement. It concerned James Somerset, who was born in Africa and brought as a slave to Virginia. His master, Charles Steuart, served in Boston as a customs officer before taking Somerset with him to England on business. On October 1, 1771, Somerset escaped. A ship captain recaptured him and prepared to sail to Jamaica to sell Somerset on Steuart's behalf. Anti-slavery advocates in England, including Granville Sharp, intervened on Somerset's behalf and a legal case made its way to the Court of King's Bench in London. The judge, Lord Mansfield, ruled that slaves had the right to claim habeas corpus to prevent their being detained in preparation for deportation and sale. Almost immediately, anti-slavery advocates (including the approximately 15,000 slaves in England) inflated the meaning of the case, arguing that the ruling abolished slavery in England. The case led a number of American slaves, particularly in Boston, to begin agitating for freedom on constitutional grounds.[11]

White colonists in Massachusetts continued to criticize the institution of slavery as well. James Swan, who would later help throw tea overboard at the Boston Tea Party, published a pamphlet in 1772 entitled *A Dissuasion to Great-Britain and the Colonies, from the Slave Trade to Africa.* Although much of the pamphlet was cobbled together from previous tracts, it was heartfelt: Swan spoke of his "tender feelings for these distressed Captives," and his warm anger at "such base, unchristian, and inhuman practices, in a land of Liberty and Christianity." Swan cited verses from the Bible and lines from the Massachusetts Charter. He spoke disgustedly of shipmasters and merchants, "Men-wolves" who stole men from Africa, incited them to war and captive-taking, and bribed and corrupted African chiefs to sell other Africans into slavery. He spoke of the horrors of the transatlantic passage, chastised slave-owners who brutally mistreated their slaves and refused to teach them the Gospels, and argued that the entire institution of slavery violated the Golden Rule. Swan mentioned, in passing, that Bostonians played a part in the slave trade. Swan's pamphlet demonstrates that at least one man at the Tea Party was thinking about freedom, not just in terms of ending taxation without representation, but in terms of ending human bondage as well.[12]

In July 1773, Harvard College hosted a debate between two of its graduating seniors on the slavery issue. The two debaters were Theodore Parsons, who was later lost at sea during the Revolutionary War, and Eliphalet Pearson, who later headed the Phillips Academy at Andover. Thomas Melvill and Joseph Pearse Palmer, who earned Harvard degrees in the 1770s and later participated in the Tea Party, would have known both of these students, and Melvill almost certainly attended this event. Parsons defended the right to hold slaves as a way of maintaining authority over inferior human beings. Pearson argued that holding slaves offended the notion of liberty for all, and that a difference in skin color or nose shape didn't justify the subjection of Africans. The debate came to an unsatisfactory conclusion, doing little to resolve the central question of whether slavery was in accordance with natural law.[13]

Regardless, the black community in Boston wasn't just waiting around for British judges, white pamphleteers, and callow Harvard students to defend their natural rights. In January 1773, "The Sons of Africa" petitioned the governor, Council, and House of Representatives of Massachusetts to stop importing slaves into the province, and provide redress to those already in bondage. Felix Holbrook, on behalf of Massachusetts slaves, spoke his mind in plaintive tones: "We have no Property! We have no Wives! No Children! We have no City! No Country!" Slaves could not "possess and enjoy any Thing, no, not even *Life itself.*" All they could do in their degraded condition was trust in God and beg for help from Massachusetts officials. The Bostonians who protested against salary grants to civil officials and the Tea Act later that year professed a similar frustration.[14]

By April, Boston's black community had become more assertive. They helped usher another copy of Swan's anti-slavery pamphlet into press, dedicated it to the three branches of Massachusetts government, and asked that it be distributed to every town in the colony.[15] Around the same time, four black Bostonians, on behalf of a committee of Massachusetts slaves, wrote a letter to the representatives of each town. "We expect great things," they wrote pointedly, "from men who have made such a noble stand against the designs of their *fellow-men* to enslave them." They asked for a shorter work week, general relief, and freedom from bondage. Black Bostonians explicitly challenged their white neighbors to expend some of their libertarian strivings on behalf of slaves.[16]

The Massachusetts House of Representatives began considering the black Bostonians' petition in June 1773, but discussion of a bill to end slave imports was postponed to January 1774, when both the House and Council passed it, but Governor Hutchinson, who said that he was acting on instructions from the British government, declined to give his consent. Governor Gage gave them the same answer when a new petition was submitted in May 1774. On some level, then, the fight against Parliament and the fight against the slave trade *did* overlap with one another during the months of the tea crisis.[17]

The African-Americans of Massachusetts had their own muse, too, in the form of a young woman named Phillis Wheatley. Like Somerset, she had been born in Africa, and was brought to Boston as a slave in 1761 (aboard the schooner *Phillis*), when she was seven or eight years old. John Wheatley, who gave her the name Phillis when he purchased her, was a merchant (he sold tea, among other things). His son Nathaniel took over the business in 1771, and had dealings with the Rotch family, John Hancock, and others in the whaling business. Susanna Wheatley, John's pious wife, helped to tutor Phillis in religion, and Phillis took communion in the Old South Meeting House in 1771. Susanna also nurtured and promoted Phillis's talent: the young girl started writing poetry at age eleven or twelve, and was first published in 1767, when she was thirteen or fourteen. In 1773, she would follow in Somerset's footsteps to England, seeking fame and freedom.[18]

Like Franklin and many Americans, Wheatley was initially quite optimistic that Lord Dartmouth, when he assumed his secretaryship for American affairs, would be a protector of liberty. While Wheatley was concerned about taxation without representation, she also argued for freedom for black Americans. After describing her own experience of being "snatch'd from Afric's fancy'd happy Seat," she wrote,

> Such once my case.—Thus I deplore the day
> When Britons weep beneath Tyrannic sway.
> To thee, our thanks for favours past are due,
> To thee, we still Solicite for the new.

By "Britons," Wheatley meant Americans, both white and black. Like many Americans, Wheatley had high hopes that the pious and moderate Lord Dartmouth could bring great changes to American affairs. Like the Boston Sons of Liberty, however, she would be disappointed.[19]

In the spring of 1773, having failed to secure enough subscriptions to publish her collected poems in Boston, Wheatley traveled to England hoping to find a publisher. There she met Lord Dartmouth, Benjamin Franklin, the anti-slavery activist Granville Sharp (who had helped to secure Somerset's freedom), the merchant Brook Watson (who was then scheming to secure an East India Company tea consignment for Joshua Winslow and Benjamin Faneuil Jr.), and others. Her *Poems on Various Subjects, Religious and Moral* appeared in September 1773 (fig. 31). Personages ranging from Governor Hutchinson to John Hancock, and many of the important Massachusetts clergymen, had vouched for her poems' authenticity. She returned to Boston in September 1773 and the *Boston Gazette* announced the return of "Phillis Wheatley, the extraordinary Poetical Genius." Phillis had also achieved her freedom that fall, by October 18 at the latest, just as Bostonians began hearing news of the Tea Act.[20]

During the Tea Act crisis in Boston, newspaper and pamphlet writers talked a lot about slavery, but it was their own enslavement that concerned them, not the enslavement of black people. An interesting exception, however, arose out of the countryside. On December 29, 1773, the inhabitants of Medfield, Massachusetts (about eighteen miles southwest of Boston), shortly after

31 This portrait of Phillis Wheatley was published along with her collected poems in 1773.

resolving that the Tea Act was designed "to fasten the Chains of Slavery upon a burden'd and distressed people," also spoke out "against that Iniquitous practice of enslaving the Affricans." In their resolves, which they sent to the Boston Committee of Correspondence, they called it "Greatly absurd for us to plead for Liberty and yet patronise the most Cruel Servitude and Bondage." Echoing the language of black petitions and white pamphlets, the Medfielders lamented that blacks "have not the least Shadow of Liberty Remaining," had nothing to call their own, and were at the disposal of slave traders. "We wish to maintain Constitutional Liberty ourselves," the Medfielders said, "and cant endure the thoughts of its being withheld from the same flesh and blood" for no other reason than skin color. Samuel Adams, Joseph Warren, and the other members of the Boston Committee of Correspondence may have been leading the conversation about liberty, but the rural people of Massachusetts felt that they could teach the Bostonians a thing or two about liberty themselves.[21]

"Liberty" and "freedom" have always had multiple meanings. The Boston Sons of Liberty emphasized the importance of legislative representation, the consent of the governed, an independent judiciary, and the constitutional safeguards that protected people and property from arbitrary government. The Boston Tea Party specifically assailed taxation without representation, the danger of a government-supported monopoly, and the injustice of American tax revenue supporting an unaccountable executive. Wheatley, Appleton, Swan, and their allies, on the other hand, emphasized another idea of liberty: one that emphasized basic individual freedom, particularly for black slaves. From this perspective, it was *Britain*, and not America, that looked like the land of liberty—Great Britain was, after all, the place where the *Somerset v. Steuart* court case had made it illegal to enforce the recapture of a slave. Although many of the people who held anti-slavery beliefs became Whigs and revolutionaries, fusing these notions of liberty into one set of ideas, many anti-slavery advocates were more skeptical of the American cause, such as the Wheatley family that had owned Phillis and the Rotch family of Nantucket and New Bedford. Perhaps, for a Quaker family like the Rotches, whale oil seemed a more morally defensible branch of trade than sugar and tea.[22]

Many of the British government's supporters in America were quick to point out the contradictions between liberty and American slavery. Writing to a friend who was embarking on a slave-trading venture, Customs Commissioner Henry Hulton wrote, "It is a necessary business," though he lamented that such commerce was "a breach on our principles of humanity." At the same time, "We Americans" he wrote sarcastically (Hulton was not

American-born and had every reason to dislike Americans), "so jealous of our own liberty, such assertors of the rights of Mankind, make no scruple to exercise the severest tyranny, over the unhappy Natives of Affrick."[23]

Black Americans themselves appear to have made these arguments as well. In February 1774, as Boston waited for the British government's response to the Boston Tea Party, the *Massachusetts Spy* printed a letter from "A Son of AFRICA." After commiserating with white colonists about the hard-hearted British, the writer asked, "Are not your hearts also hard, when you hold them in slavery who are intitled to liberty, by the law of nature, equal as yourselves?"[24]

Despite setbacks in the Massachusetts legislature, in 1773 it really looked as if there was momentum building—both in terms of black political activism and whites' public opinion—to end slavery in Massachusetts. But the Boston Tea Party put an end to all of it, in a way. The Tea Party provoked the Coercive Acts, and then suddenly in May 1774 the public conversation turned wholly to questions of protest, resistance, and revolution. For the next year, the whites of Massachusetts were too busy defending themselves from "slavery" at the hands of the British Empire to worry about blacks already in bondage. Furthermore, the leaders of Massachusetts realized they needed to rely on the southern provinces (which in turn relied on slave labor) to successfully pursue British relief or American revolt. The Boston lawyer Josiah Quincy had been to South Carolina in early 1773, both for his health and to shore up political alliances. Although he was disgusted by the practice of slavery in the southern colonies, he surely came away convinced that nothing would pry the southerners away from their system of slavery and subjection. And besides, Quincy was delighted whenever he met a southerner who was just as "Hot and zealous in the Cause of America" as he was. The Massachusetts Sons of Liberty counted on this southern zeal when Parliament closed the port of Boston in 1774, and Boston gratefully accepted a shipment of slave-grown rice from Charleston. As a delegate to the Continental Congress, John Adams had exulted when he felt certain that the other colonies would support Massachusetts. In 1777, after the Declaration of Independence had established the United States, the Massachusetts House of Representatives declined to consider a bill for emancipating the slaves, since it might, as a correspondent wrote to John Adams, "have a bad effect on the Union of the Colonies." The Massachusetts patriots had achieved union, but it would be a federal union in which slavery was still permissible.[25]

Quincy had also noticed that some Carolinians were quite paranoid about the Boston Sons of Liberty trying to boss the other colonies around.

Gradually this paranoia began to crystallize: even though New Englanders were becoming more averse to slavery, southerners didn't want New Englanders telling them what to do about their slaves. The New Englanders, as it turned out, did nothing of the sort. These states, and Massachusetts in particular, owed the southern states an immense debt of gratitude for their robust political support between the passage of the Boston Port Act in 1774 and the Declaration of Independence in 1776. And it would have been churlish for the Massachusetts delegates to the Continental Congress (most of whom were moderates when it came to slavery) to respond to demands from evangelicals, Quakers, and country towns to raise the slavery question. The delegates from the southern provinces, especially South Carolina and Georgia, had no interest in hearing these anti-slavery arguments. As John Rutledge of South Carolina said during the Constitutional Convention of 1787, "If the Convention thinks that N.C; S.C. & Georgia will ever agree to the plan, unless their right to import slaves be untouched, the expectation is in vain."[26]

When the War for American Independence began, black people did not just wait to see what the outcome would be. In the North, particularly in New England, African-Americans fought against the British Army and Navy. People of color defended Bunker Hill, they huddled in the snow at Valley Forge, and they climbed the rigging aboard privateers and warships. The spectacle of dark-skinned people fighting alongside whites led many in the North to reconsider slavery, and although it took until 1804, by then every state north of the Mason–Dixon Line had passed some form of emancipation statute. Of course, even more people of color fought for the British side—they were attracted to the promises of freedom that they sometimes heard from their patriot masters' enemies. What's more, we should not exaggerate the gains made by black people during the Revolutionary War. Slavery was weaker in the Northeast after the war, but then it had been weaker there in the first place—and in the American South, slavery had only become more strongly entrenched. The Boston Tea Party had struck a blow for liberty, but for slaves there was much more fighting to be done.[27]

The emancipation of slaves, though it may seem to be an easy call from a moral perspective, also presented a number of practical problems. Would masters be compensated for the property they had purchased? What would become of the former slaves? "MENTOR" warned Massachusetts voters against any legislator that had voted for any bill that sought "to deprive masters of their black servants." Slave-owners had purchased slaves as property and paid for their upkeep, and they deserved to have their property rights protected. "MENTOR" conjured up scenes of widows and orphans being stripped of their slave property. He struck terror in his readers, by warning that blacks would flee the southern states and make Massachusetts their safe haven. He griped that higher taxes would be needed for law enforcement officials to keep the unruly and unsupported black population in line. The only possible advantage "MENTOR" could see to emancipating black people, he said, would be if it would "extirpate that race from among us."[28]

In spite of inertia, apathy, outright hostility, and continuing prejudice, the slaves in Massachusetts did achieve their emancipation. In the 1790s, when the historian Jeremy Belknap attempted to figure out how slavery came to be abolished in Massachusetts, he had trouble finding a single answer. There had been series of wartime resolves against slavery in country town meetings. The Massachusetts Constitution of 1780 stated that "all men are born free and equal," but the meaning of this clause for black inhabitants was unclear. A few freedom lawsuits had been brought before the bench between 1781 and 1783—one of them over slaves that were captured by the brigantine *Tyrannicide*, on which George Pillsbury, a Tea Party participant, was lieutenant. In one of these cases, the chief justice of the Superior Court of Massachusetts had effectively abolished slavery, but the case was ambiguous and not widely reported. Meanwhile, people's opinions had continued to turn against slavery during the war. Driven by obscure court decisions, sluggish public distaste, and the reduced need for employment in the difficult economy of the early 1780s, slavery had died a rather slow, quiet, and undramatic death in Massachusetts. There would be no anniversary to celebrate. There would be no jubilees. And there were still quirks in the rules: slave-owners from other states could recover their fugitive slaves, in theory, but Massachusetts would do nothing to help these slave-owners. Although Massachusetts emancipated its own black population and eventually outlawed the slave trade, it also actively discouraged black people from migrating to the state.[29]

Slavery in Massachusetts was abolished with little fanfare. The black petitioners, plaintiffs, and their allies, who were so active in the 1770s and 1780s, felt scant empowerment from the state's back door emancipation, and they made only slight progress toward genuine economic and social independence. Instead, Massachusetts struck the deals that allowed it to join a constitutional union with the southern states in 1789.[30] A few delegates to the Massachusetts ratification convention spoke out against the compromises that protected slavery in the United States Constitution, but they made little impact. William Rotch wrote to the Rhode Island Quaker Moses Brown that although he was grateful that the Constitution would help protect his family's whaling business, "it is evident to me it is founded on *Slavery* and that is on *Blood*." The select group of northerners who believed in genuine, universal liberty would have to fight for over seventy more years before they would see the emancipation of slaves in the United States. Most other northerners came to see slavery as a southern problem, or even as a southern right. Meanwhile, the most dramatic story of revolutionary emancipation in the late eighteenth century was the Haitian Revolution of 1791–1804, and the spectacle of black revolutionaries rising up against a European colonial power did nothing to ease the minds of most white Americans.[31]

During the Revolutionary era, both Britons and Americans used the slavery issue to score rhetorical points against their enemies in the moral contest over empire, authority, and national character. The *Somerset* case, and the obnoxiousness of the American rebels, helped Britons to distance themselves from slavery in their own minds—it was an institution that belonged to the colonies, never mind the hefty British profits from the slave trade and the products of West Indian slave labor. Many Americans, too, worried in the abstract about the presence of slavery. After Abigail Adams heard of the British burning New England towns in 1775, she wondered, "are we become a Sodom? . . . We have done Evil or our Enemies would be at peace with us. The Sin of Slavery as well as many others is not washed away." Americans confronted the conflict between their ideals and their slaveholding in uncomfortable ways—and they forced the British to do the same. Yet heightened awareness of slavery in Great Britain didn't lead to quick action on behalf of slaves; and in New England, a desire to do away with the "Sin of Slavery" led many whites to see persons of color as a lingering problem, not as human beings in need of help.[32]

The Boston Tea Party did sound a faint echo in the struggle against the slave trade. In the early 1790s, the cause of anti-slavery in Great Britain had developed a tactic that may have been borrowed from the American tea boycotters of the 1760s and 1770s. A few Britons, particularly women, realized the connections between the sugar they consumed and the slave labor that produced it. They urged their countrymen and countrywomen to stop consuming sugar—with tea or otherwise—because it was tainted by blood and oppression. These British activists took a second look at where their luxury goods were coming from, and they saw the ways in which their tastes were bound up with slavery and imperialism in other parts of the globe. By the 1820s and 1830s, American abolitionists also connected the products of slave labor to their own consuming habits, and took steps to initiate boycotts of their own.[33]

In the decades before the American Civil War, both abolitionists and anti-abolitionists used the Boston Tea Party to justify their protests. In the *Liberator*, the newspaper of the Boston abolitionist William Lloyd Garrison, the writer "Ominous" criticized South Carolina governor James Hamilton for looking forward to a "Boston Tea Affair" that would rally the South during the nullification crisis in 1831. "Ominous" disapproved of the analogy, since it summoned "the demon of civil discord."[34] Incidents throughout the 1830s proved that this concern was well founded. In cities from Cincinnati to Philadelphia, crowds destroyed abolitionist literature and printing presses in the name of the "public good," again citing the Boston Tea Party. In response, a Boston abolitionist newspaper attacked these "American Robespierres." When a crowd in Alton, Illinois, went so far as to murder the abolitionist newspaper editor Elijah P. Lovejoy in 1837, the conservative Massachusetts attorney general, James T. Austin, approvingly compared the murderers to the tea destroyers.[35]

By the 1850s, attitudes toward abolitionism and the Tea Party had changed. Abolitionists began to argue that the Fugitive Slave Law of 1850 was every bit as deserving of Americans' disobedience as Stamp Act or the Tea Act in Revolutionary times. When the Boston Vigilance Committee rescued the fugitive slave Shadrach Minkins from U.S. marshalls in 1851, the minister Theodore Parker wrote, "I think it the most noble deed done in Boston since the destruction of the tea in 1773."[36]

The Boston Tea Party both disrupted the scattered efforts to abolish slavery, and indirectly helped inspire new efforts in that direction. During the American Revolution, white colonists, African-Americans, and Native Americans all fought for liberty, but some of them found that not all struggles for liberty were created equal. White Americans achieved their liberty, but they were also struggling to figure out their own identity—and that identity wasn't always ready to embrace people of color. It would be up to subsequent generations of Americans of all hues to give equality and freedom new meanings.[37]

Conclusion:
Secrecy and Legacy

The People should never rise, without doing something to be remembered—
something notable And striking.

John Adams, December 17, 1773[1]

The Boston Tea Party had led to the War of American Independence, and
that alone has been enough to ensure its fame. This was in some ways an
accident of history. New York City and Philadelphia radicals were in fact
further to the front of the fight against the Tea Act, but Boston was the
earliest port to receive the tea ships, and the town faced a particularly
scrupulous set of consignees and civil officials. The unknown planners of
the Boston Tea Party probably did not intend that the consequence of their
action would be a break from Great Britain and the formation of a new
nation. For all that these planners tried to maintain tight control over the
destruction of the tea, the Boston Tea Party demonstrates how little control
they actually had over the outcome of their actions. They tried to ensure
that unknown "Mohawks" rather than the entire town of Boston would be
blamed for the destruction, but Parliament's reaction—closing the port and
altering the provincial charter—affected everyone they knew. The planners
also tried to make sure no one revealed the identities of the participants; but
secrets have a habit of disclosing themselves, and over time the names of
many participants made it into the historical record. Ultimately, too, the
men of the Boston Tea Party had no way of foreseeing how future generations would perceive their actions. Was the Tea Party a lawless, dangerous
act of destruction? Or was it a heroic defense of the principle of self-deter-
mination? America—and the world—still struggles with the legacy of an
event that has infused itself into the minds of people everywhere.

After the destruction of the tea on December 16, 1773, the prominent
men of Boston took great pains to show that they were ignorant of the tea
destroyers' true identities. The merchant John Rowe wrote in his diary, "I

can truly say, I know nothing of the Matter nor who were concerned in it." John Hancock referred a London correspondent to his ship captain (the bearer of the letter) for details: "for as indeed I am not Acquainted with them myself so as to give a detail." The Bostonians seem to have anticipated that many people in Britain and America would disapprove of their destruction of private property. So the tea destroyers themselves remained mum, while wealthy and influential allies like Hancock professed ignorance, and perhaps even disdain for the dirty work of dumping the tea.[2]

The only person who is definitively named in contemporary accounts as having been aboard the tea ships is Charles Conner, the man who was clubbed and kicked off of Griffin's Wharf for pocketing tea. As a villain of sorts, Conner usually doesn't rate as a participant in the Boston Tea Party. Otherwise, the only person to name the names of tea destroyers was a possibly crazy individual named Samuel Dyer, who was a prisoner of the British Navy when he squealed. His testimony was worthless—he named John Short, a captain of one of Hancock's merchant ships, and Short wasn't even in Boston at the time.[3]

After that, a code of *omertà* gripped the town of Boston for almost fifty years. The participants had originally sworn themselves to secrecy so as to evade prosecution or a lawsuit. "For a long period apprehensions are said to have been entertained," wrote James Fenimore Cooper in his naval history, "by some engaged—men of wealth—that they might yet be made the subjects of a prosecution for damages, by the East India Company." Cooper was famous for spinning tales like *The Last of the Mohicans*, in which a white man named Natty Bumppo walked in the trappings of Hudson Valley Indians. But Cooper had trouble finding out any details about this particular story of white men in Indian guise.[4]

Even though years had passed since Americans had gained their independence, the participants may have sensed that while the public had cheered the boycotts and the resistance to Great Britain, they disapproved of the Tea Party itself—a more violent, disorderly act of rebellion. From 1783 and for years afterward, many American leaders and elites argued that the Revolution was over. It was time to accept the new government, duly elected by the people, and strive to maintain law and order. Once this belief calcified into conventional wisdom, there was less room to celebrate a ragged group of mock Mohawks wielding hatchets in defiance of government.

The violent, defiant nature of Boston's protest against the Tea Act is undeniable—the townspeople harassed and threatened the consignees at their homes and places of business until they were forced to flee the town. No doubt some of the participants harbored even darker intentions. John

Adams, writing the day after the Tea Party, intimated that "Another similar Exertion of popular Power, may produce the destruction of Lives. Many Persons wish, that as many dead Carcasses were floating in the Harbour, as there are Chests of Tea." And even Adams, a conservative when it came to the exercise "popular Power," forebodingly implied that it would only take a few carcasses (by which he meant Governor Hutchinson and his allies) to "remove the Causes of all our Calamities." Hostility crackled in the air. Within a few weeks of the Tea Party, after shoemaker George R. T. Hewes had gotten into a physical altercation with a customs informer named John Malcom, a crowd gathered and retaliated by tarring and feathering Malcom so brutally that "his flesh comes off his back in Stakes (fig. 32)."[5]

William Tudor, a biographer of James Otis, described the meetings that preceded the Boston Tea Party as seething with contained violence. "These body meetings were in fact, only an orderly, well regulated mob." In a lesson intended for his audience in 1823, he continued: "their irregular action was salutary and indispensable at the time, but the habit of interfering in this manner with public affairs was a dangerous one, and it proves the virtue of the people that it did not produce permanent evils." A country where people constantly emulated the Boston Tea Party, Tudor believed, would be a country permanently steeped in wickedness.[6]

32 As the Boston Tea Party takes place in the background, a crowd tars and feathers John Malcom, a customs informer, in January 1774.

The sense of risk and shame that surrounded the Tea Party lingered for decades. The writer Harriet Hanson Robinson waited until after the Civil War before recording the claim that her grandfather, Seth Ingersoll Browne, was present at the Tea Party. She had heard the story from her mother (who was eighteen years old when Browne died in 1809) and her aunt. Robinson wrote that her mother "always thought the tea party something disgraceful and to be kept hidden from all but the family as if it was some riot and those engaged in it were liable to suffer from it. So it was kept as secret as possible."[7] The genealogist John J. May voiced a similar sentiment toward the end of the nineteenth century. Although his ancestor, Colonel John May, was silent about his role in the Tea Party, May's wife Abigail did not doubt his participation. "It seems fairly to be inferred," wrote the younger May, "that such a man would not have allowed imputations, either favorable or unfavorable, to attach to him, unless held to silence by an obligation which he could not honorably break; and it is certain that he went to his grave knowing that his friends believed him" to have been a member of the Tea Party. The younger May cited his ancestor's honorable character as proof of his participation and his adherence to a code of secrecy. Like Robinson, he hinted that others might consider participation in the Tea Party "unfavorable."[8]

By the 1810s, it was beginning to look as if most of the tea destroyers had followed John May's example and taken the secret to their graves. In the 1830s, the printer Peter Edes, son of the *Boston Gazette* publisher Benjamin Edes, wrote, "It is a little surprising that the names of the tea-party were never made public: my father, I believe, was the only person who had a list of them." Benjamin Edes had kept the list locked in his desk, but he had died in 1803, and the list had evidently disappeared.[9]

Every once in a while, a couple of names did leak out. In a sketch of Charlestown, Massachusetts, in 1813, Josiah Bartlett was willing to let slip the initials of a recently deceased friend who "was among the *Indians*, who destroyed the tea at Boston." Otherwise the record remained largely silent for the rest of that decade.[10] "The profound secrecy in which they have held their names," John Adams wrote in 1819, proved that they were men of strong character. On the other hand, a writer for the *Boston Centinel*—probably the paper's editor, Benjamin Russell—argued that the tea destroyers did not have any extraordinary wish to remain anonymous. Indeed, he wrote, "I well remember to have heard of at least twenty of those who were actors in this scene, several of whom are now alive, and known to me personally." Russell privately believed that his own father, mason John Russell, was one of the "actors" in the destruction of the tea.[11]

Whatever private confidences Russell had shared, even fifty years after the destruction of the tea, people were reluctant to let go of the secret. Still, Americans began to embrace the story of the Tea Party for a variety of purposes. In the 1820s, the Tea Party began to take on its dual identity as a touchstone of rebellious defiance on the one hand, and a cornerstone of national patriotism on the other. In the 1820s and 1830s, two very different groups worked to recover the Tea Party, and they had very different goals. A working-class movement arose during these decades, and these organized workers hoped to revive the memory of broad-based crowd action and its contributions to the Revolutionary movement. At the same time, nine-teenth-century elites were working to soften the image of the American Revolution and erase the bits about mob violence, so as to make it palatable for the impressionable minds of middle-class schoolchildren (and their parents).[12]

As a new generation succeeded the dying veterans of the Revolutionary Era, Americans indulged a strong desire to venerate their ancestors as heroes. Charles Sprague, known as the "banker-poet" of Boston, gave an oration in honor of Independence Day on July 4, 1825. "They who endured the burden of the conflict are fast going to their rest," he said. "Every passing gale sighs over another veteran's grave; and, ere long, the last sage, and the last old soldier of the revolution, will be seen no more." A decade later, American readers would learn that Sprague's father, Samuel, had been a bricklayer's apprentice on December 16, 1773, who spontaneously joined the Boston Tea Party that evening.[13]

In 1821, a contributor to the *Boston Daily Advertiser* had begun hunting down some of the basic facts about the Tea Party, and he interviewed a few anonymous witnesses. "The contrivers of this measure, and those who carried it into effect will never be known," the author concluded, because like John May, "None of those persons who were confidently said to have been of the party (except some who were then minors or very young men) have ever admitted that they were so." Those who knew about the Tea Party wouldn't say, and those who said didn't know. The minister and author Edward Everett Hale later wrote, "So far as anyone knows, they never did mention it. Of which this curious consequence has come into history, that if, within the last seventy-five years, any old gentleman has said that he was of the Boston Tea Party, it is perfectly sure that he was *not* one of the party of men who really did throw the tea into the harbor. If, on the other hand, any nice old gentleman, asked by his grandchildren if he were of the Tea Party, smiled and put off the subject and began talking about General Washington or General Gage, it is well-nigh certain that he was one of that confederation."[14]

Beginning in 1822, however, Americans did hear scattered voices from the fringes of New England. John Adams's public correspondence about the Tea Party motivated a Vermonter named Lewis Morse to write in 1819 that his father Anthony (who died in Sharon, Vermont) and Joseph Roby (then living in Hanover, New Hampshire) had participated in the tea action. Later that year, the death notice for Colonel John Spurr of Providence, Rhode Island, revealed that he "was employed in the operation of destroying the tea."[15] In 1829, the *Providence Patriot* reported the death of longtime Warren resident Nicholas Campbell, at age ninety-seven. Campbell, born on the Mediterranean island of Malta, "was one of the ever memorable *Boston Tea Party*, who committed one of the first acts of resistance to British oppression."[16]

This use of the term "Boston Tea Party" was relatively new—there is no evidence that anyone used that now famous phrase until the middle of the 1820s. Joshua Wyeth, the former blacksmith's apprentice who was then living in Cincinnati, Ohio, probably deserves credit for popularizing the phrase. In 1826, three years before Campbell's death, a widely circulated newspaper item mentioned Wyeth as "a temperate, hardy old veteran" who "often boasts of the '*Boston tea party.*' "[17] Wyeth had already sworn before a judge in 1820 that he "was on board the East India Company's Ships in the Harbour of Boston [and] assisted in throwing the tea overboard."[18] In an account printed in July 1827, Wyeth added (and possibly embellished) further details of his participation. On the morning of December 17, he noted, "We pretended to be as zealous to find out the perpetrators as the rest, and were all so close and loyal, that the whole affair remained in Egyptian darkness."[19] Yet at least one newspaper leaped to try and discredit Wyeth's account, highlighting inaccuracies and guessing that Wyeth "was probably a spectator," or at least not a leader of the Tea Party. Among the elite, the Tea Party was not yet a safe topic for discussion.[20]

Yet the need for hushed silence about the Tea Party began to fade, as the passing of the Revolutionary generation was mourned at countless funerals. People began openly speaking about the participation of a neighbor, a spouse, or an ancestor in the Boston Tea Party. Some of these claims were no doubt fabrications, half-truths, or exaggerations. But by the 1830s, when most of the witnesses to the Tea Party were dead, who would contradict them? As the Revolution became smothered by romanticism and sentiment, it seemed churlish to try to boot men out of the Revolutionary pantheon—particularly since the Tea Party was one of the more dramatic ways that a common craftsman or laborer could claim patriotic service to his country.

Well over a dozen participants had come forward by 1830. In 1826, a Boston newspaper coyly suggested that Major Thomas Melvill, a local legend, had been a participant in the Tea Party. But by the time Melvill died in 1832, the fact that he had "formed one of the Boston 'Tea Party'" was printed as fact. Upstanding local artisans who had made good, such as the decorative painter Samuel Gore (the older brother of a Massachusetts governor) and the silversmith Paul Revere, were also first named as Tea Party participants in the early 1830s.[21]

In 1833, a New York writer named James Hawkes had located an old shoemaker and Revolutionary War veteran in Richfield Springs, New York, with the improbable name of George Robert Twelves Hewes. Hewes had not only participated in the Tea Party, but he had been a witness to the Boston Massacre and other important events. Hawkes published a biography of Hewes called *A Retrospect of the Boston Tea-Party* in 1834. The Boston press embraced this rare survivor, since most Tea Party participants were only named after they had died. Hewes journeyed with his youngest son to Boston to participate in its Fourth of July celebrations in 1835. There he had his portrait painted (fig. 33), a New England author named Benjamin Bussey Thatcher published another Hewes memoir based on interviews with the old man, and he made public appearances with another purported Tea Party survivor, a former cooper's apprentice named Henry Purkitt. In *Traits of the Tea Party*, Thatcher listed fifty-eight men who were "generally supposed . . . on traditionary or other evidence, to have been more or less actively engaged in or present at the destruction of the Tea." A few were still living.[22]

Still, even the celebrated Hewes story attracted doubters. In 1833, the *Boston Daily Courier* snidely observed that the number of people suddenly claiming to have been in the Tea Party was more than double the number of men who were actually there. Adding that the same held true for Bunker Hill veterans, the paper added, "These pretensions to saintship are quite too common. Their too frequent recurrence deprives them of all their sanctity." The writer Nathaniel Hawthorne also preferred "a tale of wild, romantic mystery." He wrote that it was probably better for the younger generations to get no answer to the question of who was there, so that "the actors in the scene should sleep without their fame." He preferred that the secrets of the Tea Party remain dead and buried. False claims of participation in the Tea Party certainly disturbed many New England printers, but even genuine claimants seemed to bother people. Many Americans, it seemed, would have preferred that the "Mohawks" keep their mouths shut.[23]

Even when the descendants of participants did step forward, they were at pains to make the action sound acceptable to a nineteenth-century audience.

33 The shoemaker George Robert Twelves Hewes, in his nineties, was celebrated for his participation in the Boston Tea Party when he returned to his hometown in 1835.

A few Tea Party families, for instance, felt the Indian disguises to be a particularly disreputable element. In a memoir by Ebenezer Stevens (as told to his descendants), he recalled, *"None of the party were painted as Indians*, nor, that I know of, disguised, excepting that some of them stopped at a paint shop and daubed their faces with paint."* (Stevens was probably describing his own small group of boarders, not the entire Tea Party.) The obituary for baker

Francis Moore mentioned that he "was distinguished on that occasion by appearing openly and without disguise, whilst his comrades were disguised, and mostly as Indians." The unsavory reputation of Indian costumes was no surprise—even after the American Revolution, the tradition of white men disguising themselves as Indians while committing acts of rebellion and violence had continued.[24]

While the tea destroyers were throwing off the veil of secrecy, others donned the cloak of mystery in order to tell phony stories about participating in the Tea Party. The temptation to exaggerate was huge. As the stories unfolded, a person who hadn't yet been born in 1773 became a witness to the Boston Tea Party. An ancestor who was merely present at the Tea Party became a participant. A man who had spontaneously joined the Tea Party on the spot became transformed into a sworn member of a premeditated conspiracy. Some descendants reached for the stars and called an ancestor a "leader of the Tea Party," and so suddenly there were dozens of faux-chiefs and not enough faux-Indians. Americans apparently reveled in the delicious paradox of Tea Party tales: some argued that the real participants were too honorable to tell, while others rushed to claim that an ancestor was a charter member of the Tea Party brotherhood. In the nineteenth century, the American audiences who patronized Phineas T. Barnum and his competitors yearned for whatever entertaining frauds and opportunistic liars came their way. David Kennison was one such man, a Chicago huckster who claimed to be over one hundred years old. He boasted that he had traveled all the way from Maine with a group called the Lebanon Club for the express purpose of dumping the tea. There is very little possibility that this story is true, but the public lapped it up all the same.[25]

In the 1840s, a series of printed death notices claimed to bear witness to the demise of the last known survivor of the Boston Tea Party, only to have a letter-writer (or another obituary) contradict them. Some descendants displayed physical relics of the Tea Party as a way of bolstering the evidence of an ancestor's participation. As Henry Bromfield wrote during the tea boycotts of 1774, "Tea is not to be purchased here, & our Patriots are so Confident of its being utterly unknown in this Country in a few years that they have preserv'd Some in Bottles, (one of which I am told they have presented to the Colledge [i.e., Harvard College]) to be laid up in the Cabinets of the Curious that Posterity may have an Opp^y of Seeing an Herb that had like to have been so fatal to their Country." Like pieces of the True Cross, these tea leaves gave Americans a way of preserving a talismanic connection to a historical event. In the 1890s people were still competing to see who was the last person alive to speak to someone who had witnessed the event.[26]

Women—wives like Lucretia Stevens, daughters like Mary Palmer Tyler, and granddaughters like Harriet Hanson Robinson—were often the ones who passed on stories of the Boston Tea Party to future generations. In the nineteenth century, most historians were men. Women had to package their history as lessons for children. These rocking-chair stories often boiled the Tea Party down to folktales with singular protagonists, simple goals, and imagined villains. Such stories and female storytellers helped to humanize, sentimentalize, and domesticate the Boston Tea Party story, making a destructive act more acceptable to nineteenth-century audiences. The stories upheld women's prescribed roles as housewives, yet lent some of the women a direct interest in patriotic action and a direct role in political mobilization. Women were republican mothers, helpful spouses who made the Tea Party (and tea boycotts) possible, and also the repositories of family tradition. While women's rights did not make significant advances during the Revolutionary Era, the example of the Boston Tea Party would inspire future generations of women. The activist Harriet Hanson Robinson and her daughter, for instance, channeled their ancestral pride in Seth Ingersoll Browne's tea destruction into their work for women's suffrage.[27]

By the time they died, claimants to the Boston Tea Party had spread far beyond eastern Massachusetts to scatter across northern New England, as far west as Cincinnati and Detroit, and as far south as Alexandria, Virginia. From Wardsborough, Vermont, to Wolfeborough, New Hampshire, to Waldoborough, Maine, death notices for Tea Party participants allowed people in small, freshly hewn frontier towns to draw a connection between themselves and the history of Revolutionary Boston. The Tea Party became an event that stitched a far-flung country together.

To tell the life stories of some of these participants is, in many cases, to describe the realization of the American dream. Many of the Tea Party participants, having started life as apprentices and manual laborers in the streets of Boston, found themselves at the end of their lives with large families, greater wealth and status, new land in the American frontier, and a home they could call their own. Many of them became civil officials (including, ironically, customs officers) and political leaders, prosperous merchants and respected military officers—revered patriarchs of a new American nation.

The carpenters John Crane and Ebenezer Stevens were two striking examples of this phenomenon. Both men were members of Boston's Train of Artillery—Crane had even had experience serving in the French and Indian War when he was fifteen years old. Both men participated in the Boston Tea

Party, and both fled occupied Boston to find work in Providence, Rhode Island. Crane received a commission to serve as captain-lieutenant of a Rhode Island artillery company, and Stevens became his first lieutenant. When this company was absorbed into the Continental Army that surrounded Boston, Crane was made a major, and Stevens a captain. Both men served in a number of Revolutionary War campaigns, received promotions during the war, and were members of the Society of the Cincinnati. Crane moved to Maine and briefly got into the lumber business with Lemuel Trescott, another alleged Tea Party participant. Crane served as a judge for the Court of Common Pleas for Washington County in the Maine district, and died in 1805 in the town of Whiting. Stevens moved to New York City, married a judge's daughter, and became a successful merchant. He served in government as a state assemblyman, city alderman, and a major general in the state militia. He entertained guests at his stately summer residence in Astoria, called "Mount Napoleon," and died in 1823.[28]

Listening to stories like these, Americans could cherish a belief in America as a land of opportunity and upward mobility. Yet other Tea Party participants, including veterans of the Revolutionary War, faced poverty and difficulty in their old age. George R. T. Hewes remained poor for his entire life. As far as the records reveal, he never owned a home of his own. He and his wife may have had eleven surviving children or more, and they were able to do little to ensure their advancement in the world. Hewes lived to ninety-eight years old, and he enjoyed fame in his last years, but he never found a way to pull himself above his station in life.[29]

Joshua Wyeth, a blacksmith's apprentice in 1773, was at the battles of Bunker Hill, Brooklyn, Harlem Heights, and White Plains. When he was in his early sixties, he told an Ohio judge that, owing to "wounds age and debility," he could no longer pursue his trade as a blacksmith. He had fathered at least twenty-one children by at least two different wives, five of his offspring were under twelve years old, but their elders had left home and "furnish no assistance." His total property was worth $70, including his tools (under execution for debt), a horse, a cow, and a calf, seven chairs, and kitchenware—though when he died in Cincinnati in 1832, he may well have owned some land.[30]

Samuel Nowell was living near Wolfeborough, New Hampshire, in 1830 when he testified before a justice of the peace, hoping to receive a pension from the federal government for his service in the Revolutionary War. He swore, "I was one of those who periled themselves in that celebrated achievement, the destruction of a cargo of Tea in the harbour of Boston." He then described how he served aboard privateers during the American

Revolution and suffered as a prisoner of war. In 1830, then in his eighties, Nowell the war hero wrote that he was so destitute and devoid of means that he depended on friends for his daily bread. "At the time he was thus actively and zealously jeopardizing himself for his Country," the court recorded, "he was happy, his Country miserable. He was happy in the conscious discharge of a duty paramount to all others." But now, "The scene is reversed. His Country is rich and happy: he is poor and miserable."[31] Samuel Nowell dumped the tea in 1773 in the hope of bringing political change, and in 1776 he probably thrilled to the Declaration of Independence and its assertion that all men had the right to "Life, Liberty and the pursuit of Happiness." Yet Nowell found in 1830 that happiness could be an elusive goal. It would be up to future generations to deliver on what the American Revolution had promised.

The American Revolution was in many respects a rite of passage for the new nation. Seen in this light, the Boston Tea Party was a national moment of adolescent rebellion—of growing up and throwing off the mantle of the mother country. As the United States grew to adulthood, Americans struggled with deep anxieties about whether they were living up to the reputation of their awesome ancestors. Had Americans of the later generations earned their place in the new nation and in the world? Was the Revolution finished, or was there still more to do? Rebels, both in the United States and abroad, have frequently drawn inspiration and idealism from the example of the Tea Party. Of course, for every rebel, there are others who think that the champions of change are going too far. To more conservative observers, protests inspired by the Tea Party often appeared to be as violent and threatening as the original act. Elite printers and writers of the nineteenth century thus suppressed or whitewashed the Tea Party tales for the middle class. Yet the romance of rebellion never went away, particularly for the Boston artisans, like George R. T. Hewes, who carried the Tea Party in their memories.[32]

Over the intervening centuries, many have emulated the tactics of the Tea Party and its attendant protests, using secrecy, disguises, non-violent disobedience, ostentatious property destruction, and boycotts. Typical protests have focused attention on a few key aspects of the original Tea Party. First, the participants' contravention of the laws of society to achieve the more fundamental right of representative government has led some to emphasize the lawlessness and riotousness of the event, others the principles behind the protest. Second, the Tea Party was (at least superficially) a fight against unjust taxes, and so anti-tax protesters have always held it dear. Finally, many have celebrated the Tea Party tale as a story of national origins. The history of the Tea Party has often been a source of conflict. Some pick and choose different pieces of the story, and others draw opposing conclusions from the event. Whatever their feelings, it is clear that there is something powerful about the Tea Party—something irresistible.

Even before the last of the Tea Party participants had died, the memory of the Boston Tea Party was being taken from them and appropriated for other political uses. A writer protesting a federal tariff in 1824 called for a boycott, "as was done in the Boston tea affair."[33] In the early 1830s, the New England labor leader Seth Luther defended workers against the idea that a labor union was an inherently dangerous "combination." He wrote, "Was there no combination, when Bostonians, in the disguise of Mohawk Indians, made a dish of TEA at the expense of *King George the Third*, using Boston harbor for a teapot?"[34] In 1833, a Pequot Methodist minister named William Apess and others prevented a group of white men from taking wood from Mashpee lands, and were arrested for inciting a riot. Their lawyer, the editor of the *Boston Daily Advocate*, compared the so-called Mashpee Revolt to the Boston Tea Party: "The persons concerned in the riot, as it was called, and imprisoned for it, I think were as justifiable in what they did, as our fathers were, who threw the tea overboard."[35] The Tea Party was also invoked against landlords in upstate New York as well as banks: the critique of powerful economic interests that motivated distrust of the East India Company in 1773 was still alive in the 1840s.[36]

If tea had once been vilified as a pernicious drink, alcohol became even more so. The argument over its prohibition saw Tea Party comparisons on both sides. In 1849, the Sons of Temperance urged its members "to throw the cargoes of King Alcohol overboard." After nine women in Marion, Illinois, were arrested for destroying a saloon in 1854, their lawyer, the politician Abraham Lincoln, argued that the Boston Tea Party was a worthy precedent for their actions. But William Randolph Hearst also championed the Tea Party decades later, after Prohibition had come into force, as a model for rebellious action against it.[37]

In the quest for civil rights, people have often imitated the Bostonians' stance as aggrieved taxpayers and consumers to justify their activism and civil disobedience. Advocates for women's suffrage celebrated the centennial anniversary of the Tea Party in December 1873 with rallies and meetings in Boston's Faneuil Hall and in New York, Philadelphia, and other cities. At these rallies, Susan B. Anthony, Frederick Douglass, Lucy Stone, Mary Livermore, and others mentioned the Boston Tea Party as a way of giving fuel to the fight against taxation without representation for women, and in some cases urged women not to pay their taxes until they had been granted the right to vote.[38] By the twentieth century, women's suffragists and women's rights advocates were imitating the tactics of the eighteenth-century tea protesters by boycotting and occasionally destroying property. Martin Luther King Jr. offered the Boston Tea Party as a historical example of civil disobedience in his famous Letter from a Birmingham Jail in 1963. Three years later, Robert F. Williams used it as a rallying cry for more violent action on behalf of civil rights: "Burn, baby, burn." These groups without equal opportunity under the law felt they had just as much right to disobey unjust laws, launch boycotts, and perhaps even attack property as the tea destroyers in Boston.[39]

Vigilantes in various masks have unleashed violence and destruction in the name of the Boston Tea Party. To these Americans, the Tea Party enshrined the idea of taking matters into one's own hands whenever government fails to protect the people. Clearly indicative of the original protest, in December 1906, armed and masked night riders burned about 200,000 pounds of tobacco in Princeton, Kentucky, as a way of extracting a higher price from the monopolistic American Tobacco Company. Their handiwork was compared (both with approval and disapproval) to the destruction of the tea 133 years earlier. Other groups invoked the general principle of the Tea Party in less specific and indeed more horrific ways. In 1915, the anti-Semitic Knights of Mary Phagan justified their killing of Leo Frank (who had supposedly murdered the thirteen-year-old Phagan) near Marietta, Georgia, by citing the Tea Party as precedent. In the 1920s, William Joseph Simmons of Alabama, the Imperial Wizard of the Ku Klux Klan, wrote that the "Ku Klux spirit" had animated the Boston Tea Party. When Salt Lake City, Utah, passed an ordinance in 1925 making it illegal to assemble in public while wearing a mask or disguise, a Klan representative argued that Klansmen were "patriots who see the need of rising to the defense of their country today just as much as did the patriots of the Boston tea party when they donned the mask in order to deliver their country from the hands of the oppressor." Another white suprema-cist fraternal organization in the 1920s and 1930s, the Black Legion, claimed that its own members had destroyed the tea back in 1773.[40]

But the legend was not only invoked by Americans. Since no one was seriously hurt at the Tea Party (other than the forgotten Charles Conner), the Tea Party appealed to the advocates of a grand global tradition of nonviolent civil disobedience. When the British government in South Africa forced the Indians resident there to be registered and fingerprinted, Mahatma Gandhi led the Indian community to burn their registration cards in 1908, in protest at racially prejudicial acts by the government. A *Daily Mail* correspondent, Gandhi later wrote, compared the action to the Boston Tea Party. Violent or nonviolent, though, agents of imperialism still scorned the memory of the Tea Party. After World War II, Lord Winterton defended the rights of white European property-owners in Northern Rhodesia (now Zambia). "If there is one thing that has been burnt into the minds of the British public," he wrote, "it is that there must never again be another 'Boston tea party' with its deplorable sequel."[41]

In fact, nationalist movements the world over have drawn inspiration from the Boston Tea Party. When Sun Yat-sen, head of the Kuomintang, threatened to seize customs revenues from Canton in late 1923, the United States and other nations sent warships to intervene. Three days after the 150th anniversary of the Tea Party, Sun addressed a cable to "the American people" defending his actions: "We must stop that money from going to Peking to buy arms to kill us," he wrote, "just as your forefathers stopped taxation going to the English coffers by throwing English tea into Boston Harbor." In 2005, the political analyst Nawaf Salam described political demonstrations in Lebanon—sometimes called the "Cedar Revolution," which sought a more independent, less Syrian-influenced leadership in the country—as "our Boston Tea Party."[42]

Since the 1970s, popular demonstrations in the United States that invoke the Boston Tea Party have often (though not exclusively) become associated with libertarians, conservatives, and tax protesters. In December 1988, a Detroit radio talk show host launched a national campaign to send tea bags to Washington, D.C., to protest a pay increase for congressmen and senior federal employees. On April 16, 1990, three libertarians drove a firebomb to a post office in Royal Oak, Michigan, wrapped it with a tea bag, addressed it to the Internal Revenue Service, and put it in a mail bin, burning the face and hands of a postal worker who noticed smoke coming from the package. In 1997, two Congressmen from Louisiana and Colorado dumped copies of the federal tax code in Boston harbor. On April 15, 2009, thousands of protesters in dozens of American cities and towns hosted "Tea Parties" to express their dissatisfaction with government spending.[43]

The struggle over the legacy of the Boston Tea Party has taken various guises throughout the intervening centuries. While some have admired its spirit of disobedience in defense of the public good, others have worried that property destruction and lawbreaking go too far. Not every group that has invoked the Tea Party has done so with historical accuracy: commentators and protesters tend to gloss over the real story of the event in favor of their own causes.

The Boston Tea Party inspired radical values, wider civic participation, and the promise of building a new nation. The men of the Tea Party, along with their families and community, spoke out against unfair competition and unjust taxation. The Boston Tea Party was not just significant because it embodied the objection to imperial rule, or because it demonstrated the economic power of self-interested traders and smugglers. It also drew together Bostonians from all walks of life, who responded to the global forces of tea and empire in a radical and risky way. Artisans, apprentices, and even mere teenagers worked alongside young merchants to dispose of the tea.

Since 1773, those who have seen the Boston Tea Party as an act of unalloyed American heroism have willfully ignored the destructive chaos that surrounded it. While some have crowed that the United States was born in a noble rebellion, the Tea Party offers a stark reminder that all rebellion involves some form of heresy and sedition, treason and parricide, or destruction and terrorism. The Tea Party will always be controversial. Was the protest unique to Boston or part of a collective intercolonial effort? Was it an act of cynical self-interest or romantic principles? Was the event public and proud, or underhanded and secret? Was a given participant authentic or fake? Was it right or wrong?

Such questions expose the enduring paradox of the Boston Tea Party. It was a nonviolent act with a distinct air of menace. It was a disorderly act that ushered in a new order. Its destruction paved the way for creation. Imperial expansion had brought both its commercial blessing and its curse, in the form of threats to liberty and livelihood. White men were dressing as Native Americans, taking aim at powerful enterprises and powerful empires, only to build new ones in their place. It was a classic example even before the cliché existed: one man's terrorist is another man's freedom fighter.

The Boston Tea Party helped to bring about American independence and the Revolutionary War. Yet what made it truly revolutionary was that it demonstrated the ability of ordinary men to engage in defiant, democratic protests. The Tea Party stands as a dramatic example of popular sovereignty in action, of the people enacting their wishes in defiance of a government that could no longer claim to represent or control them. It is a legacy that Americans and other peoples sometimes reject and sometimes embrace.

On December 16, 1773, the tea destroyers brewed a revolution in Boston harbor. The Boston Tea Party remains a poignant moment in history, and it continues to inspire people all over the globe.

Appendix:
Boston Tea Party Participants

Almost no story of Tea Party participation is verifiable with any certainty. For the purposes of this appendix, I have evaluated only Tea Party participants for whom written claims to participation existed prior to 1853, eighty years after the Boston Tea Party. After this point, few new claims to participation were likely to be verifiable by living witnesses. These parameters exclude a few men (Henry Bass, David Bradlee, Seth Ingersoll Browne, Thomas Crafts Jr., John May, Benjamin Wallcut, etc.) who are mentioned in the text; I have also eliminated a few participants named before 1853 whose participation (as opposed to presence) seems doubtful, such as Jonathan Hunnewell, Richard Hunnewell Jr., David Kennison, Peter Mackintosh, John Short, Josiah Ward, and Dr. Thomas Young.

In some cases, identifying the exact person who participated in the Tea Party is difficult due to the duplication of names and the incompleteness of records. Determining the dates of birth and death is also an imperfect process. Birth dates are approximate in some cases: for instance, I have sometimes subtracted the person's age at death (as listed in an obituary) from the date of death. People changed occupations during their lives: I have tried to determine a person's occupation (or occupational status) in 1773. Where this has not been possible, I have listed a person's occupation later in life.

The seeming preponderance of younger men at the Tea Party may simply be a consequence of timing. It took until 1835 for the first public compilation of a list of participants to appear. Sixty-two years after the event, most of the people on this list were deceased. Public acknowledgment of Tea Party participation favored the long-lived. Although more forty-year-olds may have participated, their secret was more likely to have died with them in the 1810s or earlier.

Sources for personal details of the participants include published newspapers and books, pension applications, church and court records, city directories, genealogical databases, and private correspondence. Special thanks to George A. Quintal Jr., who generously shared some of his research, with the permission of the Boston Tea Party Ships and Museum, owned by Historic Tours of America. For details about political activity, see notes in Chapters 2 and 6. Abbreviations include "NEC" for North End Caucus, "SOL" for Sons of Liberty who dined on the anniversary of the Stamp Act protests on August 14, 1769; "MAS" for members of St. Andrew's Lodge of Freemasons by 1773; "petition" for signers of November 1773 petitions to town selectmen; and "watch" for the earliest volunteers to watch the tea ships.

PARTICIPANT NAME	Birth	Death	Occupation	Political activities
Barber, Nathaniel	1728	1787	merchant, insurer	SOL, NEC, petition
Barnard, Samuel	1737	1782	(farmer)	
Beals, Adam	1754	1834	(cabinet-maker)	
Bolter (Bolton), Thomas	1735	1811	housewright or ropemaker	
Brewer, James	1742	1806	pump and block maker	watch
Brimigion, Thomas	1754	1843	(later a farmer)	
Bruce, Stephen	1746	1806	merchant	SOL, MAS, petition, watch
Burton, Benjamin	1749	1835	mariner, ship carpenter	
Cady, Jeremiah	1752	1848	mason	
Campbell, Nicholas	1732	1829	sailor	
Chase, Thomas	1739	1787	distiller	Loyal Nine, SOL, NEC, MAS, watch
Clarke, Benjamin	1727	1783		
Cochran, John	1749	1839	(later an innkeeper)	
Colesworthy, Gilbert	1744	1818	caulker	
Collson, Adam	1738	1798	leather dresser	NEC, SOL, MAS, watch
Condy, James Foster	1746	1809	bookseller	NEC, petition, watch

PARTICIPANT NAME	Birth	Death	Occupation	Political activities
Conner, Charles	1734	1793	coastal trader, innkeeper, horse trader	
Coolidge, Samuel	1753	1816		
Cooper, Samuel	1755	1840	cooper's apprentice	
Cowdrey, John	1757	1835	(later a soldier, prison supervisor)	
Crane, John	1744	1805	house carpenter	SOL, watch
Dolbeare, Edmund	1757	1796	cooper's apprentice (later ship carpenter)	
Eaton, Joseph	1750	1825	hatter	
Eayres, Joseph	1733	1790	housewright	SOL, watch
Edes, Benjamin	1732	1803	printer	Loyal Nine, SOL, NEC, watch
Etheridge, William	1739	1776	mason	
Frothingham, Nathaniel	1746	1825	coachmaker	
Gammell, John	1752	1828	carpenter	
Gerrish, Thomas			mariner	
Gore, Samuel	1751	1831	painter	
Grant, Moses	1743	1817	upholsterer	NEC, petition, watch
Greene, Nathaniel	1738	1791	merchant	SOL
Hammond, Samuel	1748	1842	farmer	
Hendley, William	1747	1830	mason	
Hewes, George Robert Twelves	1742	1840	shoemaker	
Hooton, John	1754	1844	oarmaker's apprentice	
Horton, Elisha	1757	1837	(later a papermaker)	

PARTICIPANT NAME	Birth	Death	Occupation	Political activities
Howard, Samuel	1747	1840	caulker	
Howe, Edward Compton	1741	1821	ropemaker	petition
Hunnewell, Richard	1731	1805	mason	watch
Ingollson (Ingersoll), Daniel	1750	1829	carpenter	
Larrabee, Samuel	1753	1844	coastal trader	
Lee, Joseph	1744	1831	merchant	
Lincoln, Amos	1753	1829	housewright's apprentice	
Loring, Matthew	1751	1829	leatherworker	
Mackintosh, Ebenezer	1737	1817	shoemaker	
Martin, John	1752	1817	journeyman distiller or trader	
Maxwell, Thompson	1742	1832	farmer and teamster	
McNeil, Archibald	1750	1840	ropemaker	
Mellus, Henry	1752	1832	(mariner)	
Melvill, Thomas	1751	1832	merchant's clerk	
Melvin, William	1742	1832		
Molineux, William	1717	1774	merchant	SOL, NEC
Moore, Francis	1740	1833	baker	
Moore, Thomas	1753	1813	operator of a commercial wharf	
More, William				
Morse, Anthony	1753	1803	(later a tavern-keeper)	
Newell, Eliphalet	1735	1813	(later a tavern-keeper)	
Nowell, Samuel	1744	1833	boat builder or ship carpenter	
Palmer, Joseph Pearse	1750	1797	merchant	petition, watch
Payson, Joseph	1743	1833	housewright	
Peck, Samuel			cooper	MAS, watch

PARTICIPANT NAME	Birth	Death	Occupation	Political activities
Peirce, William	1744	1840	barber	
Peters, John	1732	1832	(mariner or shopkeeper)	
Pillsbury, George	1753	1832	(schoolteacher or mariner)	
Pitts, Lendall	1747	1787	merchant	
Porter, Thomas		1800	merchant	
Prentiss, Henry	1749	1821	merchant	
Proctor, Edward	1733	1811	merchant, tavern-keeper	SOL, NEC, MAS, petition, watch
Purkitt, Henry	1755	1846	cooper's apprentice	
Randall, John	1750		(farmer)	
Revere, Paul	1734	1818	silversmith and engraver	SOL, NEC, MAS, petition, watch
Rice, Benjamin	1722	1796		
Ridgeway, Isaac	1758	1840	(caulker's son)	
Roby, Joseph	1753	1836	tinman or trader	
Russell, John		1778	mason	
Russell, William	1748	1784	schoolteacher	
Sessions, Robert	1752	1836	laborer (later a farmer)	
Shed, Joseph	1732	1812	carpenter (later a grocer)	
Simpson, Benjamin	1755	1849	bricklayer's apprentice	
Slater, Peter	1760	1831	ropemaker's apprentice	
Sloper, Samuel	1747		ship carpenter	
Smith, Ephraim	1752	1835	mariner	

PARTICIPANT NAME	Birth	Death	Occupation	Political activities
Spear, Thomas	1753	1812	blacksmith	
Sprague, Samuel	1753	1844	mason's apprentice	
Spurr, John	1749	1822	carpenter	
Starr, James	1740	1830	(cooper)	
Stearns, Phinehas	1736	1798	farmer, blacksmith	
Stevens, Ebenezer	1752	1823	carpenter	
Story, Elisha	1743	1805	physician	SOL, NEC, watch
Swan, James	1754	1831	counting-house clerk	NEC, petition
Tower, Abraham	1752	1832	shipbuilder, farmer, fisherman	
Trescott, Lemuel	1750	1826	carpenter	
Trow, Bartholomew	1736	1806	cordwainer	
Urann, Thomas	1723	1792	ship joiner	NEC, MAS, watch
Whaley, Alexander	1746	1833	(later a blacksmith or gunsmith)	
Wheeler, Josiah	1743	1817	housewright	watch
Willis, Nathaniel	1755	1831	printer's apprentice	
Wyeth, Joshua	1758	1832	blacksmith's apprentice	

Abbreviations

AAS:	American Antiquarian Society
ADM:	Admiralty
AHR:	*American Historical Review*
BCC:	Boston Committee of Correspondence
BDA:	*Boston Daily Advertiser*
BEP:	*Boston Evening-Post*
BG:	*Boston Gazette*
BL:	British Library
BNL:	*Boston News-Letter* or *Boston Weekly News-Letter*
BPB:	*Boston Post-Boy*
BPL:	Boston Public Library
BTR:	*A Report of the Record Commissioners of the City of Boston, Containing the Boston Town Records* (Boston, 1885, 1886, 1887), vol. 14, *1742–1757*, vol. 16, *1758–1769*, vol. 18, *1770–1777*
CO:	Colonial Office
DAR:	*Documents of the American Revolution, 1770–1783 (Colonial Office Series)*, 21 vols., ed. K. G. Davies (Shannon, 1972–81)
Dartmouth Papers:	The American Papers of the Second Earl of Dartmouth in the Staffordshire Record Office, D(W) 1778
DCNY:	*Documents Relative to the Colonial History of the State of New-York*, ed. E. B. O'Callaghan (Albany, NY, 1857)
EHR:	*Economic History Review*
EIC:	East India Company
HHL:	Houghton Library, Harvard University
HMC:	Historical Manuscripts Commission
HPMA:	Hutchinson Papers, Massachusetts Archives
HSP:	Historical Society of Pennsylvania
IOR:	India Office Records
JAH:	*Journal of American History*
LOC:	Library of Congress
MassSpy:	*Massachusetts Spy*
MHS:	Massachusetts Historical Society
MHSC:	*Collections of the Massachusetts Historical Society*
MHSP:	*Proceedings of the Massachusetts Historical Society*
NEHGR:	*New England Historical and Genealogical Register*
NEHGS:	New England Historic Genealogical Society
NEQ:	*New England Quarterly*
NLS:	National Library of Scotland

NM:	*Newport Mercury*
NYGWM:	*New York Gazette and the Weekly Mercury*
NYJ:	*New-York Journal*
NYPL:	New York Public Library
NYT:	*New York Times*
PBF:	*Papers of Benjamin Franklin*, ed. William B. Willcox (New Haven, CT, 1974–76, 1978), vols. 18–21
PCSM:	*Publications of the Colonial Society of Massachusetts*
PG:	*Pennsylvania Gazette*
PJ:	*Pennsylvania Journal*
PMHB:	*Pennsylvania Magazine of History and Biography*
PP:	*Pennsylvania Packet*
PRO:	Public Record Office
RWP:	Revolutionary War Pension and Bounty Land Warrant Application Files, National Archives of the United States
Selectmen's Minutes:	*A Report of the Record Commissioners of the City of Boston, containing the Selectmen's Minutes* (Boston, 1889, 1893), vol. 20, *1764–1768*, vol. 23, *1769–1775*
T:	Treasury
TH:	Thomas Hutchinson
TNA:	The National Archives of the United Kingdom
VG:	*Virginia Gazette*
WMQ:	*William and Mary Quarterly*
WO:	War Office

Notes

Any sources listed here without full references can be found in the Further Reading on pp. 289–96.

Introduction: Teapot in a Tempest

1. *Jemima Condict Her Book: Being a Transcript of the Diary of an Essex County Maid during the Revolutionary War*, in North American Women's Letters and Diaries (Newark, NJ, 1930; reprint, Alexandria, VA, 2001), 36–37.
2. Thatcher, *Traits*, 178.
3. *Diary and Autobiography of John Adams*, ed. L. H. Butterfield (Cambridge, MA, 1961), 2:85–86.
4. For contemporary definitions of terrorism in the United Kingdom and the United States, see Alexander Carlile, Baron Carlile of Berriew, "The Definition of Terrorism: A Report by Lord Carlile of Berriew Q.C., Independent Reviewer of Terrorism Legislation" (Norwich, England, March 2007); US Government Publications Office, Electronic Code of Federal Regulations, Title 28, Judicial Administration, §0.85, General functions, (l).

Chapter 1: The Empire's Corporation

1. Thomas Gage to Lord Barrington, April 13, 1772, in *Correspondence of General Thomas Gage*, ed. Clarence Edwin Carter, 2 vols. (New Haven, CT, 1931, 1933), 2:603.
2. *BG*, November 8, 1773; *BTR*, 14:180–81.
3. Mancke, "Chartered Empires"; Elizabeth Mancke, "Negotiating an Empire: Britain and its Overseas Peripheries, *c.* 1550–1780," and H. V. Bowen, "Perceptions from the Periphery: Colonial American Views of Britain's Asiatic Empire, 1756–1783," in Daniels and Kennedy, *Negotiated Empires*, 235–65, 283–300.
4. Bowen, *Business of Empire*, 29–31.
5. BL Egerton MSS 218, ff. 149–51; Kumkum Chatterjee, *Merchants, Politics and Society in Early Modern India: Bihar: 1733–1820* (Leiden, 1996), 141–42, 213–17, 226–29.
6. "An Historical Account of the late Acquisitions of the *East India* Company in *Bengal*, &c.," *The Gentleman's Magazine* 37 (March 1767), 99–101 (quote 100); Bowen, *Business of Empire*, 37–43, figure p. 39; Bowen, *Revenue and Reform*, chap. 2; Bowen, "British Conceptions"; Robins, *Corporation*, 17; Nancy F. Koehn, *The Power of Commerce: Economy and Governance in the First British Empire* (Ithaca, NY, 1994), 55, 97–99, 103–4, 132–38, 200–217; Javier Cuenca Esteban, "The British Balance of Payments, 1772–1820: India Transfers and War Finance," *EHR*, new ser., 54, 1

(February 2001): 58–86; Thomas Palmer & Co. to TH, January 29, February 6, 1767, HPMA, 25:147–54, MHS transcripts, p. 135; B. R. Mitchell with Phyllis Deane, *Abstract of British Historical Statistics* (Cambridge, 1962), 388.

7. *[London] Gazetteer and New Daily Advertiser,* November 15, 1768; Philip Lawson and Bruce Lenman, "Robert Clive, the 'Black Jagir,' and British Politics," *Historical Journal* 26, 4 (December 1983): 801–29; Datta, *Society, Economy and the Market,* 342–58; Lucy S. Sutherland, *The East India Company in Eighteenth-Century Politics* (Oxford, 1952), 58, 81, 116, 147–48, 219; Robert Travers, "Ideology and British Expansion in Bengal, 1757–72," *Journal of Imperial and Commonwealth History* 33, 1 (January 2005): 7–27; Robert Travers, *Ideology and Empire in Eighteenth-Century India: The British in Bengal* (Cambridge, 2007).

8. Douglas M. Peers, *India under Colonial Rule, 1700–1885* (New York, 2006), 107; Bankimcandra Chatterji, *Ānandamaṭh, or The Sacred Brotherhood,* trans. Julius J. Lipner (Oxford, 2005), 131–32; Sushil Chaudhury, *From Prosperity to Decline: Eighteenth-Century Bengal* (New Delhi, 1995), 2; William W. Hunter, *Annals of Rural Bengal* (London, 1868), esp. 19–34.

9. Chatterji, *Ānandamaṭh,* 132; Karam Ali, *Bihar and Bengal in the 18th Century: A Critical Edition and Translation of Muzaffarnama: A Contemporary History,* ed. Shayesta Khan (Patna, 1992), 36; David Arnold, "Hunger in the Garden of Plenty: the Bengal Famine of 1770," in Alessa Johns, ed., *Dreadful Visitations: Confronting Natural Catastrophe in the Age of Enlightenment* (New York, 1999), [81–111] 82–87, 90, 98–99.

10. For the estimate of 1.2 million, see Datta, *Society, Economy and the Market,* 29, 243–46, 249–62, 286–88, 336; Arnold, "Hunger in the Garden of Plenty," 85–86, 93–94, 102; B. Chaudhuri, "Eastern India, II," chap. 2, sec. III of *The Cambridge Economic History of India,* vol. 2: *c. 1757.–c. 1970,* ed. Dharma Kumar with Meghnad Desai (Cambridge, 1983), [295–332] 299–301.

11. *BEP,* December 9, 1771; *NYJ,* November 28, 1771; Ravi Ahuja, "State Formation and 'Famine Policy' in Early Colonial South India," in Sanjay Subrahmanyam, ed., *Land, Politics and Trade in South Asia* (New Delhi, 2004), [147–85] 150–51; Vinita Damodaran, "Famine in Bengal: A Comparison of the 1770 Famine in Bengal and the 1897 Famine in Chotanagpur," *Medieval History Journal* 10, 1/2 (October 2007): 143–181; see also BL IOR, H/105, pp. 95–96, 105–7, 305.

12. Chatterji, *Ānandamaṭh,* 140; Warren Hastings et al. to EIC Directors, November 3, 1772, in Hunter, *Annals of Rural Bengal,* 381; *NYJ,* May 23, 1771; *MassSpy,* May 23, 1771.

13. Horace Walpole, *Journal of the Reign of King George the Third, from the Year 1771 to 1783,* ed. J. Doran, 2 vols. (London, 1859), 1:75 (quote), 205–12, 239–46; William Bolts, *Considerations on India Affairs . . . ,* 2nd edn. (London, 1772), v; *The Speeches of the Right Honourable The Earl of Chatham in the Houses of Lords and Commons,* rev. edn. (London, 1848), 101; Alexander Dow, *The History of Hindostan . . .* (London, 1772), 84; Philip Lawson and Jim Phillips, " 'Our Execrable Banditti': Perceptions of Nabobs in Mid-Eighteenth Century Britain," *Albion* 16, 3 (fall 1984): 225–41; Ranajit Guha, *A Rule of Property for Bengal: An Essay on the Idea of Permanent Settlement* (Paris, 1963), chap. 2, pp. 16–17, 90, 123.

14. *BPB,* January 27, 1772; *MassSpy,* July 2, 1772; for initial accounts, see *PG,* May 9, 1771; *NYGWM,* May 20, 1771; *MassSpy,* May 23, 1771; *BEP,* September 23, 1771.

15. J. Boswell, *Reflections on the Late Alarming Bankruptcies in Scotland* (Edinburgh, 1772), 1; quoted in Julian Hoppit, "Financial Crises in Eighteenth-Century England," *EHR,* new ser., 39, 1 (February 1986): [39–58] 54; see also John Clapham, *The Bank of England: A History* (Cambridge, 1966), 1:245–49; Charles Wilson, *Anglo-Dutch Commerce and Finance in the Eighteenth Century* (Cambridge, 1941), 170–77 (quote 174); Henry Hamilton, "The Failure of the Ayr Bank, 1772," *EHR,* new ser., 8, 3 (1956): 405–17; Richard B. Sheridan, "The British Credit Crisis of 1772 and the American Colonies," *Journal of Economic History* 20, 2 (June 1960): 161–86; Bowen, *Revenue and Reform,* 126–27; Wahrman, *Making of the Modern Self,* 208–11, 216.

16. Thomas Pownall, *The Right, Interest, and Duty of Government, As Concerned in the Affairs of the East Indies* . . . (1773; rev. edn., London, 1781), 4; Bowen, *Business of Empire*, 17.

17. Richard Becher to David Anderson, January 3, 1773, BL Add. MS 45430, ff. 254–7; BL IOR L/AG/18/2/1, p. 3; Bowen, *Revenue and Reform*, 118, 125–26, 128–29.

18. This represented about 63 percent of the value of the Company's unsold goods. Bowen, "Tea, Tribute," 171; see also Labaree, *Boston Tea Party*, 6, 58–60, 67; Hoh-cheung Mui and Lorna H. Mui, "Smuggling and the British Tea Trade before 1784," *AHR* 74, 1 (October 1968): 44–73; Hoh-cheung Mui and Lorna H. Mui, " 'Trends in Eighteenth-Century Smuggling' Reconsidered," *EHR*, new ser., 28, 1 (February 1975): 28–43.

19. Bowen, *Revenue and Reform*, chap. 8.

20. Laurence Sulivan to Warren Hastings, April 28, 1773, BL Add. MS 29133, ff. 533–35; Labaree, *Boston Tea Party*, 60–62; Bowen, *Revenue and Reform*, 127–30.

21. Bowen, *Revenue and Reform*, chaps. 9–11; Sutherland, *East India Company Politics*, 241–43; Marshall, *Making and Unmaking*, 213.

22. Koehn, *Power of Commerce*; Huw V. Bowen, "A Question of Sovereignty? The Bengal Land Revenue Issue, 1765–67," *Journal of Imperial and Commonwealth History* 16, 2 (January 1988): 155–76; Sudipta Sen, *Distant Sovereignty: National Imperialism and the Origins of British India* (New York, 2002).

23. Marshall, *Making and Unmaking*, 209; Alison Gilbert Olson, *Making the Empire Work: London and American Interest Groups, 1690–1790* (Cambridge, MA, 1992), esp. chap. 11; Marguerite Appleton, "The Agents of the New England Colonies in the Revolutionary Period," *NEQ* 6, 2 (June 1933): 371–87; Mancke, "Negotiating an Empire," 252; Bowen, *Revenue and Reform*, 30–33; Bowen, *Business of Empire*, 94–96; Andrew Jackson O'Shaughnessy, *An Empire Divided: The American Revolution and the British Caribbean* (Philadelphia, 2000), 15–17, 63–69, 104–8, 128–29; Jacob M. Price, "Who Cared about the Colonies? The Impact of the Thirteen Colonies on British Society and Politics, circa 1714–1775," in Bernard Bailyn and Philip D. Morgan, eds., *Strangers within the Realm: Cultural Margins of the First British Empire* (Chapel Hill, NC, 1991), 395–436.

24. Nathaniel Rogers to TH, December 30, 1767, February 17, 1768, HPMA, 25:240–41a, 248–53, MHS transcripts, pp. 238–39 (quote), 246; John Sekora, *Luxury: The Concept in Western Thought, Eden to Smollett* (Baltimore, 1977), 232; Wylie Sypher, "The West-Indian as a 'Character' in the Eighteenth Century," *Studies in Philology* 36 (1939): 503–20; Michael Craton, "Reluctant Creoles: The Planters' World in the British West Indies," in Bailyn and Morgan, *Strangers within the Realm*, [314–63] 346–49; P. J. Marshall, "The Moral Swing to the East: British Humanitarianism, India and the West Indies," in Kenneth Ballhatchet and John Harrison, eds., *East India Company Studies: Papers Presented to Professor Sir Cyril Philips* (Hong Kong, 1986), [69–95] 70–71.

25. Thomas Palmer & Co. to TH, January 29 to February 6, 1767, HPMA, 25:147–54, MHS transcripts, pp. 134–39; Labaree, *Boston Tea Party*, 13, 20–21, 43, 45.

26. BL IOR B/85, p. 331; Labaree, *Boston Tea Party*, 14–22, 60; Robert J. Chaffin, "The Townshend Acts of 1767," *WMQ*, 3rd ser., 27, 1 (January 1970): 90–121; Thomas, *Townshend Duties Crisis*, chaps. 2, 11; Tucker and Hendrickson, *Fall*, 123–24, 238–40.

27. John Dickinson, *Letters from a Farmer in Pennsylvania, to the Inhabitants of the British Colonies* (Boston, 1768), Evans #10876, p.19; Francis Bernard to TH, March 7, 1770, Francis Bernard Papers, Sparks Manuscripts, HHL, 4.8.70–74; Labaree, *Boston Tea Party*, 21–46.

28. Earl of Hillsborough to Lords of Treasury, July 27, 1772, *DAR*, 5:152; Brown, *Revolutionary Politics*, chaps. 3–6.

29. *[London] Public Advertiser*, October 14, 1773; reprinted in *MassSpy*, January 20, 1774; Marshall, *Making and Unmaking*, chaps. 5–7; Bowen, "British Conceptions"; Travers, *Ideology and Empire*, 24; Warren M. Elofson, "The Rockingham Whigs and the Country Tradition," *Parliamentary History* 8, 1 (1989): 90–115; W. M. Elofson, "The Rockingham Whigs in Transition: The East India Company Issue, 1772–1773,"

English Historical Review 104, 413 (October 1989): 947–74; Bernard Bailyn, *The Ideological Origins of the American Revolution*, enlarged edn. (1967; Cambridge, MA, 1992), chap. 4; Bushman, *King and People*, 186–98.

30. *[London] General Evening Post*, May 25, 1773; Beverly Committee of Correspondence to BCC, January 11, 1773, MHS photostats, 1:77; Bowen, *Revenue and Reform*, 175–76.

31. BCC, circular letter, September 21, 1773, BCC minute book, NYPL, p. 234; see also *BEP*, October 25, 1773.

32. Sir George Colebrooke, *Retrospection: or Reminiscences Addressed to My Son Henry Thomas Colebrooke Esq.*, 2 vols. (London, 1898–99), 1:174, quoted in Bowen, *Revenue and Reform*, 124; see also BL IOR, B/88, esp. pp. 384, 395, 402, 434, 447–48; Hope & Co. to EIC chairman, January 12, 1773, in BL IOR, E/1/57, ff. 21–22; Bowen, "Tea, Tribute"; Labaree, *Boston Tea Party*, 67–73; Tucker and Hendrickson, *Fall*, chap. 12.

33. Massachusetts Committee of Correspondence to other Committees of Correspondence, October 21, 1773, in *The Writings of Samuel Adams*, ed. Harry Alonzo Cushing (New York, 1907), 3:67; *In Consequence of a Conference with the Committees of Correspondence in the Vicinity of Boston . . .* (Boston, 1773), Evans #12693.

34. Earl of Hillsborough to Lords of Treasury, July 27, 1772, *DAR*, 5:152; Bushman, *King and People*, 75–76, 118–120, 124–25, 137–38, 155–62, 165, 169–76, 184–86.

35. Labaree, *Boston Tea Party*, 89–91, 106, 258–59; Bushman, *King and People*, 92–93; Tyler, *Smugglers and Patriots*, 192–95, 198.

36. HAMPDEN, *The ALARM* 1, 2 (New York, October 6, 9, 1773), Evans #12799, 12800; *NM*, December 6, 1773; reprinted in *MassSpy*, December 23, 1773.

37. RUSTICUS [John Dickinson], "A Letter from the Country, To A GENTLEMAN in *PHILADELPHIA*" (Philadelphia, 1773), Evans #42457; Russ Castronovo, "Propaganda, Prenational Critique, and Early American Literature," *American Literary History* 21, 2 (summer 2009): 183–210.

38. George Macartney, *An Account of Ireland in 1773 by a Late Chief Secretary of that Kingdom* (London, 1773), 55, 68; Marshall, *Making and Unmaking*; Mancke, "Negotiating an Empire."

39. Walpole, *Journal of the Reign of King George III*, 1:242–45, 431–32.

40. *Qing Shi Lu* (Documental Chronicle of the Qing Court), Daoguang reign, chap. 227:4, 240:1–2, quoted in Zhuang Guotu, "Tea, Silver, Opium and War: From Commercial Expansion to Military Invasion," *Itinerario* 17, 2 (1993): [10–36] 30; Om Prakash, "Opium Monopoly in India and Indonesia in the Eighteenth Century," in Sanjay Subrahmanyam, "Merchants, Markets and the State in Early Modern India," *Indian Economic and Social History Review* (Delhi, 1990), 121–38; Van Dyke, *Canton Trade*, 120–34, 161–62.

41. Adam Smith, *An Inquiry into the Nature and Causes of the Wealth of Nations*, ed. Edwin Cannan (London, 1904), Library of Economics and Liberty (online), book 4, chap. 7, paras. 177 (second quote), 189 (first quote); Sankar Muthu, "Adam Smith's Critique of International Trading Companies: Theorizing 'Globalization' in the Age of Enlightenment," *Political Theory* 36, 2 (April 2008): 185–212; Emma Rothschild, "Global Commerce and the Question of Sovereignty in the Eighteenth-Century Provinces," *Modern Intellectual History* 1, 1 (2004): 3–25; Robins, *Corporation*, 101–2.

42. Chatterjee, *Merchants, Politics and Society*, 222–30; Rajat Kanta Ray, "Indian Society and the Establishment of British Supremacy, 1765–1818," in P. J. Marshall, ed., *The Eighteenth Century*, vol. 2 of *The Oxford History of the British Empire*, ed. William Roger Louis (New York, 1998), [508–29] esp. 508–10.

Chapter 2: "The Ringleader of All Violence"

1. Nathaniel Coffin to Charles Steuart, May 22, 1770, Charles Steuart Papers, 5026:56–59, NLS, quoted in Colin Nicolson, " 'McIntosh, Otis & Adams are our

demagogues': Nathaniel Coffin and the Loyalist Interpretation of the American Revolution," *MHSP* 108 (1996): 86.

2. Colin Nicolson, "Governor Francis Bernard, the Massachusetts Friends of Government, and the Advent of the Revolution," *MHSP* 103 (1991): 24–113; Bailyn, *Ordeal*, 15–30.

3. *BTR*, 16:147–48; Edwin L. Bynner, "Topography and Landmarks of the Provincial Period," in Justin Winsor, ed., *Memorial History of Boston, Including Suffolk County, Massachusetts, 1630–1880*, 4 vols. (Boston, 1881), 2:496; John Tudor, *Deacon Tudor's Diary . . .*, ed. William Tudor (Boston, 1896), 1, 2, 6–7, 15, 21.

4. Richard L. Bushman, "Shopping and Advertising in Colonial America," in Carson et al., *Of Consuming Interests*, [233–51] 239–40.

5. Edward Lillie Pierce, "Introduction," in *Letters and Diary of John Rowe*, 14–17, 24–25, 35–37; Triber, *True Republican*, 7–17, 26–27, 69–71; Steven C. Bullock, *Revolutionary Brotherhood: Freemasonry and the Transformation of the American Social Order, 1730–1840* (Chapel Hill, NC, 1996).

6. Jack Tager, *Boston Riots: Three Centuries of Social Violence* (Boston, 2001), chaps. 1–3.

7. Nash, *Urban Crucible*; William Pencak and Ralph J. Crandall, "Metropolitan Boston before the American Revolution: An Urban Interpretation of the Imperial Crisis," *Proceedings of the Bostonian Society* (1985): 57–79.

8. Abner C. Goodell Jr., "The Charges against Samuel Adams," *MHSP* 20 (1882–83): 213–23.

9. *New-York Gazette or Weekly Post-Boy*, February 12, 1770.

10. Francis Bernard to Lord Shelburne, December 22, 1766, Francis Bernard Papers, Sparks Manuscripts, HHL, 4.4.276, 282; *BG*, April 4, 11 ("lucrative posts"), 1763; L. Kinvin Wroth and Hiller B. Zobel, eds., *Legal Papers of John Adams* (Cambridge, MA, 1965), 2:107 ("prophetic glare"); Warden, *Boston*, 153–56; Shaw, *American Patriots*, chap. 4; John J. Waters and John A. Schutz, "Patterns of Massachusetts Colonial Politics: The Writs of Assistance and the Rivalry between the Otis and Hutchinson Families," *WMQ*, 3rd ser., 24, 4 (October 1967): 543–67; Bailyn, *Ordeal*, 48–62.

11. Tyler, *Smugglers and Patriots*, esp. 13–17, 28–30, 187–92; W. T. Baxter, *The House of Hancock: Business in Boston, 1724–1775* (New York, 1965), 61, 69–73, 84–85, 94, 113–18, 135, 259–60, 306–7.

12. TH to Lord Dartmouth, n.d., HPMA, 27:489–92, MHS transcripts, pp. 903–5; Morgan and Morgan, *Stamp Act Crisis*, esp. chap. 12.

13. RWP, W. #15211; Peter Orlando Hutchinson, *The Diary and Letters of His Excellency Thomas Hutchinson, Esq. . . .* (Boston, 1884), 2:228; Francis Bernard to the Earl of Hillsborough, August 29, 1768, in Bernard Papers, Sparks Manuscripts, HHL, 4.7.26; Anderson, "Ebenezer Mackintosh"; Hoerder, *Crowd Action*, 110–13, 112 n81.

14. Henry Bass to Samuel P. Savage, December 19, 1765, in Worthington Chauncey Ford, ed., "Savage Papers, 1703–1779," *MHSP* 44 (June 1911): [683–702] 688–89; *Diary and Autobiography of John Adams*, ed. L. H. Butterfield (Cambridge, MA, 1961), 1:294; Pauline Maier, *From Resistance to Revolution: Colonial Radicals and the Development of American Opposition to Britain, 1765–1776* (New York, 1972), 58, 63, 79–80, 85–87, 307; Warden, *Boston*, 163–64, 168–69.

15. TH to unknown, November 1768, HPMA, 26:324–25, MHS transcripts, p. 673; George Gregerson Wolkins, ed., "Daniel Malcom and Writs of Assistance," *MHSP* 58 (October 1924): 5–84, esp. pp. 52, 56; Carville Earle, "Boston: Vanguard of the American Revolution," in *Geographical Inquiry and American Historical Problems* (Stanford, CA, 1992), 153–72.

16. Ann Hulton to Mrs. Lightbody, undated, in *Letters of a Loyalist Lady*, 41; *BG*, March 14, 1768.

17. Fowler, *Baron of Beacon Hill*, 48–49, 82–90; D. H. Watson, "Joseph Harrison and the *Liberty* Incident," *WMQ*, 3rd ser., 20, 4 (October 1963): 585–95.

18. *Boston Chronicle*, October 26, 1769; Fowler, *Baron of Beacon Hill*, 54–61, 113–20; Zobel, *Boston Massacre*, 156–58; Hoerder, *Crowd Action*, 210; Breen, *Marketplace*, 218–19; Tyler, *Smugglers and Patriots*, chaps. 3–4.

19. *Letters and Diary of John Rowe*, 286; Nellie Zada Rice Molyneux, *History Genealogical and Biographical of the Molyneux Families* (Syracuse, NY, 1904), 152–53, 169–71; *Peter Oliver's Origin and Progress*, 117.

20. TH to Francis Bernard, May 22, 23, 1770, HPMA, 27:491–92, MHS transcripts, p. 1070; Journal of Transactions at Boston Respecting the Committee of Nonimportation, also George Mason to unknown, January 24, 1770, New England Papers, Sparks Manuscripts, HHL, 10.3.55–56, 63; *BEP*, January 22, 1770, Deposition of Thomas Hutchinson Jr. and Elisha Hutchinson, January 22, 1770, Misc. Papers, Massachusetts Archives, 88:226–28; Governor's Council Executive Records, Massachusetts Archives, 16:443–50; Shaw, *American Patriots*, chap. 7, esp. pp. 160–61; Hoerder, *Crowd Action*, 218–19.

21. *BEP*, February 26, 1770; Wroth and Zobel, *Legal Papers of John Adams*, 2:398, 417, 419; Zobel, *Boston Massacre*, 173–77.

22. Frederic Kidder, *History of the Boston Massacre, March 5, 1770: Consisting of the Narrative of the Town, the Trial of the Soldiers, and a Historical Introduction* (Albany, NY, 1870), 51; *[Baltimore] Sun*, January 31, 1840; Wall, *Historic Boston Tea Party*, 25; J. L. Bell, "Brawl at Gray's Ropewalks," *Boston 1775* (weblog), March 2, 2007; Zobel, *Boston Massacre*, 181–84.

23. Henry Prentiss to Joshua Prentiss, March 7, 1770, in Samuel Adams Drake, *History of Middlesex County, Massachusetts . . .*, 2 vols. (Boston, 1880), 1:472–73; Zobel, *Boston Massacre*, 191, 199–200, 273; RWP, W. #15211; Kidder, *History of the Boston Massacre*, 96, 135–37; Testimony of Charles Conner, March 1770, Mellen Chamberlain Collection, BPL; Young, *Shoemaker*, 33–41; *Brattleboro [VT] Messenger*, January 4, 1828; J. L. Bell, "Charles Conner Testifies About Patrick Carr," "James Brewer at the Boston Massacre, part 1," *Boston 1775* (weblog), March 17, July 17, 2007; Anderson, "Ebenezer Mackintosh," 46.

24. Hoerder, *Crowd Action*, 184, 200–203; Elbridge Henry Goss, *The Life of Colonel Paul Revere*, 2 vols. (Boston, 1891), 2:635; Brown, *Revolutionary Politics*, 59 n1; Alan Day and Katherine Day, "Another Look at the Boston 'Caucus,' " *Journal of American Studies* 5, 1 (April 1971):19–42; Nash, *Urban Crucible*, 333–35, 355–59.

25. *Orations Delivered at the Request of the Inhabitants of the Town of Boston, to Commemorate the Evening of the Fifth of March, 1770 . . .* (Boston, [1785]), Evans #18955.

26. Tucker and Hendrickson, *Fall*, 292–97.

27. William Shirley to the Lords of Trade, December 1, 1747, in *Correspondence of William Shirley . . .*, ed. Charles Henry Lincoln, 2 vols. (New York, 1912), 1:418; TH to Thomas Pownall, March 8, 1766, HPMA, 26:207–14, MHS transcripts, pp. 407–8; see also Nash, *Urban Crucible*, 273.

28. TH to Thomas Pownall, June 7, 1768, HPMA, 25:262, MHS transcripts, p. 263.

29. TH to Thomas Pownall, March 8, 1766, HPMA, 26:207–14, MHS transcripts, pp. 407–8.

30. Richard Clarke to Isaac Winslow Clarke, September 6, 1770, Richard Clarke Collection, NEHGS.

31. Samuel Cooper to Benjamin Franklin, January 1, 1771, in *PBF*, 18:3; Shaw, *American Patriots*, 101–8, 123–24, 126, 164–67; Warden, *Boston*, 251–52; Samuel Adams to James Warren, March 25, 1771, December 9, 1772, *Warren–Adams Letters*, vol. 1, *1743–1777, MHSC*, 72 (1917): 8–10, 14–15; *Diary and Autobiography of John Adams*, 2:55, 63, 66–67, 73–74; Cary, *Joseph Warren*, 46–47, 102–7, 120–22; *Letters and Diary of John Rowe*, 199, 201, 212; Clifford K. Shipton, ed., *Sibley's Harvard Graduates*, vol. 14, *1756–1760* (Boston, 1968), 516; *BNL*, November 26, 1772; Maier, *Old Revolutionaries*, esp. 105, 111, 124–26.

32. TH to unknown, June 5, 1771, TH to unknown, not sent, January 24, 1772, TH to Francis Bernard, January 29, 1772, TH to Lord Hillsborough, January 31, 1772, TH to

Francis Bernard, May 29, 1772, HPMA, 27:180–81, 284–87 (on Church), 289–90, 340–41, MHS transcripts, pp. 303 (first quote), 499 (second and third quotes), 502–3 (on Church), 509, 611–13; Warden, *Boston*, 242–46, 250–51; Stephen E. Patterson, *Political Parties in Revolutionary Massachusetts* (Madison, WI, 1973), 72–73; Fowler, *Baron of Beacon Hill*, 136–40, 145–46; Bailyn, *Ordeal*, 178; Shipton, *Sibley's Harvard Graduates*, vol. 13, *1751–1755* (Boston, 1965), 384.

33. Thomas Young to Hugh Hughes, July 30, 1769, Huntington Library; see also Young to Hughes, August 31, 1772, December 21, 1772, Miscellaneous Bound MSS, MHS; Warden, *Boston*, 150, 169, 171, 187, 189–90, 194, 207–9, 261; Schlesinger, *Colonial Merchants*; Maier, *From Resistance to Revolution*.

34. Earl of Hillsborough to Lords of Treasury, July 27, 1772, *DAR*, 5:152; Brown, *Revolutionary Politics*, chaps. 3–6.

35. *Copy of Letters Sent to Great-Britain, by His Excellency Thomas Hutchinson, the Hon. Andrew Oliver* . . . (Boston, 1773), Evans #49796, pp. 1 (second quote), 16 (first quote); William Franklin to Benjamin Franklin, July 29, 1773 (third quote), Benjamin Franklin to William Franklin, October 6, 1773 (fourth quote), in *PBF*, 20:332, 439; see also TH to the Earl of Dartmouth, June 26, 1773, *DAR*, 6:165–6; TH to Francis Bernard, June 29, 1773, HPMA, 27:502–3, MHS transcripts, pp. 922–26; Bailyn, *Ordeal*, chap. 7.

36. Ann Hulton to Mrs. Lightbody, undated, *Letters of a Loyalist Lady*, 59.

37. *Letters and Diary of John Rowe*, 245; John Boyle, "Boyle's Journal of Occurrences in Boston," *NEHGR* 84 (October 1930): 364; Massachusetts First Corps of Cadets, Records of Meetings, Bound Volumes and Notebooks, 1772–1830, Box 1, also Ephraim Eliot MS, Howard Gotlieb Archival Research Center at Boston University; *BG*, June 7, 1773; Hoerder, *Crowd Action*, 253; *BTR*, 18:139.

Chapter 3: Tea and Scandal

1. Jonas Hanway, *A Journal of Eight Days Journey from Portsmouth to Kingston upon Thames . . . To Which is Added, An Essay on Tea* (London, 1756), 275.

2. *PG*, March 25, 1742; Wilford P. Cole, "Henry Dawkins and the Quaker Comet," *Winterthur Portfolio* 4 (1968): 35–46.

3. Jamieson, "Essence of Commodification"; Kenneth Pomeranz and Steven Topik, *The World That Trade Created: Society, Culture, and the World Economy, 1400–the Present* (Armonk, NY, 1999), 77–81; Brown, *In Praise of Hot Liquors*; Shammas, *Pre-Industrial Consumer*, 299.

4. *Camellia sinensis* was named in 1753 for the Moravian Jesuit botanist George Joseph Kamel and the Latin word for "Chinese." Most "herbal teas," like South African rooibos or European and Egyptian chamomile, are tisanes infused from other plants.

5. Hohenegger, *Liquid Jade*, 182–87; Moxham, *Tea*, 36–37, 59–60; E. J. Gardner, C. H. S. Ruxton, and A. R. Leeds, "Black Tea—Helpful or Harmful? A Review of the Evidence," *European Journal of Clinical Nutrition* 61, 1 (January 2007): 3–18; Sven Wolfram, Ying Wang, and Frank Thielecke, "Anti-Obesity Effects of Green Tea: From Bedside to Bench," *Molecular Nutrition and Food Research* 50, 2 (February 2006): 176–87; J. M. Hodgson, "Effects of Tea and Tea Flavonoids on Endothelial Function and Blood Pressure: A Brief Review," *Clinical and Experimental Pharmacology and Physiology* 33, 9 (September 2006): 838–41.

6. Evans, *Tea in China*, 1–4; S. A. M. Adshead, *Material Culture in Europe and China, 1400–1800* (New York, 1997), 58–59; Walvin, *Fruits of Empire*, 9–11.

7. Gardella, *Harvesting Mountains*, 9–10; Hohenegger, *Liquid Jade*, 200–4; Liu, *Dutch East India Company's Tea Trade*, 68–71.

8. Liu, *Dutch East India Company's Tea Trade*, 68–69; Labaree, *Boston Tea Party*, 335.

9. Weijing Lu, "Beyond the Paradigm: Tea-picking Women in Imperial China," *Journal of Women's History* 15, 4 (winter 2004): 19–46; Liu, *Dutch East India Company's Tea Trade*, 68–72.

10. Van Dyke, *Canton Trade*, 1–2, 9–13, 16; Earl H. Pritchard, *The Crucial Years of Early Anglo-Chinese Relations, 1750–1800* (New York, 1970), chaps. 2–3.

11. Van Dyke, *Canton Trade*, 31, 60, 149; Labaree, *Boston Tea Party*, 5.

12. Smith, *Consumption*, 70–76.

13. Gardella, *Harvesting Mountains*, 259; Zhuang Guotu, "Tea, Silver, Opium and War: From Commercial Expansion to Military Invasion," *Itinerario* 17, 2 (1993): 10–36; Bowen, "Tea, Tribute," [158–76] 164, 170–71, 174–75; BL Add. MS 8133B, f. 362; Niels Steensgaard, "The Growth and Composition of the Long-Distance Trade of England and the Dutch Republic before 1750," in James D. Tracy ed., *The Rise of Merchant Empires: Long Distance Trade in the Early Modern World, 1350–1750* (Cambridge, 1990), [102–152] 114–18, 128, 130–32, 148–49; Smith, *Consumption*, 53–54; K. N. Chaudhuri, *The Trading World of Asia and the English East India Company, 1660–1760* (Cambridge, 1978), 97, 385–410; Pritchard, *Crucial Years*, 162–66; Philip Lawson, "Sources, Schools and Separation: The Many Faces of Parliament's Role in Anglo-American History to 1783," in *Parliament and the Atlantic Empire* (Edinburgh, 1995), [5–27] 20 n44.

14. Hoh-cheung Mui and Lorna H. Mui, "Smuggling and the British Tea Trade before 1784," *AHR* 74, 1 (October 1968): 44–73; Hoh-cheung Mui and Lorna H. Mui, " 'Trends in Eighteenth-Century Smuggling' Reconsidered," *EHR*, new ser., 28, 1 (February 1975): 28–43; Bowen, "Tea, Tribute," 165; Walvin, *Fruits of Empire*, 16–19, 169–70; Shammas, *Pre-Industrial Consumer*, 84, 146–47; S. D. Smith, "Accounting for Taste: British Coffee Consumption in Historical Perspective," *Journal of Interdisciplinary History* 27, 2 (autumn 1996): 183–214; John Coakley Lettsom, *The Natural History of the Tea-Tree . . .* (London, 1772), 62–64; Dorothy Davis, *Fairs, Shops, and Supermarkets: A History of English Shopping* (Toronto, 1966), 194, 199, 201–3, 210, 213; Mintz, *Sweetness and Power*, 114–17, 127–30, 137–49.

15. Tyler, *Smugglers and Patriots*, 109–10, 137–38, 167–69, 180–81; Richard L. Bushman, "Shopping and Advertising in Colonial America," in Carson et al., *Of Consuming Interests*, [233–51] 239–40; Breen, *Marketplace*, 111–21, 126–46.

16. TH to unknown, November 1768, TH to Thomas Palmer & Co., August 27, 1767, HPMA, 26:324–25, 25:176, MHS transcripts, pp. 673, 156; Francis Bernard to Lords of Trade, April 28, 1766, Francis Bernard Papers, Sparks Manuscripts, HHL, 4.4.222; Tyler, *Smugglers and Patriots*, 15–16, 186–92; Labaree, *Boston Tea Party*, 9–13, 36–37, 50–57; Merritt, "Tea Trade"; Peter R. Schmidt and Stephen A. Mrozowski, "Documentary Insights into the Archaeology of Smuggling," in Mary C. Beaudry ed., *Documentary Archaeology in the New World* (Cambridge, 1988), 32–42.

17. Shammas, *Pre-Industrial Consumer*, 65–67, 73 n27. A British naval officer cited an even higher figure: that £400,000 worth of tea was consumed annually in America, including smuggled tea. Extract of a letter from Boston from an officer on board the *Active*, postscript (original letter dated December 6, 1773), in Dartmouth Papers, II, 752.

18. Samuel Wharton, "Observations upon the Consumption of Teas in North America, 1773," *PMHB* 25 (1901): [139–41] 139–40, estimated that Americans bought 5 million pounds of tea every year, enough for most of the population to drink tea twice a day; Labaree, *Boston Tea Party*, 7; one historian has given a lower estimate of 0.8 pounds of tea annually in the 1760s, yet she may have been too conservative about the level of smuggling; Shammas, *Pre-Industrial Consumer*, 84–86; Merritt, "Tea Trade," 126; Tyler, *Smugglers and Patriots*, 310 n32.

19. Shammas, *Pre-Industrial Consumer*, 68; Breen, *Marketplace*, esp. chap. 2; Cary Carson, "The Consumer Revolution in Colonial British America: Why Demand?" in Carson et al., *Of Consuming Interests*, 483–697; Walvin, *Fruits of Empire*, chap. 12.

20. Smith, *Consumption*, 173–74; Berg, *Luxury and Pleasure*, 232–34; Amanda Vickery, *The Gentleman's Daughter: Women's Lives in Georgian England* (New Haven, CT, 1998), 168–69, 195–223.

21. Smith, *Consumption*, 40–43, 174–81, 204–12; Peter Earle, *The Making of the English Middle Class: Business, Society and Family Life in London, 1660–1730* (Berkeley and Los Angeles, 1989), 164, 272, 280–81, 294–95, 297–99, 383 n7, 387 n45.

22. Kenneth Pomeranz, *The Great Divergence: China, Europe, and the Making of the Modern World Economy* (Princeton, NJ, 2000), 114–15; Jan de Vries, "Between Purchasing Power and the World of Goods: Understanding the Household Economy in Early Modern Europe," in Brewer and Porter, *Consumption and the World of Goods*, 85–132.

23. Schmidt, "Caffeine and the Coming of the Enlightenment."

24. Ethan W. Lasser, "Reading Japanned Furniture," *American Furniture* (2007): 169–90; Dean A. Fales Jr., "Boston Japanned Furniture," in Walter Muir Whitehill ed., *Boston Furniture of the Eighteenth Century* (Boston, 1974), 49–69; Breen, *Marketplace*, 76–82, 166–72.

25. Sarah Neale Fayen, "Tilt-Top Tables and Eighteenth-century Consumerism," *American Furniture* (2003): 95–137; Rodris Roth, "Tea-Drinking in Eighteenth-Century America: Its Etiquette and Equipage," in Robert Blair St. George, ed., *Material Life in America, 1600–1860* (Boston, 1988), 439–62.

26. *BNL*, November 28, 1771; Berg, *Luxury and Pleasure*; Breen, *Marketplace*, xii, 84; Anne Yentsch, "The Symbolic Divisions of Pottery: Sex-related Attributes of English and Anglo-American Household Pots," in Randall H. McGuire and Robert Paynter, eds., *The Archaeology of Inequality* (Oxford, 1991), 192–230, esp. pp. 223–25; Triber, *True Republican*, 16–17, 26–27, 38–41, 60–61, 83–84, 95–96, 205 n16, 223 n26, 224 n27; Ann Hulton to Mrs. Lightbody, August 1772, November 21, 1772, in *Letters of a Loyalist Lady*, 47–48, 54–55.

27. *BTR*, 14:178, 180–84, 221 (quote), 241; *BEP*, May 14, 1750.

28. Richard Clarke & Son to Peter Contencin, June 6, 1768, in Letter-Book, 1767–69, Richard Clarke Collection, NEHGS, p. 110; see also Clarke to Contencin, May 9, 1767, p. 21; Michael D. Coe, "The Line of Forts: Archeology of the mid-Eighteenth Century on the Massachusetts Frontier," in *New England Historical Archaeology*, ed. Peter Benes, Dublin Seminar for New England Folklife Annual Proceedings 2 (1977): [44–55] 52–54; Gloria L. Main, "The Standard of Living in Southern New England, 1640–1773," *WMQ*, 3rd ser., 45, 1 (January 1988): [124–34], 129; Breen, *Marketplace*, 49–50; Carson, "Consumer Revolution," in Carson et al., *Of Consuming Interests*, 546; Shammas, *Pre-Industrial Consumer*, 183–84; Wharton, "Observations," 139; Merritt, "Tea Trade," 126–27.

29. Dr. Nicolas Tulpius, *Observationes Medicae* (Amsterdam, 1641); quoted in William H. Ukers, *All About Tea* (New York, 1935), 1:31–32; Smith, *Consumption*, 105–8, 122–30, 263 n21 ("work of Venus"); Thomas Garway, *An Exact Description of the Growth, Quality and Vertues of the Leaf TEA* (1660); Biziere, "Hot Beverages," 137–39; Walvin, *Fruits of Empire*, 10–14; Macfarlane and Macfarlane, *Empire of Tea*, 66–69.

30. South Briton, "Observations on the Effects of TEA," *Gentleman's Magazine* 7 (April 1737): [213–14] 214.

31. John Wesley, *Letter to a Friend, Concerning Tea* (1748; reprint, London, 1825), 3.

32. Hanway, *Journal of Eight Days Journey*, 217–28, 230 (second quote), 244 (first quote).

33. John Sekora, *Luxury: The Concept in Western Thought, Eden to Smollett* (Baltimore, 1977), esp. chaps. 2–3; Christopher J. Berry, *The Idea of Luxury: A Conceptual and Historical Investigation* (Cambridge, 1994), esp. chap. 6; Kowaleski-Wallace, *Consuming Subjects*, 5–10; Smith, *Consumption*, 77–80; Breen, *Marketplace*, chap. 5.

34. Smith, *Consumption*, 25–40, 69–71, 78–81; Joyce Appleby, "Consumption in Early Modern Social Thought," in Brewer and Porter, *Consumption and the World of Goods*, 162–73.

35. Hanway, *Journal of Eight Days Journey*, 282–83 (first quote), 244 (second and third quotes); see also Charlotte Sussman, *Consuming Anxieties: Consumer Protest, Gender, and British Slavery, 1713–1833* (Stanford, CA, 2000), 24–31; Kowaleski-Wallace, *Consuming Subjects*, 31–36; Walvin, *Fruits of Empire*, 22–25, 128–31; Roy Porter, "Consumption: Disease of the Consumer Society?" in Brewer and Porter, *Consumption and the World of Goods*, 58–81; Wahrman, *Making of the Modern Self*, 202–8.

36. [Samuel Johnson], review, in *Literary Magazine, or Universal Review* 2, 13 (April 1757): [161–67] 161, 166.

37. Kowaleski-Wallace, *Consuming Subjects*, 19–21, 26–30; Smith, *Consumption*, 74, 76–77, 173.

38. [Bernard de Mandeville], *The Fable of the Bees: or, Private Vices, Publick Benefits*, 6th edn. (London, 1732), 249–55, quote 254; Kowaleski-Wallace, *Consuming Subjects*, 4–5, 8, 26–32; Sussman, *Consuming Anxieties*, 27–28.

39. Eliza Fowler Haywood, *The Tea Table, or a Conversation between Some Polite Persons of Both Sexes, at a Lady's Visiting Day* (London, 1725), 2; Edward Young, "Love of Fame, the Universal Passion," 6th satire, "On Women," in *The Poetical Works of Edward Young*, 2 vols. (Boston, 1859), 2:134; Smith, *Consumption*, 139–61, 171–75; Jamieson, "Essence of Commodification," 270, 275, 281–82, 284; David S. Shields, *Civil Tongues and Polite Letters in British America* (Chapel Hill, NC, 1997), 112–14; Shammas, *Pre-Industrial Consumer*, 186–88.

40. Simon Mason, *The Good and Bad Effects of Tea Consider'd . . .* (London, 1745), 46; Kowaleski-Wallace, *Consuming Subjects*, 33–36; De Vries, "Between Purchasing Power and the World of Goods," 110–14, 118–21.

41. "An Easy and Practicable Plan for Increasing the Consumption of Tea . . ." *Gentleman's Magazine* 43 (February 1773): 59–61; Smith, *Consumption*, 127–28, 172–74, 233; Berg, *Luxury and Pleasure*, 234–46.

42. *BEP*, August 18, 1746; John E. Crowley, *This Sheba, Self: The Conceptualization of Economic Life in Eighteenth-Century America* (Baltimore, 1974), 60–65, 77–85, 101–10, 125–46; Nash, *Urban Crucible*, 137, 224, 262–63; Breen, *Marketplace*, 168–91, 204–10; Mark A. Peterson, "Life on the Margins: Boston's Anxieties of Influence in the Atlantic World," in Wim Klooster and Alfred Padula, eds., *The Atlantic World: Essays on Slavery, Migration, and Imagination* (Upper Saddle River, NJ, 2005), 45–59.

43. *The Present Melancholy Circumstances of the Province Consider'd, . . .* (Boston, 1719), Evans #2067, pp. 5, 12; Breen, *Marketplace*, 10–19, 82–101, 210–13; Walvin, *Fruits of Empire*, chap. 10.

44. *BEP*, August 25, 1746; [Joseph Bennett], "Boston in 1740," *MHSP*, ser. 1, vol. 5 (1860–1862): [108–26] 125–26; *Connecticut Courant*, June 10, 1765; see also James Murray to Jean and Anne Bennet, August 4, 1760, James Murray Letterbooks, 1732–69, MHS; Fayen, "Tilt-Top Tables," 98–99; Shields, *Civil Tongues and Polite Letters*, 104–19; Roth, "Tea-Drinking in Eighteenth Century America," 441–46; Breen, *Marketplace*, 172–82; Crane, *Ebb Tide in New England*, chap. 3.

45. *BG*, October 1, 1764; Breen, *Marketplace*, chap. 6; George Spencer to the Lords of Treasury, January 8, 1766, TNA:PRO, T 1/445, ff. 459–60, LOC transcripts; Thomas M. Truxes, *Defying Empire: Trading with the Enemy in Colonial New York* (New Haven, CT, 2008), 199.

46. *BG*, November 2, 1767; see also *BNL*, November 5, 1767; Breen, *Marketplace*, chap. 7.

47. Breen, *Marketplace*, xvi, 225–26; Crowley, *This Sheba, Self*, 125–46.

48. *BG*, October 24, 1768.

49. [John Lovell], *Freedom the First of Blessings* (Boston, [1754]), Evans #7233, p. 3; Jonathan Mayhew, *The Snare Broken: A Thankgiving-Discourse . . .*, 2nd edn. (Boston, 1766), Evans #10389, p. 26; Alfred F. Young, " 'Persons of Consequence': The Women of Boston and the Making of the American Revolution, 1765–1776," in *Liberty Tree*, [100–143] 103; Paul S. Boyer, "Borrowed Rhetoric: The Massachusetts Excise Controversy of 1754," *WMQ*, 3rd ser., 21, 3 (July 1964): 328–51; Breen, *Marketplace*, 229–34.

50. *BG*, February 26, 1770; Norton, *Liberty's Daughters*, 157–63; Young, "'Persons of Consequence,'" 115–16, 128–34.
51. *BNL*, November 5, 1767.
52. *BNL*, December 24, 1767.
53. *BG*, December 28, 1767; *Connecticut Journal, and New-Haven Post-Boy*, April 8, 1768; Shields, *Civil Tongues and Polite Letters*, 107–8; "The Drunken Husband and Tea-Drinking Wife, &c.," (n.p., 176–?), Shipton & Mooney #49066.
54. *BG*, November 21, 1768.
55. *Pennsylvania Chronicle*, December 25, 1769.
56. *BG*, February 5, 12, 1770; *BEP*, February 12, 1770.
57. *BG*, November 2, 9, December 7, 1767, January 25, May 2, 9, 1768, May 8, 1769; *BPB*, November 16, 1767; *Peter Oliver's Origin and Progress, 15*.
58. *BG*, December 21, 1767; see also *New-London Gazette*, October 16, 1767, reprinted in *BPB*, November 16, 1767.
59. *BG*, August 29, 1768.
60. *BG*, January 8, 1770; Merritt, "Tea Trade."
61. *BEP*, February 5, 1770.
62. *Peter Oliver's Origin and Progress*, 73 (first quote), 74 (second quote).
63. Abigail Dwight to Pamela Dwight [later Sedgwick], June 14, 1769, Pamela Dwight Sedgwick Family Correspondence, Sedgwick Family Papers, MHS.
64. Smith, *Consumption*, 196; Colin Campbell, "Understanding Traditional and Modern Patterns of Consumption in Eighteenth-Century England: A Character-Action Approach," in Brewer and Porter, *Consumption and the World of Goods*, 40–57.

Chapter 4: "Enemies to Their Country"

1. Reprint from a London newspaper, *MassSpy*, November 18, 1773; *BG*, November 22, 1773.
2. *BG*, October 18, 1773; *BEP*, October 11, 1773.
3. Colin Nicolson, "Governor Francis Bernard, the Massachusetts Friends of Government, and the Advent of the Revolution," *MHSP* 103 (1991): 24–113, esp. 27–39; Janice Potter, *The Liberty We Seek: Loyalist Ideology in Colonial New York and Massachusetts* (Cambridge, MA, 1983); Bailyn, *Ordeal*.
4. *Sibley's Harvard Graduates*, vol. 8, *1726–1730* (Boston, 1951), 550–62; Massachusetts Archives, 117:51–54.
5. Richard Clarke & Sons to Peter Contencin, September 25, 1767, Richard Clarke Collection, NEHGS; see also Thomas Palmer & Co. to TH, January 29, February 6, 1767, HPMA, 25:147–54, MHS transcripts, pp. 134–39.
6. Richard Clarke & Sons to Peter Contencin, December 3, 1767, Richard Clarke Collection, NEHGS.
7. TH to Thomas Pownall, January 29, 1769, TH to William Palmer, December 3, 1768, TH to Francis Bernard, February 18, 1770, HPMA, 26:340, 332, 442–44, MHS transcripts, pp. 714–15, 690, 965; Bailyn, *Ordeal*, 154.
8. Jeffrey Amherst to Earl of Dartmouth, March 9, 1774, in Dartmouth Papers, II, 852.
9. Labaree, *Boston Tea Party*, 32–37, 331.
10. TH to Francis Bernard, October 4, 5, 1769, HPMA, 26:383–84, MHS transcripts, p. 820. Clarke may have engaged previously in smuggling ventures; Tyler, *Smugglers and Patriots*, 112–13, 260, 299 n10.
11. Richard Clarke and Sons to Peter Contencin, May 10, 1768, Richard Clarke Collection, NEHGS.
12. *Boston Chronicle*, August 14–17, 17–21, 1769; Tyler, *Smugglers and Patriots*, 120–24, 129, 132–35.

13. Thomas Young to Hugh Hughes, December 21, 1772, Misc. Bound MSS, MHS; *Boston Chronicle*, October 26, 1769; Richard Clarke & Sons to Peter Contencin, April 12, 1769, Richard Clarke Collection, NEHGS; Tyler, *Smugglers and Patriots*, 124–27, 135–38, 178.

14. *BG*, August 14, 1769; Richard Clarke & Sons to Peter Contencin, September 24, 1768, Richard Clarke Collection, NEHGS; Tyler, *Smugglers and Patriots*, 109–10, 116–20, 136–38; Schlesinger, *Colonial Merchants*, 106–20, 124–34, 156–72.

15. Richard Clarke & Sons to Peter Contencin, August 19, 1769, Richard Clarke Collection, NEHGS.

16. TH to William Palmer, October 5, 1769, TH to Francis Bernard, October 4, 5, 1769, TH to [Ebenezer] Silliman, July 28, 1770, HPMA, 26:386, 383–84, 527–28; MHS transcripts, pp. 825, 820, 1149; see also Tyler, *Smugglers and Patriots*, 127–28, 139–47, Schlesinger, *Colonial Merchants*, 164, 172–76.

17. Philadelphus, *To the Public* (Philadelphia, 1770), Evans #11823; *NYJ*, June 22, 1769, January 4, 1770; *NYGWM*, August 27, 1770; *PG*, September 20, 1770; Thomas Young to Hugh Hughes, December 21, 1772, Misc. Bound MSS, MHS; Breen, *Marketplace*, 289–93; Tyler, *Smugglers and Patriots*, 148–69; Schlesinger, *Colonial Merchants*, chap. 5; Merritt, "Tea Trade," 137; Labaree, *Boston Tea Party*, 46–57.

18. Samuel Salisbury to Stephen Salisbury, November 14, 1770, Salisbury Family Papers, AAS.

19. Charles Dudley to Commissioners of Customs at Boston, April 11, 1771, *DAR*, 3:78–82; Commissioners to Collector and Comptroller at Philadelphia, [January 17, 1771], [John Swift?] to Commissioners, January 31, February 5, April 16, 30, 1771, John Swift and Joshua Loring to Commissioners, January 17, 1772, Philadelphia Custom House Papers, vols. 11, 12, HSP; TH to unknown, November 1768, TH to Thomas Pownall, January 29, 1769, HPMA, 26:324–25, 340, MHS transcripts, pp. 673–74, 714–15; Schlesinger, *Colonial Merchants*, 97–99.

20. John Swift to Commissioners, November 25, 1771, John Swift and Joshua Loring to Commissioners, November 30, 1771, Philadelphia Custom House Papers, vol. 12, HSP.

21. TH to Earl of Hillsborough, July 26, 1770, August 25, 1771, *DAR*, 2:153, 3:172–73; C. C. Smith, ed., "An Account of Part of the Sufferings and Losses of Jolley Allen, a Native of London," *MHSP* 16 (February 1878): [67–99] 69–71; John Adams diary, February 14, 1771 (quote), in *Founding Families: Digital Editions of the Papers of the Winthrops and the Adamses*, ed. C. James Taylor (Boston, 2007); Labaree, *Boston Tea Party*, 50–53.

22. William Palfrey to John Hancock, February 15, 1771, Palfrey Family Papers, HHL, f. 34; see also TH to Lord Hillsborough, January 24, 1772, HPMA, 27:285, MHS transcripts, p. 500; Jeffrey Amherst to Earl of Dartmouth, March 9, 1774, in Dartmouth Papers, II, 852.

23. The New York consignees were Pigou and Benjamin Booth, Abraham Lott, and Henry White. The Philadelphia consignees were Gilbert Barkly, Thomas and Isaac Wharton, Jonathan Browne, and Abel James and Henry Drinker. The Charleston consignees were Roger Smith and Peter Leger and William Greenwood. Drake, *Tea Leaves*, 199–247; Earl H. Pritchard, *The Crucial Years of Early Anglo-Chinese Relations, 1750–1800* (New York, 1970), 123–26; Samuel Wharton, "Observations upon the Consumption of Teas in North America, 1773," *PMHB* 25 (1901): 139–41; Merritt, "Tea Trade," 142–43; Leger & Greenwood to Greenwood & Higginson, September 20, December 4, 1773, Leger & Greenwood Letterbook, William L. Clements Library, pp. 127, 138; Leila Sellers, *Charleston Business on the Eve of the American Revolution* (Chapel Hill, NC, 1934), 220–26; Labaree, *Boston Tea Party*, 73–79, 87–91, 97.

24. Drake, *Tea Leaves*, 202–3, 203 n1, 209–11, 214–15, 222–23, 224 (quote), 238, 243; Governor Hutchinson's sons and daughter were related to the Clarkes through the politically prominent Oliver family. Richard Clarke's sister Mary had married Peter Oliver Sr.; Sarah Hutchinson had married Peter Oliver Jr., who was Richard Clarke's

nephew; Elisha Hutchinson had married Mary Oliver Watson, and the senior Clarke was her great-uncle. The younger Clarkes and younger Hutchinsons thought of each other as cousins. Jonathan Clarke to Elisha Hutchinson, April 30, 1773, TH to Elisha Hutchinson, November 30, 1773, in Correspondence of the Family of Hutchinson, 1741–1800, vol. 1, BL Egerton 2659, ff. 34, 50; W. H. Whitmore, "The Oliver Family," *NEHGR* 19, 2 (April 1865): 100–6; Bailyn, *Ordeal*, 28–31, 183–84, 382; Clifford K. Shipton, ed., *Sibley's Harvard Graduates* (Boston, 1951, 1968, 1970), 8:550–62, 14:289–95, 15:264–68; Ann Uhry Abrams, "Politics, Prints, and John Singleton Copley's *Watson and the Shark*," *Art Bulletin* 61, 2 (June 1979): 265–76, esp. pp. 267–69. An additional note: Isaac Winslow Clarke was an apprentice or clerk for George Bethune, whose brother-in-law was Benjamin Faneuil Jr. Richard Clarke to Isaac Winslow Clarke, June 21, 1762, in *PCSM* 8 (1902–4): [78–90], 79.

25. *PJ*, September 29, 1773; *BG*, October 11, 18 (quote), 1773; *BPB*, October 11, 1773; *BEP*, October 11, 1773; John Erving et al. to William Bollan, December 20, 1773, in *The Bowdoin and Temple Papers, MHSC*, 6th ser., vol. 9 (1897): 332.

26. SCÆVOLA [Thomas Mifflin], "To the COMMISSIONERS appointed by the *EAST-INDIA* COMPANY, for the SALE of TEA, in AMERICA," (Philadelphia, October 9, 1773), Evans #12999, reprinted in *PJ*, October 13, 1773; *BPB*, October 18, 1773; *BG*, October 25, 1773; *BEP*, October 18, 1773; for attribution, see L. H. Butterfield, ed., *Letters of Benjamin Rush* (Princeton, NJ: Princeton University Press, 1951), 1:81–83; for date of pamphlet, see *BEP*, November 15, 1773.

27. HAMPDEN, *The ALARM* 1 (New York, October 6, 1773), Evans #12799; for attribution, see Robert Jay Christen, "King Sears: Politician and Patriot in a Decade of Revolution," (Ph.D. diss, Columbia University, 1968), 233; William Gordon, *The History of the Rise, Progress, and Establishment of the Independence of the United States of America . . .*, 4 vols. (London, 1788), 1:332–33.

28. HAMPDEN, *The ALARM* 3, 4 (New York, October 15, 19, 1773), Evans #12801, 12802; William Tryon to Earl of Dartmouth, November 3, 1773, *DAR*, 6:238–39; *Historical Memoirs . . . of William Smith*, ed. William H. W. Sabine, 2 vols. (reprint, New York, 1969), 1:156.

29. Samuel Cooper to Benjamin Franklin, December 17, 1773, in Jared Sparks, ed., "Destruction of the Tea in the Harbor of Boston, December 16, 1773," *MHSC*, 4th ser., vol. 4 (Boston, 1858): [373–89] 373.

30. BCC to Worcester Committee of Correspondence, September 11, 1773, in *The Writings of Samuel Adams*, ed. Harry Alonzo Cushing (New York, 1907), 3:50–52, quote p. 50.

31. HAMPDEN, *The ALARM*, 5 (New York, October 27, 1773), Evans #12803.

32. *BG*, November 1, 1773; TH to Thomas Hood, February 23, 1770, HPMA, 27:444–45, MHS transcripts, p. 971; see also *MassSpy*, October 21, November 4, 26, 1773.

33. Charles Thomson to Samuel Adams and John Hancock, December 19, 1773, misc. correspondence, BCC Papers, NYPL.

34. TH to unknown, December 3, 1773 (first quote), TH to William Sanford Hutchinson, December 7, 1773, TH to William Palmer, December 9, 1773 (second quote), HPMA, 27:581–85, MHS transcripts, pp. 1097 (first quote), 1102, 1106 (second quote); Bailyn, *Ordeal*, 259.

35. HAMPDEN, *The ALARM*, 5, Evans #12803; *MassSpy*, November 4, 1773; *BPB*, November 15, 1773; Thomas Danforth to the Earl of Dartmouth, December 28, 1773, in Dartmouth Papers, II, 758.

36. *BG*, November 1, 8, 1773; Frederick Pigou Jr. to James & Drinker, May 27, 1773, Henry S. Drinker Papers, HSP.

37. John Adams diary, September 20, 1774, in Taylor, ed., *Founding Families*; Jeffrey Amherst to Earl of Dartmouth, March 9, 1774, in Dartmouth Papers, II, 852.

38. *BEP*, October 18, 1773; John Eliot, *A Biographical Dictionary Containing a Brief Account of the First Settlers and Other Eminent Characters . . .* (Boston and Salem, MA, 1809), 472; Elbridge Henry Goss, *The Life of Colonel Paul Revere*, 2 vols. (Boston, 1891), 2:641.

39. *BNL*, June 30, 1768; *BTR*, 18:17; *A Report of the Record Commissioners of the City of Boston Containing Boston Births from A.D. 1700 to A.D. 1800* (Boston: Rockwell and Churchill, 1894), 239; "Three Letters Written by an American Loyalist and His Wife, 1775–1788," ed. Edward Wheelwright, *PCSM* 3 (1895–97): [379–400] 393 n2; Delmar R. Lowell, *The Historic Genealogy of the Lowells of America from 1639 to 1899* (Rutland, VT, 1899), 35–36.

40. Triber, *True Republican*; Fischer, *Paul Revere's Ride*, 16–29.

41. Quoted in Robert C. Winthrop Jr., "Remarks," *MHSP*, 2nd ser., vol. 12 (1897–98): [138–48] 141; *Boston Births*, 246; *BG*, September 14, 1772.

42. *In Consequence of a Conference with the Committees of Correspondence in the Vicinity of Boston . . .* (Boston, 1773), Evans #12693; Benjamin Franklin to Thomas Cushing, March 9, June 4, September 12, 1773, *PBF*, 20:98–100, 226–29, 400–1.

43. *BEP*, October 25, 1773; for attribution, see Drake, *Tea Leaves*, 281.

44. *NYJ*, October 21, 1773; *BG*, November 1, 1773.

45. Henry Bromfield to Thomas Bromfield, September 4, October 16, 25, 1773, Henry Bromfield Letterbook, 4:70–71, 81 (first quote), 85 (second quote), NEHGS.

46. "Moon Phases for Boston, U.S.A.—Massachusetts: Year 1773," *Time and Date AS* (Stavanger, Norway, 1995–2008), online; Ann Hulton to Mrs. Lightbody, July 25, 1770, in *Letters of a Loyalist Lady*, 22–27.

47. Drake, *Tea Leaves*, 281–83; TH to Earl of Dartmouth, November 4, 1773, *DAR*, 6:240; Alfred F. Young, "Tar and Feathers and the Ghost of Oliver Cromwell: English Plebeian Culture and American Radicalism," in *Liberty Tree*, 144–79.

48. "The True SONS OF LIBERTY," *Tradesmen's Protest against the Proceedings of the Merchants* (Boston, November 3, 1773); *BTR*, 18:142; *BPB*, November 15, 1773; Tyler, *Smugglers and Patriots*, 201; Nathaniel Rogers to TH, December 30, 1767, HPMA, 25:240–41a, MHS transcripts, p. 239.

49. Goss, *Life of Paul Revere*, 2:642–43; W. T. Baxter, *The House of Hancock: Business in Boston, 1724–1775* (New York, 1965), 280–82; after November 3, the North End Caucus recorded no more of its anti-tea activities.

50. Drake, *Tea Leaves*, 282–84; TH to William Tryon, November 21, 1773, HPMA, 27:572–74, MHS transcripts, p. 1078.

51. Narrative for TH by Joseph Green, November 3, enclosed in TH to Earl of Dartmouth, November 4, 1773, *DAR*, 6:239–40; TH to William Tryon, November 21, 1773, HPMA, 27:572–74, MHS transcripts, p. 1078; Drake, *Tea Leaves*, 285–86.

52. *MassSpy*, November 4, 1773.

53. Drake, *Tea Leaves*, 292–94; "Diary for 1773 to the end of 1774, of Mr. Thomas Newell, Boston," *MHSP* 15 (October 1877): [335–63] 343.

54. TH to Lord Dartmouth, November 6, 1773, HPMA, 27:590, MHS transcripts, p. 1121; *BTR*, 18:141–44; *BG*, November 8, 1773.

55. Drake, *Tea Leaves*, 289; *BG*, November 8, 1773; *BTR*, 18:144–46; *MassSpy*, November 11, 1773; John Scollay to Arthur Lee, December 23, 1773, in Sparks, "Destruction of the Tea," 380–81.

56. William Paine to Isaac W. Clarke, November 7, 1773, Misc. Bound MSS, MHS.

57. *BG*, November 15, 1773.

58. TH to William Tryon, November 11, 21, 1773, HPMA, 25:559, 572–74, MHS transcripts, pp. 605, 1078–79; TH to Earl of Dartmouth, December 2, 1773, *DAR*, 6:248; "Diary of Thomas Newell," 344.

59. Drake, *Tea Leaves*, 278.

60. TH to William Tryon, November 21, 1773, HPMA, 27:572–74, MHS transcripts, p. 1079; Rough draft of Petition to Governor and Council [November 19, 1773], Richard Clarke Papers, MHS; *BNL*, November 26, 1773; *BG*, December 13, 1773; see also "Petition to the Governor and Council," *PCSM* 8 (1902–4): 84–85; TH to Earl of Dartmouth, December 2, 1773, *DAR*, 6:248–49; Ann Hulton to Mrs. Lightbody, November 25, 1773, in *Letters of a Loyalist Lady*, 64; *BPB*, November 22, 1773; William Gordon to Earl of Dartmouth, December 11, 1773, in Dartmouth Papers, II, 754.

61. *BG*, November 22, 1773; *BTR*, 18:146–48; Scollay to Lee, December 23, 1773, Dr. Hugh Williamson's examination before the Privy Council in London, February 19, 1774, in Sparks, "Destruction of the Tea," 380, 386–87.

62. Scollay to Lee, in Sparks, "Destruction of the Tea," 380–81; Drake, *Tea Leaves*, 309–10; TH to William Tryon, November 21, 1773, HPMA, 27:572–74, MHS transcripts, p. 1080; *BG*, November 22, 1773; *MassSpy*, November 26, 1773.

63. TH to Lord Dartmouth, November 15, 1773, in "Tea-Party Anniversary," ed. Robert C. Winthrop, *MHSP* 13 (December 1873): [151–216] 165; TH to William Tryon, November 21, December 1, 1773, HPMA, 27:572–74, 576, MHS transcripts, pp. 1080–81, 1085; Drake, *Tea Leaves*, 310–15; Council proceedings of November 23, 27, 29, 1773, in Dartmouth Papers, I, ii, 908; see also TH to Elisha Hutchinson, November 30, 1773, in Correspondence of the Family of Hutchinson, 1741–1800, vol. 1, 1741–1783, BL Egerton 2659, f. 50; Francis G. Walett, "The Massachusetts Council, 1766–1774: The Transformation of a Conservative Institution," *WMQ*, 3rd ser., 6, 4 (October, 1949): 605–27.

64. Minutes of Meeting of Boston Selectmen, November 24, 28, 1773, BCC Records, NYPL, Misc. correspondence, 1773; *Selectmen's Minutes*, 23:202–3; Scollay to Lee, in Sparks, "Destruction of the Tea," 381–82.

65. John Andrews to William Barrell, November 29, 1773, "Letters of John Andrews," ed. Winthrop Sargent, *MHSP* 8 (1864–65): [316–413] 324; Peleg Clarke to John Fletcher, November 28, 1773, Newport Historical Society; Extract of *Dartmouth* log, Thatcher, *Traits*, 259–60.

Chapter 5: The Detestable Tea Arrives

1. TH to William Palmer, December 9, 1773, HPMA, 27:584–85, MHS transcripts, p. 1106.

2. L. F. S. Upton, ed., "Proceedings of Ye Body Respecting the Tea," *WMQ*, 3rd ser., 22, 2 (April 1965): 287–300, quote 291; for meeting minutes, I have used "Boston Tea Party Meeting Minutes, 29–30 November 1773," in *The Coming of the American Revolution, 1764–1776* (MHS, 2008), online; *BG*, December 6, 1773; see also "Minutes of the Tea Meetings, 1773," *MHSP* 20 (November 1882): 10–17; for numbers present, see John Scollay to Arthur Lee, December 23, 1773, in Jared Sparks, ed., "Destruction of the Tea, in the Harbor of Boston, December 16, 1773," *MHSC*, 4th ser., 4 (1858): [373–89] 383; Samuel Adams to Arthur Lee, December 31, 1773, in Richard Henry Lee, *Life of Arthur Lee, LL.D.*, 2 vols. (Boston, 1829), 2:209; "Gentlemen, The Committee of Correspondence for this Town . . ." (Boston, December 1, 1773), Ford #1665, Broadside 30, Special Collections, State Library of Massachusetts; Thomas Danforth to the Earl of Dartmouth, December 28, 1773, in Dartmouth Papers, II, 758.

3. For the phrase "Body of the People," see *MassSpy*, June 4, 1772, December 9, 1773; Upton, "Proceedings," 290–91, quote 291; *BG*, August 26, 1765, December 19, 1768; *BEP*, February 22, 1767; for the shaky legality of the meeting, see TH to Lord Dartmouth, December 14, 1773, HPMA, 27:586–88, MHS transcripts, p. 1116; see also Samuel Adams to James Warren, March 31, 1774, *Warren–Adams Letters* (Boston, 1917; reprint: New York, 1972), 1:24.

4. Upton, "Proceedings," 290; *BG*, December 6, 1773.

5. "To a Gentleman on His Voyage to *Great-Britain* for the Recovery of His Health," in *The Poems of Phillis Wheatley*, ed. Julian D. Mason Jr., rev edn. (1966; Chapel Hill, NC, 1989), 91–92; John M. Bullard, *The Rotches* (New Bedford, MA, and Milford, NH, 1947), 43–45.

6. Memorial of Francis Rotch, TNA:PRO, T 1/505, f. 29; McDevitt, *House of Rotch*, 116–17, 120–34, 163–74; Abram English Brown, *John Hancock: His Book* (Boston, 1898), 41–43, 64–68, 77–79; W. T. Baxter, *The House of Hancock: Business in Boston,*

1724–1775 (New York, 1965), 171–73, 226–31, 243–46; Tyler, *Smugglers and Patriots*, 123, 167.

7. *BG*, December 6, 1773; Drake, *Tea Leaves*, 353–54.

8. Extract from *Dartmouth* log, in Thatcher, *Traits*, 260; Protest of Francis Rotch et al., December 17, 1773, TNA:PRO, T 1/505, f. 13; see also "Diary for 1773 to the end of 1774, of Mr. Thomas Newell, Boston," *MHSP* 15 (October 1877): [335–63] 345; on the warships' effect, see TH to Nathaniel Rogers, May 31, 1768, TH to Thomas Gage, April 22, 1770, HPMA, 25:258–59, 387–88, MHS transcripts, pp. 258–59, 394–95.

9. Oliver M. Dickerson, *The Navigation Acts and the American Revolution* (New York, 1951), 169–70, 202; Thomas Cushing et al. to Arthur Lee, December 21, 1773, in Sparks, "Destruction of the Tea," 378–79.

10. *Selectmen's Minutes*, 23:203–4; Minutes of Meeting of Boston Selectmen, November 24, 28, 1773, BCC Records, NYPL, Misc. correspondence, 1773; Scollay to Lee, in Sparks, "Destruction of the Tea," 381–83.

11. BCC minutes, November 19, 1773, NYPL, pp. 3:232, 6:452, 457; TH to unknown, December 3, 1773, HPMA, 27:581–82, MHS transcripts, pp. 1098; Brown, *Revolutionary Politics*, 43–49, 152–61; *In Consequence of a Conference with the Committees of Correspondence in the Vicinity of Boston . . .* (Boston, 1773), Evans #12693.

12. BCC minutes, November 28, 1773, NYPL, pp. 6:457–58; "Great Britain: Parliament— The Townshend Act, November 20, 1767," Avalon Project, Yale Law School, online; *Acts and Resolves of the Province of Massachusetts Bay*, Province Laws 1770–71, chap. 2, sect. 3, 1771–72, chap. 12, 1772–73, chap. 47, pp. 5:77–78, 171, 251; Labaree, *Boston Tea Party*, 118–20, 126–28.

13. BCC minutes, November 28, 1773, NYPL, pp. 6:458–59.

14. Scollay to Lee, in Sparks, "Destruction of the Tea," 383.

15. *BG*, November 29, 1773.

16. The "chief Speakers" at the meetings were Adams, Hancock, Warren, Quincy, Phillips, William Cooper, and Molineux; selectmen John Scollay, Timothy Newell, Thomas Marshall, and John Pitts, Church, Joseph Greenleaf, and Cushing were also present. TH to Earl of Dartmouth, December 2, 1773, *DAR*, 6:249; Warden, *Boston*, 26–33, 40–44; Brown, *Revolutionary Politics*, 3–6, 59 n1, 161–63; Labaree, *Boston Tea Party*, 124–25; Upton, "Proceedings," 300; Information of Captain James Hall to Privy Council, February 19, 1774, *DAR*, 8:53–54; Elbridge Henry Goss, *The Life of Colonel Paul Revere*, 2 vols. (Boston, 1891), 2:635–36; *BTR*, 18:110, 129.

17. *BG*, November 29, 1773; Scollay to Lee, in Sparks, "Destruction of the Tea," 383; "Boston Tea Party Meeting Minutes, 29–30 November 1773."

18. TH to Earl of Dartmouth, December 2, 1773, *DAR*, 6:249; Scollay to Lee, in Sparks, "Destruction of the Tea," 383; Thomas Danforth to the Earl of Dartmouth, December 28, 1773, in Dartmouth Papers, II, 758; Hamilton Andrews Hill, *History of the Old South Church (Third Church), Boston, 1669–1884*, 2 vols. (Boston and New York, 1890), 2:137; Jane C. Nylander, "Toward Comfort and Uniformity in New England Meeting Houses, 1750–1850," in *New England Meeting House and Church, 1630–1850*, ed. Peter Benes, Dublin Seminar for New England Folklife Annual Proceedings (1979), 86–100.

19. Scollay to Lee, in Sparks, "Destruction of the Tea," 383–84; *BG*, December 6, 1773; "Boston Tea Party Meeting Minutes, 29–30 November 1773"; Young may have proposed destroying the tea at the meeting of November 30; Information of Nathan Frazier, Information of Andrew Mackenzie, mariner, before Privy Council, February 19, 1774, TNA:PRO, CO: 5/763, ff. 85, 89.

20. Upton, "Proceedings," 290–91; *BG*, December 6, 1773; Labaree, *Boston Tea Party*, 129–32.

21. Upton, "Proceedings," 290–91; *BG*, December 6, 1773; Extract from *Dartmouth* log in Thatcher, *Traits*, 260; Information of David Black before Privy Council, February 19, 1774, TNA:PRO, CO 5/763, f. 91; Deposition of Samuel Hunt and Thomas Dade, December 30, 1773, Deposition of Thomas Kirk and George Lewis, December 28, 1773, TNA:PRO, T 1/505, ff. 15, 17; Goss, *Life of Paul Revere*, 2:635; *BTR*, 18:111.

Wardens policed the town on Sundays; see C. W. Ernst, "Municipal Scraps," in Horace W. Fuller, ed., *The Green Bag: An Entertaining Magazine for Lawyers*, vol. 4 (Boston, 1894: [219–22] 221.

22. Upton, "Proceedings," 291; see also *MassSpy*, November 4, 1773.

23. Drake, *Tea Leaves*, 315–20, quotes 316, 318.

24. TH to William Tryon, December 1, 1773, HPMA, 27:576, MHS transcripts, p. 1086; TH to Earl of Dartmouth, December 2, 1773, *DAR*, 6:249.

25. Ann Hulton to Mrs. Lightbody, June 30, 1768, July 25, 1770, January 31, 1774, in *Letters of a Loyalist Lady*, 14, 24 (quote), 69–70; *BPB*, December 6, 1773; [Henry Hulton] to Thomas [Irving], December 2, 1773, Hulton to Richard———, December 3, 1773, Hulton to unknown, December 8, 1773, in Henry Hulton Letterbooks, HHL, pp. 70–78; Richard Clarke to Jonathan and Isaac Winslow Clarke, November 23, 1773, *PCSM* 8 (1902–4): 87–88; TH to unknown, November 24, 1773, TH to William Tryon, December 1, 1773, HPMA, 27:575, 576, MHS transcripts, pp. 1083–85; Alexander Leslie to Lord Barrington, December 6, 1773, TNA:PRO, WO 40/1; Customs Commissioners at Boston to Lords of Treasury, January 4, 1774, TNA:PRO, T 1/505, ff. 1–2; TH to Elisha Hutchinson, November 30, 1773, Thomas Hutchinson Jr. to Elisha Hutchinson, December 14, 1773, in Peter Orlando Hutchinson, *The Diary and Letters of His Excellency Thomas Hutchinson, Esq. . . .* (Boston, 1884), 1:94–97; [Henry] Hulton, Some Account of the Proceedings of the People of New England . ., bound from the André deCoppet Collection of American Historical Manuscripts, Princeton University Library, MHS, p. 216; for a more cynical view of the retreat to Castle Island, see James Bowdoin to John Temple, December 13, 1773, in *The Bowdoin and Temple Papers*, MHSC, 6th ser., vol. 9 (1897): 327–30.

26. *BG*, December 6, 1773; Scollay to Lee, in Sparks, "Destruction of the Tea," 383–84; TH to William Tryon, December 1, 1773, HPMA, 27:576, MHS transcripts, p. 1086.

27. *BG*, December 6, 1773; TH to Earl of Dartmouth, December 2, 1773, *DAR*, 6:249.

28. Upton, "Proceedings," 292–93; Walmsley, *Thomas Hutchinson*, 14, 19–21, 40.

29. *BG*, December 6, 1773.

30. The other members of the committee were Samuel Adams, John Hancock, Jonathan Williams, and William Phillips. Upton, "Proceedings," 294–95; *Letters and Diary of John Rowe*, 256; *BG*, December 6, 1773.

31. TH to unknown, December 7, 1773, TH to [Thomas or John?] Lane, December 12, 1773, HPMA, 27:582, 586, MHS transcripts, pp. 1100, 1112; John Rowe to Messrs. Hutchinson, "Saturday" [December 11, 1773?], Correspondence of the Family of Hutchinson, 1741–1800, vol. 1, 1741–1783, BL Egerton 2659, f. 58; Tyler, *Smugglers and Patriots*; Labaree, *Boston Tea Party*, 134–35.

32. Upton, "Proceedings," 294; John Andrews to William Barrell, December 1, 1773, in "Letters of John Andrews," ed. Winthrop Sargent, *MHSP* 8 (1864–65), [316–413] 325; Goss, *Life of Paul Revere*, 2:636; *BTR*, 18:111; *Selectmen's Minutes*, 20:305, 23:28–29.

33. John Singleton Copley to Jonathan Clarke and Isaac Winslow Clarke, [December 1, 1773], in *Letters and Papers of John Singleton Copley and Henry Pelham, 1739–1776*, MHSC, vol. 71 (1914): 211–13; *BG*, December 6, 1773; Upton, "Proceedings," 295.

34. Upton, "Proceedings, 295; Copley to Clarke brothers, December 1, 1773, *Copley–Pelham Letters*, 211–13.

35. *BG*, December 6, 1773; quote, Upton, "Proceedings," 296; see also Information of William Turner before Privy Council, February 19, 1774, TNA:PRO, CO 5/763, f. 101.

36. Memorial of Francis Rotch to the Board of Commissioners of Customs, TNA:PRO, T 1/505, f. 29; Extract from *Dartmouth* log in Thatcher, *Traits*, 260; Alexander Leslie to Lord Barrington, December 6, 17, 1773, TNA:PRO, WO 40/1; on Griffin's Wharf, see *BPB*, August 12, 1745, October 16, 1749, October 31, 1763; *BG*, July 3, 1769, April 26, 1773.

37. TH to Lord Dartmouth, December 14, 1773, HPMA, 27:586–88, MHS transcripts, p. 1113; John Montagu to Philip Stephens, December 8, 1773, in Alexander

Wedderburn Papers, William L. Clements Library, p. 2:30; Alexander Leslie to Lord Barrington, December 6, 1773, TNA:PRO, WO 40/1; Information of John Dean Whitworth and William Turner (quote) before Privy Council, February 19, 1774, TNA:PRO, CO 5/763, ff. 87, 101 (quote); Information of Captain James Hall to Privy Council, February 19, 1774, *DAR*, 8:53. One of the Boston artillery trains supplied the men of the watch one night despite the refusal of its commander, Adino Paddock (a friend of government); John Austin Stevens, "Ebenezer Stevens: Lieut.-Col. of Artillery in the Continental Army," *Magazine of American History with Notes and Queries* 1 (1877): [588–610] 588–89. In 1821, an old man remembered that he served with Boston's Grenadier Company (along with bookseller Henry Knox, then a lieutenant of the Grenadiers) aboard one of the ships; *BDA*, November 10, 1821. The day after he was chosen a junior deacon of St. Andrew's masonic lodge, Thomas Newell (nephew of a selectman) reported serving aboard the *Eleanor* on December 3, its first night at Griffin's Wharf. Richard Frothingham, ed., "Diary for 1773 to the End of 1774, of Mr. Thomas Newell, Boston," *MHSP* 15 (October 1877): [334–63] 346.

38. *BG*, December 13, 20, 1773; BCC minutes, December 3, 7, 1773, NYPL, pp. 6:460–61; *Selectmen's Minutes*, 23:204–27; John Boyle, "Boyle's Journal of Occurrences in Boston, 1759–1778," *NEHGR* 84 (October 1930): 370–71; Protest of James Bruce et al., December 17, 1773, Protest of Hezekiah Coffin et al., December 17, 1773, TNA:PRO, T 1/505, ff. 9, 11–12; Protest of Joseph Royall Loring, John Hitch, and John Green, December 13, 1773, Protest of Joseph Royall Loring and John Green, January 24, 1774, Ezekiel Price Notarial Records, Boston Athenæum, 6:169–72, 180.

39. TH to William Palmer, December 9, 1773, HPMA, 27:584–85, MHS transcripts, p. 1108.

40. TH to Lord Dartmouth, December 14, 1773, HPMA, 27:586–88, MHS transcripts, p. 1114; see also TH to Lord Dartmouth, November 15, 1773, in "Tea-Party Anniversary," ed. Robert C. Winthrop, *MHSP* 13 (December 1873): [151–216] 170; Scollay to Lee, in Sparks, "Destruction of the Tea," 384.

41. *BG*, December 13, 1773; Scollay to Lee, in Sparks, "Destruction of the Tea," 384.

42. *Essex Gazette*, December 7, 1773; *BG*, December 13, 1773.

43. *BEP*, November 29, December 6, 13, 20, 1773; *BG*, November 29, December 6, 13, 20, 1773.

44. Andrews to Barrell, December 1, 1773, "Letters of John Andrews," 325; Abigail Adams to Mercy Otis Warren, December 5, 1773, in *Adams Family Correspondence*, ed. L. H. Butterfield (Cambridge, MA, 1963), 1:88.

45. TH to Lord Dartmouth, December 14, 1773, HPMA, 27:586–88, MHS transcripts, p. 1117.

46. *BG*, November 29, 1773.

47. *BG*, December 13, 1773.

48. TH to Lord Dartmouth, November 15, 1773, in "Tea-Party Anniversary," 166; *Rivington's New-York Gazetteer*, November 18, December 2, 1773, reprinted in *BPB*, November 29, December 13, 1773; Henry White, Abraham Lott & Co., and Pigou & Booth to Court of Directors, EIC, December 1, 1773, Memorial of Henry White, Abraham Lott, and Benjamin Booth to William Tryon, December 1, 1773, TNA:PRO, CO 5/133, ff. 24–26; At a Council held at Fort George in the City of New York, December 1, 1773, TNA:PRO, CO 5/1105, f. 9; *Rivington's New-York Gazetteer*, May 12, 1774; *NYJ*, December 2, 1773; [Pigou & Booth] to [James & Drinker], November 8, 12, 1773, Henry S. Drinker Papers, 1739–1779, HSP; Drake, *Tea Leaves*, 224–25, 240, 269–70; CASSIUS, "To the FRIENDS of LIBERTY, and COMMERCE" (New York, November 5, 1773), Evans #12711; Labaree, *Boston Tea Party*, 91–97.

49. James & Drinker to Pigou & Booth, January 1, 1774, Henry Drinker Foreign Letters, 1772–1785, Drinker Papers, HSP, p. 164; "The COMMITTEE for Tarring and Feathering," "To the Delaware Pilots" (Philadelphia, November 1773), Evans #12941;

"THE COMMITTEE FOR TARRING AND FEATHERING" "To the Delaware Pilots" and "To Capt. AYRES" (Philadelphia, November 27, 1773), Evans #12942; "The COMMITTEE for TARRING and FEATHERING," "To the DELAWARE PILOTS" (Philadelphia, December 7, 1773), Evans #12943; *BPB*, December 13, 1773; Labaree, *Boston Tea Party*, 97–102, 152–54; Carp, *Rebels Rising*, 195–96.

50. Upton, "Proceedings," 295; *BG*, December 6, 1773.

51. *BG*, December 13, 1773.

52. Andrews to Barrell, December 1, 1773, "Letters of John Andrews," 324; William Palfrey to George Peacock, January 24, 1774, Palfrey Family Papers, HHL, f. 63.

53. William Palfrey [to John Hancock or BCC], December [11?], 1773, Palfrey Family Papers, HHL, f. 92; see also *MassSpy*, November 26, 1773.

54. A ship had arrived in Charleston on December 2, but people in Boston would not learn of this until later; *MassSpy*, December 30, 1773; Labaree, *Boston Tea Party*, 135, 152–54.

55. Drake, *Tea Leaves*, 344–49, 353–56.

56. BCC minutes, December 9, 11, 1773, NYPL, pp. 6:462–63; *Letters and Diary of John Rowe*, 257.

57. TH to Lord Dartmouth, December 14, 1773, HPMA, 27:586–88, MHS transcripts, p. 1114.

58. Scollay to Lee, in Sparks, "Destruction of the Tea," 384; Upton, "Proceedings," 296, 296n 20; "Boston Tea Party Meeting Minutes, 14–16 December 1773," in *Coming of the American Revolution*; [Abijah Savage to Samuel P. Savage, September 4, 1773], Samuel P. Savage Papers II, MHS; Lawrence Park, "Old Boston Families, Number Three: The Savage Family," *NEHGR* 67 (October 1913): [309–30] 313–18; Jake Chiam, Tufts University class paper, March 2008.

59. Upton, "Proceedings," 296–97.

60. "Boston Tea Party Meeting Minutes, 14–16 December 1773"; *BPB*, December 20, 1773.

61. Joseph Harrison to Marquis of Rockingham, June 17, 1768, in D. H. Watson, ed., "Joseph Harrison and the *Liberty* Incident," *WMQ*, 3rd ser., 20, 4 (October 1963): 585–95 (quote 590); James H. Stark, *The Loyalists of Massachusetts and the Other Side of the American Revolution* (Salem, MA, 1910), 319–21.

62. Richard Harrison and Robert Hallowell to Board of Commissioners of Customs, December 16, 1773, TNA:PRO, T 1/505, f. 43. In TH to Earl of Dartmouth, December 17, 1773, *DAR*, 6:256, Hutchinson writes that Rotch then applied to the "Naval Office" (presumably Admiral John Montagu) for a permit to pass Fort William; see also John Montagu to Board of Commissioners of Customs, December 16, 1773, TNA:PRO, T 1/505, f. 39.

63. Extract from *Dartmouth* log, in Thatcher, *Traits*, 260; "Boston Tea Party Meeting Minutes, 14–16 December 1773"; *BPB*, December 20, 1773. Samuel Adams estimated "at least seven thousand men" present at this meeting: Samuel Adams to Richard Henry Lee, *Life of Arthur Lee*, 2:211. John Andrews estimated five or six thousand: Andrews to Barrell, December 18, 1773, "Letters of John Andrews," 325.

Chapter 6: The Destroyers at Griffin's Wharf

1. Josiah Quincy, *Memoir of the Life of Josiah Quincy, Junior, of Massachusetts Bay, 1744–1775*, ed. Eliza S. Quincy (Boston, 1875), 125; these words, supposedly uttered at the moment the disguised "Indians" approached the Old South Meeting House, may be apocryphal; see also Josiah Quincy to John Eagleson, September 15, 1768, *Memoir of Josiah Quincy*, 15; Daniel R. Coquillette and Neil Longley York, eds., *Portrait of a Patriot: The Major Political and Legal Papers of Josiah Quincy Junior*, vol. 74 of PCSM (2005), 1:32–33.

2. "Revolutionary Reminiscence of Throwing the Tea Overboard in Boston Harbour," *The Western Monthly Review* 1, 3 (July 1827): [145–49] 148; Thatcher, *Traits*, 178–80, 262–65; *[Washington] Daily National Intelligencer*, October 25, 1831; John Austin Stevens, "Ebenezer Stevens: Lieut.-Col. of Artillery in the Continental Army," *Magazine of American History with Notes and Queries* 1 (1877): [588–610] 590; *[Boston] Columbian Centinel*, June 16, 1819; Thomas Danforth to the Earl of Dartmouth, December 28, 1773, in Dartmouth Papers, II, 758.

3. TH to Directors, EIC, December 19, 1773, HPMA, 27:597–99, MHS transcripts, p. 1138.

4. Drake, *Tea Leaves*, 93; see also the story of Sarah Bradlee Fulton on pp. 91–92.

5. Thomas Putnam Tyler, memoranda from conversation with Elizabeth Palmer, RWP, W. #19975; see also the post-1853 story of John May in Drake, *Tea Leaves*, 128.

6. "Throwing the Tea Overboard," 147; *[Washington] Daily National Intelligencer*, October 25, 1831; "Col. Henry Purkitt," *Boston Courier*, cited in *[Charleston, SC] Southern Patriot*, March 27, 1845; Drake, *Tea Leaves*, 79; Joseph T. Buckingham, *Annals of the Massachusetts Charitable Mechanic Association* (Boston, 1853), 34; James M. Crafts and William F. Crafts, comp., *The Crafts Family* (Northampton, MA, 1893), 115. Wyeth's account, mentioning "tory masters," in 1831, may have been a distortion. Benjamin Bassett to John Davis, February 3, 1825, Lemuel Shaw Papers, MHS.

7. *BDA*, November 11, 1821; Peter Edes to Benjamin C. Edes, February 16, 1836, *MHSP* 12 (December 1871): 175.

8. Thomas Jefferson, *A Summary View of the Rights of British America* (Williamsburg, VA, 1774), Evans #13350, p.13.

9. L. F. S. Upton, ed., "Proceedings of Ye Body Respecting the Tea," *WMQ*, 3rd ser., 22, 2 (April 1965): 297; *BG*, December 20, 1773.

10. TH to Israel Mauduit, December 1773, HPMA, 27:604–6, 607, MHS transcripts, pp. 1152–53; TH to Dartmouth, December 15, 17, 1773, Information of Francis Rotch to Privy Council, February 19, 1774, *DAR*, 6:251–52, 256, 8:51–52; see also William Gordon to Earl of Dartmouth, December 11, 1773, in Dartmouth Papers, II, 754.

11. *MassSpy*, December 16, 1773.

12. *BEP*, December 20, 1773; John Andrews to William Barrell, December 18, 1773, in "Letters of John Andrews," ed. Winthrop Sargent, *MHSP* 8 (1864–65): 326; Information of Captain James Hall to Privy Council, February 19, 1774, *DAR*, 8:53.

13. Andrews to Barrell, December 18, 1773, "Letters of John Andrews," 326; TH to Israel Mauduit, December 1773, HPMA, 27:604–6, 607, MHS transcripts, p. 1153; *BEP*, December 20, 1773; John Scollay to Arthur Lee, December 23, 1773, in Jared Sparks, ed., "Destruction of the Tea, in the Harbor of Boston, December 16, 1773," *MHSC*, 4th ser., vol. 4 (1858): 385.

14. Upton, "Proceedings," 299; for similar debates that may have been taking place privately among the Sons of Liberty, see "Throwing the Tea Overboard," 147–48.

15. "Henry Ireton" [Josiah Quincy] to Abigail (Phillips) Quincy, December 14, 1774, Quincy, Wendell, Holmes, and Upham Papers, MHS; see also Josiah Quincy address in "Tea-Party Anniversary," *MHSP* 13 (December 1873): 196–97; Drake, *Tea Leaves*, 59–60.

16. Quincy, *Memoir of Josiah Quincy*, 124–25.

17. Upton, "Proceedings," 297–98.

18. *BEP*, December 20, 1773.

19. Upton, "Proceedings," 298.

20. *BG*, December 20, 1773; William Tudor, *The Life of James Otis of Massachusetts . . .* (Boston, 1823), 419–20; TH to Directors, EIC, December 19, 1773, HPMA, 27:597–99, MHS transcripts, p. 1138; Upton, "Proceedings," 298; Samuel Cooper to Benjamin Franklin, December 17, 1773, in Sparks, "Destruction of the Tea," 375. One observer believed that the war-whoop originally came from inside the meetinghouse as a signal to the disguised men outside. Extract of a letter from Boston from an officer on board the *Active*, postscript (original letter dated December 6, 1773), in Dartmouth Papers, II, 752.

21. *BDA*, November 10, 1821; Thatcher, *Traits*, 178; [James Hawkes], *A Retrospect of the Boston Tea-Party, with a Memoir of George R. T. Hewes* . . . (New York, 1834), 38; George Folsom, *History of Saco and Biddeford* . . . (Saco, ME, 1830), 288n; Extract of a letter from *Active* officer, postscript (original letter dated December 6, 1773), in Dartmouth Papers, II, 752; *New-Bedford Mercury*, December 13, 1833; Benjamin Bassett to John Davis, February 3, 1825, Lemuel Shaw Papers, MHS; James Miller and John S. Allanson, eds., "The Narrative of Major Thompson Maxwell," *Essex Institute Historical Collections*, 7, 3 (June 1865): [97–116] 106; William Willder Wheildon, ed., "A Remarkable Military Life," *NEHGR* 45 (October 1891): [271–78] 274; Michael Pfitzer, Tufts University class paper, April 2007.

22. *BG*, December 20, 1773; Upton, "Proceedings," 298; *BDA*, November 10, 1821.

23. Andrews to Barrell, December 18, 1773, "Letters of John Andrews," 326, Upton, "Proceedings," 298. In spite of this, Thatcher, *Traits*, 262, included "Dr. Young" among the Tea Party participants; see also Young, *Shoemaker*, 44, 55–57.

24. TH to Dartmouth, December 17, 1773, *DAR*, 6:256; Drake, *Tea Leaves*, 79–80; "Throwing the Tea Overboard," 148; John Adams to James Warren, December 17, 1773, in *Papers of John Adams*, ed. Robert J. Taylor et al. (Cambridge, MA, 1977), 2:2; *BNL*, December 23, 1773; *BDA*, November 10, 1821; Extract from *Dartmouth* log, in Thatcher, *Traits*, 260; *Letters and Diary of John Rowe*, 258; Peter Edes to Benjamin C. Edes, February 16, 1836, *MHSP* 12:175.

25. *NYGWM*, December 27, 1773.

26. Alexander Leslie to Lord Barrington, December 17, 1773, TNA:PRO, WO 40/1; John Montagu to Philip Stephens, December 17, 1773, CO 5/247, ff. 86–87.

27. [Henry] Hulton, *Some Account of the Proceedings of the People of New England* . . ., bound from the André deCoppet Collection of American Historical Manuscripts, Princeton University Library, MHS, p. 218; Board of Customs Commissioners at Boston to Lords of Treasury, January 4, 1774, TNA:PRO, T 1/505, f. 2; William Gordon, *The History of the Rise, Progress, and Establishment of the Independence of the United States of America* . . ., 4 vols. (London, 1788), 1:341; TH, *The History of the Province of Massachusetts Bay, from 1749 to 1774* . . . (London, 1828), 437.

28. *BG*, December 20, 1773; TH, *History*, 436.

29. Andrews to Barrell, December 18, 1773, "Letters of John Andrews," 326; Tudor, *Life of James Otis*, 420n (quote).

30. Upton, "Proceedings," 298–99; for lack of disguises, see Folsom, *History of Saco*, 288n; "An English Gentleman" [William N. Blane], *An Excursion through the United States and Canada during the Years 1822–1823* (London, 1824), 281; Stevens, "Ebenezer Stevens," 590.

31. For the tides, see [Benjamin West], *Bickerstaff's Boston Almanack, for* . . . *1773* (Boston, 1772), Evans #12613; Donald W. Olson and Russell L. Doescher, "The Boston Tea Party," *Sky and Telescope* 86, 6 (December 1993): 83–84; Fischer, *Paul Revere's Ride*, 312–13.

32. Stevens, "Ebenezer Stevens," 590–91.

33. Extract from *Dartmouth* log, in Thatcher, *Traits*, 261 (first quote); Richard Harrison and Robert Hallowell to the Board of Commissioners of Customs, December 17 (second, fifth quotes), 23, 1773, Protest of Francis Rotch et al., December 17, 1773, TNA:PRO, T 1/505, ff. 3 (second, fifth quotes), 5, 13; "Throwing the Tea Overboard," 148 (third and fourth quotes); *NYGWM*, December 27, 1773.

34. *NYGWM*, December 27, 1773; Thatcher, *Traits*, 181; Folsom, *History of Saco*, 288n.

35. Gordon, *History*, 1:341; Thatcher, *Traits*, 182; Drake, *Tea Leaves*, 97–98; "Marriages and Deaths," *NEHGR* 6, 4 (October 1852): 389–90; "Assessors' 'Taking Books' of the Town of Boston, 1780," *Bostonian Society Publications*, vol. 9 (Boston, 1912): 23; Daniel Vickers and Vince Walsh, "Young Men and the Sea: The Sociology of Seafaring in Eighteenth-Century Salem, Massachusetts," *Social History* 24, 1 (January 1999): 17–38; Carp, *Rebels Rising*, 24–33, 56–57.

36. TH to Directors, EIC, December 19, 1773, HPMA, 27:597–99, MHS transcripts, p. 1138; Reminiscences of Major Cooper Senior . . ., Papers of Samuel Cooper, 1780–1960, Special Collections, University of Virginia Library (first quote); see also "Biographical Sketch of Captain Samuel Cooper," *Southern Literary Messenger* 4, 8 (August 1838): 519–23; "Throwing the Tea Overboard," 148–49 (second quote); *NYGWM*, December 27, 1773; Stevens, "Ebenezer Stevens," 590; Drake, *Tea Leaves*, 79–80; [John Prince], *Salem [MA] Gazette*, September 24, 1833; Peter Edes to Benjamin C. Edes, February 16, 1836, *MHSP*, 12:175.

37. Upton, "Proceedings," 298; Thatcher, *Traits*, 180–81; *BG*, December 20, 1773; "Throwing the Tea Overboard," 148–49, quote 149; TH to Directors, EIC, December 19, 1773, HPMA, 27:597–99, MHS transcripts, p. 1138.

38. Thatcher, *Traits*, 182–84; Andrews to Barrell, December 18, 1773, "Letters of John Andrews," 326; *NYGWM*, December 27, 1773; Cooper to Franklin, December 17, 1773, in Sparks, "Destruction of the Tea," 375; Hawkes, *Retrospect*, 40–41; Drake, *Tea Leaves*, 80; Hugh D. McLellan, *History of Gorham, Me.*, ed. Katherine B. Lewis (Portland, ME, 1903), 764–65; Henry Bromfield to Flight & Halliday, December 17, 1773, in Henry Bromfield Letterbook, NEHGS, 4:90; see also J. L. Bell, "Captain Conner: Tea Party Thief, Scapegoat," *Boston 1775* (weblog), May 29, 2007; Young, *Shoemaker*, 45.

39. Thatcher, *Traits*, 264; compare with Andrew Walker's account of boatman Jonathan Mitchell; *Duluth [MN] Tribune*, June 5, 1891.

40. *BNL*, December 23, 1773.

41. "Throwing the Tea Overboard," 149 (first quote); Thatcher, *Traits*, 263 (second quote); TH to Directors, EIC, December 19, 1773, HPMA, 27:597–99, MHS transcripts, p. 1138 (third quote); see also *BG*, December 20, 1773; *NYGWM*, December 27, 1773; Drake, *Tea Leaves*, 78–80; John Scollay to Arthur Lee, December 23, 1773, Dr. Hugh Williamson's Examination before the Privy Council, February 19, 1774, in Sparks, "Destruction of the Tea," 385, 388; Samuel P. Savage diary, 1773, MHS.

42. Upton, "Proceedings," 298–99; Thatcher, *Traits*, 263; Folsom, *History of Saco*, 288n; *[Washington] Daily National Intelligencer*, October 25, 1831; [John Prince], *Salem [MA] Gazette*, September 24, 1833; Thomas Danforth to the Earl of Dartmouth, December 28, 1773, in Dartmouth Papers, II, 758; Olson and Doescher, "Boston Tea Party," 83–84; J. L. Bell, "Apprentices at the Tea Party," *Boston 1775*, December 14, 2006.

43. Samuel Adams Drake, *Old Landmarks and Historic Personages of Boston* (Boston, 1873), 283.

44. Samuel Nowell's petition to Congress, February 23, 1830, RWP, S. #4503.

45. Thatcher, *Traits*, 180; Protest of Hezekiah Coffin et al., December 17, 1773, TNA:PRO, T 1/505, f. 11; see also Young, *Shoemaker*, 99–100; on free movement aboard the ships, see [John Prince], *Salem [MA] Gazette*, September 24, 1833; Drake, *Tea Leaves*, 79, 146. Other figures for the number of participants include 28 or 30, in "Throwing the Tea Overboard," 147; 40, in "One of the Boston Tea-Party," *Western Recorder*, August 8, 1826; 40 or 50, in Information of John Dean Whitworth before Privy Council, February 19, 1774, TNA:PRO, CO 5/763, f. 87; 73, in Wheildon, "Remarkable Military Life," 274; 70 or 80, Stevens, "Ebenezer Stevens," 589–90; and 200 or 300, Samuel Cooper to Benjamin Franklin, December 17, 1773, Sparks, "Destruction of the Tea," 373.

46. "Throwing the Tea Overboard," 148.

47. Remarks by R. C. Winthrop Jr., *MHSP*, 2nd ser., 12 (February 1898): 140–1; Thatcher, *Traits*, 180–81, 184; "Taking Books," 23, 33; *MassSpy*, June 10, 1773; *BG*, March 9, 1772; Biographical Lists, Massachusetts 1st Corps of Cadets, Howard Gotlieb Archival Research Center at Boston University; *Mills and Hicks's British and American Register, with an Almanack for the Year 1774* (Boston, 1774), Evans #12869; Daniel Goodwin Jr., *Memorial of the Lives and Services of James Pitts and His Sons . . .* (Chicago, 1882), 16–22; Elbridge Henry Goss, *The Life of Colonel Paul Revere*, 2 vols. (Boston, 1891), 2:635–40; Zobel, *Boston Massacre*, 174; *BTR*, 18:93, 111; *Boston Births*

from A.D. 1700 to A.D. 1800 (Boston: Rockwell and Churchill, 1894), 24:312, 316, 320; TH to Thomas Pownall, June 7, 1768, HPMA, 25:262, MHS transcripts, p. 263; *Boston Chronicle*, February 16 to 20, 1769; Ellie Berg, Tufts University class paper, April 2008; see also Pauline Maier, *From Resistance to Revolution: Colonial Radicals and the Development of American Opposition to Britain, 1765–1776* (New York, 1972), chap. 6, pp. 198–200; Shaw, *American Patriots*, chap. 3.

48. Henry Bromfield to Flight & Halliday, December 17, 1773, in Henry Bromfield Letterbook, NEHGS, 4:90–91; *BDA*, November 11, 1821; Peter Edes to Benjamin C. Edes, February 16, 1836, *MHSP*, 12:175; Andrew Helms, Tufts University class paper, April 2008.

49. Hawkes, *Retrospect*, 6; Anderson, "Ebenezer Mackintosh," 53; Clifford K. Shipton, ed., *Sibley's Harvard Graduates*, vol. 17, *1768–1771* (Boston, 1975), 184–86, 584–90; Tyler, *Smugglers and Patriots*, 258–77.

50. TH to Thomas Pownall, June 7, 1768, HPMA, 25:262, MHS transcripts, p. 263; "B.," "Revolutionary Articles," *Boston News-Letter and City Record* 1, 11 (March 4, 1826): 121; Triber, *True Republican*, chaps. 2–6; Fischer, *Paul Revere's Ride*, 9–26, 306–7; Benjamin L. Carp, "Fire of Liberty: Firefighters, Urban Voluntary Culture, and the Revolutionary Movement," *WMQ* 58, 4 (October 2001): [781–818] 805–11.

51. "Boston Tea Party Meeting Minutes, 29–30 November 1773," *The Coming of the American Revolution, 1764–1776* (MHS, 2008), online; Goss, *Life of Paul Revere*, 2:635–66.

52. "An Alphabetical List of the Sons of Liberty who Dined at Liberty Tree, Dorchester, Aug. 14, 1769," *MHSP* 11 (August 1869): 140–42.

53. Reprint of minutes of St. Andrew's Lodge, Boston Tea Party File, Grand Lodge of Massachusetts A.F. & A.M., Samuel Crocker Lawrence Library, Boston; *The Lodge of Saint Andrew, and the Massachusetts Grand Lodge* (Boston, 1870), 231–34. Thomas Crafts, William Palfrey, and Joseph Warren were also brother masons.

54. Petition to the Selectmen of Boston for a Town Meeting on November 5, 1773, Loose Boston Town Papers, BPL; Petition to the Selectmen of the Town of Boston, November 17, 1773, plus petition to the Selectmen of the Town of Boston for a Town Meeting [on November 5, 1773], in Mellen Chamberlain, comp., "Samuel Adams and Joseph Warren, Sketches of their Lives with Autographs and Illustrations," 1880, BPL, pp. 79, 90.

55. Caleb Davis Papers, MHS; Drake, *Tea Leaves*, 79. I have interpreted "Daniel Ingollson" from Thatcher, *Traits*, 262, as "Ingersoll."

56. Tudor, *Life of James Otis*, 420; Wyeth's statement that "Mr. Hancock drew up" a secretly circulated paper enjoining them to meet in Indian disguise seems to support this conclusion; Benjamin Bassett to John Davis, February 3, 1825, Lemuel Shaw Papers, MHS. On the role of the BCC, see Brown, *Revolutionary Politics*, 164–65; Labaree, *Boston Tea Party*, 141–42.

57. "The 'White Hills' of New Hampshire," *Yale Literary Magazine* 10, 9 (August 1845): [415–22] 418; *[Portland, ME] Eastern Argus*, May 17, 1836; *Portsmouth [NH] Journal of Literature and Politics*, July 11, 1840.

58. Jeremiah Colburn, ed., "The Command at the Battle of Bunker Hill, as Shown in the Statement of Major Thompson Maxwell," *NEHGR* 22 (January 1868): 57–59, quote 58; Thatcher, *Traits*, 181, writes that Hewes "went on board one of the brigs"; the *Beaver* was the only brig; see also Young, *Shoemaker*, esp. 17, 28–29, 44; Nash, *Urban Crucible*, 312–15.

59. Hawkes, *Retrospect*, 37; Sarah Gammell, "The Following is a List of the Names of the Noble Men Who in the Year 1773 Destroyed the Tea in Boston Harbour," Civil War Collection, Military Order of the Loyal Legion of the United States, HHL; Charles Collyer Whittier, "The Urann Family of New England," *NEHGR* 64 (January 1910): [7–17] 16; *A Volume of Records Relating to the Early History of Boston, containing Boston Marriages from 1752 to 1809* (Boston, 1903), 30:46, 62; *Boston Births*, 24:255, 261; Marybeth Paruti, Tufts University class paper, April 2007.

60. Thatcher, *Traits*, 263; note this number of "chiefs" is consistent with the figures from Tudor, *Life of James Otis*, 419; and Gordon, *History*, 1:341, of about 17 to 20 men in Indian disguise.

61. Thatcher, *Traits*, 179; "Throwing the Tea Overboard," 147; Drake, *Tea Leaves*, 79; see also *[Washington] Daily National Intelligencer*, October 25, 1831.

62. Thatcher, *Traits*, 179, 262–63; Drake, *Tea Leaves*, 163.

63. Ebenezer Fox, *The Revolutionary Adventures of Ebenezer Fox, of Roxbury, Massachusetts* (Boston, 1838), 16–18 (quote 17); Ann Hulton to Mrs. Lightbody, undated, in *Letters of a Loyalist Lady*, 50; J. H. Benton Jr., *Early Census Making in Massachusetts, 1643–1765* (Boston, 1905), 74–75; J. L. Bell, "From Saucy Boys to Sons of Liberty: Politicizing Youth in Pre-Revolutionary Boston," in James Marten, ed., *Children in Colonial America* (New York, 2007), 204–16; William Pencak, "Play as Prelude to Revolution: Boston, 1765–1776," in Pencak et al., *Riot and Revelry*; 125–55; Jennifer Scherck, Tufts University class paper, April 2007; see also Edwin G. Burrows and Michael Wallace, "The American Revolution: The Ideology and Psychology of National Liberation," *Perspectives on American History* 6 (1972): 167–305; Pencak, *War, Politics, and Revolution*, 185–232, 275–80, 284–85.

64. John Scollay to Arthur Lee, December 23, 1773, in Sparks, "Destruction of the Tea," 385; "Throwing the Tea Overboard," 147; Drake, *Tea Leaves*, 79.

65. Drake, *Tea Leaves*, 102, 125, 129, 140, 167; Triber, *True Republican*, 7–8.

66. Miller and Allanson, "Narrative of Major Thompson Maxwell," 106; Wheildon, "Remarkable Military Life," 274; J. L. Bell, "A Teamster at the Tea Party? Exploring Thompson Maxwell's Stories of Revolutionary Massachusetts," unpublished paper, October 1999, used with permission of author.

67. *[Boston] Daily Atlas*, February 7, 1842; Samuel Francis Smith, *History of Newton, Massachusetts: Town and City from its Earliest Settlement to the Present Time, 1630–1880* (Boston, 1880), 330.

68. Deposition of Samuel Larrabee, July 7, 1837, RWP, S. #18076; Benjamin Burton to William D. Williamson, January 10, 1835, Melten Chamberlain Collection, BPL.

69. Thatcher, *Traits*, 183–84, 263; Hawkes, *Retrospect*, 6, 40; "Tea-Party Anniversary," 209; James Kimball, "The One Hundredth Anniversary of the Destruction of Tea in Boston Harbor, with a Sketch of William Russell, of Boston, One of the 'Tea Destroyers,'" *Essex Institute Historical Collections* 12 (1874): [197–239] 231.

70. Thomas Putnam Tyler, memoranda from conversation with Elizabeth Palmer, RWP, W. #19975.

71. Labaree, *Boston Tea Party*, 335; "An Account of the Invoice Amount of Teas exported to Boston . . .," TNA:PRO, CO 5/247, p. 187.

72. *BNL*, December 23, 1773; Thatcher, *Traits*, 186–87, 264–65; [John Prince], *Salem [MA] Gazette*, September 24, 1833.

73. TH to [Israel] Williams, December 23, 1773, Israel Williams Papers, MHS; [John Prince], *Salem [MA] Gazette*, September 24, 1833.

74. EIC Chairman to Earl of Dartmouth, March 23, 1774, TNA:PRO, CO 5/133, ff. 45a–b; this amount includes the American duty and commission; see also EIC Court of Directors to Earl of Dartmouth, February 16, 1774, IOR E/1/217, Miscellanies vol. 21, BL, pp. 77–78; "Amount of Teas exported by the United East India Company for Boston . . . ," in Dartmouth Papers, II, 1086; Triber, *True Republican*, 71; Bailyn, *Ordeal*, 169; Charles Bahne, "How Much Was the Tea in the Tea Party Worth?" in J. L. Bell, *Boston 1775* (weblog), December 18, 2009.

Chapter 7: "Resolute Men (Dressed as Mohawks)"

1. Samson Occom, *A Sermon, Preached at the Execution of Moses Paul, an Indian* (New Haven, CT, 1772), Evans #12494, p. 12. I have substituted a question mark for a period.

2. Henry Bromfield to Flight & Halliday, December 17, 1773, in Henry Bromfield Letterbook, NEHGS, 4:90; John Andrews to William Barrell, December 18, 1773, in "Letters of John Andrews," ed. Winthrop Sargent, *MHSP* 8 (1864–65): 326; Shannon, "Dressing for Success"; Ribiero, *Dress Worn at Masquerades*, 445–52.

3. L. F. S. Upton, ed., "Proceedings of Ye Body Respecting the Tea," *WMQ*, 3rd ser., 22, 2 (April 1965): 298 (first quote); *Dartmouth* log in Thatcher, *Traits*, 260–61 (second quote), 263 (sixth quote); *BG*, December 20, 1773 (third quote, also "Savages" and "War Whoop"); *BPB*, December 20, 1773 (fourth quote); Andrews to Barrell, December 18, 1773, in "Letters of John Andrews," 326 (fifth quote); see also *Legal Papers of John Adams*, ed. L. Kinvin Wroth and Hiller B. Zobel (Cambridge, MA, 1965), 3:246, 268; *Peter Oliver's Origin and Progress*, 74–75.

4. Thatcher, *Traits*, 180–81, 262.

5. "Revolutionary Reminiscence of Throwing the Tea Overboard in Boston Harbour," *The Western Monthly Review* 1, 3 (July 1827): [145–49] 148; *Peter Oliver's Origin and Progress*, 103; Deloria, *Playing Indian*, 6–7; Jonathan Sayward Diaries, AAS, vol. 14 (entry for December 17, 1773); McWilliams, "Indian John."

6. Edward G. Porter, "The Beginning of the Revolution," in Justin Winsor, ed., *The Memorial History of Boston . . .*, 4 vols. (Boston, 1882), 3:14 n4; *The Acts and Resolves, Public and Private, of the Province of Massachusetts Bay . . .* (Boston, 1890), 4:937; Henry Laurens to Joseph Brown, October 28, 1765, in *The Papers of Henry Laurens*, ed. George C. Rogers Jr. and David R. Chesnutt (Columbia, SC, 1976), 5:30; Deloria, *Playing Indian*, 6.

7. *Peter Oliver's Origin and Progress*, 103.

8. Wroth and Zobel, eds., *Legal Papers of John Adams*, 3:266, 269; Zobel, *Boston Massacre*, 292–93; *Peter Oliver's Origin and Progress*, 89; see also Peter Linebaugh and Marcus Rediker, *The Many-Headed Hydra: Sailors, Slaves, Commoners, and the Hidden History of the Revolutionary Atlantic* (Boston, 2000), chap. 7; Shaw, *American Patriots*, 194–95.

9. TH to Richard Jackson, June 16, 18, 1768, TH to William Tryon, November 21, 1773, HPMA, 26:310–12 (quote 310), 27:572–74, MHS transcripts, pp. 644, 1078. For other examples, see *BEP*, November 11, 1745; *BTR*, 14:127; *Journals of the House of Representatives of Massachusetts, 1747–1748* (Boston, 1949), 24:212–14; Owen Richards to William Sheaffe and Robert Hallowell, May 21, 1770, Sparks MS, New England Papers, HHL, 10.4.1; John Mein, *Sagittarius's Letters and Political Speculations* (Boston, 1775), Evans #14255, pp. 1, 44; Jack Tager, *Boston Riots: Three Centuries of Social Violence* (Boston, 2001), 45–48; Hoerder, *Crowd Action*, 94; John Lax and William Pencak, "The Knowles Riot and the Crisis of the 1740's in Massachusetts," *Perspectives in American History* 10 (1976): [163–214] 196–97, 200–1.

10. *MassSpy*, July 2, 1772; *BNL*, July 9, 1772. After John Mein was attacked, he wrote similarly that the Sons of Liberty were planning to repeat "their usual sayings . . . that it was done by Boys & Negroes, or by Nobody." John Mein to Joseph Harrison, November 5, 1769, Sparks MS, New England Papers, HHL, 10.3.51.

11. Deloria, *Playing Indian*, 15–20, 22–28; Alfred F. Young, "Tar and Feathers and the Ghost of Oliver Cromwell: English Plebeian Culture and American Radicalism," in *Liberty Tree*, 144–79; Young, *Shoemaker*, 102–5; E. P. Thompson, *Whigs and Hunters: The Origin of the Black Act* (London, 1975); E. P. Thompson, *Customs in Common* (London, 1991); Robert Blair St. George, *Conversing by Signs: Poetics of Implication in Colonial New England Culture* (Chapel Hill, NC, 1998), chap. 3.

12. *BG*, October 23, 1753; *BEP*, October 30, 1769; Tager, *Boston Riots*, 10, 14–16, 41–51.

13. Petition of Jonathan Loring and Jonathan Jackson to Governor and Council, September 1732, Box 2, Folder 4, Curwen Family Papers, AAS (first quote); *BNL*, March 24 to April 1, 1737 (second quote); [Thomas Pemberton], "A Topographical and Historical Description of Boston, 1794," *MHSC*, 1st ser., vol. 3 (1794): [241–304] 255; Morgan and Morgan, *Stamp Act Crisis*, 159; Tager, *Boston Riots*, 34–35; Hoerder, *Crowd Action*, 57; Warden, *Boston*, 121–22; *Acts and Resolves*, 4:937.

14. Ann Hulton to Mrs. Lightbody, July 25, 1770, in *Letters of a Loyalist Lady*, 25; see also John Swift and Joshua Loring to Commissioners of Customs in Boston, November 30, 1771, Custom House Papers, HSP, 12:1437.

15. Frederick Smyth to Earl of Dartmouth, February 8, 1773, *DAR*, 6:83 (first quote); William Dudingston to Admiral John Montagu, June 12, 1772, Darius Sessions to John Wanton, January 18, 1773, Deposition of William Dickinson, June 1, 1773, in John Russell Bartlett, ed., *Records of the Colony of Rhode Island and Providence Plantations in New England* (Providence, 1862; reprint, New York, 1968), 7:86 (second quote), 150 (third quote), 168; see also Wilfred Harold Munro et al., *Tales of an Old Sea Port: A General Sketch of the History of Bristol, Rhode Island . . .* (Princeton, NJ, 1917), 21; *A New Song Called the Gaspee* ([1772?]), Shipton & Mooney #42361; *BG*, August 17, 1772; Gaspee Days Committee, "Gaspee Virtual Archives" (Warwick, RI, 1997–2009), online.

16. The term "Mohawk" was used publicly, *BPB*, December 20, 1773, while the term "Narragansett" was used privately, Andrews to Barrell, December 18, 1773, "Letters of John Andrews," 326; see also *MassSpy*, March 10, 17, 1774; *BG*, March 28, 1774.

17. John Winthrop to Sir Simonds D'Ewes, July 21, 1634, in Everett Emerson, ed., *Letters from New England: The Massachusetts Bay Colony, 1629–1638* (Amherst, MA, 1976), 119; see also David S. Jones, "Virgin Soils Revisited," *WMQ*, 3rd ser., 60, 4 (October 2003): 703–42.

18. Adam J. Hirsch, "The Collision of Military Cultures in Seventeenth-Century New England," *JAH* 74, 4 (March 1988): 1187–212; Mandell, *Behind the Frontier*, esp. chaps. 1–2; Colin G. Calloway, "Introduction: Surviving the Dark Ages," in Colin G. Calloway, ed., *After King Philip's War: Presence and Persistence in Indian New England* (Hanover, NH, 1997), 1–28.

19. Mary White Rowlandson, *A Narrative of the Captivity, Sufferings and Removes of Mrs. Mary Rowlandson . . .* (Boston, 1682; reprint, Boston, 1773), Evans #12988, p. 6; Jill Lepore, *The Name of War: King Philip's War and the Origins of American Identity* (New York, 1998), esp. 187–88, 197–98; Greg Sieminski, "The Puritan Captivity Narrative and the Politics of the American Revolution," *American Quarterly* 42, 1 (March 1990): 35–56; Clarence S. Brigham, *Paul Revere's Engravings* (New York, 1969), 99–101; on "skulking," see *BPB*, December 12, 1763; Patrick M. Malone, *The Skulking Way of War: Technology and Tactics among the New England Indians* (Baltimore, 1991), esp. 31, 138 n55.

20. John Williams, *The Redeemed Captive Returning to Zion* (New London, CT, 1773), Evans #13081, pp. 6–7; Evan Haefeli and Kevin Sweeney, *Captors and Captives: The 1704 French and Indian Raid on Deerfield* (Amherst and Boston, MA, 2003).

21. William Johnson to Cadwallader Colden, June 18, 1761, *The Papers of Sir William Johnson*, ed. James Sullivan (Albany, NY, 1921), 3:410.

22. Sir William Johnson to the Earl of Dartmouth, April 22, 1773 (quote), December 16, 1773, in *DCNY*, 8:361 (quote), 405–6; see also William Wood, *New England's Prospect*, ed. Alden T. Vaughan (Amherst, MA, 1977), 75–76 (also Evans #9884); Alan Taylor, *The Divided Ground: Indians, Settlers, and the Northern Borderland of the American Revolution* (New York, 2006), 16, 45, 60–61; Jon Parmenter, "After the Mourning Wars: The Iroquois as Allies in Colonial North American Campaigns, 1676–1760," *WMQ*, 3rd ser., 64, 1 (January 2007): 39–76.

23. J. H. Benton Jr., *Early Census Making in Massachusetts, 1643–1765* (Boston, 1905), 74–75; Mandell, *Behind the Frontier*, 174–75, 177–78; Joanna Brooks, ed., *The Collected Writings of Samson Occom, Mohegan: Leadership and Literature in Eighteenth-Century Native America* (New York, 2006), 22–23; Occom, *Sermon* (Boston, 1773), Shipton & Mooney #42478, #42479; *BEP*, February 1, 1773, *BPB*, February 14, 1774.

24. Gorham Committee of Correspondence to BCC, February 10, 1774, NYPL, p. 565; Kenneth A. Lockridge, *A New England Town, the First Hundred Years: Dedham, Massachusetts, 1636–1736* (New York, 1970), esp. 83–85, 143–59.

25. Mandell, *Behind the Frontier*, chap. 6; Jean M. O'Brien, *Dispossession by Degrees: Indian Land and Identity in Natick, Massachusetts, 1650–1790* (Cambridge, 1997).

26. "Journal of James Kenny, 1761–1763," ed. John W. Jordan, in *PMHB*, 37, 2 (April 1913): [152–201] 188; Charles M. Hudson, ed., *Black Drink: A Native American Tea* (Athens, GA, 1979); Gregory Evans Dowd, *A Spirited Resistance: The North American Indian Struggle for Unity, 1745–1815* (Baltimore, 1992), 33–34, 214 nn24–25; *MassSpy*, December 9, 1773; Mercy Otis Warren to Abigail Adams, January 19, 1774, in *Adams Family Correspondence*, ed. L. H. Butterfield (Cambridge, MA, 1963), 1:91.

27. Abrahams, "Playing Indian in Early America," 279; Deloria, *Playing Indian*, 3–5, 20–22; Berkhofer, *White Man's Indian*, esp. 73–85, 113–34; Sweet, *Bodies Politic*, 191–94; Martin W. Walsh, "May Games and Noble Savages: The Native American in Early Celebrations of the Tammany Society," *Folklore* 108 (1997): 83–91; Troy O. Bickham, *Savages within the Empire: Representations of American Indians in Eighteenth-Century Britain* (Oxford, 2005).

28. Rakashi Chand, " 'Bedazzling the Eyes . . . Like an Angel of the Sun': Shem Drowne's Indian Archer Weathervane," MHS (online); Elbridge Henry Goss, *The Life of Colonel Paul Revere*, 2 vols. (Boston, 1891), 1:35–46, 58–62; *BNL*, May 22, 1766; Brigham, *Paul Revere's Engravings*, 26–31, 43–48; E. McClung Fleming, "The American Image as Indian Princess, 1765–1783," *Winterthur Portfolio* 2 (1965): 65–81.

29. [Richard Steele], *Spectator*, #324, March 12, 1712, in Donald F. Bond, ed., *The Spectator* (Oxford, 1965), 3:186–88; *BPB*, May 18, 1772; "A Mask," *Town and Country Magazine* 3 (February 1771): [81–84] 84; see sources cited in Roger D. Abrahams, "Mohawks, Mohocks, Hawkubites, Whatever: Down and Dirty in Eighteenth-century London and Boston," *Common-place* 8, 4 (July 2008), online; Stephanie Pratt, *American Indians in British Art, 1700–1840* (Norman, OK, 2005), chap. 2; Daniel Statt, "The Case of the Mohocks: Rake Violence in Augustan London," *Social History* 20, 2 (May 1995): 179–99; Jennine Hurl-Eamon, *Gender and Petty Violence in London, 1680–1720* (Columbus, OH, 2005), chap. 3.

30. John Camp, *Out of the Wilderness: The Emergence of an American Identity in Colonial New England* (Middletown, CT, 1990), 219–20, 225, 228, 236–40; Jack P. Greene, "Search for Identity: An Interpretation of the Meaning of Selected Patterns of Social Response in Eighteenth-century America," in *Imperatives, Behaviors, and Identities: Essays in Early American Cultural History* (Charlottesville, VA, 1992), 143–73; T. H. Breen, "Ideology and Nationalism on the Eve of the American Revolution: Revisions Once More in Need of Revising," *JAH*, 84, 1 (June 1997): 13–39; Wahrman, *Making of the Modern Self*, esp. chap. 3.

31. *BEP*, December 6, 1773; Douglass Adair, "The Stamp Act in Contemporary English Cartoons," *WMQ*, 3rd ser., 10, 4 (October 1953): 538–42; Fleming, "American Image as Indian Princess"; Lester C. Olson, *Emblems of American Community in the Revolutionary Era: A Study in Rhetorical Iconology* (Washington, DC, 1991); Pratt, *American Indians in British Art*, 59–69.

32. Deloria, *Playing Indian*, 4–5, 28–37; see also Shari M. Huhndorf, *Going Native: Indians in the American Cultural Imagination* (Ithaca, NY, 2001); Jean M. O'Brien, " 'Vanishing' Indians in Nineteenth-Century New England: Local Historians' Erasure of Still-Present Indian Peoples," in Sergei A. Kan and Pauline Turner Strong, eds., *New Perspectives on Native North America: Cultures, Histories, and Representations* (Lincoln, NE, 2006), 414–32; Annette Kolodny, "Fictions of American Prehistory: Indians, Archeology, and National Origin Myths," *American Literature* 75, 4 (December 2003): 693–721; Linda Colley, "Britishness and Otherness: An Argument," *Journal of British Studies*, 31, 4 (October 1992): 309–29, esp. 327–28.

33. *BG*, October 7, December 30 (quote), 1771; *NM*, July 20, 1772, December 27, 1773; Camp, *Out of the Wilderness*, 155–63.

34. Deloria, *Playing Indian*, 10–11; [Gershom Flagg], *A Strange Account of the Rising and Breaking of a Great Bubble* (Boston?, 1767), Evans #10778, p. 11; *BEP*, December 26,

1768; Alan Taylor, *Liberty Men and Great Proprietors: The Revolutionary Settlement on the Maine Frontier, 1760–1820* (Chapel Hill, NC, 1990), 264.

35. Ann Hulton to Mrs. Lightbody, June 30, 1768, in *Letters of a Loyalist Lady*, 11.
36. Francis Bernard to Earl of Halifax, December 14, 1765, Bernard Papers, Sparks Manuscripts, HHL, 4.3.199.
37. "Hopkins *v.* Ward,—An Ante-Revolutionary Lawsuit," *Monthly Law Reporter* 22, 6 (October 1859): [327–39] 338; see also John, Thomas and Samuel Freebody to Earl of Hillsborough, July 22, 1771, *DAR*, 3:140.
38. *BNL*, September 22, 1768.
39. *BPB*, December 13, 1773; reprinted from *Rivington's New-York Gazetteer*, December 2, 1773; William Tudor, *The Life of James Otis of Massachusetts . . .* (Boston, 1823), 419–20.
40. Thatcher, *Traits*, 182–83; Drake, *Tea Leaves*, 147–48; *BG*, March 28, 1774; Hoerder, *Crowd Action*, 97–98; Shaw, *American Patriots*, 12; William Pencak, "Play as Prelude to Revolution: Boston, 1765–1776," in Pencak et al., *Riot and Revelry*, 125–55.
41. TH to [Israel] Williams, December 23, 1773, Israel Williams Papers, MHS; see also Thomas Danforth to Earl of Dartmouth, December 28, 1773, in Dartmouth Papers, II, 758; Thomas Bolton, *An Oration Delivered March Fifteenth, 1775 . . .* ([Boston], 1775), Evans #13840; Mein, *Sagittarius's Letters*, 27, 44.
42. Richard Price, *Observations on the Nature of Civil Liberty . . .*, 6th edn. (London, 1776), 64; for these paragraphs, see Dror Wahrman, "The English Problem of Identity in the American Revolution," *AHR*, 106, 4 (October 2001): 1236–62; Wahrman, *Making of the Modern Self*, 218–19, 261.
43. John Wesley, *Some Observations on Liberty: Occasioned by a Late Tract* (London, 1776), 6–7.
44. John Wesley, *A Calm Address to the Inhabitants of England*, 2nd edn. (London, 1777), 10–13; see also *[London] Morning Chronicle*, January 1, 1774.

Chapter 8: Boycotting the Accursed Leaf

1. Mercy Otis Warren to Abigail Smith Adams, December 29, [1773], in *Mercy Otis Warren: Selected Letters*, ed. Jeffrey H. Richards and Sharon M. Harris (Athens, GA, 2009), 41–42.
2. Hannah Griffitts, "Beware the Ides of March," February 28, 1775, Hannah Griffitts Papers, Library Company of Philadelphia.
3. James Kimball, "The One Hundredth Anniversary of the Destruction of Tea in Boston Harbor, with a Sketch of William Russell, of Boston, One of the 'Tea Destroyers,'" *Essex Institute Historical Collections* 12 (1874): [197–239] 231; Cogliano, *American Maritime Prisoners*.
4. William Davis to R. C. Winthrop, December 16, 1873, in "Tea-Party Anniversary," ed. Robert C. Winthrop, *MHSP* 13 (December 1873): [151–216] 212; Thatcher, *Traits*, 186 (quotes); Young, *Shoemaker*, 73; "The Boston Tea Party," *[Concord] New-Hampshire Patriot*, December 10, 1873, p. 4;
5. Drake, *Tea Leaves*, 169.
6. Charles J. Stratford Reminiscences, MHS.
7. *Diary and Autobiography of John Adams*, ed. L. H. Butterfield (Cambridge, MA, 1961), 2:85–86; John Adams to James Warren, December 17, 1773, in *Papers of John Adams*, ed. Robert J. Taylor (Cambridge, MA: 1977), 2:1.
8. *Letters and Diary of John Rowe*, 258.
9. Samuel Adams for the BCC to Thomas Mifflin and George Clymer and to Philip Livingston and Samuel Broome, December 17, 1773, William Cooper to Alexander McDougall and Isaac Sears and to Thomas Mifflin and George Clymer, December 6, 1773, BCC records, NYPL, pp. 4:468–69, 470–71; Samuel Adams to James Warren, December 28, 1773, in *Warren–Adams Letters* (Boston, 1917; reprint: New York, 1972), 1:20; John Boyle, "Boyle's Journal of Occurrences in Boston, 1759–1778," *NEHGR* 84

(October 1930): 372; *NYJ*, December 23, 1773; *BG*, January 3, 1774; Brown, *Revolutionary Politics*, 165; Fischer, *Paul Revere's Ride*, 26, 299–300.

10. *MassSpy*, January 6, 1774 (first quote); Samuel Adams to James Warren, December 28, 1773 (second quote), in *Warren–Adams Letters*, 1:20; William Tryon to Earl of Dartmouth, December 1, 1773, Frederick Haldimand to Lord Dartmouth, December 28, 1773, February 2, 5, 1774, in Tea Party Papers, comp. Gilbert Elliot Minto, HHL; [Henry Hulton] to———, December 8, 1773, in Henry Hulton Letterbooks, HHL, p. 77; Frederick Haldimand to Earl of Dartmouth, May 4, 1774, Cadwallader Colden to Earl of Dartmouth, May 4, 1774, *DAR*, 6:248, 8:107–9; William Tryon to the Earl of Dartmouth, January 3, 1774, *DCNY*, 8:407–8; TH to John Montagu, December 28, 1773, HPMA, 27:601, MHS transcripts, pp. 1144–46; Drake, *Tea Leaves*, 358–60; *NYJ*, December 23, 1773, April 21, 28, 1774; *Rivington's New-York Gazetteer*, December 23, 1773, April 7, 28, May 12, 1774; *NYGWM*, December 27, 1773, April 25, 1774; *BNL*, December 30, 1773; *BG*, January 3, 1774; *PJ*, April 27, 1774; Petition of James Chambers to the Lords of Treasury, April 15, 1776, T 1/522, TNA:PRO, ff. 94–95; EIC Court of Directors to Earl of Dartmouth, March 10, 1775, BL IOR E/1/217, Miscellanies 21:238–39; *Historical Memoirs . . . of William Smith*, ed. William H. W. Sabine, 2 vols. (reprint, New York, 1969), 1:156–67, 173, 184–85; Labaree, *Boston Tea Party*, 154–56, 167, 335; Joseph S. Tiedemann, *Reluctant Revolutionaries: New York City and the Road to Independence, 1763–1776* (Ithaca, NY, 1997), 175–83; James Bowdoin to John Temple, December 13, 1773, in *The Bowdoin and Temple Papers, MHSC*, 6th ser., vol. 9 (1897): 328.

11. "Christmas-Box for the Customers of the *Pennsylvania Journal*," December 24, 1773, (Philadelphia, 1773), Shipton & Mooney #42425; *PG*, December 24 (postscript), 29, 1773; *PP*, December 27, 1773, January 3, 1774; *BG*, January 10, 24, 1774; Joseph Reed to Earl of Dartmouth, December 22, 27, in *Life and Correspondence of Joseph Reed*, ed. William B. Reed, 2 vols. (Philadelphia, 1847), 1:51–56; Thomas Wharton to Samuel Wharton, November 30, 1773, Thomas Wharton to Thomas Walpole, December 24, 1773, in "Selections from the Letter-Books of Thomas Wharton, of Philadelphia, 1773–1783," *PMHB* 33, 3 (1909): [319–39] 319–22; Philadelphia Committee of Correspondence to BCC, December 25, 1773, in BCC minutes, NYPL, p. 4:487; Protest of Samuel Ayres, December 27, 1773, Papers Pertaining to the Shipment of Tea, etc., Philadelphia, 1769–1773, HSP; James & Drinker to Pigou & Booth, December 28, 1773, Henry S. Drinker Papers, 1739–1779, HSP; John Patterson and Zachariah Hood to Customs Commissioners at Boston, December 28, 1773, T 1/505, TNA:PRO, ff. 107–8; EIC Court of Directors to Earl of Dartmouth, March 10, 1775, BL IOR E/1/217, Miscellanies 21:238–39; George Clymer and Thomas Mifflin to Adams, December 27, 1773, in Samuel Adams Papers, NYPL; Earl of Dartmouth to John Penn, February 5, 1774, John Penn to Earl of Dartmouth, May 3, 1774, *DAR*, 8:45–46, 103; Eliza Farmar to her nephew "Jack," [January 1774?], "Letters of Eliza Farmar to Her Nephew," *PMHB* 40, 2 (1916): [199–207] 199–200; see also Henry Laurens to John Laurens, January 21, 1774, in *The Papers of Henry Laurens*, ed. George C. Rogers Jr. and David R. Chesnutt (Columbia, SC, 1981), 9:244.

12. Henry Laurens to George Appleby, February 15, 1774, in *Papers of Henry Laurens*, 9:278 (quote); *MassSpy*, January 13, March 17, 1774; *PJ*, March 16, 1774; Roger Smith and Leger & Greenwood to the EIC, December 4, 18, 1773, in CO 5/133, TNA:PRO, ff. 61–62; Drake, *Tea Leaves*, 339–42; George C. Rogers Jr., "The Charleston Tea Party: The Significance of December 3, 1773," *South Carolina Historical Magazine* 75, 3 (July 1974): 153–68.

13. *BNL*, December 30, 1773; *BG*, January 10, 1774; *BEP*, January 10, 17, 1774; "Diary for 1773 to the end of 1774, of Mr. Thomas Newell, Boston," *MHSP* 15 (October 1877): [335–63] 347.

14. Samuel Adams to James Warren, December 28, 1773, in *Warren–Adams Letters*, 1:21; John Hancock to Hayley & Hopkins, December 21, 1773, Hancock Letterbook JH6,

Baker Library, Harvard Business School; *Peter Oliver's Origin and Progress*, 103; see also *The Literary Diary of Ezra Stiles, D.D., LL.D., President of Yale College*, ed. Franklin Bowditch Dexter, 3 vols. (New York, 1901), 1:427–28; Pigou & Booth to James & Drinker, December 31, 1773, Henry S. Drinker Papers, 1739–1779, HSP.

15. *Peter Oliver's Origin and Progress*, 104 (quote); William Cooper for the BCC to Samuel Cutts, [William] Bradford, George Hazard, and Jabez Bowen, December 5, 1773, NYPL, pp. 4:471–72; Brown, *Revolutionary Politics*, 167–77.

16. Samuel Adams to James Warren, December 28, 1773 (first quote), in *Warren–Adams Letters*, 1:20; *MassSpy*, January 6, 1774 (second quote); Montague Committee of Correspondence to BCC, January 20, 1774, Gorham Committee of Correspondence to BCC, February 10, 1774, NYPL, pp. 544, 565; Jonathan Sayward Diaries, AAS, vol. 15 (entry for January 20–21, 1774).

17. *BNL*, January 13, 1774; *BEP*, February 14, 1774.

18. *BEP*, February 7, 1774.

19. William Williams et al. to Charles Goodrich, January 19, 1774, in Joseph Edward Adams Smith, *The History of Pittsfield, (Berkshire County,) Massachusetts, 1734–1800* (Boston, 1869), 184–86; Worcester Selectmen to Samuel Bridge, May 13, 1774, in Albert A. Lovell, *Worcester in the War of the Revolution: Embracing the Acts of the Town from 1765 to 1783 Inclusive* (Worcester, MA, 1876), 31–33.

20. *BNL*, February 3, 1774 (first quote); *BG*, February 7, 1774; *MassSpy*, February 24, 1774 (second quote); Joseph Clarence Hagar, ed., *Marshfield: The Autobiography of a Pilgrim Town* (Marshfield, MA, 1940), 114–17; see also *BNL*, December 23, 1773; *MassSpy*, December 30, 1773; *BG*, January 24, 1774; Samuel Adams to James Warren, January 10, 1774, in "Tea-Party Anniversary," 205; James Warren to John Adams, January 3, 1774, in *Warren–Adams Letters*, 1:23–24; Frederick Haldimand to Earl of Dartmouth, January 5, 1774, *DAR*, 8:23.

21. Henry Bromfield to Flight & Halliday, December 17, 1773, in Henry Bromfield Letterbook, NEHGS, 4:90–91; Protest of John Greenough, Joseph Royall Loring, John Hitch, and John Green, December 13, 1773, Protest of Joseph Royall Loring and John Green, January 24, 1774, Ezekiel Price Notary Records, Boston Atheneum, pp. 6:169–72, 180; "Boyle's Journal," 371; John Andrews to William Barrell, December 19, 1773, in "Letters of John Andrews," ed. Winthrop Sargent, *MHSP* 8 (1864–65): 327.

22. John Adams to James Warren, December 22, 1773, in *Papers of John Adams*, 9:3–4.

23. TH to Lord Dartmouth, December 20, 1773, Tea Party Papers, Gilbert Elliot Minto, HHL, no. 17; Jonathan Clarke to Richard Clarke & Sons, Benjamin Faneuil Jr., and Thomas and Elisha Hutchinson, December 31, 1773, Misc. Bound MSS, MHS; Richard Harrison and Robert Hallowell to Commissioners of Customs at Boston, January 6, 1774, T 1/505, TNA:PRO, f. 103; *BG*, January 17, 1774; *BEP*, January 17, 1774; *MassSpy*, Feburary 17, 1774; "Boyle's Journal," 372.

24. *BG*, January 3, 17, 1774; *MassSpy*, January 6, 1774; *BEP*, January 17 (quote), 31, 1774.

25. Samuel Adams to James Warren, January 10, 1774, in "Tea-Party Anniversary," 205.

26. *BEP*, February 7, 1774.

27. *MassSpy*, October 14, 1773.

28. *MassSpy*, January 6, 1774; Nathaniel Walker Appleton to Eliphalet Pearson, December 27, 1773, in William C. Lane, ed., "Letters from Nathaniel Walker Appleton," *PCSM* 8 (February 1904): [289–324] 298; see also *MassSpy*, November 26, December 9, 30, 1773; *PJ*, December 22, 1773; reprinted in *MassSpy*, January 27, 1774; *BEP*, January 24, 1774.

29. *MassSpy*, December 23, 1773.

30. *BG*, December 20, 1773; *MassSpy*, December 30, 1773; "At a Meeting of a Number of Principal Dealers in Teas began and held at the Royal Exchange Tavern . . .," Loose Boston Town Papers, BPL; see also Samuel Lane Boardman, *Peter Edes: Pioneer Printer in Maine: A Biography* (Bangor, ME, 1901), 151–59; Joseph Gilbert to Daniel Waldow,

December 22, 1773, US Revolution Collection, AAS; *MassSpy*, December 9, 1773; *NM*, December 13, 1773; *BEP*, January 17, February 7, 1774; *BNL*, January 20, 1774; *PP*, December 6, 13, 1773; *PG*, December 8, 1773.

31. "A List of the Principal dealers of Tea in this Town, lately applied to . . .," [sometime prior to] January 20, 1774, Mss. Large, MHS (first and second quotes); *BEP*, January 24 (third quote), February 7, 1774. An informal count taken between December 2 and 23 yielded 73 merchants against all tea sales and 38 against the sale of dutied tea only; "At a Meeting of a Number of Principal Dealers in Teas . . .," BPL; see also Tyler, *Smugglers and Patriots*, 207, 272–73. Although a head count on January 20 revealed that 79 were against all tea sales and 9 were against the sale of dutied tea only, "A TRUE WHIG" caustically remarked that these 88 merchants hardly added up to the more than 150 merchants who (by his count) sold tea in town; *BEP*, January 24, 31, February 14, 1774.

32. L. F. S. Upton, ed., "Proceedings of Ye Body Respecting the Tea," *WMQ*, 3rd ser., 22, 2 (April 1965): 299.

33. *MassSpy*, January 13 (first quote), 27 (last sentence), 1774; *BEP*, January 17 (second quote), February 7, 1774; TH to Earl of Dartmouth, December 21, 1773, in Dartmouth Papers, I, ii, 921; *BG*, January 17, 1774.

34. *NM*, November 22, December 27, 1773; reprinted in *MassSpy*, November 26, 1773 (quote), January 6, 1774; *BPB*, January 31, 1774.

35. *MassSpy*, December 16, 1773; *BEP*, January 10, 1774; *NM*, December 27, 1773, reprinted in *BG*, January 10, 1774; Upton, "Proceedings," 299.

36. Upton, "Proceedings," 299; *MassSpy*, January 13, 1774; *BEP*, January 17, 24, 1774; see also *BEP*, November 22, 1773.

37. *MassSpy*, December 16, 1773; *BEP*, February 4, 1774; *Essex Gazette*, April 12, 1774.

38. *MassSpy*, January 13, 1774.

39. *BG*, February 14, 1774; *Connecticut Courant*, March 17, 1774, reprinted in *MassSpy*, March 31, 1774; for later incidents in Kingston, NH, and Leominster, MA, see Harriet S. Lacy, "Samuel Sweat's Diary, 1772–1774," *Historical New Hampshire* 30, 4 (winter 1975): [221–30] 228–29; *BG*, September 5, 1774.

40. Upton, "Proceedings," 299; *BPB*, January 24, 1774.

41. "At a Meeting of a Number of Principal Dealers in Teas . . .," BPL (first quote); *MassSpy*, January 20, 1774 (second quote); Breen, *Marketplace*, esp. chaps. 7–8.

42. *BG*, January 17, 1774; "Diary of Thomas Newell," 347; *Letters and Diary of John Rowe*, 259; *BG*, December 27, 1773 (supplement), January 3, 1774; *BEP*, January 3, 1774.

43. *MassSpy*, January 13, 1774; Frederic Scherer Withington, "Henry Withington of Dorchester, Mass., and Some of His Descendants," *NEHGR* 75 (April 1921): [142–54] 153; *BG*, January 3, 1774; *Letters and Diary of John Rowe*, 259; "Diary of Thomas Newell," 347.

44. *BEP*, January 24, 1774; *BG*, December 27, 1773 (supplement).

45. *BNL*, January 27, 1774; *BEP*, January 24, 31, 1774; "Diary of Thomas Newell," 348; "Boyle's Journal," 372.

46. *BEP*, January 10, 17, 31, February 14, 1774.

47. Nathaniel Walker Appleton to Eliphalet Pearson, January 4, [1774], in Lane, "Letters from Nathaniel Walker Appleton," 303–4; Appleton may have written as "A BATCH-ELOR," *BEP*, January 17, 1774; for responses, see *BEP*, January 24, February 7, 14, 1774.

48. *MassSpy*, January 13, 1774.

49. *BG*, March 7, 1774; "Diary of Thomas Newell," 350; *Letters and Diary of John Rowe*, 264.

50. *BG*, March 7, 1774.

51. *MassSpy*, March 10, 1774; Protest of Benjamin Gorham et al., March 8, 1774, Ezekiel Price Notary Records, Boston Athenæum, 6:186–87; *MassSpy*, March 17, 1774; *Diary and Autobiography of John Adams*, 2:91; *BNL*, March 10, 1774; *Letters and Diary of John*

Rowe, 264; Instructions to Capt. Gorham to refuse to take tea aboard his ship, October 4, 1773, transmitted March 7, 1774, in BCC Misc. Corresondence, NYPL.

52. William Palfrey to Thomas Mifflin, January 14, 1774, Palfrey Family Papers, HHL, f. 54; *BEP*, February 14, 1774; *MassSpy*, March 31, 1774.

53. Wellfleet Committee of Correspondence to BCC, January 25, 1774, Proceedings of the Wellfleet Town Meeting, January 17, 25, 1774, John Greenough to Wellfleet Committee of Correspondence, January 24, 1774, in BCC letters, NYPL, pp. 617–22; *BEP*, February 7, 1774 (first quote); John Greenough to Richard Clarke & Sons, March 26, June 2, 1774, Misc. Bound MSS, MHS; Richard Clarke & Sons to John Greenough, March 30, 1774, BPL; David Stoddard Greenough to John Greenough, January 4, 1774, John Greenough to Thomas Greenough, March 1, 1774 (second quote), John Greenough Papers, MHS (transcript).

54. *Essex Gazette*, April 12, 1774; *BEP*, July 18, 1774; Willard Knowles to John Greenough, March 1, 1774, John Greenough to Thomas Greenough, March 22, 1774, resolutions of Eastham Town Meeting, John Greenough Papers, MHS.

55. *MassSpy*, March 17, 31, April 7, 1774; *Norwich Packet*, April 7, 1774.

56. *BEP*, January 24, 1774.

57. *MassSpy*, December 2, 1773.

58. *BG*, December 13, 1773.

59. *BG*, March 21, 1774; Mercy Otis Warren, "The Squabble of the Sea Nymphs; or the Sacrifice of the Tuscararoes," in *Poems, Dramatic and Miscellaneous* (Boston, 1790), 202–5; see also Mercy Otis Warren to Abigail Adams, January 19, February 27, 1774, in *Adams Family Correspondence*, ed. L. H. Butterfield (Cambridge, MA, 1963), 1:91–94, 99–103, John Adams to James Warren, December 22, 1773, April 9, 1774, in *Papers of John Adams*, 2:3, 82–83; Jeffrey H. Richards, *Mercy Otis Warren* (New York, 1995), 53–55; Rosemarie Zagarri, *A Woman's Dilemma: Mercy Otis Warren and the American Revolution* (Wheeling, IL, 1995), 61–64, 73–77, 88–89, 93–94.

60. *VG* (Purdie & Dixon), January 20, 1774, reprinted in *MassSpy*, February 17, 1774.

61. *NM*, December 27, 1773; reprinted in *MassSpy*, January 6, 1774; *BEP*, February 7, 1774.

62. *MassSpy*, January 13, 27 (first and second quotes), 1774; "Biographical Sketch of Col. David Mason of Salem, by His Daughter, Mrs. Susan Smith," *Essex Institute Historical Collections* 48, 3 (July 1912): [197–216] 203–4 (third quote).

63. John Adams to Abigail Adams, July 6, 1774, *Adams Family Correspondence*, 1:129–30; *MassSpy*, February 17, 1774.

64. Mary Noyes to Joseph Smith, November 2, 1774, U.S. History Pre-Civil War Collection, Watkinson Library, Trinity College, CT.

65. Laurel Thatcher Ulrich, *A Midwife's Tale: The Life of Martha Ballard, Based on Her Diary, 1785–1812* (New York, 1990), 11; *Peter Oliver's Origin and Progress*, 73.

66. [William Maxwell], "My Mother [Helen Maxwell-Read]," *Lower Norfolk County Virginia Antiquary* 1, 2 (1896): [96–102] 98–99; *Grandmother Tyler's Book: The Recollections of Mary Palmer Tyler (Mrs. Royall Tyler), 1775–1866*, ed. Ferderick Tupper and Helen Tyler Brown (New York, 1925), 236–37.

67. *Peter Oliver's Origin and Progress*, 104; John Adams to Abigail Adams, April 14, 1776, *Adams Family Correspondence*, 1:382.

68. *BEP*, February 7, 1774.

69. *BPB*, January 31, 1774.

70. *BG*, November 29, 1773; *MassSpy*, December 23, 1773, January 6, 1774.

71. Abigail Adams to John Adams, March 31, 1776, in *Adams Family Correspondence*, 1:370; Norton, *Liberty's Daughters*, esp. 157–62; Alfred F. Young, " 'Persons of Consequence': The Women of Boston and the Making of the American Revolution, 1765–1776," in *Liberty Tree*, 100–43; Cynthia A. Kierner, *Beyond the Household: Women's Place in the Early South, 1700–1835* (Ithaca, NY, 1998), chap. 3; Crane, *Ebb Tide in New England.*

Chapter 9: Boston Bears the Blame

1. *The Papers of James Iredell*, ed. Don Higginbotham (Raleigh, NC, 1976), 1:338.
2. *Peter Oliver's Origin and Progress*, 103.
3. Samuel Cooper to Benjamin Franklin, December 17, 1773, Thomas Cushing et al. to Arthur Lee, December 21, 1773 (first quote), and John Scollay to Arthur Lee, December 23, 1773, in Jared Sparks, ed., "Destruction of the Tea in the Harbor of Boston, December 16, 1773," *MHSC*, 4th ser., vol. 4 (Boston, 1858): [373–89] 375, 379, 385; *Diary and Autobiography of John Adams*, ed. L. H. Butterfield (Cambridge, MA, 1961), 2:86 (second quote); see also *MassSpy*, January 13, February 3, 1774; Samuel Adams to James Warren, December 28, 1773, in *Warren–Adams Letters* (Boston, 1917; reprint: New York, 1972), 1:20; *The Bowdoin and Temple Papers, MHSC*, 6th ser., vol. 9 (1897): 327–30, 331–34.
4. *MassSpy*, December 23, 1773, January 13, 1774 (first quote); Cushing et al. to Lee, December 21, 1773 (third quote), Scollay to Lee, December 23, 1773 (second quote), in Sparks, "Destruction of the Tea," 378–79 (second quote), 385 (third quote).
5. *Diary of John Adams*, 2:86; Bushman, *King and People*, chap. 5.
6. TH, *The History of the Province of Massachusetts Bay . . .* (London, 1828), 436–38 (quote 437); TH to EIC Directors, December 19, 1773, TH to John Montagu, December 28, 1773, TH to Israel Mauduit, December 1773; TH to unknown, December 30, 1773, HPMA, 27:597–99, 601, 604–8, MHS transcripts, pp. 1138, 1144–46, 1150–54, 1158–60; TH to Francis Bernard, January 1, 1774, TH to Samuel Swift, January 4, 1774, in "Tea-Party Anniversary," *MHSP* 13 (December 1873): 174–75; *Peter Oliver's Origin and Progress*, 103; Tucker and Hendrickson, *Fall*, 297–316; Tyler, *Smugglers and Patriots*, 199; Bailyn, *Ordeal*, 262–63, 287–88.
7. TH to Earl of Dartmouth, December 20, 24, 1773, Extract of Massachusetts Council minutes, December 21, 1773 (enclosure in letter of December 24), in Tea Party Papers, comp. Gilbert Elliot Minto, HHL; John Erving et al. to William Bollan, December 20, 1773, in *Bowdoin and Temple Papers*, 334; *Diary of John Adams*, 2:97 (first quote); Nathaniel Walker Appleton to Eliphalet Pearson, December 21, [1773], in William C. Lane, ed., "Letters from Nathaniel Walker Appleton," *PCSM* 8 (February 1904): [289–324] 297 (second quote); TH, *History*, 438–39; *BG*, December 20, 27, 1773; Nathaniel Coffin to Charles Steuart, January 5, 1774, in Charles Steuart Papers, NLS, ff. 153–54.
8. Thomas Hutchinson Jr. to Elisha Hutchinson, January 9, 21, February 4, 1774, in Peter Orlando Hutchinson, *The Diary and Letters of His Excellency Thomas Hutchinson, Esq. . . .* (Boston, 1884), 1:97–98; Thomas Hutchinson Jr. to the consignees at Castle Island, January 17, 1774 (first quote), Misc. Bound MSS, MHS; *MassSpy*, December 23, 1773 (second quote), January 13, 20, 1774; *BG*, January 17, 1774 ("JOYCE, jun." quotes); *BEP*, January 24, 1774 (final quote); TH to Earl of Dartmouth, January 28, 1774, *DAR*, 8:26–27; Shaw, *American Patriots*, 189–91, 197.
9. John Singleton Copley to [Richard Clarke], [February 15, 1774,] in *Letters and Papers of John Singleton Copley and Henry Pelham, 1739–1776, MHSC*, vol. 71 (1914): 214 (first quote); *Diary of John Adams*, 2:92 (second quote); *BEP*, February 14, 1774; TH to Francis Bernard, March 9, 1774, in *Diary and Letters of Thomas Hutchinson*, 1:131; *BG*, March 28, 1774; Henry Bromfield to Thomas Bromfield, January 1, 1774, Henry Bromfield to Hughes & Whitelock, January 27, 1774, in Bromfield and Clarke Family Papers, MHS.
10. William Tryon to Earl of Dartmouth, November 3, December 1, 1773, *DCNY*, 8:400–1, 402–4; Drake, *Tea Leaves*, 260–62, 269–77; James & Drinker to Pigou & Booth, October 5, 30, November 20, 30, 1773, Henry Drinker Foreign Letters, 1772–1785, Drinker Papers, HSP, pp. 147, 152, 160, 162; Thomas, *Tea Party to Independence*, 28–33; Labaree, *Boston Tea Party*, 170–81.
11. David T. Morgan, *The Devious Dr. Franklin, Colonial Agent: Benjamin Franklin's Years in London* (Macon, GA, 1996), esp. chaps. 7–9.

12. Benjamin Franklin to William Franklin, August 17, 19[–22], November 3[–4] 1772, Benjamin Franklin to Thomas Cushing, September 3, November 4, December 2, 1772, in *PBF*, 19:243–44, 257–60, 293, 360–61, 364–65, 399–413; "JUNIUS AMERICANUS" [Arthur Lee] to the Earl of Dartmouth, *[London] Public Advertiser*, July 29, 1773, printed in *BG*, September 27, 1773; B. D. Bargar, *Lord Dartmouth and the American Revolution* (Columbia, SC, 1965); Pauline Maier, *From Resistance to Revolution: Colonial Radicals and the Development of American Opposition to Britain, 1765–1776* (New York, 1972), 228–34.

13. "The Manuscripts of Captain H. V. Knox," in HMC, *Report on Manuscripts in Various Collections* (Dublin, 1909), 6:269; William Tryon to Earl of Dartmouth, November 3, 1773, *DAR*, 6:238; John Pownall to Peter Michell, December 1773, in Dartmouth Papers, II, 760; see also Labaree, *Boston Tea Party*, 171–72; Bargar, *Lord Dartmouth*, 95–97.

14. Earl of Dartmouth to Frederick Haldimand, January 8, 1774, in BL, Add. MS 21695, f. 56; Earl of Dartmouth to William Tryon, January 8, 1774, *DCNY*, 8:408–9.

15. George III to Earl of Dartmouth, January 19, 1774, in HMC, "The Manuscripts of the Earl of Dartmouth. (Supplementary Report)," in *The Manuscripts of Rye and Hereford Corporations . . .*, Thirteenth Report, Appendix, Part IV (London, 1892), 31:499 (quote); EIC Court of Directors minutes, January 7, 1774, BL IOR B/89, pp. 678–79; EIC Court of Directors to Francis Legge, January 8, 1774, in Dartmouth Papers, I, ii, 936; P[eter] Michell to John Pownall, January 8, 1774, CO 5/133, TNA:PRO, f. 5.

16. *BNL*, December 23, 1773; *[London] Public Advertiser*, January 21, 1774; *London Evening-Post*, January 20–22, 1774; *St. James's Chronicle*, January 20–22, 1774.

17. King George III to Earl of Dartmouth, January 19, 1774, in HMC, "Manuscripts of the Earl of Dartmouth," 31:499.

18. *[London] Public Ledger*, January 27, 1774; *DAR* (1973), 4:430; EIC Court of Directors minutes, January 28, 1774, BL IOR B/89, pp. 735–36; Labaree, *Boston Tea Party*, 173; Thomas, *Tea Party to Independence*, 30.

19. *[London] Middlesex Journal*, January 22–25, 25–27, 27–29, 1774.

20. EIC Chairman and Deputy Chairman to Earl of Dartmouth, January 21, 1774, TNA:PRO, CO 5/133, f. 36a; [Peter] Michell to [Gilbert] Barkly, January 26, 1774, BL IOR E/1/217, p. 63; Earl of Dartmouth to Attorney- and Solicitor-General, February 5, 1774, *DAR*, 8:37–42; Thomas, *Tea Party to Independence*, 29–30.

21. *London Chronicle*, December 23–25, 1773, Benjamin Franklin to Thomas Cushing, January 5, 1774, William Whately's Chancery Suit against Franklin, and Franklin's answer, January 7, April 19, 1774, in *PBF*, 20:513–16; 21:5–7, 13–18, 197–202; *Diary and Letters of Thomas Hutchinson*, 1:81–93; Bailyn, *Ordeal*, chap. 7; Tucker and Henrickson, *Fall*, 308–9 n37; Morgan, *Devious Dr. Franklin*, 220–27.

22. The Final Hearing before the Privy Council . . ., January 29, 1774, A Letter from London, [on or after February 7, 1774], printed in the *Boston Gazette*, April 25, 1774, Anthony Todd to Benjamin Franklin, January 31, 1774, Benjamin Franklin to Thomas Cushing, February 15[–19?], 1774, in *PBF*, 21:37–70 (first quote p. 49, second quote p. 67), 73–74, 79–83, 86–96; Earl of Shelburne to Earl of Chatham, February 3, 1774, in *Correspondence of William Pitt, Earl of Chatham*, ed. William Stanhope Taylor and John Henry Pringle (London, 1840), 4:322–23; Thomas, *Tea Party to Independence*, 26–28; Jack P. Greene, "The Alienation of Benjamin Franklin, British American," in *Understanding the American Revolution: Issues and Actors* (Charlottesville, VA, 1995), 247–84.

23. Cabinet minute, January 29, 1774, in Dartmouth Papers, II, 799; Earl of Shelburne to Earl of Chatham, February 3, 1774, in *Correspondence of William Pitt*, 4:323–24.

24. Earl of Shelburne to Earl of Chatham, April 4, 1774, in *Correspondence of William Pitt*, 4:339 (quote); see also Tucker and Hendrickson, *Fall*, 314–16; Thomas, *Tea Party to Independence*, 14, 21, 24–25, 44–47.

25. George III to Lord North, March 14, 1774, in *The Correspondence of King George the Third with Lord North from 1768 to 1783*, ed. W. Bodham Donne, 2 vols. (London, 1867), 1:174; Cabinet minutes, February 4, 9, 19, 28, 1774, in Dartmouth Papers, II, 817, 819, 834, 839; see also James Scott to John Hancock, February 21, 1774, John Hancock, Letters from London, 1768–1771, box 16, folder 4, Hancock Family Papers, Baker Library, Harvard Business School; Thomas, *Tea Party to Independence*, 31–37, 42–43; Labaree, *Boston Tea Party*, 149–50, 174–75.

26. A Merchant's Remarks upon the People of Boston, received February 1774, in Dartmouth Papers, II, 840; Labaree, *Boston Tea Party*, 177–83.

27. Henry Bathurst, Lord Chancellor Apsley to Earl of Dartmouth, March 6, 1774, in Dartmouth Papers, 1778, II, 849; Earl of Dartmouth to TH, April 9, 1774, in "Tea-Party Anniversary," 175–76; Earl of Dartmouth to William Bull, February 5, 1774, TNA:PRO, CO 5/396, ff. 5–6; Earl of Dartmouth to William Tryon, February 5, 1774, in *DCNY*, 8:409; Earl of Dartmouth to TH, February 5, 1774, Earl of Dartmouth to John Penn, February 5, 1774, *DAR*, 8:45–46; Thomas, *Tea Party to Independence*, 30–45.

28. Earl of Dartmouth to J. Thornton, February 12, 1774, in Dartmouth Papers, II, 827.

29. Benjamin Franklin to Massachusetts House Committee of Correspondence, February 2, 1774, Benjamin Franklin to William Franklin, September 7, 1774, in *PBF*, 21:75–77, 287; Thomas, *Tea Party to Independence*, 38.

30. Speech of Lord North, March 14, 1774, in R. C. Simmons and P. D. G. Thomas, eds., *Proceedings and Debates of the British Parliaments Respecting North America, 1754–1783* (White Plains, NY, 1985), 4:75.

31. Speeches of Lord North, March 14, 1774 (first quote), Welbore Ellis, March 25, 1774 (third quote), in Simmons and Thomas, *Proceedings and Debates*, 4:57–58, 63 (first quote), 75, 78, 122 (third quote); "Message and Papers Considered, Speech of Lord North," in Peter Force, *American Archives: Fourth Series*, 6 vols. (Washington, DC, 1837) 1:39 (second quote); Benjamin Franklin to Thomas Cushing, March 22, 1774, in *PBF*, 21:152–53 (fourth quote); Thomas, *Tea Party to Independence*, chap. 4.

32. Force, *American Archives*, 1:60–66; *BNL*, May 12, 1774; Labaree, *Boston Tea Party*, 192–93.

33. David Ammerman, *In the Common Cause: American Response to the Coercive Acts of 1774* (New York, 1974), 7–8; Thomas, *Tea Party to Independence*, 62–66.

34. Force, *American Archives*, 1:104–12; Raphael, *First American Revolution*, 49–51.

35. Force, *American Archives*, 1:129–31; John Adams to Joseph Palmer, September 26, 1774, in *Founding Families: Digital Editions of the Papers of the Winthrops and the Adamses*, ed. C. James Taylor (Boston, 2007), online.

36. Force, *American Archives*, 1:170; Thomas, *Tea Party to Independence*, 79–80.

37. Speeches of Lord North and Edmund Burke, April 19, 1774, in Simmons and Thomas, *Proceedings and Debates*, 4:198 (North quote), 199–200, 226 (Burke quote); Thomas, *Tea Party to Independence*, 73–76.

38. Speech of Isaac Barré, May 2, 1774, in Simmons and Thomas, *Proceedings and Debates*, 4:344–45.

39. George III to Lord North, February 4, 1774, in *Correspondence of King George the Third*, 1:164–65; Lord North to Lord Dartmouth, February 13, 1774, and Cabinet minute, February 16, 1774, in Dartmouth Papers, II, 828, 832; Lord Dartmouth to Thomas Gage, April 9, 1774, *DAR*, 8:86–90; HMC, "Various Papers on Measures for America and American Business Generally," [early 1774], in vol. 2 of *The Manuscripts of the Earl of Dartmouth*, Fourteenth Report, Appendix, Part X (London, 1895), 20:245; Thomas, *Tea Party to Independence*, 33–35, 43, 67–70.

40. *BEP*, May 2, 1774; *BNL*, May 12, 1774; Samuel Adams to James Warren, May 14, 1774, in *The Writings of Samuel Adams*, ed. Harry Alonzo Cushing (New York, 1907), 3:112 (first quote); *BTR*, 18:174 (second quote); TH to Earl of Dartmouth, March 21, May 19, 1774, *DAR*, 8:71 (third quote), 115–16.

41. Speeches of Lord North, Constantine Phipps, April 15, 1774, in Simmons and Thomas, *Proceedings and Debates*, 4:170, 177; Earl of Dartmouth to TH, April 9, 1774, in "Tea-Party Anniversary," 175–76; Bailyn, *Ordeal*, 272–73.

42. *Diary of John Adams*, 2:86; John Adams to James Warren, December 17, 1773, in *Papers of John Adams*, ed. Robert J. Taylor (Cambridge, MA, 1977), 2:2.

43. Mason A. Green, *Springfield, 1636–1886: History of Town and City* (Springfield, MA, 1888), 276; Speech of Edmund Burke, March 25, 1774, in Simmons and Thomas, *Proceedings and Debates*, 4:124.

44. John Penn to Earl of Dartmouth, July 5, 1774, *DAR*, 8:142; *Letters and Diary of John Rowe*, 278; Thomas Gage to Earl of Dartmouth, July 5, 1774, *DAR*, 8:140–41; Stephen E. Patterson, *Political Parties in Revolutionary Massachusetts* (Madison, WI, 1973), 76–90; on fast days, see *Providence Gazette*, June 18, 1774; *NM*, June 27, 1774; *BG*, July 11, 1774; *Connecticut Journal*, July 22, 1774; *The Papers of Thomas Jefferson*, ed. Julian P. Boyd (Princeton, NJ, 1950), 1:105–7.

45. "Convention of Worcester County," in *The Journals of Each Provincial Congress of Massachusetts in 1774 and 1775*, ed. William Lincoln (Boston, 1838), 627–31; Raphael, *First American Revolution*; for examples of the "common cause" sentiment, see *BEP*, May 23, June 6, 1774; *PP*, June 6, 1774; *BTR*, 18:186, 212, 223; "Correspondence, in 1774 and 1775, between . . . Boston and Contributors of Donations for the Relief of the Sufferers . . . ," *MHSC*, 4th ser., 4 (1858): 5 n1, 11, 23–24 n1, 33 n1, 57, 64 n1; Nathaniel Coffin to Charles Steuart, July 6, 1774, Charles Steuart Papers, NLS, f. 227.

46. Benjamin Hallowell to Thomas Gage, September 8, 1774, quoted in Raphael, *First American Revolution*, 119; Patrick Johnston, "Building to a Revolution: The Powder Alarm and Popular Mobilization of the New England Countryside, 1774–1775," *Historical Journal of Massachusetts* 37, 1 (spring 2009): 123–40; Robert P. Richmond, *Powder Alarm, 1774* (Princeton, NJ, 1971).

47. "Convention of Suffolk County," in Lincoln, *Journals of Each Provincial Congress of Massachusetts*, 601–5; *Journals of the Continental Congress, 1774–1789*, ed. Worthington C. Ford et al. (Washington, DC, 1904), 1:31–41, 43, 51–53, 58 (first quote), 63–73, 75–81, 102; *Diary of John Adams*, 2:134–35 (second quote); Ammerman, *In the Common Cause*.

48. *BEP*, January 23, 1775 (Portsmouth, NH); *MassSpy*, March 17, 1775 (Providence, RI); *Maryland Gazette*, October 20, 27, November 3, 10, 1774; "Account of the Destruction of the Brig 'Peggy Stewart,' at Annapolis, 1774," *PMHB* 25, 2 (1901): 248–54; Richard D. Fisher, comp., "The Burning of the 'Peggy Stewart,' " *Maryland Historical Magazine* 5, 3 (September 1910): 235–45; *PP*, January 9, 1775 (Greenwich, NJ); *Philip Vickers Fithian: Journal, 1775–1776*, ed. Robert Greenhalgh Albion and Leonidas Dodson (Princeton, NJ, 1934), 247–48; for York River, VA, see *VG* (Purdie and Dixon, also Pinkney), November 24, 1774; *VG* (Dixon and Hunter), May 6, 1775; for public burnings of tea in Charleston, SC, on November 5, 1774, see *VG* (Pinkney), December 15, 1774; bonfire before the Northampton, VA, County Courthouse on January 11, 1775, in *VG* (Dixon and Hunter), February 4, 1775.

49. Thomas Gage to Earl of Dartmouth, October 30, 1774, *DAR*, 8:222.

50. George III to Lord North, November 14, 1774, *Correspondence of King George the Third*, 1:215; Earl of Dartmouth to Thomas Gage, January 27, 1775, in *The Correspondence of General Thomas Gage . . .*, ed. Clarence Edwin Carter, 2 vols. (New Haven, CT, 1931, 1933), 2:181.

51. Samuel Nowell's petition to Congress, February 23, 1830, RWP, S. #4503.

52. *BEP*, October 24, 1774; Thomas Bolton, *An Oration Delivered March Fifteenth, 1775 . . .* ([Boston], 1775), Evans #13840, p. 6; *Peter Oliver's Origin and Progress*, 117; "A Citizen of New-York" [James Hawkes], in *A Retrospect of the Boston Tea-Party, with a Memoir of George R. T. Hewes . . .* (New York, 1834), 44.

53. Daniel R. Coquillette and Neil Longley York, eds., *Portrait of a Patriot: The Major Political and Legal Papers of Josiah Quincy Junior*, vol. 74 of *PCSM* (2005), 1:41–44;

Cary, *Joseph Warren*, 221; Clifford K. Shipton, ed., *Sibley's Harvard Graduates* (Boston, 1965, 1968), 13:380–98, 14:510–27; Maier, *Old Revolutionaries*, 123–24; David James Kiracofe, "Dr. Benjamin Church and the Dilemma of Treason in Revolutionary Massachusetts," *NEQ* 70, 3 (September 1997): 443–62; William Tudor, *The Life of James Otis of Massachusetts . . .* (Boston, 1823), 481–86.

54. Edward Lillie Pierce, "Introduction," in *Letters and Diary of John Rowe*, 1–60; McDevitt, *House of Rotch*.

55. James Warren to John Adams, May 18, 1787, in *Warren–Adams Letters*, *MHSC*, vol. 73 (1925), 2:292–93; Maier, *Old Revolutionaries*, 3–16, 31.

56. Bailyn, *Ordeal*, 373; *Diary and Letters of Thomas Hutchinson*, 2:353–55; Shipton, *Sibley's Harvard Graduates* (1951, 1968, 1970), 8:550–62, 14:289–95, 15:264–68; *BNL*, March 23, 1775; Drake, *Tea Leaves*, 223 n1, 294 n1; James H. Stark, *The Loyalists of Massachusetts and the Other Side of the American Revolution* (Salem, MA, 1910), 232, 408–9.

57. Bowen, *Business of Empire*; Lawson, *East India Company*; Robins, *Corporation*.

58. Michelle Craig McDonald and Steven Topik, "Americanizing Coffee: Refashioning a Consumer Culture," in Alexander Nützenadel and Frank Trentmann, eds., *Food and Globalization: Consumption, Markets and Politics in the Modern World* (New York, 2008), 109–27.

Chapter 10: Sugar, Slaves, and the Shadow of the Tea Party

1. *The Poems of Phillis Wheatley*, ed. Julian D. Mason Jr., rev edn. (1966; Chapel Hill, NC, 1989), 59.

2. James Swan, *A Dissuasion to Great-Britain and the Colonies, from the Slave Trade to Africa . . .* (Boston, [1772]), Evans #12572, p. viii.

3. F. Nwabueze Okoye, "Chattel Slavery as the Nightmare of the American Revolutionaries," *WMQ*, 3rd ser., 37, 1 (January 1980): 4–28, esp. pp. 7–8; Brown, *Moral Capital*, 156–59, 170–71, 210–28; Eliga H. Gould, *The Persistence of Empire: British Political Culture in the Age of the American Revolution* (Chapel Hill, NC, 2000); Melish, *Disowning Slavery*, chap. 4.

4. David Richardson, "Slavery, Trade, and Economic Growth in Eighteenth-century New England," in Barbara L. Solow, ed., *Slavery and the Rise of the Atlantic System* (Cambridge, 1991), 237–64.

5. Mintz, *Sweetness and Power*; Walvin, *Fruits of Empire*, 128–31; Shammas, *Pre-Industrial Consumer*, 299.

6. Morgan and Morgan, *Stamp Act Crisis*, chap. 3; Tyler, *Smugglers and Patriots*, chap. 2.

7. Lorenzo J. Greene, *The Negro in Colonial New England, 1620–1776* (1942; Port Washington, NY, 1966); Melish, *Disowning Slavery*, 12–23; Robert E. Desrochers Jr., "Slave-For-Sale Advertisements and Slavery in Massachusetts, 1704–1781," *WMQ*, 3rd ser., 59, 3 (July 2002): 623–64.

8. James Otis, *The Rights of the British Colonies Asserted and Proved* (Boston, 1764), Evans #9773, p. 29 (quote); Allegro, "Law, Politics, and the Antislavery Movement"; Brown, *Moral Capital*, 17, 24–29.

9. *The Journal and Essays of John Woolman*, ed., Amelia Mott Gummere (New York, 1922), 117 (quote), 283; *Nantucket Inquirer*, February 14, 1822; George H. Moore, *Notes on the History of Slavery in Massachusetts* (New York, 1866), 117; Thomas E. Drake, *Quakers and Slavery in America* (New Haven, CT, 1950), 88; McDevitt, *House of Rotch*, 115–17; Brown, *Moral Capital*; Melish, *Disowning Slavery*, 52–56.

10. *Diary and Autobiography of John Adams*, ed. L. H. Butterfield (Cambridge, MA, 1961), 1:321; *BTR*, 16:183, 200; Nathaniel Appleton, *Considerations on Slavery in a Letter to a Friend* (Boston, 1767), Evans #10546, pp. 5–6, 19 (quote); Bernard Rosenthal, "Puritan Conscience and New England Slavery," *NEQ* 46, 1 (March 1973): 62–81; Brown, *Revolutionary Politics*, 59 n1, 64.

11. *MassSpy*, August 27, 1772; *BEP*, August 31, 1772; *BG*, September 21, 1772; James Oldham, "New Light on Mansfield and Slavery," *Journal of British Studies* 27, 1 (January 1988): 45–68; Mark S. Weiner, "New Biographical Evidence on Somerset's Case," *Slavery & Abolition* 23, 1 (April 2002): 121–36.

12. Swan, *Dissuasion to Great-Britain and the Colonies*, 17 (first quote), 33 (second quote), 64 (Boston mentioned).

13. [Theodore Parsons and Eliphalet Pearson], *A Forensic Dispute on the Legality of Enslaving the Africans, Held at the Public Commencement in Cambridge, New-England, July 21st, 1773* (Boston, 1773), Evans #12917; Larry E. Tise, *Proslavery: A History of the Defense of Slavery in America, 1701–1840* (Athens, GA, 1987), 30–32.

14. *The Appendix; or, Some Observations on the Expediency of the Petition of the Africans, Living in Boston, &c. . . .* (Boston, [1773]), Evans #12651, p. 10; Davis, "Emancipation Rhetoric"; Sinha, "Black Radicalism."

15. Swan, *Dissuasion to Great-Britain*, 2nd edn. (Boston, 1773), Evans #13034, p. ix.

16. Peter Bestes, Sambo Freeman, Felix Holbrook, Chester Joie to the town representatives, April 20, 1773, in *Sir, The Efforts Made by the Legislative . . .* ([Boston, 1773]), Shipton & Mooney #42416.

17. St. George Tucker and Jeremy Belknap, "Queries respecting the Slavery and Emancipation of Negroes in Massachusetts," *MHSC* 4 (1795): [191–211] 201–2; Moore, *Notes on the History of Slavery*, 135–43; "Negro Petitions for Freedom," *MHSC*, 5th ser., 3 (1877): 432–37; Benjamin Quarles, *The Negro in the American Revolution* (1961; Chapel Hill, NC, 1996), 39–40.

18. William H. Robinson, "On Phillis Wheatley and Her Boston," in *Phillis Wheatley and Her Writings* (New York, 1984), 3–69; David Grimsted, "Anglo-American Racism and Phillis Wheatley's 'Sable Veil,' 'Length'ned Chain,' and 'Knitted Heart,'" in Ronald Hoffman and Peter J. Albert, eds., *Women in the Age of the American Revolution* (Charlottesville, VA, 1989), 338–444; Vincent Caretta, "Phillis Wheatley, the Mansfield Decision of 1772, and the Choice of Identity," in Klaus H. Schmidt and Fritz Fleischmann, eds., *Early America Re-Explored: New Readings in Colonial, Early National, and Antebellum Culture* (New York, 2000), 201–23; see also Joseph Rotch & Co. to Aaron Lopez, January 30, 1764, Lopez Papers, Haight Collection, Newport Historical Society; "An Account of What Tea Has Been Imported into Boston since the Year 1768 . . .," British North American Customs Papers, 1765–1774, MHS, p. 29; the Wheatleys were related to Benjamin Wallcut, later said to be a Tea Party participant; see Charles J. Stratford Reminiscences, MHS.

19. Mason, ed., *Poems of Phillis Wheatley*, 82–83, 148–51 (quote 150), 192–93.

20. *BG*, September 20, 1773; Phillis Wheatley to David Worcester [Wooster], October 18, 1773, in Mason, ed., *Poems of Phillis Wheatley*, 195–98; Charles W. Akers, " 'Our Modern Egyptians': Phillis Wheatley and the Whig Campaign against Slavery in Revolutionary Boston," *Journal of Negro History* 60, 3 (July 1975): 397–410; Carla Willard, "Wheatley's Turns of Praise: Heroic Entrapment and the Paradox of Revolution," *American Literature* 67, 2 (June 1995): 233–56; Kirstin Wilcox, "The Body into Print: Marketing Phillis Wheatley," *American Literature* 71, 1 (March 1999): 1–29.

21. "At a Legal Meeting of the Freeholders and Inhabitants of the Town of Medfield on the 29ᵗʰ of Decem.ʳ 1773," BCC Minutes, January 4, 1774, NYPL, pp. 524, 526; Brown, *Revolutionary Politics*, 173–74; Lee Nathaniel Newcomer, *The Embattled Farmers: A Massachusetts Countryside in the American Revolution* (New York, 1953), 160–62.

22. Caretta, "Phillis Wheatley"; Bernard Bailyn, *The Ideological Origins of the American Revolution*, enlarged edn. (1967; Cambridge, MA, 1992); Brown, *Moral Capital*, 46–48; Van Gosse, " 'As a Nation, the English Are Our Friends': The Emergence of African American Politics in the British Atlantic World, 1772–1861," *AHR* 113, 4 (October 2008): 1003–28.

23. [Henry Hulton] to unknown, February 1775, in Henry Hulton Letterbooks, HHL, p.111; John Mein, *Sagittarius's Letters and Political Speculations* (Boston, 1775), Evans #14255, pp. 38–39; Brown, *Moral Capital*, chap. 2.

24. *MassSpy*, February 10, 1774.
25. Daniel R. Coquillette and Neil Longley York, eds., *Portrait of a Patriot: The Major Political and Legal Papers of Josiah Quincy Junior*, vol. 76 of *PCSM* (2007), 3:28–40, 211–26 (quote 225); *Diary of John Adams*, 2:134–35; James Warren to John Adams, June 22, 1777, in *Warren–Adams Letters*, vol. 1, *1743–1777, MHSC*, vol. 72 (1917): 335.
26. Max Farrand, ed., *The Records of the Federal Convention of 1787* (New Haven, CT, 1911), 2:373; Coquillette and York, *Portrait of a Patriot*, 3:163–68; Paul Finkelman, "Slavery and the Constitutional Convention: Making a Covenant with Death," in Richard Beeman, Stephen Botein, and Edward C. Carter II, eds., *Beyond Confederation: Origins of the Constitution and American National Identity* (Chapel Hill, NC, 1987), 188–225.
27. Quarles, *Negro in the American Revolution*; William W. Freehling, "The Founding Fathers, Conditional Antislavery, and the Nonradicalism of the American Revolution," in *The Reintegration of American History: Slavery and the Civil War* (New York, 1994), [12–33] 14, 30–31; Alfred F. Young, "Afterword: How Radical Was the American Revolution?" in *Beyond the American Revolution: Explorations in the History of American Radicalism* (DeKalb, IL, 1993), [317–64] 338–40.
28. *BEP*, May 3, 1783; see also *[Boston] Independent Ledger*, March 10, 1783.
29. "Queries respecting the Slavery and Emancipation of Negroes in Massachusetts"; "Queries relating to Slavery in Massachusetts," Belknap Papers, *MHSC*, 5th ser., 3 (1877): 373–431; Breen, "Making History"; Blanck, "Seventeen Eighty-Three"; Sweet, *Bodies Politic*, 248–67; Zilversmit, *First Emancipation*, 109–116; Melish, *Disowning Slavery*, 64–65, 84, 95–97; on the *Tyrannicide*, see RWP, W. #15211.
30. Brown, *Moral Capital*, 100, 109n, 451; Patricia Bradley, *Slavery, Propaganda, and the American Revolution* (Jackson, MS, 1998), 155.
31. William Rotch to Moses Brown, November 8, 1787, Austin Collection, Moses Brown School, Brown University, in John P. Kaminski, ed., *A Necessary Evil?: Slavery and the Debate over the Constitution* (Madison, WI, 1995), 74 (quote), see also chap. 3; Jordan, *White over Black*, chaps. 8–10; Melish, *Disowning Slavery*, chap. 6; Kathryn Grover, *The Fugitive's Gibraltar: Escaping Slaves and Abolitionism in New Bedford, Massachusetts* (Amherst, MA, 2001), 34–36.
32. Abigail Adams to John Adams, October 25, 1775, in *Adams Family Correspondence*, ed., L. H. Butterfield (Cambridge, MA, 1963), 1:313; Brown, *Moral Capital*; Eliga H. Gould, "Zones of Law, Zones of Violence: The Legal Geography of the British Atlantic, circa 1772," *WMQ*, 3rd ser., 60, 3 (July 2003): 471–510; Melish, *Disowning Slavery*, pp. 50–64, 79, chap. 5; see also *MassSpy*, March 3, 1774.
33. Berg, *Luxury and Pleasure*, 327; Charlotte Sussman, "Women and the Politics of Sugar, 1792," *Representations* 48 (autumn 1994): 48–69; Clare Midgely, *Women Against Slavery: The British Campaigns, 1780–1870* (London, 1992); Clare Midgely, "Slave Sugar Boycotts, Female Activism and the Domestic Base of British Anti-Slavery Culture," *Slavery & Abolition* 17, 3 (December 1996): 137–62; Lawrence B. Glickman: " 'Buy for the Sake of the Slave': Abolitionism and the Origins of American Consumer Activism," *American Quarterly* 56, 4 (December 2004): 889–912.
34. *Liberator* 1, 38 (September 17, 1831): 152.
35. *[Cincinnati] Philanthropist* 1, 30 (July 22, 1836); "American Robespierres," *Boston Recorder* 21, 34 (August 19, 1836): 134; *Speeches, Lectures, and Letters by Wendell Phillips* (1863; Boston, 1872), 1–3; Henry Wilson, *History of the Rise and Fall of the Slave Power in America*, 4th edn. (Boston, 1875), 1:383–87; Tise, *Proslavery*, chap. 10; Leonard L. Richards, *Gentlemen of Property and Standing: Anti-Abolition Mobs in Jacksonian America* (New York, 1970), 69, 97–98.
36. John Weiss, *Life and Correspondence of Theodore Parker . . .* (New York, 1864), 2:103; see also John G. Richardson, *Obedience to Human Law Considered in the Light of Divine Truth: A Discourse Delivered in the First Baptist Meeting House, Lawrence, Mass., July 4, 1852* (Lawrence, MA, 1852), 12–13; *Speeches by Wendell Phillips*, 417.

37. Jordan, *White over Black*; Deloria, *Playing Indian*, 5, 34–37, 190–91; Sweet, *Bodies Politic*; Nancy Shoemaker, *A Strange Likeness: Becoming Red and White in Eighteenth-Century North America* (New York, 2004), esp. chap. 6.

Conclusion: Secrecy and Legacy

1. *Diary and Autobiography of John Adams*, ed. L. H. Butterfield (Cambridge, MA, 1961), 2:86.
2. *Letters and Diary of John Rowe*, 257–58; John Hancock to Hayley & Hopkins, December 21, 1773, Hancock Letterbook, JH6, Hancock Collection, 1712–1854, Baker Library, Harvard Business School, pp. 423–24.
3. Depositions of Samuel Dyer and Samuel Mouat, enclosed in John Montagu to Philip Stevens, August 1, 1774, ADM 1/484, TNA:PRO, transcripts, LOC, pp. 529–30; see also advertisement in *BG*, June 16, 1766; *MassSpy*, March 5, 1772, *BNL*, April 23, 1772, January 24, 1774.
4. James Fenimore Cooper, *The History of the Navy of the United States of America*, 2 vols. (Paris, 1839), 1:36.
5. *Diary of John Adams*, 2:86; Ann Hulton to Mrs. Lightbody, January 31, 1774, in *Letters of a Loyalist Lady*, 70–72; *BNL*, January 27, February 3, 1774; *BEP*, January 31, 1774; TH to Earl of Dartmouth, January 28, 1774, *DAR*, 8:25–27; Frank W. C. Hersey, "Tar and Feathers: The Adventures of Captain John Malcom," *PCSM* 34 (1937–42): 429–73; Young, *Shoemaker*, 46–51.
6. William Tudor, *The Life of James Otis of Massachusetts* . . . (Boston, 1823), 418n.
7. Notes on Browne genealogy, Papers of Harriet Jane Hanson Robinson and Harriette Lucy Robinson Shattuck, 1833–1937, series II, Schlesinger Library, Radcliffe Institute, Harvard University.
8. John J. May to R. C. Waterson, [1873?], in *MHSP* 13 (December 1873): 185–86.
9. Peter Edes to Benjamin C. Edes, February 16, 1836, in *MHSP* 12 (December 1871): 175. Edes may have confused the list of Tea Party participants with the list of watchmen aboard the ships prior to the destruction of the tea, which was kept at the *Gazette* offices: see *BG*, December 6, 1773.
10. Josiah Bartlett, "An Historical Sketch of Charlestown, in the County of Middlesex, and Commonwealth of Massachusetts," [1813], *MHSC*, 2nd ser., vol. 1 (1838): 175.
11. John Adams to Hezekiah Niles, May 10, 1819, also "A Bostonian," June 12, 1819, in *[Boston] Columbian Centinel*, June 16, 1819; Drake, *Tea Leaves*, 90; Edward L. Pierce, "Recollections as a Source of History," *MHSP*, 2nd ser., vol. 10 (1895–96): [473–90] 476; J. L. Bell, "Who Identified Men at the Boston Tea Party?" *Boston 1775* (weblog), December 16, 2006; Thatcher, *Traits*, 265.
12. "Trades' Unions," *The Man* 1, 2 (February 20, 1834); Young, *Shoemaker*, 148.
13. Remarks by Robert C. Winthrop, *MHSP* 14 (September 1875): [153–56] 154; Charles Sprague, "American Independence: An Oration Pronounced before the Inhabitants of Boston, July 4, 1825," in *The Poetical and Prose Writings of Charles Sprague*, rev. edn. (Boston, 1851), [147–75] 167; Thatcher, *Traits*, 264.
14. *BDA*, November 11, 1821; Edward Everett Hale, *Historic Boston and its Neighborhood* . . . (New York, 1898), 72; J. L. Bell, "Who Threw the Tea into Boston Harbor?" *Boston 1775* (weblog), December 15, 2006.
15. Lewis R. M. Morse to Hezekiah Niles, June 22, 1819, in Hezekiah Niles, *Principles and Acts of the Revolution in America* . . . (Baltimore, 1822), 326; *Boston Commercial Gazette*, November 7, 1822; Cameron Tung, Tufts University class paper, April 2007.
16. *Providence Patriot*, July 29, 1829; Young, *Shoemaker*, 156; Aaron B. Chaleff, Tufts University class paper, April 2007.
17. *Baltimore Patriot and Mercantile Advertiser*, January 28, 1826; see also *Providence Patriot and Columbian Phenix*, February 4, 1826; *[Portsmouth] New-Hampshire Gazette*,

February 6, 1826; *Middlesex [CT] Gazette*, February 8, 1826; *[Windsor] Vermont Journal*, February 13, 1826; Solomon Lincoln Jr., *History of the Town of Hingham, Plymouth County, Massachusetts* (Hingham, MA, 1827), 149.

18. RWP, S. #40734.

19. "Throwing the Tea Overboard," from *Flint's Western Monthly Review*, July 1827, reprinted in *[Baltimore] Niles' Weekly Register*, September 29, 1827; Drake, *Tea Leaves*, 72.

20. *Pittsfield [MA] Sun*, September 20, 1827.

21. "Recollections of Characters: Thomas Melville," April 8, 1826, in Jerome V. C. Smith, ed., *Bowen's Boston News-Letter, and City Record* (Boston, 1826), 1:185; *The American Almanac and Repository of Useful Knowledge* (1834), 312 (quote); see also Daniel A. Cohen, "Passing the Torch: Boston Firemen, 'Tea Party' Patriots, and the Burning of the Charlestown Convent," *Journal of the Early Republic* 24, 4 (winter 2004): 527–86; on Gore, see *Salem Gazette*, November 29, 1831; on Revere, see "Early American Artists and Mechanics, No. II, Paul Revere," *New England Magazine* (October 1832): [305–14] 310.

22. "A Citizen of New-York" [James Hawkes], *A Retrospect of the Boston Tea-Party, with a Memoir of George R. T. Hewes . . .* (New York, 1834); Thatcher, *Traits*, 261 (quote); Young, *Shoemaker*, esp. pp. 79–81, 155–56, 166–79.

23. *Boston Daily Courier*, December 26, 1833; [Nathaniel Hawthorne], "The Boston Tea Party," *The American Magazine of Useful and Entertaining Knowledge* 2, 8 (April 1, 1836).

24. John Austin Stevens, "Ebenezer Stevens: Lieut.-Col. of Artillery in the Continental Army," *Magazine of American History with Notes and Queries* 1 (1877): [588–610] 590; *New-London [CT] Gazette, and General Advertiser*, September 18, 1833; Alan Taylor, *Liberty Men and Great Proprietors: The Revolutionary Settlement on the Maine Frontier, 1760–1820* (Chapel Hill, NC, 1990); Charles W. McCurdy, *The Anti-Rent Era in New York Law and Politics, 1839–1865* (Chapel Hill, NC, 2001).

25. Henry C. Watson, *The Yankee Tea-Party: or, Boston in 1773* (Philadelphia, 1851) was a children's book based on the fake Kennison claims; Labaree, *Boston Tea Party*, 143, mistakenly credits a "Lebanon Club" based on Watson. See also [Albert G. Overton], "David Kennison and the Chicago Sting" (typescript, 1980), NEHGS.

26. Henry Bromfield to Thomas Bromfield, March 24, 1774, Bromfield and Clarke Family Papers, MHS; *Barre [MA] Gazette*, February 4, 1842; *[Boston] Daily Evening Traveller*, December 16, 1873, p. 4., c. 2; *Duluth [MN] News-Tribune*, June 5, 1891; Letter from Samuel C. Clarke, April 6, 1891, in S. Arthur Bent, clerk, "Report of the Committee on the Rooms," January 12, 1892, *Proceedings of the Bostonian Society*, vol. 2 (1888–92): [25–31], 30. See Objects #0005.1892 (Thomas Melvill family) and #0005.1895 (John Crane family), Bostonian Society, Old State House; "Tea from lot thrown into Boston Harbor, Dec. 16, 1773," Object #106,951 (Cheever family), Peabody Essex Museum; *BDA*, December 17, 1873; Howard Kendall Sanderson, *Lynn in the Revolution* (Boston, 1909), 2:252; M. Louise Hawkes to Russell Leigh Jackson, Jan. 18, 1950, Peabody Essex Museum; Drake, *Tea Leaves*, 129.

27. J. L. Bell, "Listening to the Old Lady in the Kitchen: How Grandmothers' Tales Became Legends for a Nation," paper prepared for the Heroism, Nationalism, & Human Rights Conference, University of Connecticut, February 24, 2006, MS cited with author's permission; Claudia L. Bushman, *"A Good Poor Man's Wife": Being a Chronicle of Harriet Hanson Robinson and Her Family in Nineteenth-Century New England* (Hanover, NH, 1981), xvi, 1, 4–5, 12, 221.

28. Drake, *Tea Leaves*, 150–8, 165–66; *Pittsfield [MA] Sun*, September 20, 1827; Justin Horton, Tufts University class paper, May 2007; Stevens, "Ebenezer Stevens."

29. Young, *Shoemaker*, pt. 1, chaps. 10–12.

30. Joshua Wyeth's petition to Congress, RWP, S. #40734; William Richard Cutter and Benjamin Cutter, "Papers Connected with the Settlement of Benjamin Cutter's Estate," in *A History of the Cutter Family of New England*, rev edn. (Boston, 1871), 327–34.

31. Samuel Nowell's petition to Congress, February 23, 1830, in RWP, S. #4503.
32. Michael Kammen: *A Season of Youth: The American Revolution and the Historical Imagination* (Ithaca, NY, 1978), esp. chap. 6.
33. "Political Economy," *American Farmer* 5, 48 (February 20, 1824): 377.
34. Seth Luther, *An Address to the Working Men of New England* . . . (New York, 1833), 27; Young, *Shoemaker*, 80, 147–48, 157.
35. Benjamin F. Hallett to whom it may concern, October 2, 1834 (quote), and "Marshpee," *Barnstable [MA] Journal*, July 25, 1833, in *On Our Own Ground: The Writings of William Apess, a Pequot*, ed. Barry O'Connell (Amherst, MA, 1992), xxxvii–xxxviii, 167 (quote), 195.
36. "The Boston Tea Party: A True Tale of Anti-Rentism," *Young America* 2, 18 (July 26, 1845): 4; "Bank and Tariff Taxation," *Subterranean, United with the Workingman's Advocate* 1, 34 (November 16, 1844): 3; Young, *Shoemaker*, 183.
37. "Editors' Table," *Mistletoe*, January 1, 1849, p. 23; Jed Dannenbaum, "The Origins of Temperance Activism and Militancy among American Women," *Journal of Social History* 15, 2 (winter 1981): [235–52] 243; Paul A. Carter, "Prohibition and Democracy: The Noble Experiment Reassessed," *Wisconsin Magazine of History* 56, 3 (spring 1973): [189–201] 193.
38. "The Boston Tea Party: Centennial Anniversary To-morrow," *NYT*, December 15, 1873, p. 5; "The New-York Woman's Suffrage Society," *NYT*, December 17, 1873, p. 5; Sally G. McMillen, *Seneca Falls and the Origins of the Women's Rights Movement* (New York, 2008), 186; Elizabeth Cady Stanton, Susan B. Anthony, and Matilda Joslyn Gage, eds., *History of Woman Suffrage*, vol. 1 (New York, 1881), vols. 2–3 (Rochester, NY, 1881, 1886).
39. Editorial, "Boycott of Meat Gaining Recruits," *NYT*, January 30, 1910, p. 16; "She Defends London Window Smashing," *NYT*, March 12, 1912, p. 1; Editorial, "Safeguard Democracy!" *Equal Rights* 24, 23 (December 1938): 370; Marilyn Kneeland, "The Modern Boston Tea Party: The San Diego Suffrage Campaign of 1911," *Journal of San Diego History* 23, 4 (fall 1977): 35–42; Martin Luther King Jr. to "My Dear Fellow Clergymen," April 16, 1963, in *Why We Can't Wait* (New York, 1963), 87; "U.S. Negro Puts Out Paper from Peking," *NYT*, December 7, 1966, p. 42; Martha R. Simms, Jennifer Scherck, Kevin Kistler Jr., Cameron Tung, Alec Wescott, Tufts University class papers, February 2007.
40. Theodore Saloutos, "The American Society of Equity in Kentucky: A Recent Attempt in Agrarian Reform," *Journal of Southern History* 5, 3 (August 1939): [347–63] 357 n41; Charles William Eliot, *Lawlessness: An Address Delivered before the Civic Forum, Carnegie Hall, New York City, December 12, 1908* (New York, 1909), 23–24; Nancy MacLean, "The Leo Frank Case Reconsidered: Gender and Sexual Politics in the Making of Reactionary Populism," *JAH* 78, 3 (December 1991): [917–48] 943–44; Nancy MacLean, *Behind the Mask of Chivalry: The Making of the Second Ku Klux Klan* (New York, 1993), 159 (first quote); William M. Cortner quoted in Larry R. Gerlach, "A Battle of Empires: The Klan in Salt Lake City," in Shawn Lay, ed., *The Invisible Empire in the West: Toward a New Historical Appraisal of the Ku Klux Klan in the 1920s* (Urbana and Chicago, IL, 1992), [121–52] 140–42; Peter H. Amann, "Vigilante Fascism: The Black Legion as an American Hybrid," *Comparative Studies in Society and History* 25, 3 (July 1983): [490–524] 497 n16; Robert H. Churchill, *To Shake Their Guns in the Tyrant's Face: Libertarian Political Violence and the Origins of the Militia Movement* (Ann Arbor, MI, 2009), 165.
41. M. K. Gandhi, *Satyagraha in South Africa*, trans. Valji Govindji Desai, 2nd edn. (1928; Ahmedabad, 1950), 203; Lord Winterton, "Europeans in Africa," *The [London] Times*, March 6, 1952, p. 7 (quote); see also "AFRICANUS," "The War Contribution of the Transvaal," *The [London] Times*, October 20, 1902, p. 5; editorial, "South of Algeria," *The [London] Times*, May 22, 1958, p. 11; W. M. Macmillan, "Situation in Rhodesia: Why a Compromise Is Needed," *The [London] Times*, June 19, 1965, p. 9; James Bone,

" 'Boston Tea Party' as US Radicals Defy Canterbury," *The [London] Times,* June 21, 2006, p. 2; Aaron Chaleff, Justin Horton, Sarina Mathai, Tufts University class papers, February 2007.

42. "Sun Scores America for Action at Canton," *NYT,* December 20, 1923, p. 4; C. Martin Wilbur, *Sun-Yat-sen: Frustrated Patriot* (New York, 1976), 183–90; Thomas L. Friedman, "The Beirut Tea Party," *NYT,* March 10, 2005, p. A27; Jake Chiam, Jun Lee, Tufts University class papers, February 2008.

43. Bill McAllister, "Taxpayer Discontent Coming to a Boil?" *Washington Post,* December 30, 1988, p. A17; Jason Zengerle, "Hell Nay, We Won't Pay!" *NYT Magazine,* March 29, 2009, p. MM40; Matthew Taylor, "Tax Code Protest to Replay Tea Party: Federal Forms To Be Dumped in Harbor," *Boston Globe,* April 14, 1997, p. B2; Liz Robbins, "Protesters Air Views on Government Spending at Tax Day Tea Parties Across U.S.," *NYT,* April 16, 2009, p. A16; Benjamin L. Carp, "Nice Party, But Not So Revolutionary," *Washington Post,* April 19, 2009, Outlook, p. B03.

Manuscript Sources Cited

American Antiquarian Society
  Curwen Family Papers, 1637–1808
  Salisbury Family Papers
  Jonathan Sayward Diaries
  US Revolution Collection, 1754–1773
Baker Library, Harvard Business School
  Hancock Family Papers, 1712–1854
  Hancock Letterbook, JH6, Hancock Collection, 1712–1854
Boston Athenæum
  Ezekiel Price Notarial Records
Boston Public Library
  Boston Town Papers, Loose
  Mellen Chamberlain Collection
  Mellen Chamberlain, comp., "Samuel Adams and Joseph Warren, Sketches of their Lives
    with Autographs and Illustrations," 1880
British Library
  Additional Manuscripts 8133B
  Additional Manuscripts 21695: Haldimand Papers
  Additional Manuscripts 29133: Hastings Papers
  Additional Manuscripts 45430: Anderson Papers
  Egerton Manuscripts 218: Parliamentary Diary of Henry Cavendish
  Egerton Manuscripts 2659: Correspondence of the Family of Hutchinson, 1741–1800
  India Office Records
    B/85, 88, 89: Minutes of the Court of Directors
    E/1/57, 217: EIC General Correspondence, Miscellanies
    H/105: Miscellaneous Series
    L/AG/18/2/1: Accountant-General's Records
Daughters of the American Revolution Library
  Application Files (record copies)
David Library of the American Revolution
  The American Papers of the Second Earl of Dartmouth (microfilm from Staffordshire
    Record Office)
Historical Society of Pennsylvania
  Henry Drinker Foreign Letters, 1772–1785, Drinker Papers
  Henry S. Drinker Papers, 1739–1779

Papers Pertaining to the Shipment of Tea, etc., Philadelphia, 1769–1773
Philadelphia Custom House Papers
Houghton Library, Harvard University
  Civil War Collection, 1724–1933, Military Order of the Loyal Legion of the United
    States
  Henry Hulton Letterbooks, 1768–1780
  Palfrey Family Papers, 1713–1915
  Sparks Manuscripts
    Francis Bernard Papers
    New England Papers
  Tea Party Papers, 1773–1774, comp. Gilbert Elliot Minto
Howard Gotlieb Archival Research Center, Boston University
  Massachusetts First Corps of Cadets
    Biographical Lists
    Ephraim Eliot Manuscript
    Records of Meetings, Bound Volumes and Notebooks, 1772–1830
Huntington Library
  Thomas Young Letters
Library Company of Philadelphia
  Hannah Griffits Papers
Massachusetts Archives
  Governor's Council Executive Records, 1765–1774, Volume 16
  Massachusetts Archives Collection
    Hutchinson's Correspondence, 1741–1774, Volumes 25–27
    Miscellaneous Papers, 1648–1775, Volume 88
    Towns, 1755–1762, Volume 117
Massachusetts Historical Society
  Boston Committee of Correspondence Records (photostats from NYPL)
  British North American Customs Papers, 1765–1774
  Bromfield and Clarke Family Papers, 1672–1861
  Richard Clarke Papers, 1763–1775, in the Henry Herbert Edes Collection, 1648–1917
  Caleb Davis Papers, 1684–1831
  John Greenough Papers, 1766–1820 (also transcripts)
  [Henry] Hulton, "Some Account of the Proceedings of the People of New England from
    the Establishment of a Board of Customs in America to the Breaking Out of the
    Rebellion in 1775," bound from the André de Coppet Collection of American
    Historical Manuscripts (microfilm from Princeton University Library)
  Thomas Hutchinson Letterbooks (Massachusetts Archives transcripts)
  Manuscripts Large
  Miscellaneous Bound Manuscripts
  Miscellaneous Manuscripts
  James Murray Papers, 1732–1781 (microfilm)
  Quincy, Wendell, Holmes, and Upham Family Papers, 1633–1910 (microfilm)
  Samuel P. Savage Diaries, 1770–1795 (microfilm)
  Samuel P. Savage Papers II, 1710–1810
  Sedgwick Family Papers, 1717–1946
  Lemuel Shaw Papers, 1648–1923 (microfilm)
  Charles J. Stratford Reminiscences
  Israel Williams Papers, 1728–1785 (microfilm)

National Archives and Records Administration, United States
   Revolutionary War Pension and Bounty Land Warrant Application Files (microfilm)
The National Archives of the United Kingdom, Public Record Office
   Admiralty Office, 1/484 (LOC transcripts)
   Colonial Office 5/133, 247, 396, 763, 1105
   Treasury 1/445 (LOC transcripts), 505, 522
   War Office 40/1
National Library of Scotland
   Charles Steuart Papers
New England Historic Genealogical Society
   Henry Bromfield Letterbook
   Richard Clarke Collection
   [Albert G. Overton], "David Kennison and the Chicago Sting" (typescript, 1980)
New York Public Library
   Boston Committee of Correspondence Papers (microfilm)
   Samuel Adams Papers (microfilm)
Newport Historical Society
   Peleg Clarke to John Fletcher, November 28, 1773
   Lopez Papers, Haight Collection
Peabody Essex Museum
   M. Louise Hawkes to Russell Leigh Jackson, January 18, 1950
Samuel Crocker Lawrence Library, Grand Lodge of Massachusetts A.F. & A.M.
   Boston Tea Party File
Schlesinger Library, Radcliffe Institute, Harvard University
   Papers of Harriet Jane Hanson Robinson and Harriette Lucy Robinson Shattuck,
      1833–1937, series II
University of Virginia Special Collections
   Papers of Samuel Cooper, 1780–1960
Watkinson Library, Trinity College
   U.S. History Pre-Civil War Collection
William L. Clements Library, University of Michigan
   Alexander Wedderburn Papers
   Leger & Greenwood Letterbook

Further Reading

Benjamin Woods Labaree, *The Boston Tea Party* (London, 1966), was the last full, scholarly treatment of the Boston Tea Party. Labaree's excellent research illuminated the Boston Tea Party in an imperial context, using debates in Parliament and sources from the executive branch of the British government; and in a proto-national context, focusing on the ways that Boston and Massachusetts were drawn together with the other American colonies during the period in question. Most other published books about the Boston Tea Party are geared for children, for whom the Tea Party appears to have a natural and instant appeal. Trade books on the subject for adults include Wesley S. Griswold, *The Night the Revolution Began: The Boston Tea Party, 1773* (Brattleboro, VT, 1972); and Robert J. Allison, *The Boston Tea Party*, (Beverly, MA, 2007). Alfred F. Young, *The Shoemaker and the Tea Party: Memory and the American Revolution* (Boston, 1999) pairs two essays on particular topics related to the Tea Party of 1773: one (drawn from an award-winning essay in the *William and Mary Quarterly*) about the shoemaker George Robert Twelves Hewes, who participated in the Tea Party, and the other on the memory of the Boston Tea Party during the nineteenth century.

John W. Tyler, *Smugglers and Patriots: Boston Merchants and the Advent of the American Revolution* (Boston, 1986), revisited the role of Boston merchants in the coming of the American Revolution, a topic previously covered by Arthur Meier Schlesinger, *The Colonial Merchants and the American Revolution, 1763–1776*, in Studies in History, Economics and Public Law, vol. 78, no. 182 (New York, 1918). Tyler argues that Labaree placed insufficient emphasis on the American fears of an East India Company monopoly (199, 311 n42). Furthermore, he argues that Labaree simplified the tea resistance as a two-sided conflict between the friends of government and the Sons of Liberty. Instead, Tyler argues, there were also conflicts within the merchant community, such as the rivalry between legitimate tea sellers and smugglers.

Revolutionary Boston

Other works have also helped illuminate a broader picture of Revolutionary Boston. G. B. Warden, *Boston, 1689–1776* (Boston, 1970), is a wonderfully researched narrative, anchored on the Boston Town Meeting. Edmund S. Morgan and Helen M. Morgan, *The Stamp Act Crisis: Prologue to Revolution*, rev. edn (1953; New York, 1963), and Hiller B. Zobel, *The Boston Massacre* (New York, 1970), are largely skeptical toward the major crowd actions that preceded the Tea Party. Dirk Hoerder, *Crowd Action in Revolutionary Massachusetts, 1765–1780* (New York, 1977), and Gary B. Nash, *The Urban Crucible: Social Change, Political Consciousness, and the Origins of the American Revolution* (Cambridge, MA, 1979), are more sympathetic to these actions as forces for radical change. Peter Shaw, *American Patriots and the Rituals of Revolution* (Cambridge, MA, 1981), and the essays in William Pencak, Matthew Dennis, and Simon P. Newman, *Riot and Revelry in Early America* (University Park, PA, 2002), also provide useful perspectives on crowd action and festive culture. The essays in Alfred F. Young, *Liberty Tree: Ordinary People and the American Revolution* (New York, 2006), offer further insights into crowd actions and social relations.

For further discussion of Massachusetts politics, see Richard D. Brown, *Revolutionary Politics in Massachusetts: The Boston Committee of Correspondence and the Towns, 1772–1774* (Cambridge, MA, 1970; reprint, New York, 1976), which discusses reactions to the tea crisis throughout the colony. Richard L. Bushman, *King and People in Provincial Massachusetts*, paperback edn. (1985; Chapel Hill, NC, 1992), analyzes the political culture of colonial Massachusetts. Benjamin L. Carp, *Rebels Rising: Cities and the American Revolution* (New York, 2007), chap. 1, explores political mobilization in Boston's waterfront community. Mary Beth Norton, *Liberty's Daughters: The Revolutionary Experience of American Women, 1750–1800* (Ithaca, NY, 1980), broke open a discussion of women's participation in revolutionary protests. Elaine Forman Crane, *Ebb Tide in New England: Women, Seaports, and Social Change, 1630–1800* (Boston, 1998), has more to say about the lives of Boston women, and she is skeptical of the idea that the Revolutionary Era ushered in any real change for women. Ray Raphael, *The First American Revolution: Before Lexington and Concord* (New York, 2002), explores political developments in Massachusetts following the Boston Tea Party.

Biographies, Prosopographies, and Printed Correspondence

A few earlier works have attempted to compile and analyze lists of Tea Party participants. Benjamin Bussey Thatcher wrote as "A Bostonian," *Traits of the Tea Party: Being a Memoir of George R. T. Hewes,* ... (New York, 1835), and rather modestly claimed that he listed "persons generally supposed . . . on traditionary or other evidence, to have been more or less actively engaged in or present at the destruction of the Tea" (261–62). Thatcher regarded it as neither correct nor complete, yet this list became the foundation for all subsequent lists. Benson J. Lossing, *The Pictorial Field-Book of the Revolution,* 2 vols. (New York, 1850), 1:499 n3, copied Thatcher's list and added David Kennison. A descendant of the English-born ropemaker Peter Slater established a monument in honor of the Tea Party participants in a Worcester cemetery in 1870; Caleb A. Wall, *The Historic Boston Tea Party of December 16, 1773* (Worcester, MA, 1896), 21–22, printed the list (which included a handful of new names). When Francis S. Drake, *Tea Leaves: Being a Collection of Letters and Documents Relating to the Shipment of Tea to the American Colonies in the Year 1773 . . .* (Boston, 1884), assembled his larger list, he had also incorporated "Additional names of the tea party [though he ignored some from the monument], derived principally from family tradition" (92–94). Drake also includes a narrative of the Tea Party and biographies of numerous actors (both real and purported) in the drama of the tea crisis.

Historians have used these later lists of Tea Party participants to provide rough social and political data about a sample of Revolutionary actors, though they were unable to interrogate the quality or nature of these lists. This is understandable, because the process of verification is maddening even to the determined researcher. See Griswold, *Night the Revolution Began,* 141–43; James Barton Hunt, "The Crowd and the American Revolution, A Study of Urban Political Violence in Boston and Philadelphia, 1763–1776" (Ph.D., University of Washington, 1973), 482–85; John Harris, ed., *Boston Tea Party: The Trigger of our Revolution* (Boston, 1974), 76–79; William Pencak, *War, Politics, and Revolution in Provincial Massachusetts* (Boston, 1981), 275–77; David Hackett Fischer, *Paul Revere's Ride* (New York, 1994), 301–7. More recently, the Boston Tea Party Ships & Museum (part of Historic Tours of America, Inc.), though it has not yet reopened at the time of this writing, has maintained a website with a newer list, based on the research of genealogist and independent historian George A. Quintal Jr. See http://www.bostonteapartyship.com/participants.asp.

There are two recent biographies of Thomas Hutchinson: Bernard Bailyn, *The Ordeal of Thomas Hutchinson* (Cambridge, MA, 1974); and Andrew Stephen Walmsley, *Thomas Hutchinson and the Origins of the American Revolution* (New York, 1999). For more on the consignees, I consulted *Sibley's Harvard Graduates*, 18 vols. (Boston, 1873–1999); and James H. Stark, *The Loyalists of Massachusetts and the Other Side of the American Revolution* (Salem, MA, 1910). Joseph L. McDevitt, *The House of Rotch: Massachusetts Whaling Merchants, 1734–1828* (New York, 1986), is a thoroughly researched study of the Rotch family.

There are numerous biographies of the leaders of the Boston Sons of Liberty. Pauline Maier, *The Old Revolutionaries: Political Lives in the Age of Samuel Adams* (New York, 1980), examines Samuel Adams as well as Thomas Young. I also consulted John K. Alexander, *Samuel Adams: America's Revolutionary Politician* (Lanham, MD, 2002); John Cary, *Joseph Warren Physician, Politician, Patriot* (Urbana, IL, 1961); William M. Fowler Jr., *The Baron of Beacon Hill: A Biography of John Hancock* (Boston, 1979); and *Sibley's Harvard Graduates*.

The printed writings and correspondence of Samuel Adams, John Adams, Benjamin Franklin, and Josiah Quincy are useful resources, as are *Letters of a Loyalist Lady: Being the Letters of Ann Hulton, Sister of Henry Hulton, Commissioner of Customs at Boston, 1767–1776* (Cambridge, MA, 1927; reprint, New York, 1971); *Peter Oliver's Origin and Progress of the American Rebellion: A Tory View*, ed. Douglass Adair and John A. Schutz (Stanford, CA, 1961); *Letters and Diary of John Rowe, Boston Merchant, 1759–1762, 1764–1779*, ed. Anne Rowe Cunningham (Boston, 1903).

There are only a few book-length biographies of Tea Party participants. In addition to Young, *Shoemaker and the Tea Party*, see Jayne E. Triber, *A True Republican: The Life of Paul Revere* (Amherst, MA, 1998); and Francis D. Cogliano, *American Maritime Prisoners in the Revolutionary War: The Captivity of William Russell* (Annapolis, MD, 2001). George P. Anderson, "Ebenezer Mackintosh: Stamp Act Rioter and Patriot," and "A Note on Ebenezer Mackintosh," *PCSM* 26 (1924–26): 15–64, 348–61, gave details about this important crowd leader. Short biographical vignettes can be found scattered throughout other sources, and books about prominent people who descended from Tea Party participants (such as Herman Melville, the Peabody sisters, Joseph Story, or Edith Wharton) also provide some biographical information.

The British Empire and the East India Company

For a book that takes a global approach to the Boston Tea Party, see Marc Aronson, *The Real Revolution: The Global Story of American Independence* (New York, 2005), which is written for younger readers; see also P. J. Marshall, *The Making and Unmaking of Empires: Britain, India, and America c. 1750–1783* (New York, 2005); and works cited in Philip J. Stern, "British Asia and British Atlantic: Comparisons and Connections," *WMQ*, 3rd ser., 63, 4 (October 2006): 693–712. Robert W. Tucker and David C. Hendrickson, *The Fall of the First British Empire: Origins of the War of American Independence* (Baltimore, 1982), is an excellent imperial approach to the American Revolution; for the parliamentary perspective, see Peter D. G. Thomas, *The Townshend Duties Crisis: The Second Phase of the American Revolution, 1767–1773* (Oxford, 1987); and Peter D. G. Thomas, *Tea Party to Independence: The Third Phase of the American Revolution, 1773–1776* (Oxford, 1991).

I consulted numerous recent works on the East India Company. Philip Lawson, *The East India Company: A History* (London, 1993), is a short survey. H. V. Bowen, *Revenue and Reform: The Indian Problem in British Politics, 1757–1773* (Cambridge, 1991), gives the wider context leading up to the passage of the Tea Act. Bowen also offers useful interpretations in H. V. Bowen, "British Conceptions of Global Empire, 1756–83," *Journal of Imperial and Commonwealth History* 26, 3 (September 1998): 1–27; and H. V. Bowen, "Tea, Tribute and the East India Company, c. 1750–c. 1775," in Stephen Taylor, Richard Connors, and Clyve Jones, eds., *Hanoverian Britain and Empire: Essays in Memory of Philip Lawson* (Woodbridge, Suffolk, 1998), 158–76. Elizabeth Mancke and Bowen contributed useful essays about the British Empire in Christine Daniels and Michael V. Kennedy, eds., *Negotiated Empires: Centers and Peripheries in the Americas, 1500–1820* (New York, 2002); see also Elizabeth Mancke, "Chartered Empires and the Evolution of the British Atlantic World," in Elizabeth Mancke and Carole Shammas, eds., *The Creation of the British Atlantic World* (Baltimore, 2005), 237–62. Nick Robins, *The Corporation that Changed the World: How the East India Company Shaped the Modern Multinational* (London, 2006), gives a rather caustic account of the Company's history. H. V. Bowen, *The Business of Empire: The East India Company and Imperial Britain, 1756–1833* (Cambridge, 2006), delves into the Company's inner workings.

Tea and Consumption

For the general reader, the following recent books are comprehensive histories of tea: Roy Moxham, *Tea: Addiction, Exploitation, and Empire* (New York, 2003); Alan Macfarlane and Iris Macfarlane, *The Empire of Tea: The Remarkable History of the Plant that Took Over the World* (Woodstock, NY, 2003); and Beatrice Hohenegger, *Liquid Jade: The Story of Tea from East to West* (New York, 2006).

For recent scholarly discussions of the global tea trade, see John C. Evans, *Tea in China: The History of China's National Drink* (New York, 1992); Robert Paul Gardella, *Harvesting Mountains: Fujian and the China Tea Trade, 1757–1937* (Berkeley, CA, 1994); Paul Arthur Van Dyke, *The Canton Trade: Life and Enterprise on the China Coast, 1700–1845* (Hong Kong, 2005); Yong Liu, *The Dutch East India Company's Tea Trade with China, 1757–1781* (Leiden, 2007).

A number of scholars have discussed the cultural importance of tea in the eighteenth century: see Jean Maurice Biziere, "Hot Beverages and the Enterprising Spirit in 18th-Century Europe," *Journal of Psychohistory* 7, 2 (fall 1979): 135–45; Peter B. Brown, *In Praise of Hot Liquors: The Study of Chocolate, Coffee and Tea-Drinking, 1600–1850* (York, 1995); Ross W. Jamieson, "The Essence of Commodification: Caffeine Dependencies in the Early Modern World," *Journal of Social History* 35, 2 (winter 2001): 269–94; Roger Schmidt, "Caffeine and the Coming of the Enlightenment," *Raritan* 23, 1 (spring 2003): 129–49; Jane T. Merritt, "Tea Trade, Consumption, and the Republican Paradox in Revolutionary Philadelphia," *PMHB* 128, 2 (April 2004): 117–48.

On consumption more generally, see Sidney W. Mintz, *Sweetness and Power: The Place of Sugar in Modern History* (New York, 1985); Carole Shammas, *The Pre-Industrial Consumer in England and America* (Oxford, 1990); various essays in John Brewer and Roy Porter, eds., *Consumption and the World of Goods* (London, 1993); Cary Carson, Ronald Hoffman, and Peter J. Albert, eds., *Of Consuming Interests: The Style of Life in the Eighteenth Century* (Charlottesville, VA, 1994); Elizabeth Kowaleski-Wallace, *Consuming Subjects: Women, Shopping, and Business in the Eighteenth Century* (New York, 1997); James Walvin, *Fruits of Empire: Exotic Produce and British Taste, 1660–1800* (New York, 1997); Woodruff D. Smith, *Consumption and the Making of Respectability, 1600–1800* (New York, 2002); T. H. Breen, *The Marketplace of Revolution: How Consumer Politics Shaped American Independence* (New York, 2004); Maxine Berg, *Luxury and Pleasure in Eighteenth-century Britain* (Oxford, 2005).

Race, Slavery, and Indian Disguises

Scholars have only begun to probe the subjects of Indian disguises and eighteenth-century masquerades. See, for instance, Calvin Martin and Steven Crain, "The Indian behind the Mask at the Boston Tea Party," *Indian Historian* 7, 1 (winter 1974): 45–47; Aileen Ribiero, *The Dress Worn at Masquerades in England, 1730 to 1790, and its Relation to Fancy Dress in Portraiture* (New York, 1984); Terry Castle, *Masquerade and Civilization: The Carnivalesque in Eighteenth-century English Culture and Fiction* (Stanford, CA, 1986); Rayna Green, "The Tribe Called Wannabee: Playing Indian in America and Europe," *Folklore* 99, 1 (1988): 30–55; Roger D. Abrahams, "History and Folklore: Luck-Visits, House-Attacks, and Playing Indian in Early America," in Ralph Cohen and Michael S. Roth, eds., *History and . . .: Histories within the Human Sciences* (Charlottesville, VA, 1995), 268–95; Timothy J. Shannon, "Dressing for Success on the Mohawk Frontier: Hendrick, William Johnson, and the Indian Fashion," *WMQ*, 3rd ser., 53, 1 (January 1996): 13–42; Philip J. Deloria, *Playing Indian* (New Haven, CT, 1998); Roxann Wheeler, *The Complexion of Race: Categories of Difference in Eighteenth-century British Culture* (Philadelphia, 2000); Ann M. Little, " 'Shoot That Rogue, for He Hath an Englishman's Coat On!': Cultural Cross-Dressing on the New England Frontier, 1620–1760," *NEQ* 74, 2 (June 2001): 238–73; Dror Wahrman, *The Making of the Modern Self: Identity and Culture in Eighteenth-century England* (New Haven, CT, 2004).

Numerous scholars have examined attempts to abolish the slave trade or put an end to slavery. See Arthur Zilversmit, *The First Emancipation: The Abolition of Slavery in the North* (Chicago, 1967); David Brion Davis, *The Problem of Slavery in the Age of Revolution, 1770–1823* (1975; New York, 1999); Paul Thomas, "Changing Attitudes in an Expanding Empire: The Anti-slavery Movement, 1760–1783," *Slavery & Abolition* 5, 1 (May 1984): 50–72; Thomas J. Davis, "Emancipation Rhetoric, Natural Rights, and Revolutionary New England: A Note on Four Black Petitions in Massachusetts, 1773–1777," *NEQ* 62, 2 (June 1989): 248–63; T. H. Breen, "Making History: The Force of Public Opinion and the Last Years of Slavery in Revolutionary Massachusetts," in Ronald Hoffman, Mechal Sobel, and Fredrika J. Teute, eds., *Through a Glass Darkly: Reflections on Personal Identity in Early America* (Chapel Hill, NC, 1997), 67–95; Emily Blanck, "Seventeen Eighty-Three: The Turning Point in the Law of Slavery and Freedom in Massachusetts," *NEQ* 75, 1 (March 2002): 24–51; James J. Allegro, " 'Increasing and Strengthening the Country': Law, Politics, and the

Antislavery Movement in Early-Eighteenth-century Massachusetts Bay,"
NEQ 75, 1 (March 2002): 5–23; Christopher Leslie Brown, *Moral Capital:
Foundations of British Abolitionism* (Chapel Hill, NC, 2006); Manisha Sinha,
"To 'cast just obliquy' on Oppressors: Black Radicalism in the Age of
Revolution," *WMQ*, 3rd ser., 64, 1 (January 2007): 149–60.

Winthrop D. Jordan, *White over Black: American Attitudes toward the
Negro, 1550–1812* (Chapel Hill, NC, 1968), is still the cornerstone of any
reading list about eighteenth-century racial relations. Robert F. Berkhofer
Jr., *The White Man's Indian: Images of the American Indian from Columbus to
the Present* (New York, 1978), offered an early discussion of white percep-
tions of Native Americans. William S. Simmons, "Cultural Bias in the New
England Puritans' Perception of Indians," *WMQ*, 3rd ser., 38, 1 (January
1981): 56–72; and Alden T. Vaughan, "From White Man to Redskin:
Changing Anglo-American Perceptions of the American Indian," *AHR* 87,
4 (October 1982): 917–53, helped continue this discussion. Daniel R.
Mandell, *Behind the Frontier: Indians in Eighteenth-century Eastern
Massachusetts* (Lincoln, NE, 1996), is a useful discussion of the Indians near
Boston in 1773. John McWilliams, "Indian John and the Northern
Tawnies," *NEQ* 69, 4 (December 1996): 580–604, discusses earlier attitudes
toward skin color in New England. Two excellent recent books on race in
New England are Joanne Pope Melish, *Disowning Slavery: Gradual
Emancipation and "Race" in New England, 1780–1860* (Ithaca, NY, 1998);
and John Wood Sweet, *Bodies Politic: Negotiating Race in the American North,
1730–1830* (Baltimore, 2003).

Index

Note: Illustrations have page numbers in *italics*.